T0338237

# Additional Praise for *Risk Transfer*

"Culp provides us with a thought-provoking and extremely valuable contribution to risk management literature. His analysis gives insight into using derivatives for risk transfer. High-powered theory translated into cutting-edge practice."

—Rudolf Ferscha, CEO, Eurex

"Christopher Culp has written a thorough, yet accessible, guide to modern financial risk management. The text presents a well-balanced blend of theory and application, highlighting many practical lessons gleaned from Culp's years of experience in the field."

—James Overdahl, Author of *Financial Derivatives*

"Chris Culp's *Risk Transfer* is an extraordinary book for the addressed reader, simply because it masterfully links the theoretical aspects of risk with the practical aspects used in the financial world to obtain control over risk. The interrelationship among risk, uncertainty, and the expected outcome, profit, are dependent on business decisions, influenced by the correct implementation of the appropriate use of derivative instruments to 'complete the market.' All this is shown in this book to be not only viable but mostly necessary. Risk, being inherent to business transactions, cannot itself be eliminated. The objective ought to be to achieve the appropriate (partial or full) transfer of risk. Culp gives us an excellent review of this vital subject."

—Rodolfo H. Ibáñez, Head of Investment Research
and Asset Management, BBVA (Switzerland) Ltd.

"Christopher Culp has written an outstanding book about risk transfer. He derives his ideas from both a historical and a general economic perspective. This enables him to demystify derivative instruments and to show their true value. He combines financial innovation and practical experience to develop modern concepts of risk transfer using derivative instruments."

—Cuno Pümpin, Professor of Management,
University of St. Gallen (Switzerland)

# Risk
# Transfer

Founded in 1807, John Wiley & Sons is the oldest independent publishing company in the United States. With offices in North America, Europe, Australia, and Asia, Wiley is globally committed to developing and marketing print and electronic products and services for our customers' professional and personal knowledge and understanding.

The Wiley Finance series contains books written specifically for finance and investment professionals as well as sophisticated individual investors and their financial advisors. Book topics range from portfolio management to e-commerce, risk management, financial engineering, valuation, and financial instrument analysis, as well as much more.

For a list of available titles, visit our Web site at www.WileyFinance.com.

# Risk
# Transfer

*Derivatives in Theory
and Practice*

# CHRISTOPHER L. CULP

**WILEY**

John Wiley & Sons, Inc.

Published by John Wiley & Sons, Inc., Hoboken, New Jersey.
Published simultaneously in Canada.

For general information on our other products and services please contact our Customer Care Department within the U.S. at (800) 762-2974, outside the United States at (317) 572-3993 or fax (317) 572-4002.

Wiley also publishes its books in a variety of electronic formats. Some content that appears in print may not be available in electronic books.

For more information about Wiley products, visit our web site at www.wiley.com.

*Library of Congress Cataloging-in-Publication Data:*

Culp, Christopher L.
    Risk transfer : derivatives in theory and practice / Christopher L. Culp.
        p.   cm.
    ISBN 0-471-46498-8 (cloth)
    1. Derivative securities.   2. Risk management.   I. Title.
    HG6024 .A3C85   2004
    332.64'57—dc22                                    2003020245

Printed in the United States of America.

10  9  8  7  6  5  4  3  2  1

# Acknowledgments and Dedication

This book is based on a graduate course I teach every autumn at the University of Chicago's Graduate School of Business (GSB) entitled "Futures, Forwards, Options, and Swaps: Theory and Practice"—a.k.a. B35101 (formerly B339). I am grateful to all the students who have survived my course over the years, many of whom provided honest feedback that has helped me refine and refocus both the course and this book. I also am grateful to Professors Terry Belton and Galen Burgardt, who teach the winter and spring quarter sections respectively, of B35101, for their consistent willingness to share both their materials and expertise. Although our three sections of B35101 have many differences, the basic themes explored are the same, and I am grateful to them for sharing with me their insights and expertise about those themes.

I also owe a significant debt of gratitude to my predecessor, Professor Todd E. Petzel, whose section of B35101 I took over when he left the city of Chicago in 1998. I originally took B35101 from Todd when I was a Ph.D. student, and I then served as his teaching assistant for the class for six years. Todd is a brilliant University of Chicago–trained economist and was then a senior executive at the Chicago Mercantile Exchange; his blend of theory and practice was unique and made for a fantastic class. Many of the ideas and concepts that Todd emphasized in his course are still alive and well in mine, and in this book. I am very grateful to Todd for all that he has taught me and for his friendship.

Several other friends and colleagues have also provided me with helpful comments and insights about this particular subject and work. My thanks in that regard go to Keith Bockus, John Cochrane, George Constantinides, Ken French, J. B. Heaton and Barb Kavanagh. Thanks also to Rotchy Barker and Keith Bronstein, both exceptional traders, for sharing with me over time a wealth of practical insights on how derivatives *really* work.

I am especially appreciative of the effort and time spent by Andrea Neves, who read and commented thoughtfully on the entire manuscript. Her suggestions and insights were tremendously valuable. Those same types of insights and ideas have made Andrea one of my most valued professional colleagues over the past decade, and I remain grateful to have her as both a professional collaborator and a very good friend.

I am as grateful as ever to Bill Falloon and Melissa Scuereb at John Wiley & Sons. Their professionalism and skill have once again been matched only by their thoughtful suggestions and seemingly infinite patience.

As things turned out, much of the last part of this book was written—and the entire book was copyedited—during several periods when I was in London. Special thanks to Michael, Tony, Andy, Paul, Ron, and Roy—the Hall Porters at The Ritz Hotel in London—for their infinite patience and tireless efforts in helping me bring this book to completion. Their dedication to service is exceeded only by their enthusiasm and efficiency.

Finally, this book would never have come into existence without the years of instruction, guidance, and advice I have received from Professor Steve H. Hanke. As a freshman in college at Johns Hopkins, I first encountered concepts like "backwardation" and "own interest rates" and first read the writings of economists like Pierro Sraffa and Holbrook Working in Professor Hanke's "Economics of Commodity Markets" class. I continued to learn from Professor Hanke as his research assistant at Hopkins, and later as his co-author on a variety of eclectic topics ranging from the Hong Kong monetary system to inflation hedging with commodity futures. He is now a partner at Chicago Partners LLC, where we both consult together on projects regularly. We continue to write together, and it is highly unusual for even a week to pass without at least one lengthy phone conversation between the two of us. He taught me the true meaning of a "full-court press," so it is not at all unusual for that phone call to occur around five o'clock on a Saturday morning, when we are both in our respective offices already at work.

I am also quite fortunate that Professor Hanke—and his brilliant and delightful wife Lilliane—are both also among my closest personal friends and confidants. I cannot imagine a major decision I would make about much of anything in my life—career or personal—without first soliciting and then seriously considering their opinions.

Steve Hanke's fingerprints are all over this book in pretty much every way possible. He is an exceptional economist and a true example for me to follow as an academic, a trader, a public policy advocate, a gentleman, and a scholar. He is more than a mentor and more than a friend, and he has indelibly shaped the way I think about derivatives. I take great pleasure in dedicating this work to Professor Hanke.

I would be remiss, however, in not adding the usual disclaimer that all remaining errors of omission and commission here are my responsibility alone. Furthermore, the views expressed here do not necessarily represent the views of any institution with which I am affiliated or any clients by whom I am regularly engaged.

CHRISTOPHER L. CULP

*London*
*July 26, 2003*

# Contents

# Preface:
# The Demonization of Derivatives

In his March 2003 letter to Berkshire Hathaway shareholders, investment guru Warren Buffett described derivatives as "financial weapons of mass destruction, carrying dangers that . . . are potentially lethal." George Soros has similarly argued that derivatives serve no useful purpose but to encourage destabilizing speculation. Indeed, more than 200 proposals to prohibit, limit, tax, or regulate derivatives have appeared in the United States in the past century. Freddie Mac's massive derivatives accounting restatement and Enron's active participation in derivatives have recently exacerbated popular fears of these products. What's all the fuss about?

## DERIVATIVES: FICTION AND REALITY

"Derivatives" are financial instruments whose payoffs are based on the performance of some specific underlying asset, reference rate, or index. Popular types include futures, forwards, options, and swaps. Futures and options on futures are standardized, traded on organized exchanges, margined and marked to market at least daily, and settled through a central counterparty called a clearinghouse. At the end of 2002, the Bank for International Settlements reports 28.2 million futures contracts and 55.2 million option contracts outstanding on the world's major organized exchanges. At the same time, $141.8 trillion in notional principal was outstanding in over-the-counter (OTC) derivatives such as swaps. That amount is not ever exchanged and thus is not a measure of capital at risk, but it does provide some indication of the popularity of swaps.

Many portrayals of derivatives characterize them as excessively complex by-products of modern financial engineering that dupe their users and expose the financial system to unjustified systemic risks. These portrayals are misleading.

---

Portions of this Preface are based on Culp (2003a, 2003b, 2003c).

Derivatives are hardly novel and are usually remarkably simple. One of the oldest and most versatile derivatives is a simple forward contract in which A agrees to buy some asset such as corn or wheat from B at a fixed price on some date in the future. As Chapter 5 discusses in more detail, derivatives like that can be traced to Babylonian and Assyrian agribusiness from 1900 to 1400 B.C.—the famed Code of Hammurabi even includes an explicit reference to derivatives. Since then, long periods of sustained derivatives activity have regularly resurfaced. The Medici Bank, for example, relied extensively on derivatives during the fourteenth and fifteenth centuries. A handful of the Medici's derivatives were fairly complex, but most were plain-vanilla forward agreements used to promote trade finance.

Nor are derivatives financial weapons of mass destruction. In fact, derivatives are more akin to smart bombs with which corporations can apply laserlike accuracy and precision to remove unwanted risks. In most cases, the risks to which a business is naturally exposed are greater than the risks that shareholders perceive as essential to running that business. Derivatives can be used like smart bombs to target those nonessential risks and surgically remove them.

The historical appeal of derivatives is that they do hit their marks—their payoffs can be defined very precisely to eliminate highly specific risks. That derivatives correctly hit their marks does not mean, of course, that the right marks are always painted. In the mid-1990s, for example, a number of corporate treasurers used derivatives to bet that short-term interest rates would stay low relative to long-term rates. When short rates rose instead, the derivatives performed just as they were designed to, but the companies lost hundreds of millions of dollars by aiming at the wrong interest rate target. And, for that matter, remember that a misidentified target can be destroyed by sticks and stones as well as a misguided smart bomb.

## THE BENEFITS OF DERIVATIVES TO CORPORATIONS

Perhaps most importantly, derivatives can help firms manage the risks to which their businesses expose them but to which shareholders of the firm may be unable to fully diversify away on their own or at a reasonable cost. Specifically, derivatives can be used as a means of engaging in *risk transfer*, or the shifting of risk to another firm from the firm whose business creates a natural exposure to that risk.

Derivatives can be used to facilitate the transfer of multiple risk types. By far the most popular are market and credit risk. Consider some common examples of how derivatives can be used to engage in market risk transfer: A firm that has issued fixed-rate debt can protect itself against interest rate declines by entering into a pay-fixed swap or can go long a strip of Eurodollar futures; a firm that has issued floating-rate debt can protect itself against interest rate increases by entering into a pay-floating swap or can go short a strip of Eurodollar futures; a firm concerned about the cost of issuing new equity in the future to honor the eventual exercise of a stock options program could manage its equity price risk by entering into equity forwards; a multinational can protect its revenues from unanticipated exchange rate fluctuations with currency derivatives; a chocolate candy manufacturer can lock in its profit margin by using derivatives as a hedge against rising cocoa purchase costs; an oil refinery can lock in the refining spread by using derivatives to hedge crude oil purchased at variable prices for refining into heating oil and gasoline for sale at variable prices; and so on.

A very important benefit of derivatives is their flexibility. Different firms have different strategic risk management objectives. In any given transaction, a firm may be focused on reducing the risk of its assets and/or liabilities, its capital or net worth, its per-period cash flows, its economic profit margin, or its accounting earnings. Although the mechanics of hedging each of these risks may differ, derivatives can be used to accomplish any of these specific risk management goals.

A second important benefit of derivatives traces to the economic and functional equivalent of derivatives as asset loans—borrowing cash to buy an asset today and storing it for 90 days is economically equivalent to entering into a forward contract today for the purchase of an asset 90 days hence at a price that is paid in 90 days but that is negotiated today. The absence of arbitrage and a competitive equilibrium ensure that derivatives are priced to make firms essentially indifferent at the margin to owning the asset now or in the future. This means that firms can also use derivatives to engage in what is known as "synthetic" asset purchases or sales—buying or selling the asset *economically* without buying or selling it *physically*.

Suppose, for example, that a corporate pension plan has a long-term target of 80 percent large-cap U.K. stocks and 20 percent cash, but that it is worried about a temporary correction in the stock market and prefers a 60 percent/40 percent asset mix for the next three months. The pension plan could sell stocks now and repurchase them later—likely for huge transaction costs—or could short stock index futures to reduce synthetically its equity position for three months. Similarly, consider a bank whose assets (fully funded) and liabilities have a duration of seven and five years on average, respectively. If the bank is worried about short-term rate increases eroding its net interest income, the bank could increase the duration of its liabilities by incurring new longer-dated liabilities *or* could synthetically immunize its duration gap with interest rate derivatives. And so on.

Third, derivatives can help corporations hedge their economic profits when price and quantity are correlated and shifts to one imply shifts in the other. Risk management programs of that kind can be directed at managing the costs of input purchases, the revenues of output sales, or both.

All of these potential benefits of derivatives relate in some way to helping firms manage their risks—that is, to achieve an expected return/risk profile that is in line with shareholder preferences. In the world of perfect capital markets that many of us were introduced to in business school, however, corporate risk management was largely a matter of indifference to the company's stockholders. Because such investors could diversify away the risks associated with fluctuations in interest rates or commodity prices simply by holding well-diversified portfolios, they would not pay a higher price-earnings (P/E) multiple (or, what amounts to the same thing, lower the cost of capital) for companies that chose to hedge such risk. So if hedging was unlikely to affect a firm's cost of capital and value, then why do it?

Two decades of theoretical and empirical work on the issue of "why firms hedge" have produced a number of plausible explanations for how risk management can increase firm value—that is, how it can increase the firm's expected cash flows even after taking account of the costs of setting up and administering the risk management program. Summarized briefly, such research suggests that risk management can help companies increase (or protect) their expected net cash flows mainly in the following ways:

- By reducing expected tax liabilities when the firm faces tax rates that rise with different levels of taxable income.
- By reducing the expected costs of financial distress caused by a downturn in cash flow or earnings, or a shortfall in the value of assets below liabilities. Although such costs include the out-of-pocket expenses associated with any formal (or informal) reorganization, more important considerations are the diversion of management time and focus, loss of valuable investment opportunities, and potential alienation of other important corporate stakeholders (customers, suppliers, and employees) that can stem from financial trouble.
- By reducing potential conflicts between a company's creditors and stockholders, including the possibility that "debt overhang" results in the sacrifice of valuable strategic investments.
- By overcoming the managerial risk aversion that (in the absence of hedging) could lead managers to invest in excessively conservative projects to protect their annual income and, ultimately, their job security—or vice versa for managers who like to take risks.
- By reducing the possibility of corporate underinvestment that arises from unexpected depletions of internal cash when the firm faces costs of external finance that are high enough to outweigh the benefits of undertaking the new investment.

As this list suggests, value-increasing risk management has little to do with dampening swings in reported earnings (or even, as many academics have suggested, minimizing the variance of cash flows). For most companies, the main contribution of risk management is likely to be its role in minimizing the probability of a *costly* financial distress. In this sense, a common use of derivatives is to protect a firm against worst-case scenarios or catastrophic outcomes. And even when the company has relatively little debt, management may choose to purchase such catastrophic insurance to protect the company's ability to carry out the major investments that are part of its strategic plan. In the process of ensuring against catastrophic outcomes and preserving a minimal level of cash flow, companies will generally discover that they can operate with less capital (or at least less equity capital) than if they left their exposures unmanaged. And to the extent that hedging proves to be a cheap substitute for capital, risk management is a value-adding proposition.

## THE ANTIDERIVATIVES CRUSADE

Despite their enormous popularity and numerous potential benefits, public outcries toward derivatives like those voiced by Messrs. Buffett and Soros—generally followed by demands for stricter derivatives regulation—are the historical rule rather than the exception. In the 1930s, politicians initially sought to blame "speculative excesses" for the Great Depression. Included in the post-Depression political response was legislation that banned financial contracts called "privileges," which we now know as "options." Senator Arthur Capper, a sponsor of the Grain Futures Act regulating futures markets in 1921, referred to the Chicago Board of Trade as a "gambling hell" and "the world's greatest gambling house." In 1947, President Harry S Truman claimed that futures trading accounted for the high prices of food and that "the government may find it necessary to limit the amount of trading." He continued, "I say this because the cost of living in this country must not be a football to be kicked about by gamblers in grain" (Smith, 2003).

In the 1990s, politicians trained their sights on OTC derivatives like swaps following the widely publicized losses supposedly involving derivatives at firms like Procter & Gamble, Gibson Greetings, Air Products, Metallgesellschaft, Barings Bank, and the Orange County Investment Pool. Representative Henry Gonzalez characterized swaps activity as a "gambling orgy" in the business world. He criticized the very names of the products—"swaps, options, swaptions, futures, floors"—as nothing more than "gambler's language" (Smith, 2003). One of my own corporate clients one day went so far as to say he thought that derivatives "were sent to the earth by the Devil to destroy corporate America."

On the heels of the so-called swap-related losses in the 1990s, numerous government agencies and private groups undertook studies of derivatives to determine whether they were inherently dangerous, in need of greater regulation, or both. Similarly, the failure of Long-Term Capital Management in 1998 led to cries for the regulation of derivatives in the hedge fund world. And of course, let us not forget the 2001 collapse of Enron—the bankruptcy of this major energy derivatives dealer has spawned the latest round of calls for greater supervision and regulation of derivatives.

Such a long track record of controversy and enmity naturally begs the question whether derivatives are, indeed, the instruments of Satan on earth—or whether these concerns are perhaps simply misplaced and unfounded. But if the latter is true, then why are derivatives repeatedly subject to such a firestorm of controversy?

First, although derivatives have "social benefits" such as promoting a more resilient financial system and helping firms avoid risks that are not core to their primary businesses, derivatives are *at the transactional level* zero-sum games. For every dollar one party makes, the counterparty loses. Unlike a bull stock market in which everyone (except the shorts) wins, a bull market in derivatives always means one of the two parties is a loser. When those losses get big enough, a loud chorus of whining derivatives losers can arise with stunning alacrity. Derivatives were not, of course, the reason for the firms' losses, merely the instrument. Nevertheless, it is often easier to blame the messenger than admit the firm's fundamental hedging or trading strategy was wrong. In short, derivatives don't kill companies, Mr. Buffett, people kill companies.

Second, derivatives markets do sometimes attract speculators—firms and individuals that enter into derivatives to bet on future prices. Despite assertions of the kind made by Mr. Soros that speculation is destabilizing, most empirical evidence shows that speculators provide a *stabilizing* influence on balance because they increase market liquidity, lower trading costs, and enhance market depth.

Finally, derivatives are not unique in their condemnation by critics. In fact, most novel financial innovations are pilloried and criticized when they are first introduced. People have consistently clung to the status quo under the mistaken belief that it is safer. In fact, though, one of the greatest risks to a society or to a company is the risk of *too little* innovation. The risk of stagnation can be far greater than the risk of change (Smith, 2003).

Firms like Enron have been castigated not only for allegedly defrauding and misleading investors but for their development of increasingly novel financial instruments, including derivatives. What few people realize, however, is that most of Enron's fraud and deception came from its accounting and disclosure practices, not its use of derivatives. In other words, the financial innovations themselves were not to blame either for Enron's bankruptcy or for its deception. The inappropriate way that Enron booked and disclosed those activities has little to do with the inherent legitimacy of the activities themselves (Culp and Niskanen, 2003).

## RISKS AND COSTS OF DERIVATIVES

Like any other financial activity, derivatives do expose their corporate users to various risks. Because derivatives are themselves used to manage some risks, you can often think of derivatives as trading one type of risk for another. Derivatives often involve trading market risk for credit risk, for example. If a firm enters into a swap to manage the interest rate risk on its outstanding debt, it has reduced its interest rate risk *in return* for bearing credit risk that the swap counterparty will not perform. A firm can then use credit derivatives or insurance to manage the credit risk of nonperformance on the interest rate swap, but that original credit risk has really just been exchanged for credit risk to the credit derivatives or insurance counterparty. And so on.

Derivatives also expose users to operational risks, such as the potential for abuse of derivatives by a rogue trader. Or to the risk that a contract might be declared legally unenforceable. Or to the risk that the cash flow servicing requirements on a marked-to-market futures hedge depletes a firm's cash reserves. But recognize that none of these risks are unique to derivatives. Most financial activities already expose firms to these sorts of risks. Provided a firm has in place a judiciously designed risk management process that is properly aligned with the firm's strategic risk management and business objectives, the risks of using derivatives—and all other financial instruments—can be controlled fairly effectively.

Some critics of derivatives, however, argue that certain derivatives risks are "systemic" in nature and thus beyond the control of individual firms. Most recently, some have voiced the concern that the exit by a single large swap dealer would cause liquidity in the market to dry up, making it impossible for users of derivatives to implement their hedging programs. This risk is not a particularly compelling one, however. Different market participants pursue different hedging objectives and have different exposures, thus generally leading to plenty of supply. Dealers *intermediate* that supply, but do not usually take on the full force of a counterparty's risk exposure. And if the dealer's intermediation activities do not result in a relatively neutral risk position, the dealers themselves may turn to other related markets that are more than deep enough to absorb net hedging needs. True, the exit of a dealer from one market will reduce liquidity in that market, but provided liquidity is deep enough in the related markets (on which the derivatives themselves are usually based), the market could resiliently weather the storm of a dealer exit decision.

A gloomier take on systemic risk holds that the failure of a major derivatives dealer with numerous linkages to others could turn into a global payment gridlock. This is, frankly, a very plausible horror scenario. But it is just that—a horror scenario. The failures of large firms like Bankhaus Herstatt, Drexel Burnham Lambert, Barings, and Enron all resulted in relatively little disruption to the global financial market. Indeed, in the failures of firms like Drexel and Enron, the role of derivatives was generally to help mitigate the impact of the failure, not exacerbate it. Concerns about systemic risk likely will remain a favorite justification for calls for greater political regulation of financial markets, but these concerns play much more on fear than on any actual empirical evidence legitimating the concern.

## CONCLUSION

Because innovation will continue to be met with skepticism and because derivatives remain an explosive source of financial innovation, criticisms of derivatives by policy makers and whining losers should be expected to continue. But firms should not be blinded by these often vacant accusations and negative characterizations. Derivatives are an essential weapon in the corporate arsenal for managing risk, controlling cost, and increasing shareholder value. They are *not* weapons of mass destruction, but rather smart bombs that can be very precisely targeted at specific risks or areas of concern.

Misfires involving derivatives will occur—some of the Medici Bank customers *did* use derivatives to circumvent deceptively the medieval church's prohibition on usury, Barings *did* blow up, Freddie Mac *did* restate its derivatives book, and so on. But caution must be exercised not to confuse flaws in corporate risk management, internal controls, and governance that lead to bad management decisions or poorly selected risk targets with flaws in derivatives themselves.

Indeed, perhaps the greatest risk of derivatives to a firm is the risk of *not* using them when it is appropriate to do so. Firms would then be forced to bear *all* the risks to which their businesses expose them, leaving shareholders scrambling to manage those risks on their own, or, worse, leaving shareholders vulnerable to the full impact of nearly any adverse financial market event. In that world, every single precipitous market move could become a financial weapon of mass destruction. Far from being such a weapon, derivatives may well be a corporation's best defense against them.

# Introduction and Structure of the Book

**A**s Sir John Hicks emphasized in his 1939 treatise, *Value and Capital*, the essential feature of derivatives that distinguishes them from traditional agreements to purchase or sell a physical or financial asset on the spot is the explicit treatment in derivatives contracts of time and space. A spot transaction is the purchase or sale of an asset for immediate delivery by the seller to the purchaser, whereas derivatives involve the purchase or sale of an asset at a specified place and time that differ from the here and now. As a result, derivatives are essentially contracts to facilitate asset loans over space and time.

Derivatives originated historically as alternatives to explicit commodity loans—for example, a farmer might borrow wheat to feed his family and workers until his actual harvest came in. Unlike a money loan, such commodity-backed loans were subject to the risk of fluctuations in commodity prices and production levels. This meant that when the payoff of a commodity loan was viewed in isolation, it was highly correlated with the price and quantity risk associated with the underlying commodity business. In turn, this made it possible for firms to combine derivatives with existing assets and liabilities to achieve a net reduction in their risks—a "transfer" of risk, as it were, to other firms in the marketplace.

Without a firm understanding of how derivatives are related to and can be viewed as asset loan markets, it is very difficult for users to take full advantage of their numerous applications for risk transfer. Accordingly, this book develops this single central theme—that the capacity of firms to transfer certain risk to other firms using derivatives is inextricably related to the economic foundations of derivatives as asset lending instruments.

This book emphasizes the economic and financial foundations of derivatives. It is not a manual about products and contract specifications. It is not an introduction to option pricing techniques. It is not a menu or technical guide for trading strategies on a product-by-product or market-by-market basis. Nor is the book an economic theory text. Rather, the book builds a bridge between how the underlying theory of derivatives as asset loan instruments affects the theory and practice of using derivatives for risk transfer.

## ORGANIZATION OF THE BOOK

The book is divided into three parts. Part One is largely theoretical and presents the micro and macro foundations underlying risk transfer as a financial activity and derivatives as an efficient—often *the most efficient*—means of exploiting risk transfer opportunities. Chapter 1 begins by reviewing the functions performed by an economic system in general and a financial system more specifically. We will see in particular that most financial innovations—including the evolution of many derivatives over time—do not enable firms to do "new things." Most innovation either enables firms to perform one of a constant set of functions of the financial system *in a more efficient manner* than was possible without the innovation or enables firms to avoid the costs of unexpected changes in taxes and regulations. As a result, financial institutions and products are constantly changing and evolving to meet consumers' needs, but the functions performed by these institutions and products are relatively stable over time.

Chapter 2 presents a discussion of the foundational distinctions in economic theory between risk and uncertainty and how those distinctions are related to the elusive but critically important notions of "profit" and "equilibrium." Heavy use of the history of economic thought is made in this chapter to illustrate these somewhat abstract but essential concepts that lie at the base of questions like: "When should firms consider hedging?" "What sources of randomness are essential drivers of corporate profits, and which ones can be shifted to other firms without significantly attenuating the bottom line?" "How do speculators make money?" The ideas developed in Chapter 2 are used throughout the book.

We then consider in Chapter 3 the methods by which firms can control risk and uncertainty that they have decided to reduce. We emphasize that of four methods available to firms, only one—risk transfer—involves the explicit agreement by some other firm to help the original firm manage its risks. But this method is a crucial one.

Chapter 4 discusses in general terms how risk transfer can be accomplished using contracts like derivatives. Risk is not simply moved from one firm to another by decree. We develop the notion that the payoff function of financial contracts plays an essential role in the degree to which risk transfer is possible, even when the payoff of a contract is not explicitly designed to facilitate risk transfer. We also consider for the first time—but hardly the last—the cost of risk transfer.

We conclude Part One in Chapters 5 and 6 with a discussion of how derivatives evolved historically, emphasizing the migration of derivatives along two dimensions: from asset lending contracts into risk transfer mechanisms, and from bilateral contracts into traded financial instruments. Chapter 6 then explores the mechanics of the derivatives "supply chain"—trading, clearing, and settlement.

In Part Two of the book, we explore in significant detail the function of derivatives as intertemporal and interspatial resource allocation markets. We begin in Chapter 7 with an examination of derivatives in a general equilibrium setting. Using the modern theory of financial asset valuation, we see how derivatives can be used to shift resources from states of nature in which higher consumption is relatively less valuable into states of nature in which a small increase in consumption is particularly highly valued. We explore the implications of this for the valuation of derivatives payoffs and the compensation of firms for bearing systematic risk associated with derivatives.

In Chapter 8, we reconcile the modern general equilibrium view of derivatives valuation with historical conceptions of derivatives as commodity loan markets. We develop the concept of an own or commodity interest rate—the cost of carry—for physical and financial assets, and we see how that concept acts as the central linkage between derivatives as risk transfer instruments and the basic microeconomics of derivatives as asset loans.

In Chapter 9, we consider in more detail the element of *time* in derivatives. We develop concepts of the term structure of futures and forward prices and see how those concepts relate to physical asset storage, inventory management, and the rationing of scarcity over time.

Chapter 10 explores briefly the term structure of interest rates and how this can be viewed as a *special case* of the term structure of forward prices for an asset called money. Basic similarities between money and derivatives are presented. We illustrate the application of these historical concepts to the more contemporary London Interbank Offered Rate (LIBOR) swap curve.

In Chapter 11 we introduce the concept of basis or spread relations. We define the basis as the price of transforming an asset over time and/or space, and review some of the most common basis and spread relations in derivatives.

Part Three explores the practical aspects of speculation and hedging in light of the theoretical foundations laid in Parts One and Two. We consider in Chapter 12 the role of speculators, including their sources of perceived profits and whether they demand a risk premium over and above the systematic risk premium to engage in risk transfer with hedgers. We then explore in Chapter 13 the rich array of concepts implied by the term *hedging*. Chapter 14 then presents a discussion of how firms determine their specific hedge ratios in the context of the hedging objectives a firm sets forth along the lines presented in Chapter 13. Chapters 15 and 16 illustrate the concepts of quality and calendar basis risk—that is, how basis relations can lead to imperfections in risk transfer strategies.

## RELATION TO OTHER BOOKS

This is my third full-length sole-authored book. The first—*The Risk Management Process: Business Strategy and Tactics* (Wiley, 2001)—explored when and how risk management as a process may be value-enhancing for corporations. The second—*The ART of Risk Management: Alternative Risk Transfer, Capital Structure, and the Convergence of Insurance and Capital Markets* (Wiley, 2002)—emphasized the risk finance and risk transfer aspects of a corporation's risk management process. As the title suggests, the emphasis in the second book was on alternative risk transfer (ART) products, representing the convergence of insurance, derivatives, and securities. The second book also emphasized the inherent symmetry between corporate financing and risk management decisions.

Both of my earlier books took very much a "corporate finance" perspective. They considered risk management as a part of corporate finance, and emphasized how any individual firm should analyze and undertake risk management decisions. In sharp contrast, this book deals much more with a macro-market or microeconomic perspective of risk transfer. Whereas the other books were written from the bottom-up perspective of single firms, this book is written with a top-down perspective of the broad risk transfer and derivatives marketplace. With the exception of a brief part of Chapter 13 (a discussion of hedging objectives by value-maximizing firms), there is essentially no overlap in this book with my other two.

In terms of where this book stands relative to what others have written, everyone has their favorite bookshelf items. Far be it from me to try to propose some ideal reading list, thus both imposing my preferences on you and insulting other able authors by the inevitable omissions from such a list. Nevertheless, mainly to clarify further by example what this book does and does not cover in terms of subject matter, allow me to comment on a few other offerings in the market. Specifically, allow me to comment on things that this book *is not*.

First, this book is not a substitute for a general textbook introduction to derivatives. On the contrary, this book actually assumes you have already digested or are concurrently digesting such a general text. For a first course on derivatives, the excellent new book by Robert MacDonald (*Derivatives Markets*, 2003) is the one to beat. Or, for derivatives with a risk management emphasis, try the new text by René Stulz (*Risk Management and Derivatives*, 2003). The texts by John Hull (*Options, Futures, and Other Derivatives*, 2003) and Robert Jarrow and Stuart Turnbull (*Derivative Securities*, 1999) also remain reliable introductions to both the institutional aspects and the valuation of derivatives. And, of course, there are others well worth reading but too numerous to list here.

All the books just mentioned place a heavy emphasis on the analytical aspects of derivatives pricing. For those wishing a slightly less technical and more institutional introduction to derivatives, the third edition of *Financial Derivatives* by Robert Kolb and Jim Overdahl (Wiley, 2003) is very nice. If you want a heavier mixture of product information with a current and thorough treatment of tax and regulatory issues, see Andie Kramer's *Financial Products: Taxation, Regulation and Design* (2003). And if you want more of a focus on how derivatives fit into practical hedging and trading strategies, Todd Petzel's *Financial Futures and Options* (1989) will never disappoint.

Second, this book is not a product manual. It provides neither an overview of major products by asset class—MacDonald and the others noted earlier do that nicely—nor an in-depth focus on any single product or market. If you are looking for product-specific depth, you will not be disappointed by the numerous high-quality offerings in the market today.

In the interest rate area, look to Galen Burghardt. The 1991 Eurodollar book by Burghardt, Belton, Lane, Luce, and McVey (1991) is dated but remains a classic. Happily, Burghardt recently undertook a complete revision and update of that early offering that culminated in his new *Eurodollar Futures and Options Handbook* (2003). No serious practitioner of derivatives can justify not owning this one. Together with Terry Belton, Professor Burghardt has also given us *the* book on bond futures and options, *The Treasury Bond Basis*.

For currency products, J. Orlin Grabbe's *International Financial Markets* (1996) provides a balanced mixture of monetary history, economics, financial products (down to pips and bid/ask quote conventions), and strategies. For a deeper look at currency derivatives in particular, David DeRosa's *Currency Derivatives* (1998) and *Options on Foreign Exchange* (2000) are the deserved frontrunners.

Equity derivatives represent a more difficult area in which books tend to be highly subspecialized. At the overview level, probably the best bets are the new edition of Francis, Toy, and Whittaker's edited volume *The Handbook of Equity Derivatives* (Wiley, 1999) and Harry Kat's *Structured Equity Derivatives* (Wiley, 2001). Beyond those, it depends on whether your interest lies in convertibles, structured products, futures and swaps, or other products. Fortunately, there is no shortage of material in any of these specific areas.

A standard reference for anyone on the commodities side is still the Chicago Board of Trade's *Commodity Trading Manual*. I also recommend getting a used copy of Jeff Williams's *The Economic Function of Futures Markets*. Cambridge University Press should be chastised for letting this gem of a book go out of print. In addition, try to obtain from the Chicago Board of

Trade the Selected Readings in Futures Markets Research series edited by Anne Peck. The collected works of Holbrook Working are especially commendable to commodity derivatives aficionados.

When you get into more specialized commodity products—natural gas, oil, weather, electricity, and so on—the choices get more limited and harder to find. But there is a lot of good stuff out there; you just have to look around and be sure to choose judiciously.

Finally, in the rapidly emerging area of credit derivatives, you'll find more choices than you can shake a stick at. As in any "hot" area, some of the books are great, whereas others are more opportunistic and won't last long. Fortunately, the former outnumber the latter in this area. My own personal favorite is the recent contribution by one of the true gurus of derivatives, Charles Smithson. His *Credit Portfolio Management* (Wiley, 2003) provides a balanced mixture of analytics, economics, products, and strategies. (His *Managing Financial Risk* is also still well worth owning.)

## AUDIENCE

Those most likely to find this book interesting are researchers and practitioners of derivatives (including traders and corporate risk managers) with an interest in learning more about the theoretical underpinnings of derivatives as risk transfer instruments. This book is not a recipe book or a how-to guide; nor is it pure theory for the sake of theory. The book strives to draw explicit connections between theory and practice in derivatives and thus is intended to appeal to those with an interest in both.

Please note that a book like this, which attempts to take theory and practice equally seriously, will not suit people at either extreme. If you are looking for how-tos, you will be disappointed in this book. It doesn't present gift-wrapped solutions to anything—it provides you with a way of thinking about the issues. If you are a research specialist or academic, you will be equally disappointed. The literature surveyed here is not intended to be complete, and the models of speculation and hedging presented are a small fraction of the current academic literature. But if you are looking to straddle these two worlds and see how theory and practice meet, I hope you will find the book of some value.

Finally, students and instructors may find this book useful either as a supplementary text to a first course on derivatives or as the sole text for a more specialized second course on derivatives. A suggested curriculum for a second MBA-level derivatives course relying on this book plus a packet of supplementary readings can be found on my Web site at http://gsb.uchicago.edu/fac/christopher.culp/—go to the "Teaching" section and choose "Business 35101."

## ERRATA AND WEB SITE

Errors inevitably survive the edits of even the most conservative publishers and meticulous authors. They are facts of life in publishing. Accordingly, I will maintain an updated errata list on my Web site under the "Research" section for those interested. Similarly, those who spot errors in need of correction are encouraged to send me e-mail—my address is also listed on my Web site.

# Mathematical Notation

| | |
|---|---|
| $\partial x$ | Very small or continuous rate of change in $x$ |
| $\partial x / \partial y$ | First partial derivatives of $x$ w.r.t. $y$ |
| $\partial^2 x / \partial y^2$ | Second partial derivatives of $x$ w.r.t. $y$ |
| $\Delta x$ | A discrete rate of change in $x$ |
| $\Delta_h$ | Delta of a hedge exposure $H$ to underlying price $P$, or $\partial M / \partial P$ |
| $\Delta_u$ | Delta of a risk exposure $U$ to underlying price $P$, or $\partial U / \partial P$ |
| $\Gamma$ | Gamma, or $\partial^2 U / \partial P^2 = \partial \Delta_u / \partial P$ |
| $\kappa$ | Kappa, or $\partial U / \partial \sigma^2$—also known as Gamma |
| $\theta$ | Theta, or $\partial U / \partial (T - t)$ |
| $\rho$ | Rho, or $\partial U / \partial r$ |
| $\rho_{t,T}$ | Asset repo rate for asset sale at $t$ and repurchase at $T$ |
| $\pi_1$ | Probability of the good state in a two-state model |
| $\pi_2$ | Probability of the bad state in a two-state model |
| $\pi_T^l$ | Cash flow on a long position with value date $T$ |
| $\pi_T^s$ | Cash flow on a short position with value date $T$ |
| $\Pi$ | Terminal net profit on a hedging strategy |
| $\zeta$ | Pure rate of time preference |
| $\sigma$ | Volatility or standard deviation |
| $\sigma^2$ | Variance |
| $\psi$ | Speculative risk premium $= f_{t,T} - E_t(S_T)$ |
| $\omega$ | Speculative risk premium as a proportion of $S_t$ |
| $A/360$ | Actual/360 day-count convention |
| $A/365$ | Actual/365 day-count convention |
| $b_{t,T}$ | Calendar basis or net cost of carry from $t$ to $T$ as a proportion of $S_t$ |
| $c_t$ | Consumption at time $t$ |
| $c_{t,T}$ | Physical storage cost from $t$ to $T$ as a proportion of $S_t$ |

$d_{t,T}$      Number of calendar days between $t$ and $T$ (inclusive)

$D$        Macaulay duration

$DCB$    Day-count basis, or number of days in the quotation year for an annualized interest rate

$DV01$   Dollar (or foreign currency equivalent) value of a basis point or tick

$E[x]$      Mathematical expectation or expected value (unconditional)

$E_t[x]$     Conditional expectation or expected value of $x$ conditional on information available at time $t$

$E_t[m_T]$ Risk-free discount factor from $t$ to $T$, or $1/R^f$

$f_{t,T}$       Fixed price paid by the long to the short in a forward contract with trade date $t$ and value/maturity date $T$

$F_{t,T}$      Quoted price on date $t$ for a futures contract maturing on date $T$

$H$        Value of a hedge position

$K$        Fixed price or rate parameter—strike price for an option, fixed interest rate in a swap, and so on

$l_{t,T}$       Asset liquidity yield from $t$ to $T$ as a proportion of $S_t$

$m_T$      Stochastic discount factor—generally, the intertemporal marginal rate of substitution—applied to time $T$ payoff

$MD$     Modified duration

$N$        Number of futures contracts corresponding to hedge ratio $h$

$PV_t[x]$ Expected discounted present value of $x$ as of date $t$; this assumes the correct discount rate is used but does not require us to write out or define what the correct discount rate is—$x$ can be known or random

$PV01$   Present value of a DV01, or $PV_t(DV01)$

$q_{t,T}$      Asset or convenience yield from $t$ to $T$ as a proportion of $S_t$

$Q$        Quantity of a risk exposure to be hedged

$r^f$        Net risk-free return

$r_{t,T}$      Money rate of interest from $t$ to $T$ $or$ net return (Chapter 7 only)

$R_j$       Floating reference rate corresponding to settlement date $j$ or gross asset return with end of holding period at date $j$ (Chapter 7 only)

$R_j^e$       Excess return, or $R_j - R^f$

$R^f$       Gross risk-free return, or $(1 + r^f)$

$S_t$        Spot price of an asset for immediate delivery

$t$         Trade date

$T$      Value/maturity date

$u(c_t)$      Von Neumann–Morgenstern utility of date $t$ consumption for a risk-averse representative consumer or investor—$u_c > 0$, $u_{cc} < 0$

$U$      Value of an unhedged exposure to be hedged

$U(c)$      Utility value function corresponding to probability-weighted von Neumann–Morgenstern component additive utility functions

$V$      Net value of a hedge position and unhedged exposure, or $H + U$

$x_{t,T}$      Real own rate of interest from $t$ to $T$ as a proportion of $S_t$ and expressed in terms of the asset

$y_{t,T}$      Real own rate of interest from $t$ to $T$ as a proportion of $S_t$, or $x_{t,T} - r_{t,T}$

$Y$      Nominal size of a futures contract in contract specifications

$z_T$      Cash flow or payoff at time $T$

$Z$      Quantity of exposure to be hedged that is actually hedged with derivatives

$\mathbf{Z}$      A hedging strategy defined as a vector of hedging quantities

# PART One

# The Economics of Risk Transfer

# CHAPTER 1

# The Determinants of Financial Innovation

The range of financial products and instruments available today is quite literally mind-boggling. Corporate securities no longer include only plain-vanilla stocks, bonds, and convertibles, but all manner of preferred stock, commodity- and equity-indexed debt, amortizing principal notes, and more. Depository instruments, once limited to fixed-interest demand and term deposits, now encompass products that pay interest based on stock market returns, election results, and other eclectic variables. And with the advent of alternative risk transfer (ART), insurance solutions now transcend their traditional role and provide indemnity against risks like exchange rate shifts, credit downgrades, and investment losses.

Perhaps nowhere has the sheer breadth of financial products grown more than in the area of derivatives activity. The conventional definition of a "derivative" is a bilateral contract that derives its value from one or more underlying asset prices, indexes, or references rates.[1] As we will see again throughout the text, the definition of derivatives that will prove most useful for our purposes is a contract for the purchase or sale of some asset (or its cash equivalent) in which time and space are explicitly defined and differ in some way from the here and now.

The most common types of derivatives include futures, forwards, swaps, and options, all of which are available on a huge range of underlying assets (e.g., metals, interest rates, electric power, currencies, etc.) and for maturities ranging from days to many years. The terms of these agreements can be so customized and varied that the array of products available to their users is essentially boundless. In addition, derivatives are frequently embedded into other products like bonds to create instruments like commodity-linked debt.[2]

Many public and social commentators have questioned whether all of these diverse financial products available today play a legitimate economic function. Or, even if most new financial products do serve some purpose, how big is the benefit and who appropriates it? The question is rather like asking how badly society really needs another breakfast cereal in the grocery aisle—one more surely cannot hurt, but how much does it really help?[3]

To understand the benefits and functions of derivatives, we need to begin with a broader discussion of the functions of the economy in general and financial markets (as distinct from physical asset markets) in particular. We then consider what determines the rate and types of financial innovations that emerge to help provide the functions of the economy and the financial system.

## THE ECONOMIC AND FINANCIAL SYSTEMS

Academics have advanced a number of hypotheses to explain the range of financial instruments available and the rate at which they are developed, but remarkably little common agreement has been reached on which explanation is most consistent with the data.[4] One explanation must surely be that not all innovations occur for the same reason. As a result, the historical data available to test competing hypotheses for explaining innovation is too limited relative to the multiplicity of possible explanations that the data reflects. Indeed, we can identify anecdotal examples that are consistent with virtually *all* of the proposed theories.

The overarching theme underlying most explanations for legitimate financial innovation is the idea that financial products arise to help perform the functions of the economic system. Products like derivatives, in turn, are generally considered part of the financial system, the component of the broader economic system that provides a well-functioning capital market.

### The Economic System

Economic behavior includes all the actions taken by humans to achieve certain ends when those objectives are in the face of scarce means with numerous potential uses. An *economic system*, in turn, is a social mechanism to help humans address those resource scarcity problems. Knight (1933) argued that any properly functioning economic system must perform five main interconnected functions.[5]

#### Fixing Standards
The economic system should "fix standards" for the purpose of maximizing the efficient allocation of resources. An economic system must somehow allow a heterogeneous group of individuals and firms to coordinate their activities with one another using a common and consistent set of indicators about

the value of scarce resources. This is the classic rationale for a free price system—to signal relative scarcity on the supply side and the intensity of consumer wants and needs on the demand side (Hayek, 1945).

## Allocation
The economic system should actually facilitate the allocation of those scarce resources to their most highly valued uses. In a capitalist system, the counterpart to the free price system—which serves to indicate relative scarcity and the value of alternative resource allocations—is free trade. By facilitating the exchange of assets and goods at freely determined prices, resources may actually flow from their original endowments to those individuals and firms that value those resources the most.

## Distribution
The third function of an economic system is distributional. The free price system and open markets together help ensure that resources are allocated to their most highly valued uses. This in turn generally leads to *efficiency*, or the situation in which social resources are collectively the greatest. Distribution then may seek to reallocate those resources based on the particular wants and needs of certain consumers and producers. To repeat a common analogy, allocative efficiency helps ensure that the social pie is baked as big as possible. Once the size of the pie is maximized, distribution then seeks to determine the size of each pie slice.

## Maintenance and Accumulation of Factors of Production
An economic system should promote the maintenance and efficient accumulation of factors of production. Specifically, an economic system should support the growth of population and the labor force relative to basic resource constraints (i.e., to avoid the Malthusian trap). In addition, the system should facilitate the processes of capital formation and capital accumulation, where "capital" may be taken to mean any factor that facilitates production over a period of time (Hicks, 1939).

## Ensuring Consistency in Short-Term Plans
Finally, the economic system must reconcile consumption and production plans over short periods of time. The system thus must serve a *coordination* function to keep the consumption and production plans of a huge number of different individuals and firms consistent with one another.

## The Capital Market and the Financial System
Derivatives and other financial products are part of what we call the *capital market*, a specific component of a broader economic system whose particular

function is facilitating the allocation and distribution of resources *across space and time*. Interspatial resource allocation and distribution involve the shifting or transfer of resources between different places or among different economic agents, whereas intertemporal resource management involves the movement of resources across periods of time. Consumption smoothing, for example, is the process by which economic agents reduce consumption in plentiful periods in order to prevent consumption from dipping too far during periods of want. Similarly, as Part Two explains in detail, inventory management is essentially the borrowing and lending of physical commodities over time.

Like all the basic functions of the economic system, intertemporal and interspatial resource allocation is strongly interconnected with the other functions of the system. In that sense, the capital market does not play a completely unique role, except to the extent that capital itself as a factor of production is unique.

Providing a mechanism for interspatial and intertemporal resource management, however, is no small task. An organized *financial system* thus is generally required to enable the capital market to perform its allocative and distributional functions. The financial system includes a combination of institutions, markets, and financial products that together provide a payments system, a mechanism for the pooling of capital to facilitate investment, and the provision of information that facilitates coordination and resource allocation[6] (cf. Merton, 1992, 1995a, 1995b). In addition, a critical function of the capital market and the financial system is providing economic agents with a formal mechanism for controlling their exposure to randomness—that is, the management of risk and uncertainty. In particular, the financial system should facilitate efficient risk bearing, risk sharing, and risk transfer.

## "BENEFICIAL" AND "SUCCESSFUL" FINANCIAL INNOVATION

Miller (1986) distinguishes among an *innovation*; a *successful innovation*; and a *successful, significant innovation*, all of which are separate from a mere *improvement*. In order to be an innovation rather than an improvement, the financial product must arise or evolve *unexpectedly*. Technological change, for example, often gives rise to new products that can be considered improvements, but not really innovations. Innovations, in short, cannot be forecast.

A successful innovation is any innovation that "earns an immediate reward for its adopters," whereas a "successful *and* significant innovation" must cause a permanent and lasting change to the financial landscape (Miller, 1986, p. 461). To Miller, innovations that are both successful and significant "manage not only to survive, but to continue to grow, sometimes very substantially, *even after their initiating force has been removed"* (Miller, 1986, p. 462).

Most successful and significant innovations help provide one or more of the functions of the capital market in particular and the economic system in general. The discontinuation of a new financial product, in turn, likely indicates that particular innovation had at best a marginal long-term role to play in the economic system. But that hardly means the innovation was pointless.

A well-functioning capitalist economic system relies on trial and error. Successes *and* failures of market participants thus are normal characteristics of progress—you cannot have one without the possibility of the other. As a result, we should not expect all financial innovations to be successful *ex post*, despite all good intentions of the designers *ex ante*. As an example, four out of every five new futures contracts are delisted within a few years of their introduction (Carlton, 1984). Innovation thus must be regarded as evidence of what Schumpeter calls the "creative destruction" of capitalism. It is a necessary component of progress.

## THE TIMING OF INNOVATION

The universe of financial products available in the capital market at any point in time may generally be classified in one of Miller's three categories—as an unexpected improvement (i.e., an innovation), a successful innovation, or both a successful and significant new product. But apart from this snapshot of the capital market at any point in time, Miller's taxonomy also implies certain drivers affecting the *timing* and *rate* of financial innovation. We consider here some of the most common factors that are believed to explain exactly when new financial products are most likely to emerge.

### Taxes and Regulations

To Miller (1986, 1992), the impulses that are most often responsible for innovation; successful innovation; and successful, significant innovation are changes in taxes or regulations. Consider some of the examples he offers, such as the Eurodollar market or the market in which commercial banks borrow and lend in dollars offshore. This market arose as a fairly direct response to Regulation Q, which specified a maximum interest rate payable on *domestic* time deposits without placing a similar ceiling on *foreign* dollar-denominated time deposits. Similarly, a 30 percent tax on interest payments from bonds issued in the United States to foreign investors gave rise to the development of the Eurobond market, in which dollar bonds issued abroad to foreign investors were exempt from the special tax. And so on.

Miller also explains that a surprisingly large number of lasting and significant innovations in derivatives have been a result of liberalization or clarification in the relevant regulations and laws governing derivatives and comparable transactions. As an example, until the 1970s most derivatives involved the physical delivery of the asset on which the price or settlement value of the contract was based. But "cash settlement" became popular in the 1970s as an often cheaper alternative to physical delivery. As the discussion later in Part One clarifies, cash settlement simply means that instead of the short delivering a physical asset to the long, the short delivers an amount of cash to the long exactly equal to the then-current value of a physical delivery. Unless the long in a derivatives contract actually needs the physical asset—not often the case if the primary objective of the contract is to promote risk transfer—cash settlement is much more efficient.

Allowing cash settlement instead of physical delivery was hardly a revolutionary idea. Why, then, did it occur only in the mid-1970s? As Miller explains, prior to some important legislative reforms in the mid-1970s, cash settlement often inadvertently turned derivatives into "gambling contracts," which were quite simply illegal in certain states. So, the great significant and lasting innovation of cash settlement was attributable entirely to a legislative change that clarified the distinction between derivatives and lottery tickets. In like fashion, Miller maintains that the reason the 1970s and 1980s were such a significant period of genuine innovation was that many of the encumbering regulations adopted in the New Deal and post-Depression era of the 1930s were finally dismantled during the 1970s and 1980s, thus freeing market participants to achieve their financial objectives in a more direct fashion than had been possible before.

The changes to regulations adopted in the 1920s and 1930s that occurred in the 1970s and 1980s illustrate Kane's (1999) argument that regulation both influences *and is influenced by* financial innovation. Kane (1988) emphasizes that regulatory agencies must be treated as *dynamically interactive* institutions in the financial market. He refers to that process as the "political dialectic of controls"—now called the *regulatory dialectic*—whereby regulators acting and reacting to change can precipitate other changes in innovation, which precipitate additional reactions by regulators, and so on.

Miller also believes that significant and successful innovations tend to be luxury goods. The more impoverished a society, the more it will focus on innovations that are merely successful in the transitory sense, and less important will be the need to identify longer-term efficiency gains. In other words, regulatory and tax inefficiencies are not likely to be "binding constraints" during periods of relative poverty. Miller explains:

> By the middle and late 1960s, . . . the recovery in world wealth (and trade) had proceeded so far that the taxes, interest rate ceilings, foreign exchange restrictions, security sales regulations, and other anticompeti-

*tive controls slapped on in the 1930s and -40s were becoming increasingly onerous. It was not so much that new tax and regulatory burdens were being imposed (though that was happening too), but more that the existing burdens were increasingly binding, particularly so given the surges in the level and volatility of prices, interest rates, and exchange rates that were erupting in those years. (Miller, 1986, p. 471)*

## Risk Transfer and "Completing the Market"

Certainly one of the most appealing explanations for financial innovation is the notion that new products can facilitate risk transfer—a key function of the financial system, to be sure. Without the innovation, so the story goes, some risk or uncertainty affects at least one individual or firm that wishes to transfer that risk or uncertainty to a counterparty but cannot. This rather grand notion of the role played by new financial products is called *completing the market*.[7]

If markets exist for every commodity in every state of nature or under every contingency, then markets are said to be complete and the universe of available securities is said to span the known states of nature. One of the most powerful results in price theory is the result that under complete markets, a competitive general equilibrium exists that leads to an efficient allocation of risk bearing (Arrow, 1953; Debreu, 1959). The proof is nightmarish, but the intuition is basic. If we imagine that everyone starts off with some random allocation of commodities and risks, it is logical to assume that this initial allocation may well *not* correspond to people's preferences. When markets are complete, people can trade with one another away from their initial endowments in order to achieve their own optimal allocation of resources. When markets are *not* complete, you can still get a general equilibrium, but the result is no longer efficient—there are potential further reallocations that would still make at least one person better off without making anyone worse off (Radner, 1968; Arrow, 1978).

A market is said to be *dynamically complete* if all of the *nontrivial* states of nature are spanned by existing assets or trading strategies. A dynamically complete market still gives way to efficient risk bearing. Unlike a statically complete market, however, a dynamically complete market may have certain states of nature that are not spanned by existing assets or trading strategies. For efficiency to still obtain, it must simply be the case that economic agents basically attach no practical importance to those contingencies that are not covered by markets. In other words, the unspanned states of nature are *economically trivial*.

Similarly, a dynamically complete market may also exhibit nontrivial states of nature that are spanned not by specific financial instruments, but rather by "replication strategies." A good example of this might be the absence of extremely long-term contracts to deal with long-run uncertainty. As long as enough short-dated financial products exist to span the *information set*, markets can be dynamically completed by sequential trading strategies (Ross, 1999). See Chapter 16.

For static market completeness, securities markets alone are often the basis for risk sharing in an economy. After all, the corporation itself is essentially a limited liability mechanism to facilitate capital formation. And even within the corporation, risk-sharing arrangements and risk transfer occur between employees and owners (through incentive compensation), shareholders and creditors (through seniority and priority rules), and the like. The ability of individuals and institutional investors to select the securities they hold and achieve their desired optimal portfolios is an essential ingredient to a well-functioning capital market.

Whereas corporate securities are mainly intended to promote capital formation and static market completeness, derivatives are primarily designed to facilitate the transfer of capital, earnings, or cash flows at risk from one party to another, and they often do so in a dynamic way. A common belief thus is that innovations of new derivatives contracts are *dynamically market-completing*. Specifically, by creating markets in which certain risks and contingent outcomes can be explicitly traded or sequentially replicated, derivatives are thought to move the market closer to dynamic completeness, and hence closer to a Pareto efficient allocation of resources.

The temptation to assume that the development of new derivatives helps complete the market doubtless comes from the fact that derivatives can be defined to cover essentially any kind of risk. To facilitate the full transfer of a given risk or contingency, the contract just needs to have a payoff or cash flow that is perfectly correlated to the risk or contingency in question. As will become clear later, the relatively simple mechanics of derivatives makes it fairly easy to achieve this objective.

That derivatives are *capable* of playing a market-completing function thus is beyond doubt. The question remains open as to whether derivatives actually *have* completed markets when they were introduced. Importantly, if the market for the underlying asset on which the derivatives contract is based can be traded, then the derivatives transaction is known as a *redundant asset*. This means that the cash flows on the derivatives position can be dynamically replicated by holding some amount of the underlying asset over time, and perhaps adjusting that amount as time passes. But if true, then derivatives *cannot* serve a market-completing function. The available trading markets already span the state space as long as the underlying asset can be traded. The introduction of new derivatives thus does not actually make it possible for any new risks or contingencies to be covered that could not already have been covered. And there is the paradox. If derivatives are based on a traded underlying asset, then they cannot have been developed to complete the market (Ross, 1999).

The belief that derivatives complete the market is intuitively appealing, but it rests fairly strongly on an implicit assumption that transaction costs do not really matter. If we allow for the possibility of sometimes significant transaction costs and market participants that have varying degrees of knowledge about the true impact of new information on the prices of existing assets, then successful and significant financial innovation can arise purely as a way of spanning certain states of nature *more efficiently*.

In other words, derivatives may well be beneficial in facilitating risk transfer, but this is not really because derivatives *truly* allow firms to hedge and contract over certain states of nature that were inaccessible before. Derivatives provide access to those states of nature *at a lower cost* than dynamic replication strategies.

As noted earlier, markets can be dynamically complete in the absence of long-term derivatives contracts if sequential replication strategies involving short-term instruments are used. But in the presence of positive transaction costs and asymmetric information, this may be prohibitively expensive (Ross, 1999). Long-dated derivatives thus may arise *as a practical response* to the demand for a *cheaper* way of dealing with the uncertainty in that long-run state of nature. Strictly speaking, this is not a market-completing innovation because the long-dated source of uncertainty was *theoretically* already spanned by the mere possibility of short-term sequential trading. But this sort of innovation can still be efficient, successful, and significant because it allows market participants to manage the risk of a given source of uncertainty at a much lower cost.

This line of reasoning can be extended well beyond just risk transfer and can, in fact, apply to *any* function of the financial or economic system that a new innovation helps to provide. A primary economic function of derivatives, for example, is to facilitate the intertemporal and interspatial allocation of resources. New derivatives may be developed not only to allocate resources across time and space that are currently immobile along one of those dimensions, but also to allocate resources more efficiently and at a lower cost than through currently available means.

Merton (1989) emphasizes that pure transaction costs explanations for financial innovations should not be underestimated. A significant amount of financial innovation appears to be driven by the manner in which the innovations enable market participants to do something that was already possible *in a more efficient manner*.

In the context of the timing of innovations, new financial products whose primary function is to help firms manage risk or uncertainty tend to arise when the cost of existing risk management solutions becomes too high relative to the cost of the new innovation. This might occur, for example, because a technological improvement gives rise to a lower-cost innovation. Options trading, for example, predated the development of the Black-Scholes option pricing formula and the use of high-speed computers by more than 50 years, but trading never really became active until technology significantly reduced the costs of pricing and hedging an option portfolio.

## Institutional Demands and Financial Marketing

In an interesting twist on the market completeness explanation for successful and significant financial innovation, Ross (1989) argues that innovation can sometimes unexpectedly complete the market in such a way where the benefit is not clear. If a new derivatives contract is developed, for example, that is highly esoteric and complex—many of those in the late 1980s and early 1990s would qualify—any uncertainty among market participants about the nature of the payoffs of the contract will essentially generate new states of nature that are not yet spanned. These states may or may not be "empirically relevant."

To Ross, the role of financial marketing is "to leave as little nonspanned uncertainty as is efficient" (Ross, 1989, p. 543). The task of financial marketing is thus to explain the empirical benefits of the payoffs of a new instrument up to the point where those benefits of the proposed new transaction equal the marginal cost of explanation. More complex innovations thus tend to have higher marketing costs.

Unlike the standard market-completing case, Ross thus argues that innovation is much more of a cycle in which new financial products first arise that are tailored to very specific needs of individuals or particular institutions. In some cases, the benefits of the product are limited to that handful of participants, and the innovations either disappear after a time or persist in a highly customized capacity (i.e., as successful but not significant innovations). In other cases, the benefits of the product are available to a wide range of market participants, but the product emerges in such a customized form that the costs of marketing these products to other participants are prohibitively high initially. Gradually over time, marketing costs fall as the product's benefits become more tangible, and merely successful innovations among a small class of institutions give way to successful *and significant* innovations.

In the Ross model, products whose benefits are far-reaching but initially unclear thus always begin as customized financial instruments available to only a handful of sophisticated market participants. As the benefits of the product become more empirically obvious, marketing kicks in. This has the effect not only of distributing the product to a wider range of users, but the financial innovation itself also tends to undergo a type of mutation in which the product becomes less tailored to a few institutions and more standardized.

As an example, the institutionalization of the asset markets in Switzerland clearly led to a significant amount of innovation for the reasons hypothesized by Ross. (See Zimmermann, 1999.) Initially sparked by a regulatory reform of the Swiss Federal Pension law (*Bundesgesetz über die berufliche Vorsorge*) in 1985 (shades of Miller's explanation for the key driver of innovation), the rapid increase in the prominence and participation of pension funds led to a significant increase in product design aimed at those institutions. A product called "covered options" (*Stillhalteroptionen*) was an extremely narrowly defined product aimed by marketers at helping pension plans meet regulatory requirements. But as marketing efforts intensified, these products evolved and became more general. Soon thereafter, passive funds, stock-index derivatives, and exchange-traded single-security derivatives became standard features of the typical institutional investor's portfolio.

In retrospect, one can argue that the regulatory shift provided a catalyst for an institutional marketing effort that in turn led to the development of highly customized products followed by the development of more standardized products. Marketing seems to have been largely responsible for helping new participants identify new states to be spanned and new products with which to span them.

## Addressing Agency Costs

University of Chicago economist and Nobel laureate in economics George Stigler used to tell his graduate students that the most influential book of the twentieth century was *The Modern Corporation and Private Property* by Berle and Means, published in 1932. There we encounter for the first time the important concept of "agency costs," or the costs that principals like shareholders and creditors must incur to monitor the actions of their managerial agents.[8] When agency costs are high and/or the actions of agents are unobservable by principals, agents acting in their own best interests may sometimes take actions that do not coincide with the preferences of the principals in the organization.

The timing of financial innovation is often explained as a response to a change in agency costs. Ross (1989), for example, sees some innovations as responses to the agency costs affecting large, opaque financial intermediaries.[9] Equity options, for example, are derivatives that emerged first as primarily a retail trading instrument. Ross explains this as a response by large intermediaries to the agency problems associated with extending credit to clients that preferred riskier leveraged strategies. Instead of incurring that kind of risk and the associated agency and monitoring costs, institutions developed limited liability options as leveraged retail instruments that could better serve their customer needs.

Another popular belief is that the design of new financial instruments is intended to force managers to reveal information they have that investors do not have. This is a slightly different mechanism by which agency costs affect innovation than Ross's institutional explanation, but it is an agency cost–based explanation, to be sure.

Harris and Raviv (1989), Allen and Gale (1994), and Tufano (2003), among others, survey the implications of agency costs on the supply of financial products.

## THE FINANCIAL-INNOVATION SPIRAL

The role of the capital markets and financial system in the economic system is, of course, not characterized completely by the availability of financial products like derivatives. The financial system is the combination of institutions, products, and markets that *together* constitute the fabric of the capital market. An important dimension of financial innovation is how such innovations affect the institutional landscape of the marketplace.

Most financial innovations begin as relatively customized transactions and then gradually evolve into more standardized, homogeneous contracts. In the process, financial products tend to begin through bilateral negotiation among institutions and intermediaries and then evolve toward organized financial markets in the process known as commodization (Merton, 1989, 1992, 1995a,b; Ross, 1989).

Securitization is a good example of commodization in traditional security markets. Securitization is the process by which the assets of an institution are repackaged and transformed into securities that can be traded in a transparent market. The principal and interest receivables on mortgage loans made by banks and thrifts, for example, are often securitized and transformed into mortgage-backed securities, now a relatively liquid and well-developed security market. In turn, mortgage-backed securities then become the basis of securitized products (e.g., collateralized mortgage obligations) and derivatives (e.g., mortgage swaps).

Not all customized contracts evolve into standardized, traded financial instruments through the process of commodization. No market exists for homogenous financial contracts based on shoes, for example, despite the existence of long-term contracts between retailers and wholesalers to buy and sell shoe inventories in the future. Those contracts that do evolve into "markets" through commodization, moreover, often spawn further evolutionary changes in the process by which the *original* contracts are negotiated. Innovation that begins with customization thus evolves into standardization, which in turn begets further innovation. Merton (1992) refers to this as the "financial-innovation spiral."

## NOTES

1. See, for example, Global Derivatives Study Group (1993). This traditional definition is unfortunately broad enough to include the moon and stars, as

well as plain-vanilla securities like common stock, which literally derives its value from the prices of the underlying assets owned by the firm. Ultimately, there is no good way to define derivatives without including almost everything. Instead, we resort to the tactic used by U.S. Justice Potter Stewart in defining pornography, who quipped that he had no idea how to define it but would know it when he saw it.

2. See Culp and Mackay (1996, 1997).
3. Some hard-core populist critics contend that many of the financial products available today were invented "by Wall Street" in an effort to take advantage of a less informed group of end users and to generate transactions that really serve no economic purpose except to line the pockets of the masters of the universe. Such assertions are pure public policy rhetoric— no meaningful empirical support is ever offered to back these claims.
4. For a much more comprehensive survey of financial innovation than is presented here, see Tufano (2003).
5. Knight was certainly not the only one to articulate the functions of an economic system, but his description happens to fit particularly well into our discussion here.
6. Several of the items on Merton's list were omitted because they are redundant with the functions of the whole economic system already presented. Tufano (2003) summarizes the functions of the financial system proposed by some other authors.
7. Duffie and Rahi (1995) and Tufano (2003) survey the literature on financial innovation and market completion.
8. As noted in the next chapter, Adam Smith anticipated agency costs, as did others before Berle and Means. But Berle and Means were the first to give the issue serious and detailed consideration, especially in the context of the modern corporation.
9. The Ross (1989) model actually combines the earlier-discussed marketing rationale for innovation with institutional agency costs, but it is easier to present the two separately here.

# CHAPTER 2

# Risk, Uncertainty, and Profit

As Chapter 1 suggests, two major functions of the economic system are the efficient allocation and distribution of resources to their most highly valued uses. This includes the allocation of resources across time and space and the redistribution of resources among economic agents. Derivatives provide a very efficient mechanism for the shifting of risk over time and space, to other market participants, and across different states of nature.

To appreciate this economic function of derivatives more fully and to understand more clearly how derivatives actually work, we first need to develop some basic economic concepts that underlie the vast majority of what follows in this book. In particular, we focus in this chapter on developing a complete understanding of two fundamental and distinct economic concepts that lie at the core of the theory of risk transfer in general and modern derivatives activity in particular—risk and uncertainty. Perhaps more important than our consideration of either of these terms in isolation, we also want to consider fully the relations between each of these terms to the concept of profit. Without this basic foundation, it will be nearly impossible for us to consider later questions like: When and how do traders make money? Why should firms transfer away risks to which they are exposed? How can a firm distinguish between sources of randomness that are core to the business and the profits of that business from those which are merely incidental? And the like.

Much of this chapter relies on some basic concepts from traditional neoclassical price theory. In several places, moreover, the ideas depart from the traditional neoclassical paradigm and stray into other, alternative branches of economic theory. Although not essential for this chapter, before proceeding readers may wish to review Appendix 1, in which a brief summary of the primary economic theories is considered with specific attention to differences across the theories in what is meant by the concept of equilibrium.

## RISK, UNCERTAINTY, AND THE FIRM

The standard neoclassical treatment of choice under risk and uncertainty involves an axiomatic approach pioneered by von Neumann and Morgenstern (1944), Savage (1954), and others in which individuals' preferences are expressed using a mathematical functional that maps wealth or consumption over time into "units of happiness." Consumers are presumed to maximize their utility of wealth or, in the face of risk or uncertainty, to maximize the *expected value* of their utility of wealth across different random states of nature. For an introduction to this methodology, see Laffont (1989), Kreps (1990), and Gollier (2001). Machina and Rothschild (1987) provide a short but useful survey.

For the most part, however, we will not get into expected utility analysis in this book. That might seem unusual to some experienced readers—how can we ignore this huge branch of economic theory in a book about risk transfer? The simple reason is that we do not need it. Expected utility analysis may be useful for the analysis of *individual* choice under risk and uncertainty, but these methods have more limited applications when it comes to analyzing *business enterprises*. And indeed, corporations are the economic agents with which this book is primarily concerned.

The distinction between individuals and firms is often downplayed, especially for pedagogical and analytical purposes. In rigorous analysis, for example, it is tempting to simplify things by assuming that a firm's behavior can be described with the same tool used to model individual behavior—an expected utility function.[1] That allows us as modelers to make simplifying assumptions, such as the presumption that the firm is risk averse. Outside of rigorous analysis in the classroom or public dialogue, such personifications of the firm are even more tempting, even to the most seasoned theoretician or practitioner. Casual references to a firm that hedges as "risk averse," a firm that pollutes the air as "socially irresponsible," a firm that donates to the local symphony as "community involved," and the like are all useful as tools of pedagogy and discourse.

Despite its seductive appeal, the depiction of a firm as a single-acting economic agent is simply not realistic at all. Consider, for example, the seemingly clear statement that "Company Pacino prefers to take less market risk than Company DeNiro." What does it really mean to say that Company Pacino prefers one thing to another? Or that Company Pacino prefers less risk than Company DeNiro? Do we mean that the managers making the decisions at Company Pacino prefer less risk? Or that Pacino's shareholders prefer less risk? Or perhaps the creditors and customers of the firm prefer less risk? All of these questions underscore the reality that the firm is not simply an organic whole that makes its own decisions, bears its risks, and deals with those risks.[2]

In the end, a firm is just a collection of people bound together in various ways by a set of contracts. Economic theory offers several alternative explanations for when and why individuals find it sensible to form these sorts of associations by setting up corporations. Several of the dominant theories of the firm include:

- A firm is formed when the transaction costs of internal bargaining are below the transaction costs of external dealing across would-be participants in the firm (Coase, 1937).
- A firm is a risk-sharing entity designed to spread the full force of impact of the market on producers across multiple economic agents who may be able to bear such shocks collectively but might not be capable of doing so on their own (Wilson, 1969).
- A firm is an entity formed to exploit specific human capital and the benefits of "team production" (Alchian and Demsetz, 1972).
- A firm evolves to reduce the costs of disputes or bargaining among and across factors of production (Williamson, 1975).
- A firm is a nexus of contracts designed to minimize the costs arising from the separation of ownership and control (Jensen and Meckling, 1976).

No matter what role one ascribes to organizations and firms or why one believes they come into existence, the common thread across all these theories—that the firm is a collection of individuals legally bound together in some way—gives rise to certain problems. Adam Smith recognized this as early as 1776 in his treatise *An Enquiry into the Nature and Causes of the Wealth of Nations*, when he observed the potential for conflicting incentives to exist or arise across the varying numbers and types of heterogeneous individuals that comprise "the firm." Incompatible incentives not only complicate our ability to explain the actions and decisions of firms, but they also render difficult our capacity to visualize and analyze the firm as a single coherent, integrated, holistic economic agent. If a firm is a collection of individuals whose objectives and incentives are not aligned, *to whose objectives do we look* when considering "the firm"?

We could easily stop here and proceed to undertake an entire book on the subject of agency costs, the theory of the firm, and organizational decision making. But that is not our task, and, indeed, such books exist.[3] Yet, in a book about corporate risk transfer and derivatives activity, we cannot simply ignore the complex organizational conundrum underlying the organic firm whose collective decisions we seek to analyze. An immediate implication of agency costs, after all, is that it is generally impossible to ascribe to firms the same basic attitudes that individuals have toward risk; that is, the expected utility framework fails us, at least when applied directly to the firm as a single-acting economic agent.

Just consider a simple example to appreciate the practical importance of this issue. Suppose a Swiss firm has most of its costs denominated in francs and most of its revenues denominated in pounds to reflect the bulk of its sales in the United Kingdom. The firm thus has a significant amount of its business that is influenced *structurally* by exchange rate fluctuations. Now imagine that shareholders of the firm knew this when they purchased their stock, and either have preferences that are consistent with bearing franc/sterling exchange rate risk or have diversified that risk away by holding the stocks of firms whose revenues rise at the same time franc/sterling fluctuations impose losses on the Swiss firm.

Now suppose that the managers of the Swiss firm receive all of their compensation from the Swiss firm in the form of a fixed salary plus a bonus that does not exceed 20 percent of salary.[4] Suppose further that the managers are risk averse—they prefer (in an expected utility context) a fixed level of wealth to a random allocation of wealth with the same mathematical expectation as the fixed level. In the event of significant adverse exchange rate moves, the managers personally suffer—there is less from which the firm can pay the bonus, and, in the extreme, the firm goes bust and the managers lose their salaries and jobs. In the event of *favorable* exchange rate swings, the managers have a very limited upside: They can at most make a 20 percent bonus, and it is not clear that exchange rate gains will go into the bonus pool. If the managers are vested with decision-making responsibility for the firm's risk management program, their natural, rational economic tendency thus will be to hedge the company's exchange rate risk despite the inconsistency of that decision with shareholders' desires and expectations. This will make the firm as a whole appear to be averse to franc/sterling risk. Alternatively, if the shareholders are in control of the hedging decision, they will do nothing, thus making the firm appear neutral or indifferent to exchange rate risk.

When the preferences of the different parties that comprise a firm are at odds in the face of positive agency costs, there is no clear way to describe the "preferences" of "the firm." We can describe the *decisions* the firm makes—either it does or does not hedge—but we have some trouble modeling where those decisions come from without getting into a much deeper level of detail.

Culp (2001) considers the implications of agency costs like these on corporate risk management strategies in some detail. Partly for this reason but mainly because it is not central to our topic, we will simply sidestep these issues here. We cannot simply assume the firm acts like an individual—we lose too much going that route—but we *can* make an intermediate assumption that allows us to consider the firm as a collection of coordinated individuals without worrying about conflicts between different parties. Specifically and unless otherwise stated, we shall assume in this book that the decisions made by "the firm" are in fact made by the managers of the firm, and that those managers act *ex ante* (i.e., based on the information they have at the time) to maximize the market value of the firm's assets. Known as the *market value rule*, this is equivalent to assuming that managers always pursue strategies designed *ex ante* to maximize the combined wealth of all the firm's security holders.

Assuming that corporate managers follow the market value rule is not terribly implausible. As Fama (1976) explains, the market value rule is the only criterion that maximizes the value of the firm. A company whose managers do *not* adhere to the market value rule thus cannot survive in the long run—it will be acquired by a management team that *will* pursue the market value rule. So, all we really have done in making this assumption is to gloss over the various internal contracting and incentive mechanisms that firms use to enforce the market value rule.

## RISK, UNCERTAINTY, AND PROFIT

The first serious effort to explore how *firms* deal with an unknown future that did not simply presuppose a firm had an expected utility function like an individual was undertaken by Frank H. Knight. Raised as a farmer, Knight matriculated to the University of Tennessee when he was in his twenties, and graduated in 1913 with a bachelor's degree in natural sciences and a master's degree in German. From there he went to Cornell, where he worked under Alvin Johnson and Allyn Young[5] on his dissertation until its completion in 1916.

Knight's thesis was the outgrowth of a suggestion by Professor Johnson that he make an examination of "the entrepreneur" as the central figure of the economic system—in particular, of the forces that lead to the renumeration of the entrepreneur through what we call "profits." Surprising as it may seem, despite all the advances in economic theory that occurred in the "marginalist revolution" that brought classical Ricardian economics into the new era of neoclassical economics (see Appendix 1), none had concerned themselves with the firm in quite this manner. In particular, no one had undertaken any serious effort to answer questions like these: If markets are perfectly competitive as in most orthodox models so that no firms earn positive economic profits in the long run, what is the raison d'être for firms even to exist? What is the real driver of a firm's corporate profits? How does the element of randomness surrounding future events affect corporate profits? How does a firm's management decide when the randomness it faces is a problem that needs to be addressed versus when randomness is the key to the firm's competitive edge? And so on.

The fruit of Knight's exploration of these sorts of questions was a highly acclaimed dissertation called *Cost, Value, and Profit* that won second prize in a competition by Hart, Schaffner, and Marx and that helped secure Knight a coveted faculty position in the University of Chicago's department of economics.

Knight remained at Chicago from 1917 to 1919, at which point a lack of open positions forced him to leave, whereupon he joined the faculty at the University of Iowa. During his two years at Chicago, Knight did little else but substantively revise his thesis, drawing heavily on comments and feedback from colleagues that included J. M. Clark, Jacob Viner, and Charles O. Hardy—all of whom were renowned thinkers in their own right. The final result was the publication in 1921 of his revised thesis under the title *Risk, Uncertainty, and Profit*.

Knight's *Risk, Uncertainty, and Profit* is widely considered to be one of the five most important economic texts published in the twentieth century,[6] and Knight himself went on to become one of the most influential economists of all time. He returned to Chicago in 1928 where he remained until his death in 1972.

Known as the "Grand Old Man of Chicago," Knight quickly became one of the leading intellectuals in the development of the Chicago school of economic thought—a branch of the neoclassical school of economic theory with a particular emphasis on the idea that economics is an empirical science and not a normative philosophical paradigm. (See Appendix 1.) Nobel laureate and Chicago economics professor George Stigler (1987, p. 56) called Knight "the dominant intellectual influence" at Chicago during the interwar period. In 1928, he became co-editor (with Viner) of the *Journal of Political Economy*, a journal that played a pivotal role in the evolution of the Chicago school and that is still arguably the top refereed academic journal in economics today.

Knight fostered the development of the Chicago school in part through his intellectual progeny. Among his students were three who themselves subsequently became towering figures of the Chicago school: Milton Friedman, George Stigler, and James Buchanan. All three eventually became Nobel laureates in economics. Knight himself would surely have won the economics Nobel Prize, but it was not awarded until just three years before he died. He *did* win in 1957 the Francis Walker Medal for lifetime achievement in economics, granted every five years "to the living American economist who has made the greatest contribution to economics" and generally regarded as the precursor to the economics Nobel Prize.[7]

Not content to remain limited to economic problem solving, Knight also often strayed into other social sciences to conduct research. Rather than be beaten into retreat from such incursions into related fields, as many scientists are, Knight persevered and vigorously defended his scholarly explorations. In

1942, Knight received a joint appointment from the University of Chicago as a professor of the social sciences and a joint appointment as a professor of philosophy in 1945. During these years Knight helped establish (together with economic historian John Nef and sociologist Robert Redfield) the University of Chicago's Committee on Social Thought, arguably the first formalized interdisciplinary program of its kind. The Committee would later play host to other great economists, including F. A. Hayek, another famous "economic imperialist" whose work outside of economics—specifically, in philosophy— was almost as well known as his work *in* economics, which itself secured Hayek the Nobel Prize.

## Risk versus Uncertainty

Despite the voluminous modern literature on the subject, it is remarkably difficult to find a more insightful contemporary discussion of the nature of the problems faced by businesses operating in an uncertain world than the 80-year-old *Risk, Uncertainty, and Profit.* Knight's treatise about risk and how firms deal with it was theoretically path-breaking at the time, and it remains absolutely relevant today from a *practical* perspective, as well.

As the title suggests, Knight went to great lengths to distinguish between *risk* and *uncertainty.* Modern usage generally equates the two terms, at least to a first approximation. But for Knight, the two different notions of economic randomness were fundamentally distinct:

> *The practical difference between the two categories, risk and uncertainty, is that in the former the distribution of the outcome in a group of instances is known (either through calculation* a priori *or from statistics of the past experience), while in the case of uncertainty this is not true, the reason being in general that it is impossible to form a group of instances, because the situation dealt with is in a high degree unique. (Knight, 1921, p. 233)*

Risk thus represents a *quantifiable* source of randomness, whereas uncertainty is inherently *unquantifiable.*

The evaluation of an unknown future invariably involves the process of defining possible outcomes or events and associating probabilities with them. Knight (1921) and Hardy (1923) argued that there are essentially three ways of assessing probabilities once the outcomes or events to be analyzed have been defined. First, the probabilities may be purely mathematical in nature— for example, the chances of one pip showing face up when a fair die is cast. Second, the probabilities may be based on statistical inference—for example, forecasting and prediction of the weather based on a mixture of prior beliefs with actual data on comparable weather events and outcomes that have already occurred under similar circumstances. Finally come those probabilities that cannot be systematically associated with future events given the unique nature of the underlying randomness. To the extent probabilities in that circumstance can be defined and decisions about the future made, they are each based essentially on pure judgment rather than formal analysis. Hardy (1923) explains:

> An *"act of business judgment"* may denote anything from an instantaneous sizing-up of and acting on a relatively simple situation, to the involved investigations and prolonged deliberation leading up to a momentous business decision or the adoptions of far-reaching business policies. Sometimes the basic data of the judgment are definite and complete; sometimes so obscure that a judgment is almost a leap in the dark, and even the shrewd executive cannot put his finger on the specific factors which determine his decision. (p. 53)

With the explosion in the popularity of quantitative measures of risk like value at risk and earnings at risk over the past decade, many specialists increasingly argue to their commercial colleagues that *all* randomness is quantifiable. Perhaps the precision of the estimate will differ based on the methodology used, but ultimately everything can—and *should*—be thrown into a black box that will churn out an "enterprise-wide risk measure"—or so says the orthodoxy.

Contributing to this trend in thinking has been a steady move by certain regulatory and supervisory organizations to the same end. In its revision of the 1988 Basel Accord specifying minimum capital requirements for banks, for example, the Bank for International Settlements places great emphasis on the quantification of operational risks for capital adequacy purposes. When it comes to a low-severity, high-frequency risks like dollars lost from errant funds transfers, this requirement at least has some basis to it. But for low-frequency, high-severity events—for example, the disastrous events of September 11th or the Great Chicago Flood of 1991—we are getting much further away from risk and much closer to uncertainty. In fact, even those examples may still be true risks in Knight's sense, and if they are difficult to measure, then true uncertainty must be beyond the pale.

So, we are increasingly instructed by those in the risk management world that we must "think quantitatively" about virtually everything. In today's world of value at risk and Basel II and real options and everything else underlying the "enterprise-wide risk measurement" movement, Knight's distinction between risk and uncertainty is clearly heterodox, if not heretical. But to Knight, the distinction was far more than just teleology. On the contrary, Knight forcefully argued that uncertainty is a vital part of a growing economy and an emergent aspect of a well-functioning economic system.

## The Causal Relation between Risk, Uncertainty, and Profit

One of the most important theoretical implications of Knight's work is that firms cannot earn positive economic profits in the long run if the only source of randomness they face is quantifiable risk. Only *true uncertainty* can be the basis of a firm's ability to earn positive economic profits sustainably and regularly:

> *That higher form of uncertainty not susceptible to measurement and hence to elimination . . . is this* true uncertainty *which by preventing the theoretically perfect outworking of the tendencies of competition gives the characteristic form of "enterprise" to economic organization as a whole and accounts for the peculiar income of the entrepreneur. (Knight, 1921, p. 232)*

The reasons that firms can sometimes earn profits in a world of uncertainty are several. One is the specialization of firms in areas where they perceive some comparative advantage in information or knowledge of a given kind. This is a sort of "division of labor" argument for the corporate sector. Less informed firms will forgo entry into industries occupied with such specialists and focus on those areas where they perceive themselves as relatively better informed, thus leaving room for both firms to earn supranormal returns in their different information specializations.

In other cases, some companies earn profits from bearing uncertainty because other firms are not willing to do so. If the production of some good is subject to such uncertainty and the good remains demanded even when sold at a price high enough to compensate the firm for bearing the commercial uncertainty associated with its production, then some firms will collect this "uncertainty premium" for undertaking to bear the uncertainty and supply the good.

Finally, as Chapter 3 will make clearer, entrepreneurial profits can sometimes be earned when firms become specialists in assuming uncertainty from those firms that are naturally vulnerable to such uncertainty but do not wish to bear it on an ongoing basis.

### The Revolutionary Nature of Knight's Ideas

Knight's thinking at the time was no less than revolutionary. Until Knight, mainstream microeconomic theory did not readily admit to firms earning positive economic profits in the long run for any reason apart from imperfect competition. In classical Ricardian economics (see Appendix 1), profits simply tended toward some "natural rate" determined entirely by exogenous factors such as the aggregate endowment of land or technology in the economy.

The relative distribution of profits might vary across firms depending on their ownership of the factors of production, but not the *rate*.

In the late 1800s Walras, Jevons, Menger, Cournot, and others ushered in the "marginalist revolution" to economic theory. By Marshall (1890), the marginalist revolution had evolved into a unified theory of the price system—the neoclassical theory—that replaced the earlier classical theories. The archetypical neoclassical perspective on long-run corporate profits was articulated by Marshall, who argued that there was no natural rate of profit. Instead, each firm made its own optimal production decisions by producing more goods until the cost of the last good produced equaled the revenue from the last good produced.[8] In the short run—Marshall is perhaps most famous for introducing the concepts of a "short" and "long" run (see Appendix 1)—production optimality could yield profits to any given "inframarginal" firm. But in the long run, those profits would attract new firms into the market, and price would fall until production optimality occurred at the minimum average cost. This meant zero economic profits.

The assumption of zero economic profits in a long-run Marshallian equilibrium continues to permeate modern microeconomic analysis. As a result, positive economic profits are often regarded—even today despite Knight's insights—as attributable to some source of market power that prevents the full force of competition from attracting new firms and driving profits to zero. But all of these models presupposing that long-run profits are attributable only to market power assume all market participants are equally well informed.

Knight debunked the notion that profits could come only from market power by arguing forcefully for the importance of differential or asymmetric knowledge and information. That idea had been largely absent from prior mainstream economic theory, with the notable exception of Menger—the founder of the Austrian school of economics (see Appendix 1)—whose work first was published in German in 1871 (*Grundsätze der Volkswirthschaftslehre*) but which did not appear in English until 1950. When Menger's text was finally published in English, Knight penned the Foreword.

### Risk and Uncertainty in the Real World

Imagine an economic theoretician in her white lab coat and a practicing businessman in his Brioni suit sharing a coffee at Deux Magots in Saint Germaine des Prés and discussing the role of economic modeling in the daily life of the Paris businessman. The discussion turns to Knight. Neither would really disagree with Knight's conclusions that some firms could make sustainable long-run profits when market participants do not share a common set of probabilities about the future. But the businessman might be expected to argue that despite Knight's accomplishments as a part of the history of economic thought, his accomplishments were just that and little more.

No, the economist responds. The task of economics is to make certain assumptions in order to develop baseline explanations for economic phenomena. Real-world deviations from those ideals coming out of admittedly unrealistic models, she would contend, can often be explained by looking for violations in the underlying assumptions. So, not only is work like Knight's important because it advances the state of intellectual knowledge and economic theory, but it also has practical relevance.

Our Brioni-clad businessman might then reply that although true in principle, many of the major neoclassical economic models are too abstract—in either their assumptions, their object of investigation, or both—to be of any *practical* use. Knowing something about the history of economic thought himself—he must have read Appendix 1—he offers the example of Walras, who developed a system of simultaneous equations in 1874 to characterize the prices of multiple goods in a competitive general equilibrium. The work of Walras was an absolutely essential step forward in the progress of economics as a science—it was perhaps *the* founding work of "general equilibrium" theory—but it had absolutely no direct implications for the modern business. Our businessman then sips his café au lait and asks whether Knight might not be in the same category—a great thinker, perhaps, but not relevant for day-to-day corporate decision making.

Being an economic scientist and not a businesswoman, our economist may well not know how to respond to this last comment. Even if Knight demonstrated the possibility of information-driven corporate profits, what *did* he say that is relevant in the real world—that can affect the decisions the businessman has to confront later that day when he returns to his Champs d'Elysees office?

The answer lies in Knight's very distinction between risk and uncertainty—*that* is relevant in the real world. That may not yet be obvious to readers, but probably only because of differences in terminology. Corporate risk managers, after all, clearly do not show up at board meetings and present summaries of the "risk" and "uncertainty" affecting their firms.

From a practical perspective and to make things operationally easier, managers generally subclassify risks into "financial" and "nonfinancial" risks. Financial risks are those sources of randomness that can adversely affect a firm's value, cash flows, or earnings, and typically are further divided into market, credit, liquidity, and funding risks.[9] Nonfinancial risks, or those risks whose adverse outcomes are not financial per se but rather "physical," include fire, flood, personal injury or disability, contamination, and so on. "Operational" risk lies in between, and generally involves nonfinancial events that have both financial and nonfinancial repercussions. An oil company that bears the risk of losing a tanker at sea in a storm, for example, has financial and nonfinancial risks. The financial risks include the replacement cost of the ship, the loss of the oil, the consequences of defaulting on delivery promises, and the like. But to the men and women on the ship, the nonfinancial risk of drowning is arguably more important.

Financial and nonfinancial risks in turn generally can be classified as either "core" or "noncore" (Culp, 2001, 2002a). The core risks facing a firm may be defined as those risks that the firm is in business to bear and manage so that it can earn excess economic profits. Noncore risks, by contrast, are risks to which a firm's primary business exposes it but that the firm does not necessarily need to retain in order to engage in its primary business line. The firm may well be exposed to noncore risks, but it may not wish to *remain* exposed to those risks. Core risks, by contrast, are those risks the firm is literally in business *not* to get rid of—at least not all of them.

The distinction between core and noncore risk is entirely subjective and varies firm by firm. What is a core risk for one firm may not be for another one, even when the companies are in the same sector and industry. The classification of a risk as core by any given firm, moreover, depends not just on the quality of information the firm actually has, but also on the firm's *perceived* comparative advantage in digesting that information.

As you can probably see, there is a direct correspondence between what we call core and noncore risk in current risk management lingo and what Knight called risk and uncertainty—namely, uncertainty is core risk, and risk is noncore risk.

Consider, for example, regional electricity markets. What determines the degree to which power price fluctuations represent a source of risk or uncertainty depends entirely on the degree to which the power company and the consumers and investors in the community agree on the probability distribution of power prices. If there is complete agreement about the probability distribution of power prices, it is a risk to everyone. Power price fluctuations in that case cannot be the power company's true source of comparative advantage and profitability.

Alternatively, it is quite plausible that the local power company managers have relatively better judgment about power prices than the average local investor. Knowing all its customers' basic demands *and* the capacity constraints of the local transmission system, for example, the power company managers may be able to use their experience and judgment to anticipate transmission congestion and its impact on local prices better than the rest of the market. In that case, power price fluctuations would represent a core risk and a comparative advantage to be exploited—a source of Knightian uncertainty. Of course, the moment that transmission congestion becomes amenable to formal and systematic quantification and goes beyond the good judgment of the plant managers, the possibility of changes in power prices will become a risk and a firm's opportunity to profit from its perceived superior information will vanish.

Although there is a clear relation between core risk and Knightian uncertainty and between noncore risk and Knightian risk, we *cannot*, however, draw any conclusions about whether a firm may wish to reduce its susceptibility to risk or uncertainty based on that distinction alone. To return to our previous example, the local power company may consider power price fluctuations as a source of uncertainty and, hence, profits. At the same time, huge unanticipated price swings might devastate the firm financially. Accordingly, the firm might wish to take some actions to reduce its uncertainty about price volatility *in that extreme range*. So, the firm's decision about whether to tolerate the random outcomes to which its business exposes it does not really depend on whether the randomness is risk or uncertainty.

The counterexample proves the same point. Before power markets were deregulated, power prices were not very volatile and firms were allowed to charge customers a rate based on a cost-plus tariff formula. Production costs were generally known across firms, so, together with the lack of price volatility, it is hard to believe that power companies would have viewed power price fluctuations as uncertainty. And as a matter of fact, power price fluctuations were not the source of power companies' profits in those days; profits were essentially a regulatory rent created entirely by the permissible markup in consumer tariffs above costs.

Knowing the difference between risk and uncertainty may not affect managers' and shareholders' tolerances for remaining exposed to those sources of randomness, but the distinction is of practical importance for two reasons. First, at a basic level, a firm that cannot identify the relation between randomness and corporate profits will not long survive in a competitive market. In that sense, proper identification of risk and uncertainty is an essential task of strategic management. Second, whether randomness is risk or uncertainty can affect the method a firm may choose to reduce that source of randomness *if* it wishes to do so. Explanations for when and why firms may sometimes opt to reduce their exposure to risk and uncertainty are reviewed in the last section of this chapter.

## Practical Determinants of the Distinction between Risk and Uncertainty

Now that we have explored the practical importance of the distinction between risk and uncertainty, we need to determine some means by which corporate executives and risk managers can differentiate the two. Virtually by definition, this will be a hard task. That which cannot be quantitified, after all, cannot necessarily even be identified. And remember, a given source of randomness may be perceived by different firms in entirely different ways.

So, there is no single right way to differentiate between risk and uncertainty. All we can do instead is look for specific factors and telltale signs that tend to be associated with one or the other. Some of these broad determinants are discussed next.

## The Role of Judgment

Fundamental to the distinction between risk and uncertainty—and the unique capacity of a firm to earn profits only from the latter—is the role of *business judgment* exercised by managers and security holders in their financial and production decisions. Business decisions, to Knight, are often based not on "true knowledge"—we will return to that slippery notion in the next subsection—but rather on managerial judgment when perfect, quantifiable knowledge is elusive. Knight explains:

> *The most important result of this survey is the emphatic contrast between knowledge as the scientist and the logician of science uses the term and the convictions or opinions upon which conduct is based outside of laboratory experiments. The opinions upon which we act in everyday affairs and those which govern the decisions of responsible business managers for the most part have little similarity with conclusions reached by exhaustive analysis and accurate measurement. (Knight, 1921, p. 230)*

In his *General Theory of Employment, Interest, and Money*, Keynes advocated an essentially similar view that business decisions rest more often on individual judgment than on quantified probabilities about the evolution of randomness. Keynes referred to this vital role of judgment in the capacity of a firm to earn a profit as "animal spirits":

> *A large proportion of our positive activities depend on spontaneous optimism rather than on a mathematical expectation, whether moral or hedonistic or economic. Most, probably, of our decisions to do something positive, the full consequences of which will be drawn out over many days to come, can only be taken as a result of animal spirits—of a spontaneous urge to action rather than inaction, and not as the outcome of a weighted average of quantitative benefits multiplied by quantitative probabilities. Enterprise only pretends to itself to be mainly actuated by the statements in its own prospectus, however candid and sincere. Only a little more than an expedition to the South Pole, is it based on an exact calculation of benefits to come. Thus if the animal spirits are dimmed and the spontaneous optimism falters, leaving us to depend on nothing but a mathematical expectation, enterprise will fade and die. (Keynes, 1936, pp. 161–162)*

The earlier example of the regional power company provides a useful illustration of the importance of judgment. A power plant manager with years of experience dealing with the same customers in the same grid may gradually learn literally to anticipate variables like transmission congestion. This judgment, in turn, can create an informational advantage for the firm that companies lacking comparable experience cannot exploit.

This sort of judgment in some ways is the best possible example of uncertainty as a nonquantifiable source of randomness and a potential driver of profits. Of course, market participants can assign *some* probability to congestion in an electricity grid—probabilities are just numbers, after all, and can in the worst case be picked randomly. But if uncertainty is viewed as judgment intensive, there is no way for a large number of market participants to incorporate that judgment into probability estimates. So, there will be a lack of agreement, uncertainty will persist, and, in the end, only the firm with the best judgment will be able to formulate *meaningful* probabilistic estimates of the future.

Music may provide us with an even better example. Suppose we are about to attend a performance of Beethoven's Ninth Symphony by the Chicago Symphony Orchestra (CSO) under the baton of its music director, Daniel Barenboim. We wonder how the performance will be in terms of tempo. Recognizing that there are plenty of prior performances of this piece by the CSO under Barenboim, we might look at the prior tempi and infer what the tempo will be tonight. But only if we believe the performance is itself a stable repeating event.

Adopting more of an "uncertainty" perspective in considering the tempo of the forthcoming concert, we might argue that each performance of Beethoven's Ninth is completely unique. The piece itself has no meaning as notes on a page. It becomes an organic, living thing when it is performed, but it began as silence and ended as silence and was alive only for a finite period between the two silences. In that way, every performance is a unique event—it never happened before, and it will never happen again (Barenboim and Said, 2002). True, you can assign probabilities to how the CSO will play the piece and what the tempo will be like, and those probabilities may even be guided by prior experience. But, fundamentally, the event being predicted is unique, so the inference must be based almost entirely on judgment. And as far as judgment goes, who would dare to argue that an audience member's judgment about the tempo of an upcoming performance would be superior to Maestro Barenboim's? The Maestro is clearly in a better position to analyze the uncertainty than the rest of us are.

### Classification and the Knowledge Problem

Underlying Knight's distinction between risk and uncertainty is what he refers to as "the problem of knowledge," where the "problem" essentially refers to how individuals in a business setting make decisions today based on the knowledge they have today, which is by definition only partial given our inability to predict the future:

> *We live only by knowing something about the future; while the problems of life, or of conduct at least, arise from the fact that we know so little. . . . The essence of the situation is action according to opinion, of greater or less foundation and value, neither entire ignorance nor complete and perfect information, but partial knowledge. (Knight, 1921, p. 199)*

Knight considers knowledge to be essentially inference based on perception about a random and uncertain future: "We *perceive* the world before we react to it, and we react not to what we perceive, but always to what we *infer*" (Knight, 1921, p. 201). This in turn leads Knight to his conception of what is meant by knowledge:

> *We have, then, our dogma which is the presupposition of knowledge, in this form; that the world is made up of things, which, under the same circumstances, always behave in the same way. The practical problem of inference or prediction in any particular situation centers around the first two of these three factors: what things are we dealing with, and what are the circumstances which condition their action? From knowledge of these two sets of facts it must be possible to say what behavior is to be expected. The chief logical problem, as already noticed, lies in the conception of a "thing." For it is obvious that the "circumstances" which condition the behavior of any particular thing are composed of other things and their behavior. The assumption that under the same circumstances the same things behave in the same ways thus raises the single question of how far and in what sense the universe is really made up of such "things" which preserve an unvarying identity (mode of behavior). (Knight, 1921, pp. 204–205)*

So, Knight felt that the ability to formulate probabilistic predictions about the future was based on how well "things" could be grouped into homogeneous categories. This is also generally consistent with the notion of probability developed by Keynes (1921) in his seminal *Treatise on Probability*, published the same year as *Risk, Uncertainty, and Profit*. When people agree on how "things" can be classified, the common classification will lead to common inference, and then we have risk, not uncertainty.

A common misconception is the view that whenever the future is presumed to behave like the past, we have Knightian risk instead of uncertainty. In statistical terminology, that would imply a pure "frequentist" approach in which the true probability of a thing's occurring would be equal to the proportion of times that thing *actually has occurred* and *will continue to occur* in a long enough time series. That is at odds with the "subjectivist" approach to probability of Savage (1954) and others in which any given random event is unique, and the probabilities associated with that event are true for that event only.

The frequentist and subjectivist perspectives represent different philosophical notions of what we mean by "probability" and what we are doing when we engage in "probabilistic inference." As a purely mechanical issue, Knight did allow for the possibility of incorporating a mixture of subjective and objective information into probabilistic estimates in a Bayesian framework. In a typical Bayesian probabilistic inference problem, prior subjective beliefs are combined with historical data or some underlying data generation process called the likelihood function into a "posterior" distribution representing both the available data and the modeler's beliefs. Knight allowed for the possibility that in such analysis, essentially *any* subjective weight could be given to the two components. A special case involves the use of a "diffuse prior" in which the modeler essentially has no opinion about the future. In this case, the posterior distribution reflects only the likelihood function based on the data itself.

Note in this connection that there is some difference between the frequentist/subjectivist debate *methodologically* and *philosophically*. From a methodology standpoint, the Bayesian approach works perfectly well to allow pure data-driven inference to be mixed with a priori opinions. But from a philosophical standpoint, there is still a question of the uniqueness of the event being predicted. Returning to Beethoven, we can combine and recombine our opinions with the available data, but that does not change the fundamental uniqueness of the event being predicted. In that sense, the event defies data-driven prediction entirely. What determines the nature of the randomness thus is not the scientific method by which the probabilities are computed, but the nature of the event itself.

What sets risk apart from uncertainty for Knight thus is not agreement or disagreement about the process by which probabilities are formed and associated with outcomes, but rather agreement or disagreement on a classification scheme to describe the outcomes themselves. In fact, Knight considered the assignment of probabilities to future events as fairly mechanical once the events were defined. *That* was the hard part.

Consider a natural disaster like a catastrophic earthquake that could impose significant property damage on a West Coast real estate developer. Prior data alone will never facilitate the prediction of "the big one" by either the developer or a prospective insurance company, but the event itself can be clearly defined. And once it is defined, probabilities can be assigned to it using some kind of nonarbitrary quantitative process. The earthquake is a *risk*.

Alternatively, Knight would probably consider directors and officers (D&O) insurance to be "uninsurable" (*sic*) and a source of uncertainty for firms, despite the existence of policies designed to manage this randomness.

(We will see in Chapter 3 that the existence of certain mechanisms like insurance can act to transform uncertainty into risk by forcing two parties to agree on a market price for a contingent claim.) D&O insurance coverage includes items like unfavorable liability outcomes in jury trials. Once a case is filed, Knight would contend that probabilities could be assigned to the outcome. And so we have a risk. But before a case is filed, people would have to be able to assign probabilities to the filing of the case itself as well as the judgment. And to go one step further back, what about the situation in which D&O insurance covers the liability for an action not yet taken? In that case, a probability would have to be defined for all the possible liability-sensitive actions of all the officers and directors, as well as the probability of detection and the outcome of adjudication. The sheer volume of quite heterogeneous possibilities essentially renders a classification scheme impossible, hence leading Knight to consider many legal risks as sources of uncertainty rather than true risk.

## Time

One key component of business decisions about a random future that forces some of them into the category of decision making under uncertainty rather than risk is, quite simply, the passage of time or the dynamic nature of the decision-making process. If the world were a static place, one might imagine that almost everything could fall into the definition of risk. But as Knight emphasized, the world is not a static place. This results in a constant state of change in knowledge and in the knowledge problem. Specifically, when people's inferences and classifications of future outcomes are constantly evolving, there is no "stopping rule" that tells managers when to stop, take the knowledge they have, formulate probabilities, and act.

In any snapshot of time, knowledge may be fixed and the assessment of probabilities based on mathematical or statistical means feasible. But because business judgments typically occur over a period in which time is *not* a constant, the dynamic nature of knowledge forces the manager to exercise *some* judgment. The decision when to stop and use the knowledge available to make a probabilistic assessment (as opposed to waiting for new information to come along) is itself an exercise in judgment, which creates uncertainty for reasons discussed earlier in the judgment section. Hardy notes: "Seldom is it possible to [separate the exercise of business judgment into] temporally distinct and successive stages, so varied are the modes in which they may be subordinated, merged, reversed, and repeated" (Hardy, 1923, p. 53).

The dynamic nature of many business problems can also create uncertainty by inhibiting classification, thus creating uncertainty as in the immediately preceding section. In the D&O example, the scenarios in which directors and officers can incur liability for the firm that results in a complaint and a trial become much more limited if we consider, say, a one-day time horizon. But over the span of a year, a lot more is possible. What is risk in extremely short frequencies or durations thus may become uncertainty as time is allowed to elapse for longer periods.

### Endogeneity of the Underlying Source of Randomness

Uncertainty can also arise when either the probabilities of future events or the classification of events are *endogenous* to the problem being solved. Keynes (1936) offers a useful anecodotal example:

> [*The problem*] *may be likened to those newspaper competitions in which the competitors have to pick out the six prettiest faces from a hundred photographs, the prize being awarded to the competitor whose choice most nearly corresponds to the average preferences of the competitors as a whole; so that each competitor has to pick, not those faces which he himself finds prettiest, but those which he thinks likeliest to catch the fancy of the other competitors, all of whom are looking at the problem from the same point of view. It is not a case of choosing those which, to the best of one's judgment, are really the prettiest, nor even those which average opinion genuinely thinks the prettiest. We have reached the third degree where we devote our intelligences to anticipating what average opinion expects the average opinion to be. (p. 156)*

In this example, each contestant has an incentive to acquire as much information as possible to gain an advantage—or perhaps to stop the other contestants from gaining the advantage. But the information in question is not some exogenous fact, like the value of a car. Even if the value of a car is itself subjective—for example, a car may matter less to an eight-year-old than to her parents—enough information can eventually be acquired to formulate some systematic quantitative valuation of the car. In the Keynesian beauty contest, however, the relevant information that needs to be acquired is information about the predictions of others. O'Driscoll and Rizzo (1996) summarize: "Knowledge gained over time by [contestants] will necessarily affect the objects of each agent's prediction . . . [and] the very activity designed to cope with uncertainty (i.e., the acquisition of knowledge) is responsible for its continued existence" (p. 74).

In the Keynesian beauty contest, uncertainty is endogenous because of the essentially rivalrous nature of knowledge and the competitive nature of knowledge acquisition. But the example also reinforces the importance of the dynamic nature of the problem. In the example, the probabilities of the outcomes are unknowable because they depend on the dynamic behavior of the participants in the process. At any given point in time, the contestants might well be able to form some kind of static prior distribution about the average contestant's guess. Endogeneity thus vanishes in a static setting. As time passes, however, the behavior of the contestants is gradually revealed, and the distributions change. And they keep changing as long as contestants keep guessing. No matter how much time passes, the probability distributions never really become stable.

Uncertainty in the Keynesian beauty contest is also easy to see because the probabilities themselves are a direct result of competitive interaction and are thus constantly changing. But we can have uncertainty that is one step removed from the probabilities, as well, simply by postulating that the model governing the behavior of a participant engaged in prediction depends on other the models used by other people engaged in prediction of the same economic phenomenon. In other words, even if the probabilities themselves are not explicitly interdependent, and interdependence in behavior is enough to create endogenous uncertainty.

An example of this type of endogeneity is the "Lucas Critique." Specifically, Nobel laureate Robert Lucas (1972) criticized the use of structural economic models for government determinations of fiscal and monetary policy. Because either the structural form or the parameters of such models depend on market participants' beliefs about what government policy would be, those same models could not in turn be used to determine that policy.

### Confidence and Expectations

Knight's work inspired significant subsequent research into modeling expectations and the economics of asymmetric information (Emmett, 1999). Despite those advances and the mathematical and statistical tractability of the expectations operator (both conditional and unconditional), expectations are relatively hard to incorporate into economic modeling. Lachmann (1978) explains:

> [Expectations] always embody . . . an experience which requires interpretation. *It is the task of the theory of expectations to elucidate the problems our experience (and that of others insofar as it is accessible to us) sets us in judging the uncertain future, as well as to clarify the* modus interpretandi. *It is a task with which economists thus far do not seem to have come to grapple. (pp. 20–21)*

Put another way, we can model the stochastic processes from which expectations arise, but different people's opinions about why circumstances arise make it quite difficult, if not impossible, to model the *economic* processes from which expectations are formed. This, in turn, obfuscates agreement among people about expectations and thus generates uncertainty.

Stated differently, defining a nontautological learning process that meaning-fully captures people's changing expectations about other people's expecta-tions is no easy task[10] (O'Driscoll and Rizzo, 1996).

Keynes (1936) usefully summarized the problem of modeling expecta-tions in terms of *confidence*:

> *The state of long-term expectation, upon which our decisions are based, does not solely depend, therefore, on the most probable forecast we can make. It also depends on the* confidence *with which we make this fore-cast—on how highly we rate the likelihood of our best forecast turning out quite wrong. If we expect large changes but are very uncertain as to what precise form these changes will take, then our confidence will be weak. The state of confidence, as they term it, is a matter to which practi-cal men always pay the closest and most anxious attention. But econo-mists have not analysed it carefully and have been content, as a rule, to discuss it in general terms. (pp. 148–149)*

In other words, firms make decisions based on their probabilistic assessments of the future. But when a firm has no confidence in the precision or stability of its expectations, its decisions will be influenced accordingly. Uncertainty thus arises when confidence is so low that any probabilistic estimates that can be assigned to the future simply cannot be taken seriously enough to put the firm's capital at risk.

Nobel laureate Sir John Hicks (1939) emphasizes that confidence—or lack thereof—can have important implications for *ex post* efficiency: "Lack of confidence in one's foresight is not necessarily a source of waste. The loss only accrues if the expectations would have been right after all. Putting insufficient faith in good judgments is a source of inefficiency; but skepticism about bad judgments may be better than trust" (pp. 134–135).

The mere existence of uncertainty is no guarantee of profits. In fact, un-certainty generated by a lack of confidence can sometimes deter entrepre-neurs from taking legitimate actions that would have led to profits. As we have seen, a firm's perception of its own comparative informational advan-tage is the key issue, and this perception can be wrong. Hicks's quote is a useful reminder that being wrong can mean a lack of confidence in a legiti-mate advantage, just as it can imply the opposite. Uncertainty is a double-edged sword.

The important relation between confidence and expectations as a deter-minant of uncertainty became fairly pervasive in economic analysis in the twentieth century. Robinson (1951), for example, argues that "the degree of uncertainty in the market as a whole then depends on the variety of opinion within it. The same effects follow where everyone is alike, but no one feels confident that his own best guess of what the future holds will turn out to be right" (pp. 99–100).

### Putting the Pieces Together

Clearly, no simple litmus test is possible to enable any given firm to distinguish risk and uncertainty. But at least now we have some guiding principles. Uncertainty may be said to exist in the following situations: when the future cannot be described in terms of homogeneous events; when probabilities are based on the individual judgment of a business manager; when the dynamic nature of a problem requires judgment to determine when to stop and make a decision based on the available information; when the dynamic nature of a problem or some other factors endogenize the variable being predicted; or when any effort to assign probabilities results in estimates that—absent some other consideration—at least some firms are unwilling to trust for their decision-making purposes.

All of these determinants of uncertainty invariably involve some degree of abstractness. We dislike that in finance because it tends to feel very unscientific. And it well may be dissatisfying for you as a reader that we have not produced a clean way to differentiate risk from uncertainty. But as an entrepreneur, you should be thrilled. If our ability to identify uncertainty is too precise, then it isn't uncertainty anymore and the potential to profit from it goes away.

## RISK AND UNCERTAINTY IN THE THEORY OF CORPORATE FINANCE

As emphasized earlier in this chapter, the motivations for a firm to reduce on occasion the randomness it faces do not depend solely on whether that randomness is risk or uncertainty. The method chosen for dealing with risk and uncertainty depends on which one the firm is facing, but not the rationale.

Why firms sometimes choose to reduce their risks and uncertainties is not a topic that Knight explored. For insight into this topic, we must turn to the theory of corporation finance.

### Value Creation from the Management of Risk and Uncertainty

In the world of perfect capital markets to which many of us were introduced in business school, deliberate efforts by corporate managers to reduce risk are largely a matter of indifference to a company's stockholders. Because such investors could diversify away the risks associated with fluctuations in interest rates or commodity prices simply by holding well-diversified portfolios, they would not pay a higher price-earnings (P/E) multiple (or, what amounts to the same thing, lower the cost of capital) for companies that choose to hedge such risk. So if hedging is unlikely to affect a firm's cost of capital and value, then why do it?

The irrelevance of risk management is an implication of the same assumptions that led to the celebrated Modigliani and Miller (1958) or "M&M" capital structure propositions—namely, that a corporation's value is independent of its capital structure, leverage, and dividend policy, and that the value of an investment project is invariant to the type of financing used to fund it.[11] The assumptions under which these irrelevance propositions hold include:

- Capital markets are perfect (in the sense of no transaction costs, taxes, costs of financial distress, restrictions on short sales, and the like).
- All firms and investors have equal access to the capital markets—that is, the terms on which a security can be issued do not depend on who or what is issuing it.
- All investors have homogeneous expectations and exhibit complete agreement about the unknown future.
- A firm's investment opportunities are not affected by its financing alternatives (apart from the impact of the latter on the relative distribution of security holder wealth).

Two decades of theoretical and empirical work on the issue of why firms hedge have produced a number of plausible explanations for how risk management can increase firm value—that is, how it can increase the firm's expected cash flows even after taking account of the costs of setting up and administering the risk management program.[12] Not surprisingly, these explanations for how risk management can add value are generally based on the violation of one or more of the M&M assumptions. Summarized briefly, such research suggests that risk management can help companies increase (or protect) their expected net cash flows mainly in the following ways:[13]

- Reducing expected tax liabilities when the firm faces tax rates that rise with different levels of taxable income.
- Reducing the expected costs of financial distress caused by a downturn in cash flow or earnings or a shortfall in the value of assets below liabilities.[14]
- Reducing potential agency conflicts between a company's creditors and stockholders, including the possibility that "debt overhang" results in the sacrifice of valuable strategic investments; overcoming the managerial risk aversion that (in the absence of explicit and formal risk management)

could lead managers to invest in excessively conservative projects to protect their annual incomes and, ultimately, their job security.

■ Reducing the possibility of corporate underinvestment that arises from unexpected depletions of internal cash when the firm faces costs of external financing that are high enough to outweigh the benefits of undertaking the new investment.

As these reasons suggest, value-increasing risk management has little to do with dampening swings in reported earnings (or even, as many academics have suggested, minimizing the variance of cash flows). For most companies, the main contribution of risk management is likely to be its role in minimizing the probability of a *costly*[15] financial distress. In this sense, the optimal risk management policy may be one that provides a kind of insurance against worst-case scenarios or, to use an actual insurance term, *catastrophic* outcomes. And even when the company has relatively little debt, management may choose to purchase such catastrophic insurance to protect the company's ability to carry out the major investments that are part of its strategic plan. In the process of insuring against catastrophic outcomes and preserving a minimal level of cash flow, companies will generally discover that they can operate with less capital (or at least less equity capital) than if they left their exposures unmanaged. And to the extent that hedging proves to be a cheap substitute for capital, risk management is a value-adding proposition.

## Risk versus Uncertainty Again

Knight's world itself is antithetical to the M&M world. The third assumption under which the M&M irrelevance propositions hold, after all, is complete agreement among investors. Fama (1976) describes the import of this assumption: "Any information available is costlessly available to all market agents (investors and firms), and *all agents correctly assess the implications of the information for the future prospects of firms and securities* [emphasis added]" (p. 273).

In other words, the M&M propositions hold only in a world where firms are affected *by risk*. If uncertainty affects a firm, then we cannot by definition have complete agreement and cannot be living in an M&M world. This means that deliberate actions taken by a firm to manage uncertainty *can* be a source of value added. Such actions must be traded off against any possible reduction in profits that accompanies a reduction in uncertainty, of course, but the two are not mutually exclusive. Again, as our earlier power company example shows, a firm may wish to reduce financial distress costs by managing its uncertain exposure to *large* price moves, while actively facing the uncertainties of smaller and less catastrophic price changes.

Firms also may wish to engage in the active management and control of the true risks to which they are subject. In this case, investors and firms may completely agree about the probabilities associated with a given firm encountering financial distress. That complete agreement does not mean there will be no incentive for the firm bearing those positive expected distress costs to try to reduce those costs through risk management. By engaging in a transaction like a derivatives contract, for example, the firm may reduce its own expected financial distress costs without necessarily increasing the expected costs of distress for the other firm.

## NOTES

1. Culp and Miller (1995b,c) offer some examples but are highly critical of these sorts of simplifications.
2. See Jensen and Meckling (1976).
3. See, for example, Coase (1988), Jensen (2001a,b), Williamson (1998), and Williamson and Winter (1993).
4. For completeness, suppose the managers' compensation from the firm is their primary source of income.
5. Young, in particular, is not a terribly well-known economist, but his handful of contributions to economic theory are regarded by most economic historians as truly pathbreaking. See, for example, Robbins (1998).
6. See, for example, Telser (1986).
7. When the Bank of Sweden (Sveriges Riksbank) created the Bank of Sweden Prize in Economic Sciences in Memory of Alfred Nobel in 1968, the Walker Medal was discontinued.
8. Under perfect competition, demand and marginal revenue schedules are one and the same. With imperfect competition, production optimality occurs where marginal cost equals marginal revenue.
9. Culp (2001) provides definitions.
10. This is also another form of endogeneity.
11. The irrelevance of risk management and financing decisions are not independent. In many ways, risk management decisions are simply corporate financing decisions by another name. See Culp (2002a).
12. In principle, risk management can also reduce the firm's cost of capital. For example, managing risk can lower the capital cost for a partnership whose shareholders have most of their own wealth tied up in the firm. See especially Culp (2002a) for some other reasons.
13. Recent summaries of this extensive body of academic research can be found in Culp (2001) and Stulz (2002).
14. Although such costs include the out-of-pocket expenses associated with

any formal (or informal) reorganization, more important considerations are the diversion of management time and focus, loss of valuable investment opportunities, and potential alienation of other important corporate stakeholders (customers, suppliers, and employees) that can stem from financial trouble.

15. As the italics are meant to suggest, the possibility of financial distress is not necessarily value-reducing for all firms; in fact, for mature companies with large and stable operating cash flow and limited investment opportunities, high leverage, which, of course, raises the probability of financial distress, is likely to be a value-increasing strategy by reducing managers' natural tendency to spend (and thereby waste) excess cash flow.

# CHAPTER 3

# Methods of Controlling Risk and Uncertainty

The preceding chapter laid the foundations for understanding the important economic distinctions between risk and uncertainty and why those distinctions are of practical relevance. We now put that discussion from Chapter 2 in context and explore the various structures and methods by which firms can deal with the risks and uncertainties to which they are subject. As will become evident, many of these mechanisms involve the use of the capital market and the financial system—many, *but not all*.

Presuming there is some net benefit to the firm from controlling the risk and/or uncertainty it faces, there are four broad methods by which firms can manage risk or uncertainty: retention, reduction, consolidation, and specialization. Risk transfer is specialization by another name.

## RETENTION

Borrowing some terminology from the insurance industry, we can define a *retention* as any source of risk or uncertainty to which a firm is naturally exposed in the course of its business operations and to which the firm *remains* exposed over time. A retention may be planned or unplanned. In the case of unplanned retentions a firm's managers either do not know about the risk or uncertainty they face or have misdiagnosed it somehow—for example, a miscalculated hedge ratio that leaves a position more exposed to risk than managers think (see Chapter 14).

The more interesting case involves a *planned* retention of some source(s) of risk and/or uncertainty. In that case, the firm's managers perceive the potential for adverse outcomes to result in losses but opt not to take any actions that would shelter the firm's shareholders from bearing the brunt of any such adverse outcomes. Planned retentions can occur for essentially two reasons. Either the firm believes that the retention is a necessary determinant of its expected profits, or the cost of reducing the risk or uncertainty in question (through one of the other means discussed in the rest of this chapter) is above the benefit at the margin. Either may be a perfectly legitimate management decision *ex ante*.

Planned retentions often do not require that a firm does much of anything other than go about its business. In some cases, however, firms may wish to engage in what Hardy calls the "accumulation of reserves to provide for meeting the risks" (Hardy, 1923, p. 11).

## Rationales for Reserves

Reserves must be funded somehow. Either a firm diverts free cash flows into a reserve account and funds the account out of operating profits, or it must raise new cash—generally by issuing new securities and using the cash proceeds from that securities issue to fund the account. In either case, the firm is "withholding . . . resources from use to have them in readiness for a contingency which may or may not appear" (Hardy, 1923, p. 23). This creates an opportunity cost for the firm—and possibly explicit outlays, as well.

Reserves do not, however, alter the fact that shareholders are ultimately responsible for absorbing any losses arising from the retained risk or uncertainty. But economic reserves can make sense for other reasons. The benefits differ slightly depending on whether the reserves are intended to cover risk or uncertainty.

### Risk Reserves
Reserves can be allocated to sources of perceived risk or uncertainty. In the case of risk, reserves are often used for two different reasons: to prefund expected losses that are a cost of doing business for the firm, and to maintain a buffer of "risk capital" that helps the firm avoid the costs of financial distress.

For risks that give rise to positive expected losses (i.e., a loss times a positive probability) reserves are commonly set aside as a cost of doing business. A bank that expects some proportion of all loans to default, for example, may set aside funds to cover those expected or anticipated credit default losses. Similarly, an insurance company sets aside reserves to reflect expected claims it will have to honor on policies it has written.

Presumably, firms engaged in business lines with positive expected losses must believe that the discounted expected profits on those businesses exceed these expected losses. Otherwise, the business as a whole would be a negative net present value (NPV) business and inconsistent with the market value rule.

When the unexpected component of losses arising from a given risk is high, firms may also seek to hold reserves—now to help ensure the losses do not actually push the company into financial distress. Figure 3.1 illustrates the distinction between reserves held to cover expected losses—loss the firm anticipates incurring as a part of its business line, denoted $E[L]$—and some quantity intended to express "unexpected losses," denoted $L^*$. The quantity $E[L]$ represents the expected loss reserve, or the amount the firm sets aside to cover planned losses, whereas the quantity $L^* - E[L]$ is typically known as the firm's *risk capital* allocated to a given potential loss. $L^*$ may be determined from a probability distribution of potential losses, where $L^*$ is generally chosen to correspond to the firm's "maximum tolerable loss" or to the point at which a loss would expose the firm to financial distress costs. $L^*$ is often approximated probabilistically—for example, the 99th percentile of the shown distribution, intended to reflect the worst 99 percent of all estimated potential losses.

When it comes to determining the size of the reserve, the fashionable methodology for defining optimal reserve quantities is "risk-adjusted capital allocation," or the process by which firms allocate risk capital to business lines and risk exposures in an effort to maximize shareholder value. Operationally, this often involves hurdle rates, targets, or optimization programs

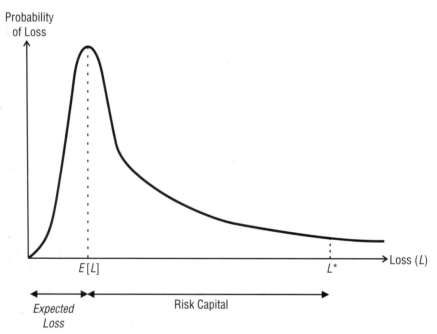

**FIGURE 3.1** Risk Capital Reserves

based on a metric known as risk-adjusted return on capital (RAROC), defined generally as the ratio of the expected economic profits of a business line (i.e., expected revenues less expected costs and expected losses) to the capital at risk in that business line. In a typical RAROC-based capital allocation regime, a business line receives a RAROC allocation for its activities only as long as RAROC exceeds some hurdle rate like economic value added (EVA).

Interestingly, most of the theoretical attention to risk-adjusted capital allocation focuses on the estimate of capital at risk required to support the program—either $L^*$ itself or $L^* - E[L]$ in Figure 3.1. But as a matter of actual practice, the main reason few firms seem to implement formalized RAROC allocation programs comes from the difficulties they encounter in accurately measuring *expected profits* at the level of the business line. Matten (2000); Crouhy, Galai, and Mark (2000); and Culp (2001) all provide more detailed discussions of risk-adjusted capital allocation techniques.

### Reserves against Uncertainty

As Figure 3.1 suggests, quantifiable randomness is a prerequisite to the determination of optimal risk reserves. By our definition of the term, explicit reserve allocations *to uncertainty* thus are impossible because the quantification of adverse outcomes arising from uncertainty is itself impossible. Certainly firms could allocate a reserve to uncertainty *in principle*, but the calculation of the amount needed in that reserve would be an essentially arbitrary process.

In essence, the firm's equity capital is itself an uncertainty reserve. In that context, perhaps the primary benefit of reserves is to allow a loss to be absorbed by equity holders gradually over time rather than all at once for liquidity and funds management purposes. This can help firms avoid the costs of the so-called "underinvestment" problem noted at the end of Chapter 2. If a large loss causes a significant depletion to the firm's cash balances, for example, the company may be forced to forgo positive net present value (NPV) investment projects that it otherwise would have undertaken purely because of the cash shortfall.

True, in a perfect capital market, firms can always issue new debt to raise the cash required to fund the new investment—whether accumulated free cash flows or a new debt issue fund the reserve or pay for the new investment directly does not really matter. But if the loss was a large one and the firm is already heavily leveraged, the company could face distress penalties when it seeks external funding following a large loss. And with asymmetric information, investors might misperceive the bond issue as raising funds to cover the loss itself, thus further raising the cost of external finance. Myers (1977, 1984) discusses in more detail this underinvestment problem that can arise when a firm has too little financial slack or liquid cash.

Maintaining financial slack (with or without reserves) to mitigate under-investment can be considered a method of reducing uncertainty when the cash flow volatility that the reserve is intended to absorb is either firmwide or not attributable to a specific risk. As Froot, Scharfstein, and Stein (1993) explain, a liquidity reserve can also be set aside, in principle, to deal with potential underinvestment problems arising from specific quantifiable risks. If excessive cash flow volatility is specifically attributable to currency fluctuations, for example, then holding reserves can make sense to ensure that adequate funding is on hand to allow positive NPV investment opportunities to be exploited.

More often than not, however, a firm concerned with avoiding underinvestment will be concerned with *anything* that increases cash flow volatility, and thus a more general reserve is a more sensible structural response. As noted, uncertainty reserves and financial slack are essentially the same things. Assuming too much specificity in the determinants of this cash buffer is likely to result in an underestimation of the true optimum amount.

### Reserve Management and Capital Markets

Although a planned retention as a response to risk or uncertainty does not require the capital market, the use of reserves *does* presuppose a financial architecture. One method of reserve management includes setting aside funds in earmarked reserve accounts, but this already presumes the availability of a stable banking system. In addition, if the firm must fund the reserve by issuing new securities rather than diverting free cash flows, then a security market must exist.

Other reserve management methods include the use of "captives" (i.e., wholly owned subsidiaries with insurance licenses that use the parent's own capital to sell insurance back to the parent in an organized self-insurance program), or participating in a mutual or cooperative insurance arrangement, including vehicles like "protected cell companies" and "rent-a-captives."[1] Much of the distinction between these sorts of alternatives owes to institutional considerations such as tax and accounting treatment, as discussed in Culp (2002a) and elsewhere. Again, these structures rely on a well-functioning security market—specifically, a market for proportional residual claims with limited liability.

## REDUCTION

Now let us suppose that a firm does not intentionally wish to retain a source of risk or uncertainty. Knight (1921) and Hardy (1923) argue that one way firms can deal with risk or uncertainty is by *reduction*.[2] The methods of dealing with risk and uncertainty that fall into this category are, as Knight puts it, "so obvious as hardly to call for discussion" (Knight, 1921, p. 239). In addition, reduction is the one mechanism for addressing risk that does *not* rely on a capital market or financial system. Accordingly, we will spend very little time with these. But the obviousness of these solutions should not belie their importance. As such, *some* mention of them is warranted.

## Technological Advancement and Research

Risk and uncertainty are often reduced by the inevitable march forward of time together with economic progress. Some risks can be eliminated through the advancement of technology or the use of research. The risk of serious harm or death from botulism, for example, was significantly reduced by the advent of canning. The sanitary and public health problems created by too many horses on crowded city streets during the age of the horse-drawn buggy were risks that the development of the automobile helped reduce. And so on. Diamond (1999) and Smith (1992, 2003) provide additional interesting historical examples.

The rate of technological progress is not some exogenous constant, despite what many classical economists used to believe (see Appendix 1). Technological progress is very much an *endogenous* variable in any economic system, and, as such, is at least somewhat under control of societies. New solutions for managing risk thus tend to evolve at a rate determined in no small part by social and cultural factors (Douglas and Wildavsky, 1982). The desire for better environmental risk management, for example, is a luxury good confined primarily to wealthy countries; starving, developing nations would generally prefer a new factory dumping pollution into the air because, at the margin, the jobs are more highly valued than is avoiding the small increased health risks from the effluent.

In this connection, wealthy countries in particular often find their true foe to be the desire for *too much* risk management and *too little* economic progress. Wildavsky (1988) often emphasized that the biggest risk to a society is the risk of pursuing too little change.[3] The wealthy comforts of the status quo often lead such societies to forget the costs of *underinnovation* (Wildavsky, 1988, 1991; Douglas and Wildavsky, 1982).

The reduction in the degree of randomness facing a firm due to technological progress can result in both diminished risk and diminished uncertainty. The risk of bacterial infection arising from eating spoiled dairy products, for example, is probably something we could all agree is a true risk. There is a stable series of data from which we can confidently draw statistical inferences about which there is likely to be little disagreement. In that connection, we can regard innovations like refrigeration and pasteurization as *risk-reducing*.

When it comes to uncertainty, technological advance and research have proven useful tools for firms mainly through the avenue of how such progress affects the information available to firms in making certain decisions. A major uncertainty faced by a medical insurance provider, for example, is the uncertainty concerning the health of insurance purchasers. If the insurer cannot distinguish between low- and high-risk types and charges a single price for both, it likely will collect too little premium to finance all its future claims.

As the discussion and examples in Chapter 2 help illustrate, such problems are *endogenous* because they depend on the behavior of others with objectives at odds to the insurance company, as well as on the passage of time. Judgment inevitably must supplant stable quantification, which is possible only in a purely static context.

Advances in customer profiling methods, medical assessments, and computer technology have all helped such insurers engage in better "customer profiling," which in turn leads to a reduction in uncertainty and a more sustainable risk profile. Technological advance also plays a role in an example like this by allowing insurers the technological capacity to track the actual experience of their policyholders, which in turn allows the insurer to use "experience ratings" in order to charge customers for their actual risk type. And here we say risk because over time the uncertainty does give way to risk as the "true type" of the individual is revealed.

One might be tempted to say this was a risk from the outset; whether a person is sick or healthy is a knowable fact with a given distribution. But then take into account that the existence of the insurance contract itself affects what the policyholder will spend on preventive medicine, and that affects the distribution. Over time, the behavior of the insured and insurer affect the outcome and hence the quantifiability of the outcome. In the absence of tools that allow the insurer to peel away the layers surrounding such behavioral issues and to charge experience-based prices, the uncertainty will persist (Rothschild and Stiglitz, 1976).

## Prevention

As suggested by the word *prevention*, risk can be reduced or eliminated in many situations through prudential *ex ante* measures taken to reduce the probability of a risk becoming an adverse outcome or loss. Consider preventive methods aimed at reducing the severity of fire: smoke detectors, fireproof doors and walls, sprinkler systems, fire hoses and extinguishers, and so on. Or preventive techniques to eliminate the risk of catching cold in the rain: umbrellas, raincoats, hats, and the like.

The practicality of eliminating risk through *ex ante* prevention depends mainly on the technology of risk prevention, including the cost of that technology. In many cases, complete risk elimination is possible only at an extremely high cost, although substantial risk reduction can often be achieved for a minimal expenditure on prevention. To utterly eliminate the risk of fire in a wooden chalet, for example, would surely be prohibitively expensive. At the same time, a failure to take simple low-cost steps like putting a hearth around an open fireplace and keeping a fire extinguisher around would be pure folly. Somewhere between the two extremes, the cost of reducing the probability of a fire will rise to the point where the incremental benefit of fire risk reduction is below the marginal cost. Nevertheless, in many situations a substantial amount of risk can be reduced or eliminated before the cost exceeds the benefit at the margin.

Risk elimination through *ex ante* prevention is fairly easy to conceptualize for nonfinancial risks, as examples like fire prevention illustrate. Less intuitive but equally relevant are preventive measures used to eliminate financial risks. Consider, for example, a limit system in which the risk of counterparty default is kept below a certain threshold by requiring traders to have an authorization number from a credit risk manager prior to entering into a new credit risk–sensitive transaction. Or, to take another example, a market risk limit system might allow news transactions only if they do not increase the firm's total "value at risk." These are clear examples of situations in which a firm takes active steps *ex ante* to avoid putting itself in risk's way—that is, prevention.

When it comes to reducing *true uncertainty*, however, prevention is not an arrow in the quiver. What does it mean, after all, to prevent being subject to a source of randomness that depends largely on the judgment of those facing it together with the passage of time? A firm would literally have to cease its operations to engage in true uncertainty prevention.

## Can Risk Ever *Really* Be Eliminated?

A widespread popular conception is that some "law of conservation of risk" exists akin to the law of conservation of matter and energy (i.e., matter and energy are never created or destroyed, merely changed from one form to the other). This supposed law of risk holds that risk can never truly be eliminated, but can only be passed from one person or firm to another like a hot potato. The *aggregate* amount of risk in an economy, so this theory holds, is constant. But as is plainly illustrated by the following discussion of the various methods of eliminating risk, risk *can* be eliminated, at least in principle—and at least for some types of risk. But not all.

The distinction between risk that can be eliminated and that which cannot lies at the heart of the modern theory of finance. Risks that can truly be eliminated are what economists refer to as "diversifiable" or "idiosyncratic" risks. From the vantage point of the risk manager, these are the risks that are often responsible for shocks to asset and liability values and cash flows that precipitate unintended fluctuations in the value of a specific firm. Certain aspects of market risk, most credit risk, and nearly all operational risks typically fall into this category. And as we shall see later in this chapter, certain aspects of uncertainty can also be eliminated, just like risk.

A risk that *cannot* simply be eliminated is systematic risk. Systematic risk is a risk affecting all assets that gives rise to an expected return at a premium to the risk-free rate. We will explore systematic risk in much more detail later in Chapter 7. Put another way, systematic risk is reflected in the asset prices that characterize a competitive general equilibrium.

Idiosyncratic risks do not generally affect equilibrium asset prices because they can, in fact, usually be eliminated. There may be certain circumstances when those risks cannot be eliminated through any of the means mentioned, however, in which case idiosyncratic risk can in principle affect asset prices. One such situation relevant to the discussion in this book is the nontradability of certain financial claims that can prevent investors from eliminating risk through traditional means. We return to how this may affect asset prices— and the cost of risk transfer in particular—in Chapter 12.

Are there sources of true uncertainty that cannot be eliminated? No. Almost by definition, *any* randomness about the future that cannot be eliminated by any means must affect asset prices,[4] and hence must be systematic in nature. The reason we refer to this as systematic risk rather than uncertainty is that judgment and inference play no role in systematic risk. Systematic risk, then, is *risk* in the sense of Knight—it is quantifiable, and the probability distribution is generally subject to complete agreement. As Chapter 7 explains in more detail, this doesn't mean that systematic risk is easy to measure or identify, but this is an *empirical* problem. As a matter of pure theory, systematic risk is *risk*.

## CONSOLIDATION

When sources of risk or uncertainty are reduced by aggregating multiple sources of randomness into a single portfolio of outcomes, the process can be called *consolidation* and can be achieved by combination, diffusion, or compensation (Knight, 1921; Hardy, 1923). Apart from helping firms reduce the risks to which they are exposed, consolidation also helps firms transform uncertainty into risk, where it can be more easily managed.

## Combination

Combination is the process by which random events can be aggregated in a manner that reduces the risk for the consolidator. Combination can lead to risk reduction for two largely distinct reasons, one structural and the other informational. We shall discuss each in turn.

### Structural Risk Reduction through Diversification

The concept of portfolio diversification is one of the most fundamental and important ideas in finance (Markowitz, 1952, 1959). Although systematic risk cannot be diversified away, idiosyncratic risk *can*. In other words, provided the returns on multiple assets are not perfectly correlated, the sum of the component risks will always exceed the portfolio of combined risks.

More formally, consider a class of $N$ risk exposures or potential liabilities, where the $k$th exposure unit is denoted $L_k$. The expected value and volatility of the $k$th exposure are $E[L_k] = \mu_k$ and $\sigma_k$ respectively. If the exposures are aggregated such that $w_i$ represents the nominal currency amount of the $k$th exposure (i.e., its portfolio weight), the total *actual* liability on the combined aggregate exposure is:

$$L = \sum_{i=1}^{N} w_i L_i$$

and the *expected* aggregate liability is:

$$E[L] = \mu = \sum_{i=1}^{N} w_i E[L_i] = \sum_{i=1}^{N} w_i \mu_i$$

The variance of the combined risk exposure is:

$$\sigma^2 = \sum_{i=1}^{N} w_i^2 \sigma_i^2 + \sum_{i=1}^{N} \sum_{i \neq k} w_i w_k \, \text{cov}(L_i, L_k) = \sum_{i=1}^{N} w_i^2 \sigma_i^2 + \sum_{i=1}^{N} \sum_{\substack{k=1 \\ i \neq k}}^{N} w_i w_k \sigma_{ik}$$

To illustrate the principle of diversification, let us suppose that $w_i = 1/N$ so that each risk in the combined portfolio is assumed in equal proportions. Then,

$$E[L] = \mu = \frac{1}{N} \sum_{i=1}^{N} E[L_i] = \frac{1}{N} \sum_{i=1}^{N} \mu_i$$

$$\sigma^2 = \frac{1}{N^2}\left(\sum_{i=1}^{N}\sigma_i^2 + \sum_{i=1}^{N}\sum_{\substack{k=1\\i\neq k}}^{N}\sigma_{ik}\right) = \frac{1}{N^2}\left(\sum_{i=1}^{N}\sigma_i^2 + \sum_{i=1}^{N}\sum_{\substack{k=1\\i\neq k}}^{N}\sigma_i\sigma_k\rho_{ik}\right)$$

Where $\rho$ denotes the correlation coefficient. To further simplify the example, let us define the *average* variance and covariance as

$$\overline{\sigma^2} = \frac{1}{N}\sum_{i=1}^{N}\sigma_i^2 \qquad \overline{\rho\sigma^2} = \frac{1}{N(N-1)}\sum_{i=1}^{N}\sum_{\substack{k=1\\i\neq k}}^{N}\sigma_{ik}$$

so that the variance of the combined risk is

$$\sigma^2 = \frac{1}{N}\overline{\sigma^2} + \frac{N-1}{N}\overline{\rho\sigma^2}$$

The diversification principle essentially says that adding exposures to the combined portfolio will reduce the risk of the combined position when the exposures are anything less than perfectly correlated. In the simplest case, suppose the average covariance is zero—then,

$$\lim_{N\to\infty}\sigma^2 = 0$$

so that the risk of the combined exposure actually approaches zero as $N$ gets large.

If the average correlation is positive but less than one, diversification will still reduce the risk of the combined exposure vis-à-vis the individual components, but the total reduction in risk possible is bounded by the covariance/correlation. See Figure 3.2.

This simple stylized example nevertheless sheds light on a very important part of finance and risk management—namely, that increasing the exposure units in a portfolio of less than perfectly correlated liabilities leads to some structural risk reduction.

### Risk Reduction through Improved Prediction

A second reason that combination can lead to risk reduction is driven by the informational benefits often associated with aggregation. Specifically, probabilistic inference is often more reliable when performed at the portfolio level. We already encountered in Knight the basic idea of reducing risk

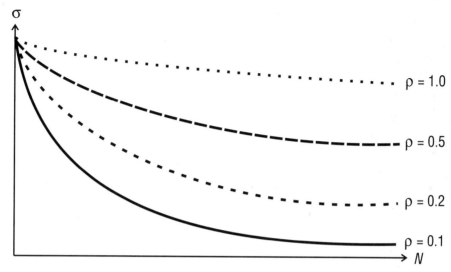

**FIGURE 3.2**   Portfolio Risk and Correlation of Component Exposures

and uncertainty by the improved prediction arising from combination. For Knight, combination through classification is the whole basis for the distinction between risk and uncertainty. The elimination of risk by combination is no less amenable to the same analysis—firms often have more confidence in the information they have about a group of risks than individual risk components. This in turn makes it easier to control the risk of the group as a whole, through prevention or other mechanisms. Hardy explains:

> *A single event defies prediction, but the mass remains always practically the same or varies in ways in which we can predict. It is obvious that any device by which we can base our business decisions on the average which we can predict, instead of on the single event, which is uncertain, means the elimination of risk. The larger the number of cases observed the less is the deviation of results from those which a priori were most probable. (Hardy, 1999, pp. 21–22)*

To illustrate, consider again $N$ possible risk exposures, and now suppose each exposure is mutually independent of every other exposure (i.e., the covariance between any two exposures is zero). For concreteness, you might imagine these as $N$ different counterparties to which you have credit exposure whose default probabilities are unrelated to one another, or all $N$ of your employees who are at risk of personal injury on the job but whose workers' compensation claims are independent of each other.

Now suppose combination involves the simple addition of exposures, rather than an equal-weighted portfolio comprised of components of each exposure. In this case the average or expected total liability is just:

$$E[L] = \mu = \frac{1}{N} \sum_{i=1}^{N} L_i$$

We can further assume that each $L_k$ is independent and identically distributed (i.i.d.) with mean $\mu$ and variance $\sigma^2$—that is, $L_k \sim f(\mu, \sigma^2)$ where $f$ is the probability density function from which losses are drawn.

In statistics, the *central limit theorem* tells us that the distribution of the *average risk* from a large group of i.i.d. random variables is approximately normal, regardless of the shapes and properties of the individual risk distributions.[5] See Figure 3.3.[6] Whereas any individual distribution may be difficult to use for statistical inference, the normal distribution certainly is not. So, combination of risk greatly enhances our capacity to draw reliable inferences about the nature of the underlying group of risks.

Note carefully that Figure 3.3 shows the *average* loss in a portfolio. Any given individual liability $k$, however, is still drawn from distribution $f_k$ and thus may be arbitrarily large. We thus have not necessarily reduced our *maxi-*

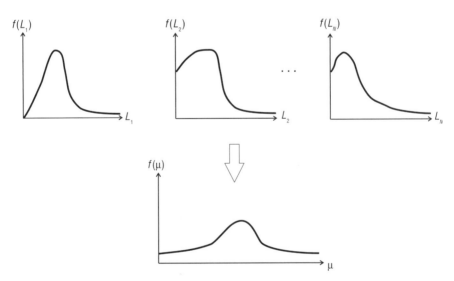

**FIGURE 3.3**   Improved Prediction by Combination

*mum* loss on any given component risk. But in reducing the volatility of our average loss, we have significantly increased our ability to manage the consolidated exposure by improving our ability to *measure* that risk and thus to predict our losses.

The classic example of how combination can be used by businesses to address risks in this manner—that is, exploiting the informational benefits of combination as opposed to the pure structural benefits of diversification—is the traditional insurance market.[7] Insurance as a type of contract essentially provides the policyholder with a reimbursement for economic damages in the event that a specific triggering event occurs. By providing a large number of similar policies to policyholders that are hopefully somewhat homogeneous, the insurance company can exploit the statistical relations described earlier. The average policy loss, in fact, typically becomes quite predictable in a large, diversified insurance portfolio.

From a practical perspective, students and practitioners of insurance will already have recognized our discussion of "classification" in Chapter 2. To an insurer, classification is perhaps *the* critical determinant of underwriting profits. An insurance company does not merely engage in classification to consolidate its risks for the purpose of improved statistical estimation of average and aggregate losses. Perhaps even more importantly, classification is generally the basis for how insurers quote the prices of the policies they sell to groups of purchasers in an effort to recover the expected loss from each group. The process by which an insurer sets premiums or rates[8] is actually often even called the classification or "class rating" process (Outreville, 1998). Knight (1921, p. 246) emphasizes the importance classification can play for insurers in their determination of what price to charge policyholders:

> *The application of the insurance principle, converting a larger contingent loss into a smaller fixed charge, depends upon the measurement of probability on the basis of a fairly accurate grouping into classes. It is in general not enough that the insurer who takes the "risk" of a large number of cases be able to predict his aggregate losses with sufficient accuracy to quote premiums which will keep his business solvent while at the same time imposing a burden on the insurer which is not too large a fraction of his contingent loss. In addition he must be able to present a fairly plausible contention that the particular insured is contributing to the total fund out of which losses are paid as they accrue in an amount corresponding reasonably well with his real probability of loss; i.e., that he is bearing his fair share of the burden.*

Proper classification of policyholders into risk categories on insurance rates is especially important for insurance companies when market participants do not all possess the same information and have the same expectations, as is virtually always the case. Insurance companies inevitably must address two practical problems arising from those information asymmetries.

First, *moral hazard*—the problem of "hidden action"—occurs when the insurer cannot perfectly observe the risk management activities of the insurance purchaser (e.g., prevention as discussed earlier) and when those activities are costly. The insurance itself will reduce the optimal quantity of risk management activities undertaken. To combat this problem, insurers use a variety of institutional contracting futures like deductibles, co-insurance, co-payment provisions, and policy limits. Although such contractual means by which moral hazard can be mitigated are usually the preferred solution to this problem, the insurer's assessment of a fair premium can also be driven by moral hazard considerations. When the risk management activities of an insurance purchaser can be observed *ex post* but not *ex ante*, for example, insurers can use classification systems to assess more accurate premiums over time as experience about the insured is acquired.

A second problem endemic to insurance markets is *adverse selection*—the problem of "hidden information"—and occurs when the insurer cannot differentiate between low-risk and high-risk types. If the insurer charges an average price, the low-risk types will view the price as excessive relative to their true risk and will not buy insurance. The result is that only high-risk types buy insurance. But in this case, the average premium is too low relative to the true expected loss and the insurer will eventually go out of business. Again, classification is an answer for insurers. The more precisely policyholders can be distinguished into risk types and homogeneous groups, the more accurate the premium will be.

In principle, risk combination of the form described earlier can be used to turn many individual risks into a more manageable—and, as explained, better-priced—agglomeration.

Combination can also sometimes be used to transform uncertainty into risk, but this is generally less true when dealing with firm-specific sources of business uncertainty. Knight (1921, p. 251) explains:

> *The fact which limits the application of the insurance principle to business risks generally is not . . . their inherent uniqueness alone. . . . First, the typical uninsurable (because unmeasurable and this because unclassifiable) business risk relates to the exercise of judgment in the making of decisions by the business man; second, although such estimates do tend to fall into groups within which fluctuations cancel out and hence to approach constancy and measurability, this happens only after the fact and, especially in view of the brevity of a man's active life, can only to a limited extent be made the basis of prediction. Furthermore, the classification or grouping can only to a limited extent be carried out by any agency outside the person himself who makes the decisions, because of the pecu-*

*liarly obstinate connection of a moral hazard with this sort of risks. The
decisive factors in the case are so largely on the inside of the person making the decisions that the "instances" are not amenable to objective description and external control.*

Although insurance as an essentially direct reimbursement for damages
has typically proven less attractive in helping firms deal with firm-specific
business uncertainties, that does not mean the market has not developed
other means by which highly idiosyncratic uncertainties can be reduced or
managed.

## Diffusion

Quite closely related to the principle of combination as a mechanism of risk
and uncertainty reduction through consolidation is what Knight (1921) calls
*diffusion*:

> *The minute divisibility of ownership and ease of transfer of shares en-
> ables an investor to distribute his holdings over a large number of enter-
> prises in addition to increasing the size of a single enterprise. The effect of
> this distribution on risk is evidently twofold. In the first place, there is to
> the investor a further offsetting through consolidation; the losses and
> gains in different corporations in which he owns stock must tend to can-
> cel out in large measure and provide a higher degree of regularity and
> predictability in his total returns. And again, the chance of loss of a small
> fraction of his total resources is of less moment even proportionally than
> a chance of losing a larger part. (Knight, 1921, p. 254)*

Diffusion does not really require diversification or imperfect correlation
in order to be beneficial. The main point here is to *distribute the risks across
multiple parties*. In this sense, the stock market is the archetypical risk- and
uncertainty-sharing device. In effect, a corporation acts as an insurance company to facilitate combination of all the risks and uncertainties that would
otherwise have to be borne separately by the numerous participants in the
corporate structure.

Without a corporation, the full impact of all production decisions would
come to bear on a single entrepreneur. By allowing multiple entrepreneurs to
invest proportionately in a single enterprise, the risks of that venture also become proportionate. An unexpected shock to demand could wipe out the capital of a single entrepreneur, but, when spread across numerous investors,
might have the same absolute impact without causing the same relative damage. As noted in Chapter 2, one entire "theory of the firm" is predicated on the
belief that organizations arise mainly as a response to the need for risk sharing.

Recall that a corporation is basically just an agglomeration of individuals tied together through contracts. In that sense, the corporation not only shelters each participant from the full force of the market to which he or she would otherwise be subject, but also protects each participant from the impact of his or her own actions and the actions of others by mutualizing the financial consequences of those actions. Laborers supply productivity and expertise, and capitalists supply funds. But the risk is now shared between them, so that capitalists help absorb the impact of adverse production outcomes and laborers help shoulder the burden of disappointing market performance (Hardy, 1923).

If corporations solve the problem of risk, why then do we observe firms of different sizes and specializations? One answer must be that we have left uncertainty out of the picture. Because uncertainty and not risk is the driving force behind profits, the guiding principle of the organizational form has been brushed aside for this discussion, but it surely cannot be brushed aside in actual contemplation of the problem.

Another problem recognized by Knight (1921)—anticipating Berle and Means (1932)—is the agency costs that can complicate the task of organizations. We have assumed that firms simply follow the market value rule, but in actual fact this may well not be the case. The larger a corporation, the greater the agency cost. Knight refers to this as a type of "moral hazard":

> The superiority of the higher form of organization over the lower from this point of view consists both in the extension of the scope of operations to include a larger number of individual decisions, ventures, or "instances," and in the more effective unification of interest which reduces the moral hazard connected with the assumption by one person of the consequences of another person's decisions. The close connection between these two considerations is manifest. It is the special "risk" to which large amounts of capital loaned to a single enterpriser are subject which limits the scope of operations of this form of business unit by making it impossible to secure the necessary property resources. On the other hand, it is the inefficiency of organization, the failure to secure effective unity of interest, and the consequent large risk due to moral hazard when a partnership grows to considerable size, which in turn limit its extension to still larger magnitudes and bring about the substitution of the corporate form of organization. (Knight, 1921, pp. 252–253)

## Compensation

Closely akin to the principle of risk elimination through combination is risk elimination through what Hardy (1923) calls *compensation*. Hardy defines compensation to be "the adjustment of business affairs in such a way that losses of a given kind will be directly associated with profits of another kind" (Hardy, 1923, p. 29). As an example, he indicates that a farmer could plant dry-weather and wet-weather crops in the same crop year in order to compensate for the risk of unknown future precipitation patterns.

Compensation is sometimes also known as *risk neutralization* or as *natural hedging*. This is the essential point of traditional hedging, as well, but hedging involves a third party, and this is not strictly necessary to achieve the desired result. Hedging, moreover, is compensation through risk transfer and thus is discussed later in the next section, on risk transfer.

An important special case of compensation occurs when a firm neutralizes the risk of an asset with the risk of a liability, often known more commonly as *balance sheet hedging*. Consider, for example, a U.S.-based airline that sells a large amount of its tickets in the United Kingdom. Suppose the airline has a capital structure consisting of 50 percent debt and 50 percent equity, and that it forecasts U.K. ticket sales at £10,000,000 per quarter. Those ticket revenues must be repatriated to dollars, and this exposes the airline to currency risk. As a solution, the firm could choose to issue part of its debt in the United Kingdom denominated in sterling, so that the airline expects to make £10,000,000 in quarterly sterling-denominated interest payments. As long as ticket sales and interest costs are equal to their expected values, the firm has eliminated its exchange rate risk.

## SPECIALIZATION AND RISK TRANSFER

Risk transfer is the explicit process by which the adverse impacts of a risk are shifted from the shareholders of one firm to either one or more individuals or to the shareholders of one or more other firms. The risk to be transferred can be systematic or idiosyncratic, financial or nonfinancial, and either core or incidental to the primary business of the firm dealing with the original risk. About the only limitation on what risk or bundle of risks can be transferred is the ability to define the risk in a contract to which both the original party and at least one counterparty can agree on terms of trade. Even uncertainty can be transferred—in the process, of course, being *transformed into risk* by virtue of the need for the two parties to agree on a price at which the transfer will occur.

Risk or uncertainty transfer can, of course, be accomplished in many different ways. We have already discussed the way that an insurer manages its own risks through consolidation. Implicit in that is the supply of risk transfer services—that is, the insurer would have no ability to consolidate risks were those risks not being transferred to the insurer through insurance contracts!

Similarly, certain types of arrangements endemic to the process of a market economy can and should be considered as mechanisms of risk transfer. As discussed, risk sharing within a corporation, for example, is essentially a form of risk transfer from laborers to capitalists and vice versa. And more broadly, the sale of a corporation by one set of owners to another will surely transfer the uncertainties facing that business enterprise from the original capitalists to the new ones.

Buying and selling assets can also be considered—in crude terms—a form of risk transfer. A Swiss chemical company that owns a factory in Brazil and is concerned about the risk of an adverse change in the price of the Brazilian real that could reduce its effective profits to be repatriated, for example, could simply sell the factory to, say, a German chemical company. In so doing, the risk of fluctuations in the price of the real are transferred from the Swiss firm to the German purchaser of the factory. The asset sale, however, also transfers all other risks and revenues to the purchaser of the factory. Risk transfer thus is a consequence of the sale of the factory, but only in certain situations is it likely to be a motivation.

Our real focus in this book, of course, is on *derivatives* as instruments of risk (and, to some degree, uncertainty) transfer. What sets apart derivatives from most other forms of risk transfer is their capacity to allow firms to *specialize* the risks being shifted. If a firm wishes only to protect its total capital or total net asset value, issuing new equity is generally a substitute for engaging in risk transfers (Culp, 2002a). But more often than not, a firm is interested in protecting some specific set of assets or liabilities from fluctuations in value, not the whole capital base of the firm. Alternatively, a firm may be focused on managing the risk of something other than value, such as fluctuations in per-period cash flows or accounting earnings. In any of these cases, derivatives enable a firm to pursue a customized risk transfer solution. A foreign exchange (forex or FX) derivatives contract, to return to our previous example, allows the Swiss chemical company to transfer its vulnerability to exchange rate changes *without selling the factory*.

Risk transfer involving derivatives presupposes that at least one of the two firms has a risk that its managers and security holders have decided is not a determinant of its core profits. The firm thus has a risk tolerance that lies below its actual risk exposure along at least some dimension. But what about the party on the other side of the transaction?

## Risk Transfer to Specialists

For many firms, intermediating risk and uncertainty is itself a perceived source of economic profits—the insurance company that perceives itself as better able to engage in consolidation than individual policyholders, the swap dealer that perceives itself better able to match a long and short than two end users, and so on. In short, some firms help other firms eradicate or reduce risk and uncertainty through their own specialization in facilitating risk transfer (Knight, 1921).

Risk transfer specialists are, quite literally, specialists in the supply of financial products designed to facilitate risk transfers. They are known by such terms of art as *middlemen, merchants,* or *dealers,* but we shall refer to firms that perceive themselves as being in the business of facilitating risk transfers as risk transfer specialists.

Risk transfer specialists are not always—or even often—specialists in *risk bearing.* In many cases, an insurance company "reinsures" or "retrocedes" a large portfolio of the risks it assumes by supplying insurance contracts. Similarly, most derivatives dealers seek to run a "matched book" in which a risk assumed in one contract is offset by another such contract. And when a matched book does not naturally result from the demands of different firms seeking risk transfer, the derivatives dealer may well turn to another risk management mechanism to deal with its "residual" risk.

Risk transfer specialists are thus often active users of risk transfer contracts. As said, insurers buy insurance actively. And derivatives dealers are in turn active users of derivatives. In many cases, risk transfer specialists also rely on the other methods by which firms can deal with risk explored in this chapter. Insurance companies first seek to reduce their risks through consolidation, and *then* turn to reinsurance. Derivatives dealers likewise rely strongly on prevention as well as consolidation to keep their own risk profiles in line with their risk tolerances (Culp, 2001).

The common features of risk transfer specialists thus do not really concern the tastes of their managers and security holders for assuming risk. Instead, risk transfer specialists tend to have some other comparative advantages. A risk transfer specialist, for example, generally faces lower search costs than individual firms seeking risk transfer (often called end users), thereby enabling those specialists to identify offsetting risk transfer demands among a customer base more easily than if, say, the Swiss chemical company had to go out and find for itself a firm that wanted to go *long* the Brazilian real against the Swiss franc.

Not surprisingly, the largest derivatives dealers thus are those firms with a large number of customers and a significant depth of information about those customers, such as commercial and investment banks. Depth of customer information is important for several reasons. First, dealers assume credit risk on the transactions into which they enter, and some expertise in identifying and managing such risks is essential in order for a dealer to survive. Second, as explained in Chapter 2, better derivatives dealers are those that have enough information about their customers' needs to anticipate their demands for often customized risk transfer solutions. Similarly, organized financial exchanges that list derivatives for trading must have extensive information about what it is exactly that customers want to trade.

Apart from economies of scope, depth, and breadth of customer information, a risk transfer specialist must also appear to be fully creditworthy to be a reliable counterparty in a risk transfer contract. A firm seeking to transfer its risks must have full confidence that the risk transfer specialist will be around to honor its commitments. An insurance company perceived to lack funds to pay off claims will not likely get many buyers of a new policy, and so, too, with derivatives dealers. Perceived creditworthiness is correlated with the credit rating assigned to the risk transfer specialist. Generally, it is difficult for a firm with below a single-A credit rating to maintain an active risk transfer business.

In addition, risk transfer specialists typically have significant amounts of equity capital, both in absolute terms and as a proportion of their capital structure. Excessively leveraged firms and firms with low market values of equity generally do not fare well as derivatives dealers or insurance providers.

A good reputation is also an essential characteristic of any true risk transfer specialist. Holistic risk transfer solutions like corporate mergers and acquisitions generally focus on an entire spectrum of risks bundled with the firm's operating profits. Risk transfer solutions, by contrast, are essentially transactional, undertaken one contract at a time to realize the benefits of tailoring and customization of risk transfer needs to risk transfer mechanisms. Because of the transactional nature of the risk transfer business, the commercial reputation of the counterparty is critical. Firms seeking risk transfer solutions are, of course, quite focused on the price of that risk transfer (much more on this later in Part Two). But assuming that competition keeps prices of comparable transactions roughly in line, reputation plays a critical secondary role in helping end users identify an appropriate risk transfer counterparty. Similarly, satisfied customers tend to engage in significant repeat business once a relationship to a risk transfer counterparty is established.

In the mid-1990s, a number of organizations received widespread media attention for their so-called "derivatives-related losses."[9] A disproportionate number of these losses arose from transactions negotiated by nonfinancial corporations like Procter & Gamble, Air Products, and Gibson Greetings with Bankers Trust (BT). In public and courtroom forums alike, these firms accused BT of selling excessively complicated and risky transactions. Not helping matters, tape-recorded transcripts were released in which BT derivatives sales representatives seem to be gloating over "sticking it to" their customers.

Regardless of BT's actual guilt or innocence in the legal context, the bank's reputation was irreparably damaged by the public accusations and the release of the tape-recorded conversations. End users and other derivatives dealers quickly began to back away from BT as a counterparty. Because its risk transfer area had been such a large profit center for the bank up to that point, the institution as a whole was unable to survive on its own after its derivatives dealing business dried up, and BT merged with Deutsche Bank in 1999.

## Risk Transfer between Hedgers

An early and important result of economic theory is that markets for the trading of risks between different individuals or firms can significantly increase the efficiency by which resources are allocated across agents in an economy (Arrow, 1953; Debreu, 1959). Sometimes it is sufficient that two firms or individuals are endowed with risk profiles they prefer not to retain. That may be enough reason for the two firms to transfer their risks to *one another*.

A firm that is seeking to enter into a derivatives contract in order to engage in risk transfer is generally called an end user of risk transfer products like derivatives. In some cases, end users simply exchange risks with other end users. In effect, two firms together engage in a joint compensation method of risk consolidation—technically risk transfer, though, because two firms are involved.

An excellent example of this was a $450 million "risk swap" undertaken in 2001 by Swiss Re and Tokio Marine, both large reinsurers of property damage arising from natural catastrophes. Swiss Re's catastrophic reinsurance portfolio is biased toward U.S. and European property damage, whereas Tokio Marine's major risk exposure lies in Japan. Under the agreement, Swiss Re agreed to make payments to Tokio Marine in the event of Japanese earthquake-, cyclone-, or typhoon-related property damage, in return for which Tokio Marine agreed to compensate Swiss Re in the event of a California earthquake, Florida hurricane, or French windstorm. The companies literally swapped risks.

Although never a dominant feature of derivatives, swapping risks between end users is not that unusual historically. A farmer concerned with falling crop prices might simply agree with a miller to a fixed-price forward sale of his crop. This would not only protect the farmer against falling prices, but also the miller against rising prices.

In general, however, it is quite costly for firms to identify risk transfer counterparties based solely on whether those firms have an offsetting or compensating risk exposure. It happens, but not very often.

## Risk Transfer to Speculators

If an end user does not engage in a transfer of risk to another end user (with a compensating, offsetting risk exposure) or to a risk transfer specialist, all that remains is for the end user to transact with speculators. A speculator is essentially a market participant—a firm, or perhaps a wealthy individual—that agrees to assume a risk or uncertainty from another market participant for which no natural offsetting exposure exists. Speculation thus involves *the net assumption of risk or uncertainty*.

The *hedge load* in a financial market is defined as the amount of depth in a market to absorb the demands of hedgers for the transfer of risk. As we have said already and will see again in Chapters 12 and 13, firms seeking to transfer risk to one or more other firms have several types of counterparties available in addition to speculators. Yet, there can be little doubt that the addition of speculators to the market, all else being equal, increases the hedge load. Even when speculators are trading with one another more than with hedgers, the presence and active participation by speculators tends to add depth to markets and thus reduce transaction costs for all participants (Gray, 1967).

One of the most articulate explanations of the beneficial role played by speculators was undertaken by Adam Smith in *An Enquiry into the Nature and Causes of the Wealth of Nations* in his analysis of the economic impact of the British laws governing the trade of corn—the insidious Corn Laws. Smith was particularly concerned about political restrictions in the Corn Laws on the trading activities of corn "merchants" and "dealers," or what we would call speculators.

"Forestalling" was the epithet assigned to an activity in which corn merchants "bought up [corn] in order to be sold again soon after in the same market, so as to hurt the people" (Smith, 1776, p. 700). Implicit in prohibitions on forestalling was the firmly rooted belief that this variety of speculation was inherently destabilizing—that it would raise prices and adversely impact consumers. But Smith argued that forestalling was a *stabilizing* activity:

> But if a merchant ever buys up corn, either going to a particular in the same market, it must be because he judges that the market cannot be so liberally supplied through the whole season as upon that particular occasion, and that the price, therefore, must soon rise. If he judges wrong in this, and if the price does not rise, he not only loses the whole profit of the stock which he employs in this manner, but a part of the stock itself, by the expense and loss which necessarily attend the storing and keeping of corn. He hurts himself, therefore, much more essentially than he can hurt even the particular people whom he may hinder from supplying themselves upon that particular market day, because they may afterwards supply themselves just as cheap upon any other market day. If he judges right, instead of hurting the great body of the people, he renders them a most important service. By making them feel the inconveniencies of a dearth somewhat earlier than they otherwise might do, he prevents their

*feeling them afterwards so severely as they certainly would do, if the cheapness of price encouraged them to consume faster than suited the real scarcity of the season. When the scarcity is real, the best thing that can be done for the people is to divide the inconveniencies of it as equally as possible through all the different months, and weeks, and days of the year. The interest of the corn merchant makes him study to do this as exactly as he can: and as no other person can have either the same interest, or the same knowledge, or the same abilities to do it so exactly as he, this most important operation of commerce ought to be trusted entirely to him. (Smith, 1776, p. 700)*

Smith made similar arguments in his seminal treatise about other forms of corn speculation (e.g., "engrossing"), which he considered to have equally stabilizing influences.[10] In the end, he argued that restrictions on a free corn trade—especially those aimed at mitigating speculative activities— were themselves significantly more destabilizing than the banned trading practices: "The freedom of the corn trade . . . in many countries is confined by such absurd regulations as frequently aggravate the unavoidable misfortune of a dearth into the dreadful calamity of a famine" (Smith, 1776, pp. 708–709).

Contemporary efforts to restrict or inhibit speculation today—often aimed at new financial instruments—are often based on the same fundamental belief as in the eighteenth century: that speculators are profiteers who undertake their activities at the expense of the public good. Now as then, evidence does not really support this.

One reason that these sorts of arguments about speculation have a tendency to resurface is public perception. What is not understood is often condemned, and few people historically understand the true value of financial entrepreneurialism, specialization in risk consolidation, and speculation. Smith aptly summarizes:

*The popular fear of engrossing and forestalling may be compared to the popular terrors and suspicions of witchcraft. The unfortunate wretches accused of this latter crime were not more innocent of the misfortunes imputed to them than those who have been accused of the former. The law which put an end to all prosecutions against witchcraft, which put it out of any man's power to gratify his own malice by accusing his neighbour of that imaginary crime, seems effectually to have put an end to those fears and suspicions by taking away the great cause which encouraged and supported them. The law which should restore entire freedom to the inland trade of corn would probably prove as effectual to put an end to the popular fears of engrossing and forestalling. (Smith, 1776, pp. 701–702)*

We will return to our discussion of speculators and the nature of speculation—as well as the expected return to speculation—in more detail in Chapter 12.

## NOTES

1. Captives and other similar structures like protected cell companies are discussed in Wöhrmann (1998, 1999, 2001) and Wöhrmann and Bürer (2001).
2. This grouping is a hybrid of Knight, Hardy, and my own effort to modernize their terminology a bit. All the ideas expressed in the rest of the chapter are really attributable to either Knight or Hardy, but I have attempted to organize them along more friendly and contemporary lines of demarcation.
3. See also Smith (2003).
4. Systematic risk may very well affect asset prices *with a zero price.*
5. In turn, the law of large numbers tells us that the mean of the (approximately normal) distribution of the sum of a large number of i.i.d. random variables is the same as the mean of the underlying distributions from which the samples were drawn.
6. See, for example, Doherty (2000).
7. Hicks (1989) suggests that same is true for many banks.
8. The *premium* usually refers to the total price paid by the policyholder for coverage, whereas the *rate* is the price per unit of coverage.
9. These losses were for the most part not caused by derivatives. See Miller (1997); Culp, Miller, and Neves (1998); and Culp, Hanke, and Neves (1999).
10. See Culp and Smith (1989) for a more detailed analysis of the passages from Adam Smith concerning the social benefits of speculation.

# CHAPTER 4

# Risk Transfer
# and Contracting Structures

**A**s we saw in Chapter 3, firms can use the principle of *compensation* to reduce their risk and uncertainty by finding two exposures within the firm's portfolio whose payoffs are negatively correlated in different states of nature. We called that a *natural hedge*. Risk transfer involves the same basic idea, except now the firm must go outside to achieve the desired result of risk reduction.

Risk transfer is not simply magically accomplished, however, when one firm tells another hedger, a risk-transfer specialist, or a speculator, "Okay, you take my risk now." The idea is to construct a *consolidation* of two exposures—the new exposure deliberately assumed in the risk transfer arrangement that generates a positive payoff at the same time the other existing exposure results in an economic loss. The key to risk transfer thus lies in the definition of the payoff structure of the risk transfer contract.

In this sense, the term *risk transfer* is itself a bit deceiving. By entering into a contract that produces positive payoffs in the same states of nature that you would otherwise experience a loss, you are essentially transferring income into what was previously a bad state of nature, but that income had to come from somewhere. Strictly speaking, it comes from the counterparty. And risk transfer contracts, after all, are bilateral and zero-sum in the sense that a gain for you necessarily implies a loss for your counterparty.

We have to be a bit careful here, though. In a *portfolio* context, you have entered into a contract that has a positive payoff in states of nature otherwise deleterious for your firm. And true, your positive payoff means a negative payoff for your counterparty. But this does *not* mean that the same contract, when viewed from the *counterparty's* portfolio perspective, increases that firm's overall risk. In other words, although the cash that came from your counterparty is being *used* by you to generate a positive payoff in a bad state of nature, the counterparty may not have the same perspective on things.

Consider a call option on platinum struck at $700 per ounce at-the-money. Suppose the call option buyer is an automotive manufacturer and the seller is a platinum mining firm. At the transactional level, the auto firm achieves risk transfer—in exchange for a known, fixed, up-front premium payment, the firm receives a payoff that rises as platinum prices rise. A platinum price increase is thus "good" for the auto firm and "bad" for the mine *transactionally*.

Now consider the *portfolio* perspective of how the individual payoff might interact with the firm's other risks to achieve some risk reduction by combination. The auto firm must put catalytic converters in its cars, which requires large amounts of platinum. If prices rise unexpectedly, the auto firm will experience an unexpected increase in costs and decline in its net margin. The payoff on the option at least partly offsets this. At the same time, the mine that wrote the option experiences a loss on the option itself, but rising platinum prices are generally good for the mine. So in this sense, the auto company has not really transferred its earnings at risk to the mine—merely the cash flows at risk *on the transaction*.

The "risk transfer" that occurred thus is not really from one firm to another, but from one state of nature to another. The auto firm is willing to part with a fixed payment in all states of nature in order to increase its cash flows in a state that would otherwise be bad, and the mine has accepted a payment of premium in all states of nature in return for agreeing to pay out some of its earnings in a state that would otherwise be good. Both firms have moved resources from the state of nature in which they were originally deployed into a state of nature where the resource gain is more highly valued and the loss less highly valued at the margin. Each additional dollar of earnings in a high-price environment is more useful to the firm than an additional dollar in a low-price stable profits environment.

As implied in Chapters 1 through 3, risk transfer thus is really about intertemporal and interspatial resource and risk allocation. They key is that *you need a counterparty in order to do it*. In fact, the situations in which risk transfer means paying one firm to absorb a hit you prefer not to take are pretty few and far between. Much more likely is that two firms simply have different definitions of "good" and "bad" states of nature, thus creating a gain from the trade.

We turn now to examine in a bit more detail the types of arrangements that can be used to facilitate risk transfer between firms in the manner just described. We follow that discussion with a more detailed look at how transactional risk transfer products facilitate risk transfer in a broader portfolio context, and we conclude this chapter with a brief look at how risk transfer is priced.

# RISK TRANSFER ARRANGEMENTS AND PAYOFF FUNCTIONS

Risk transfer is accomplished when a firm engages in a contractual arrangement that generates a positive payoff in the same states of nature that some risk imposes a negative payoff on the firm's normal business operations. We can distinguish between different types of mechanisms that facilitate risk transfer in this manner along at least two different dimensions: the nature of the underlying variable that is specified to determine the payoff on the risk transfer arrangement, and the specific manner in which changes in that underlying variable affect gains and losses on the risk transfer contract. These are not mutually exclusive from one another but are both important descriptors of the risk transfer arrangement.

## Nature of the Underlying

An extremely important distinction between different risk transfer vehicles concerns the nature of the underlying that gives the contract its value. As long as two parties can define an underlying, it is a candidate for a risk transfer arrangement. The possibilities are limitless and include: interest rates, exchange rates, commodity prices, quantities produced of an asset, property values, insurance losses, credit-sensitive assets, equity indexes, bank loan indexes, and so on.

A very useful way to distinguish between risk transfer arrangements based on the nature of the underlying is to consider whether the underlying is under the direct control of the hedger. An *indemnity* contract is a contract that makes a reimbursement to the hedger for economic damage actually sustained. The underlying of an indemnity contract is thus some variable or variables *specific to the hedger*. A *parametric* contract, by contrast, has a payoff based on one or more underlyings that are not directly related to the hedger.

## Indemnity Insurance Contracts

In an indemnity insurance contract,[1] the hedger—often called the *cedant* in insurance markets—makes a fixed up-front payment (called the *premium*) to an insurance company in exchange for the right to call on the insurer for reimbursement of certain kinds of damages sustained following the occurrence of one or more triggering events. Traditional examples include property and professional liability insurance. If a building owned by the purchaser of fire insurance burns down, for example, the owner may collect an amount from the insurer that is directly tied to the loss in value of the building due to the fire.

Because indemnity contracts are based on actual economic damage sustained, such contracts generally require that the hedger must have what is called an *insurable interest* before entering into the contract. This means that a firm cannot enter into an indemnity contract that entitles it to receive compensation in the event that some other firm sustains damages. Only the damaged party is eligible for reimbursement. American Airlines, for example, cannot purchase an insurance contract that pays off when another company loses an aircraft in a crash—for obvious reasons, given the perverse incentives that might create.

The problem of moral hazard is introduced and discussed briefly in Chapter 3. Now you can see even more clearly why moral hazard is a problem for insurance markets. When asymmetric information prevents the insurer from monitoring the risk management activities of the insurance purchaser, the insurance purchaser may not only be less willing to incur the costs of prevention but could in the extreme be tempted to overstate or even create damages just to receive the reimbursement. This is an immediate implication of the nature of indemnity contracts as reimbursements for actual damages sustained—that is, the variable that determines the payment to the insurance purchaser is *under the direct control of the insured party*.

Indemnity contracts generally contain several features specifically intended to mitigate moral hazard problems. These include deductibles, co-insurance and co-payment provisions, policy limits, and escape clauses that allow the insurer not to pay in the event of fraud or breach of warranty.

### Parametric Contracts

A parametric risk transfer contract involves an underlying that is a market-determined asset price, interest rate, or index. In other words, the variables that determines the payoff on parametric risk transfer contracts are not usually under the direct control of the hedger. Derivatives are generally parametric contracts.

Parametric contracts do not require an insurable interest on the part of the hedger. Because a firm engaging in a parametric contract is not being reimbursed for actual sustained damage, the firm need not experience any such damages in order to receive a positive payoff from the contract. A firm entering into a forward agreement to purchase Swiss francs for British pounds, for example, need not have any natural risk exposure to either the franc or to sterling in order to receive a positive payoff from its counterparty.

The absence of an insurable interest and the indexation of parametric contracts like derivatives to market-determined variables generally means that moral hazard is not an issue in parametric contracts. To continue with the previous example, any single firm entering into a forward contract to buy Swiss francs for pounds is highly unlikely to be able to influence the franc/sterling exchange rate in any meaningful way. Sometimes hedgers do possess some "market power," but as we explain later in Chapter 5, too much market power will render a derivatives market nonviable. So, if a viable market exists, it is generally true that there are sufficient competitors to prevent any single firm from manipulating the payoff on a derivatives transaction in that market.

Eliminating moral hazard by indexing the payoff of a parametric contract to a variable beyond the control of the hedger, however, comes at a price. Namely, because the contract does not pay the hedger an amount based on actual damage sustained, it is entirely possible—likely, actually—that the payoff on the parametric contract will not precisely compensate the hedger for actual losses. When the payoff on a derivatives contract is imperfectly correlated with the firm-specific risk exposure being hedged, we refer to this as *quality basis risk*. We will explore this issue extensively later in Chapter 15. For now, it is enough to recognize that there is a clear trade-off between moral hazard and basis risk; it is generally impossible to eliminate one without creating the other.

## Relation of the Payoff to the Underlying

A second useful way to distinguish between risk transfer contracts involves the "symmetry" of the payoff to the hedger created by the contract. By symmetry, we mean the extent to which a change in the underlying can give rise to a gain *or* a loss for the hedger if the transaction is viewed in isolation.

### Forward- and Option-Based Contracts

*Forward-based* risk transfer contracts have cash flows or payoffs that are linear and symmetric in the value of the underlying on their value dates, whereas *option-based* contacts do not. Consider a contract with trade date $t$ and maturity or value date $T$ that is designed to help firms shift the risk of corn price increases to the counterparty in the contract. Let $S_t$ denote the price per bushel of corn on any date $t$, and suppose one contract is based on a single bushel of corn. On the value date $T$, the value of the payoff to the long is:

$$z_T = S_T - K \tag{4.1}$$

where $K$ is the fixed purchase price.

The sensitivity of the contract payoff to a small change in the underlying asset price, known as the *delta* of the contract, can be defined as:

$$\Delta = \frac{\partial z_T}{\partial S_T} = 1 \tag{4.2}$$

which is a constant and is thus continuous for any value of $S_T$. We refer to this as a *symmetric-payoff* contract because the sensitivity of the payoff to a small change in $S_T$ is not affected by the value of $S_T$. The absolute impact of some arbitrary increase in price $\Delta S$ on $z_T$ is the same as the impact of a price decline of the same magnitude. The direction is, of course, different ($\Delta S > 0$ results in a gain, whereas $\Delta S < 0$ results in a loss), but the magnitudes are the same in absolute value. The payoff thus is *symmetric* in the sense that a price change of $\Delta S$ results in a change in the contract's payoff of the same amount, regardless of whether that represents a gain or a loss.

Now consider a second contract with similar terms as before, also intended to help firms shift the risk of corn price increases to the counterparty in the contract. But now suppose that on the value date $T$, the value of the payoff to the long is

$$z_T = \max(S_T - K, 0) \qquad (4.3)$$

which we recognize as the terminal payoff on a standard European call option. The sensitivity of this contract's payoff to a small change in the underlying asset price, or the delta of the contract, can be defined at maturity as:[2]

$$(4.4)$$

$$\Delta = \frac{\partial z_T}{\partial S_T} = 1 \quad \forall S_T \geq K$$

$$\Delta = \frac{\partial z_T}{\partial S_T} = 0 \quad \forall S_T < K$$

which is a constant and is thus continuous for any value of $S_T$ above $K$. The payoff function is thus *discontinuous* at $S_T = K$.

We refer to this second type of contract as an *asymmetric-payoff* contract because the sensitivity of the payoff to a small change in $S_T$ is affected by the relation of $S_T$ to $K$. The absolute impact of some arbitrary increase in price $\Delta S$ on $z_T$ is not the same as the impact of a price decline of the same magnitude. More specifically, this contract cannot result in a negative payout for the long on the value date $T$.

### Related Terminology

Symmetric-payoff derivatives are the same as forward-based derivatives, and asymmetric-payoff contracts are option-based contracts in this lingo. You can use the terms interchangeably without concern. Likewise, some refer to forward-based contracts as "unlimited liability" contracts and option-based contracts as "limited liability" contracts. You may *not* use *these* terms interchangeably—the comparison is not accurate.

Figure 4.1 depicts the time $T$ value of a long forward contract whose pay-

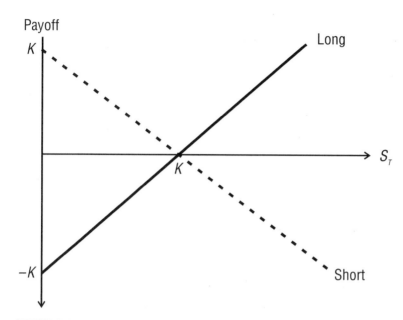

**FIGURE 4.1** Payoff on Value Date of Forward-Based Contracts

off was shown earlier in equation (4.1), as well as a short position in the same contract whose payoff is

$$z_T = K - S_T \qquad (4.5)$$

Assuming that the price of the underlying is a traditional asset, the price cannot be negative. In principle, however, the price could grow essentially without bounds, so that we have $0 \le S_T \le \infty$. As the figure shows, this means that the long position can gain in value without limit, but can never lose more than $K$. Conversely, the short can never gain more than $K$ but faces unlimited liability if prices rise. So, only the short forward is "unlimited liability."

### Relation to the Nature of the Underlying

Can we draw any conclusions about the relation between the symmetry of the payoff on a risk transfer arrangement and the nature of the underlying? Yes, but only in one direction. Specifically, indemnity contracts are always asymmetric-payoff or option-based contracts, whereas parametric contracts may be either symmetric- or asymmetric-payoff contracts.

Because indemnity contracts provide the economic equivalent of a reimbursement to the hedger, they pay off only when the hedger sustains damage. An important implication of this is that a hedger can never make money on an indemnity contract. This is also related to the principle of insurable interest, which essentially prohibits the hedger from using an indemnity contract to speculate. The requirement that the hedger has an insurable interest means, by definition, that the *net* of the indemnity contract and the natural position of the hedger cannot ever be positive.

Parametric contracts face no such constraints. Because a hedger need not have an insurable interest to engage in a parametric contract, there is absolutely nothing to prevent the use of such contracts for speculative purposes, for "anticipatory hedging" (i.e., hedging a planned future exposure that does not exist at the time the contract is initiated) and the like. Nevertheless, hedgers sometimes prefer option-based or asymmetric-payoff contracts. The choice is entirely theirs.

## MECHANICS OF RISK TRANSFER

To illustrate the mechanics of how the payoff function is the key to achieving risk transfer, let us examine a simple example of a farming corporation that seeks to reduce the variability of its revenues by hedging or transferring price risk. We will first review a hedge involving an option- or insurance-like contract provided by a risk-transfer specialist, and then a forward-based hedge negotiated either with another hedger or a speculator.

### An Asymmetric-Payoff Hedge with a Risk-Transfer Specialist

Consider a corn farming corporation in southern Illinois that produces $y$ bushels of corn in a given harvest. When the harvest comes in, the price per bushel of corn is $p$. Suppose there is a $\pi_1$ probability that the price of corn will be commensurate with a good harvest and a $\pi_2$ probability that the price of corn will decline from $p$ to $p'$ as a result of a bad-weather year. Revenues in the two states of nature may be denoted $z_k$ for $k = 1, 2$ such that:

> *State 1:*     $z_1 = yp$
> *State 2:*     $z_2 = yp'$

Now suppose that the value of the farm as a corporation $v(z)$ is a function of revenues, production costs, and some exogenous financial distress costs. As discussed in Chapter 2, a firm must have some reason for even considering risk transfer. To keep things simple, let us assume a constant marginal cost of production and then let exogenous costs of financial distress be a known and decreasing function of revenues (i.e., distress costs rise at an increasing rate as revenues fall). By assumption, then, $V_z > 0$ and $V_{zz} < 0$, where subscripts denote partial derivatives.[3]

The market risk facing the firm is the risk that state 2 occurs, in which case the firm experiences a loss in revenues of $y(p - p')$. Because distress costs rise as revenues fall, the value of the firm will fall by more than $y(p - p')$. In a portfolio context, the firm thus seeks to compensate for this risk by entering into a transaction with a counterparty whose payoff is *positive* in state 2. Ideally, the payoff should be something similar to $y(p - p')$, as well. In short, the firm will find it beneficial to reduce its revenues and pay something in state 1 in order to increase its revenues in state 2. In economic terms, the risk transfer thus allows the firm to shift resources across states of nature.

Specifically, suppose a European put option is available with a strike price set so that the option is at-the-money when the harvest comes in. The payoff of the option is thus $h(p - p')$ where $h$ is the amount the firm might wish to hedge using the option. Let us suppose that the price the firm must pay for the put option is proportional to the protection the option will provide per bushel and the number of bushels hedged, where $\phi$ denotes our proportionality factor. The total cost of the option (payable in both states) thus is $\phi h(p - p')$.

## The Optimal Hedge
We discuss different possible hedging objectives in detail in Chapter 13. For now, let us just assume that the managers of the farming company want to choose an amount to hedge $h$ to solve the following problem:

$$\max_h \pi_1 V(z_1) + \pi_1 V(z_2)$$
$$s.t. \quad z_1 = py - \phi h(p - p')$$
$$s.t. \quad z_2 = p'y - \phi h(p - p') + h(p - p')$$
(4.6)

Substituting the constraints into the objective function in equation (4.6) and setting the first-order condition equal to zero reveals that the "optimal" hedge is the $h$ that satisfies[4]

$$\pi_1 \phi V'(z_1) = \pi_2(1 - \phi) V'(z_2)$$
(4.7)

Efficient production in this world occurs when the farm reduces its corn sales in a good year up to the point that the lost value from forgoing an extra unit of corn following a good harvest is *exactly equal* to the gain in value from a small increase in corn following a bad harvest. This point occurs at exactly the ratio of the probabilities of bad and good harvests.

Now, let us assume that the probability of a price decline is exactly equal to the price of the put option per unit of intrinsic value and per bushel, so that $\phi = \pi_2$. In this case, the first-order condition is equal to zero and optimal hedging occurs when $z_1 = z_2$, or when $h = y$. In other words, the firm *fully hedges*.

Figure 4.2 illustrates the optimal hedging solution graphically, where the x-axis represents revenue in a good-weather year and the y-axis depicts revenue in a bad-weather year. The 45-degree line represents the combinations of production under the two states of nature in which the corn can be sold at the same price regardless of the weather. The family of curves convex to the origin represent the trade-off the farm is willing to make between good-weather corn and bad-weather corn[5]—each curve represents a different value of the firm, with value increasing as we move northeast, so that $V(1) < V(2) < V(3)$, but value is constant along any given curve. Finally, the line tangent to the curves has a slope of $-\pi_2 / \pi_1$, or the ratio of probabilities of a bad and good harvest.

To see the efficiency effects of risk transfer most clearly, suppose the farm's revenues in a good-weather year are originally $w_1$ and are $w_2$ in a bad-harvest year. If the corn price in a good year can be explicitly traded

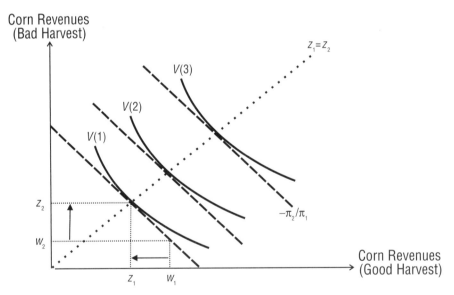

**FIGURE 4.2**   An Option Hedge of Weather Risk to Farming Revenues

for the corn price in a bad year at the price ratio $-\pi_2/\pi_1$, then the farm will engage in a trade to achieve an optimal production plan in the face of weather risk at $z_1 = z_2$. In other words, the farm will be willing to sacrifice revenue in a good-weather year in order to increase revenue following a bad harvest.

### Hedging as Insurance Purchasing

Figure 4.2 can be interpreted in an insurance or hedging context very easily. The premium paid will equal $\alpha = w_1 - z_1$ and the hedge will pay off an amount equal to $H = z_2 - w_2$ in the event that a bad-weather year occurs. The risk transfer specialist has no financial distress costs and thus has isovalue curves in Figure 4.2 that have the same slope as the budget constraint (i.e., the negatively sloped line with a slope equal to the ratio of the probabilities of the two states). The specialist thus is willing to take a payment of $\alpha$ in return for promising to make a payment of $H$ in the event that bad weather adversely affects the corn crop.

Note in the context of Chapter 2, moreover, that this transaction is genuine *risk* transfer. Paying a risk transfer specialist to assume this weather risk does not require that the agent and insurer have different information or beliefs. For the reasons discussed earlier, the insurance company acting as a risk transfer specialist may simply be willing to assume the weather risk that the agent wishes to avoid, provided the price of the risk transfer is fair.

This is a fairly standard result that should be familiar to students of insurance markets. Often called the *Bernoulli principle* when applied to people rather than firms, the result in an expected utility theory context tells us that risk-averse individuals (i.e., individuals whose utility functions are concave in wealth) purchase full insurance at actuarially fair prices, where "actuarially fair" means that the price per unit of coverage is exactly equal to the probability of the bad state of nature occurring.

In the context of the farming corporation, we assumed financial distress costs that create a concavity in the firm's value function, and this motivates the same result; as long as the put option has an actuarially fair price, the farming corporation will hedge its entire crop against price declines over the week between harvest and the sale of the crop. In economics parlance, the farming company has reduced its revenues in state 1 when financial distress costs are relatively low in order to raise its revenues in state 2 when distress costs are high.

To accomplish its risk transfer objectives, the farmer simply enters into a transaction with a risk transfer specialist for a contract whose payoff is $p - p'$ in exchange for receiving a payment of $\phi$ per bushel and per unit of coverage (i.e., intrinsic value). In other words, the counterparty is willing to accept $\phi h(p - p')$ in states 1 and 2 in exchange for an obligation to make a payment to the farm of $h(p - p')$ only in state 2. Especially under the assumption made about prices, this is perfectly intuitive. From the counterparty's perspective the expected payoff on the contract is just

$$E[z] = \phi h(p - p') - \pi_2 h(p - p') = (\phi - \pi_2) h(p - p') \qquad (4.8)$$

so that the counterparty breaks even on an expected value basis when the option price is actuarially fair (i.e., when $\phi = \pi_2$).

The expected value of the option *in isolation* is, of course, the same for the farm as it is for the counterparty. So, the price the farm corporation pays is equal to the probability-weighted payoff the farm will receive in state 2. But because the option enables the firm to shift revenue from state 2 to state 1, the firm's financial distress costs fall and the value of the firm rises. This is the *portfolio benefit* of risk transfer that we have been discussing.

The actuarially fair price in this simple example (i.e., the true price of the option) is essentially the expected discounted payoff on the risk transfer contract. Chapter 7 characterizes this much more explicitly for both symmetric- and asymmetric-payoff contracts. This aspect of the price of risk transfer will *not* depend on the nature of the counterparty. If the actuarial price of risk transfer charged by one firm differs from another, an arbitrage opportunity will exist. But this does not mean the *all-in cost* to the hedger will always be the same.

Risk transfer specialists are in the business of providing risk transfer arrangements to hedgers. To the extent this is costly, they may try to recover some of those costs from customers by adding what some call a "load" to the actuarially fair price of a risk transfer contract. This is essentially a markup that enables the risk transfer specialist to recover the costs of hedging or reinsurance, the cost of maintaining a presence in the market, and the like. On many derivatives, a portion of the load may be earned through the bid/ask spread instead of as an explicit markup to price.

### Symmetric-Payoff Hedge between Two Hedgers with Offsetting Exposures

When two parties agree about the probabilities and outcomes that define risks to which both firms are subject but in an opposite way, risk transfer can be accomplished in a manner that does *not* require an explicit payment. All that we need is to ensure that the distribution of risk *after* the transaction is more efficient for both parties than the natural risks to which both parties were originally subject. Specifically, risk transfer need not involve an explicit payment by one firm to the other if a simple bilateral exchange represents a *Pareto improvement*—an exchange that makes at least one party better off without making the other party any worse off.

To keep things easy, let's extend the analysis from the prior section by now assuming there are two agents. We will use the same variables as before, where superscripts now denote the two agents. They are identical except that Agent 1 is the farm as before and Agent 2 is now a miller. And instead of scenario 1 representing a stable price, now let's imagine that scenario 1 is a corn price increase—a good thing for the farmer and a bad thing for the miller—and that scenario 2 is a price decline.

To illustrate the concept of a Pareto improvement in risk sharing that two parties should be willing to undertake, Figure 4.3 shows what economists call an Edgeworth Box. Viewed from the bottom left, the figure is the same as Figure 4.2. But viewed from the top right and moving southwesterly, the figure is the analogue to Figure 4.2 for Agent 2. To keep things simple, we are assuming here that $w_1^1 + w_1^2 = w_2^1 + w_2^2$ (where superscripts indicate the agent number) so that there is no systematic risk.

In Figure 4.3, the farmer sacrifices revenue in the high-price state in order to increase revenue in a bad-harvest, low-price year. But now we see that it is *also* optimal for the miller to give up revenue in the low-price, bad-harvest year in order to increase revenue in the good-harvest, high-price year. By meeting in the middle, as it were, both parties are better off (i.e., both parties are on higher indifference curves) than if they retained their initial endowments. Both parties end up with less variable revenues, and both parties like that.

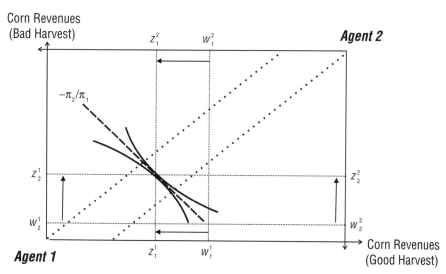

**FIGURE 4.3** Efficient Risk-Sharing Between Hedgers

The gain from trade illustrated in Figure 4.3 is called a Pareto improvement because at least one party is better off and the other party is no worse off. In fact, in this example both parties are better off than if they stuck to their original risk exposures. This is classic risk sharing involving a symmetric-payoff contract (e.g., a forward contract) instead of the optionlike contract we saw in the previous section. It does not require that the agents have any disagreement about the future, nor does it require one party to make a net cash payment to the other. All that is required is that corn in good and bad years is traded at the rate of $\pi_2/\pi_1$.[6]

Importantly, neither party will add a load in this situation because it represents pure, efficient exchange. There are no hedging or reinsurance costs, no market-making costs, and no cost of maintaining a market presence to recover from the other party. In addition, this transaction involves no extra payment from one party to the other to compensate for a shift in risk. Both parties have lower revenue volatility as a result of the outright exchange and thus do not require any such compensation.[7]

At the same time, by *not* using a risk transfer specialist, these two parties must be able to locate one another, and this may be costly in itself. If the load charged by a risk transfer specialist is lower than the search costs of the farmer and miller finding one another, the risk transfer specialist may still win the day as the preferred counterparty.

Nevertheless, it would be a mistake to trivialize the volume of risk transfer that can be accomplished among participants that have no disagreement whatsoever about the probabilities associated with future states of the world and that can exploit efficiency gains using derivatives as a substitute for bilateral exchange. Even when a specialist in risk bearing acts as an intermediary, the ability of firms to exchange offsetting exposures using derivatives is a powerful benefit of these markets.

## Speculation

If the contract entered into by the farmer—either the option depicted in Figure 4.2 or the forward in Figure 4.3—is negotiated with a speculator rather than a hedger, the basic analytical framework established can still be used. As Laffont (1989) and Weller and Yano (1992) both demonstrate using the same Edgeworth Box analysis we just went through, risk transfer can also be depicted even when the transfer involves a disagreement about the nature of the randomness. If two parties can agree to the classification of states of nature and merely disagree on the probabilities they will occur, recall from Chapter 2 that is still a *risk* in the sense of Knight. Accordingly, risk transfer can occur.

When the counterparty was a risk transfer specialist, the load was enough to compensate the firm for its market presence and the risk it assumed. When the counterparty was another hedger, the simple exchange of negatively correlated exposures at actuarially fair terms of trade was the only thing required to make both parties better off. But now when dealing with a speculator, the big question is whether the speculator will require any compensation above the actuarial fair price and any fixed load.

Some contend that speculators will demand a "risk premium" to compensate them for assuming a risk that hedgers prefer to avoid. Others argue that speculators agree to risk transfer contracts only when they firmly believe their information is superior and their expected profits thus are positive. But that, too, can lead to higher costs for hedgers because it could affect the equilibrium futures price. So, in either case it may be that firms are better off transacting with other hedgers or risk transfer specialists than speculators to avoid this added cost.

Speculators do not *always* offer more expensive risk transfer solutions, however. Indeed, this is a point of considerable debate to which we return in Chapter 12. For now, we have accomplished what we set out to show—how efficient risk transfer works mechanically using symmetric- and asymmetric-payoff contracts, and how the actuarially fair price differs using the two different types of contracting structures. We have also seen that some difference in all-in cost may be observed depending on the counterparty type, but competitive forces will tend to drive those to equality over time, as well.

## NOTES

1. Insurance contracts may also be "value contracts" rather than indemnity contracts. A value contract pays a specific, fixed amount to the insured party upon occurrence of one or more defined triggering events. Life insurance is an example of a value contract. The analogue of value contracts in the world of derivatives is a *binary option*, which pays off a fixed amount if it is in-the-money and nothing otherwise. Unlike traditional options, the payoff on a binary option does not rise the deeper in-the-money the option moves. See Culp (2002a).
2. Be careful to recognize this will not be true prior to maturity. Even an asymmetric-payoff contract that is deeply out-of-the-money before maturity could move into-the-money later.
3. This sort of approach to explaining corporate risk management by "concavifying" the value function of the firm has been criticized extensively in Culp and Miller (1999c) and Culp (2001). The approach is adopted here purely for pedagogical purposes and to keep the example brief. No pretense of realism is assumed. We return to this issue again in Chapter 13.
4. The hedge *h* is only really optimal relative to the presumed hedging objective and not necessarily in any global sense. See Chapter 13.

5. The shape of these curves owes to our financial distress cost assumption.
6. In the language we will develop in Chapter 12, this analysis also requires that the forward price be unbiased.
7. If we revisit Figure 4.2, you can think of this figure as also being an Edgeworth Box. Agent 2 would simply have no distress costs and linear indifference curves. Such a risk transfer specialist thus is indifferent between bearing the risk of its natural position and receiving actuarially fair compensation to write an option that shifts the hedger toward the certainty line.

# CHAPTER 5

# The Evolution
# of Derivatives Activity

**A**s the financial innovation spiral (see Chapter 1) has played itself out over time, the institutions performing risk transfer functions of the financial system have undergone significant changes. Along with that evolution, contractual arrangements and financial products used to engage in risk transfer along the lines discussed in the preceding chapter have also evolved.

Considerable time is spent later in this book exploring how derivatives function economically as mechanisms for borrowing and lending assets across time and space, and it is this feature of derivatives that makes them so useful today primarily as instruments by which firms can engage in the transfer of risk. And as this chapter discusses, the capacity of derivatives to function as asset borrowing and lending tools is how derivatives really got started. Specifically, as some of the examples early in this chapter illustrate, derivatives were originally popular because they provided a mechanism for commodity-based financing.[1] As derivatives evolved over time, their popularity as instruments of risk transfer grew, but this use of derivatives for risk transfer is really possible only because of their economic foundations in an intertemporal and interspatial asset lending context.

This chapter begins with a discussion of the importance of *time* in distinguishing derivatives from other types of financial transactions and products. We then review how the time element endemic to derivatives contracting led to the significant early adoption of derivatives for commodity-based finance.

In addition to the dimension of time in derivatives, the chapter also emphasizes one other particular aspect of the historical evolution of derivatives— the migration of derivatives from purely private bilateral contracting structures into more organized dealer and exchange trading markets. You may recall from your first course on derivatives the important institutional distinctions between over-the-counter (OTC) or privately negotiated derivatives like swaps and forwards and their exchange-traded futures contract cousins. Futures are marked to market and resettled twice daily, whereas OTC derivatives are only sometimes resettled in cash and rarely does that occur even as often as daily. Futures require their users to maintain adequate margin at least daily, whereas OTC derivatives either have no such requirement or involve collateral and other credit enhancements that are only periodically assessed. Futures cannot be customized, but OTC derivatives can. Futures traders do not care about the credit risk of their trading counterparty, whereas OTC derivatives participants do. And so on. Rather than repeat these distinctions you already know, in this chapter we focus on analyzing why these distinctions came about, where they come from, and why they persist.[2]

## TIME AS THE ESSENTIAL FEATURE OF DERIVATIVES

The single most important characteristic of derivatives that distinguishes them from other financial products is the explicit time dimension of a derivatives contract. In that sense, it is perhaps more useful to think of derivatives as types of transactions rather than types of financial products.

Nobel laureate Sir John Hicks (1989, p. 42) argues that any purchase or sale of an asset (real or financial) can be divided into three parts: (1) a contract between parties, including a promise to pay and a promise to deliver; (2) the actual payment of cash by the asset buyer to the seller; and (3) the actual delivery of the asset by the seller to the buyer. We generally assume that the negotiation of the contract itself in (1) is the trade or the transaction—and, by extension, that the date on which the deal is negotiated is the trade date.[3]

With the trade date in hand, we can characterize four elemental types of transactions by simply considering variations in the timing of the second and third components of a deal vis-à-vis the trade date. (This chapter ignores any settlement lags between the initiation and completion of cash and asset deliveries. Never fear, we return to this issue in Chapter 6.) When the payment of cash by the buyer and the delivery of the asset by the seller occur immediately after the trade is consummated, we call that a *spot* transaction, or the purchase of an asset "on the spot." When the buyer agrees to remit a payment in the future for an asset that he will receive in the future, the parties have engaged in a *forward* transaction, or the purchase of an asset for future/deferred delivery. When a buyer remits immediate payment to the seller for receipt of the asset in the future, the parties have engaged in a *prepaid forward* contract. Finally, when a seller makes immediate delivery of an asset and agrees to defer payment from the buyer to the future, the counterparties have negotiated a *payment-in-arrears* forward contract. The first three types of transactions are routinely observed in financial markets. The fourth is sometimes observed in commercial or retail sales contracts (e.g., buying a magazine subscription now for payment later) but is less common in a financial market context.

Derivatives are distinguished by some explicit element of delay in the delivery of the underlying asset or the transfer of cash. A swap involves the periodic exchange of assets or cash flows on several dates following the trade date. An option requires a payment up front by the purchaser but conveys a right to buy or sell the underlying asset for some length of time after the trade date.

The element of "futurity" that is common to all derivatives is perhaps best illustrated by comparing the payoff on a spot asset purchase (i.e., purchase for immediate delivery) with the payoff on traditional and prepaid forward transactions (i.e., contracts requiring the short to deliver an asset on a later date). The timing distinctions among these contracts are shown in Figure 5.1. In this and subsequent similar figures, an up arrow indicates a cash or asset inflow, whereas a down arrow indicates a cash payment or asset delivery. All three transactions depicted in Figure 5.1 are shown from the perspective of the purchaser of $Z$ units of some asset (e.g., $Z$ barrels of oil, $Z$ units of foreign currency, $Z$ mortgage-backed securities, etc.).

Notice in Figure 5.1 that there are two differences among the transactions: the timing of the payoffs and the amount paid by the long to the short. In the spot transaction, the payment of $S_t$ per unit simply denotes the current spot price. In the traditional forward, the payment by the long to the short is the price at time $t$ for forward delivery of the asset at time $T$, denoted $f_{t,T}$. And in the prepaid forward, the time $t$ payment by the long for delivery of the asset at time $T$ is just the present value of the price the purchaser would have paid by deferring her payment until date $T$.

The reason that the price paid by the long is comparable between the traditional and prepaid forwards but not in the spot transaction is quite simply that the two forwards give the purchaser the same thing—$Z$ units of the asset at time $T$, then worth $S_T$. In the spot transaction, by contrast, the long gets $Z$ units of the asset *now* worth $S_t$. As we see again in Chapter 8, there is a relationship between the price of an asset bought today and the price of an asset bought for future delivery, but it is premature to get into that discussion here. For now, we just want to focus a bit more on the structure of typical forward contracts.

### Terms of a Typical Forward Contract

In a typical forward purchase or sale agreement, the terms of trade (price per unit, quality, number of units, location and time of delivery, etc.) are specified when the contract is negotiated, but neither payment nor physical delivery occurs until the appointed date in the future. Forward delivery contracts are popular for facilitating the exchange of numerous underlying assets, including both physical assets like oil or gold and financial assets like bonds or foreign

### Spot Purchase

### Traditional Forward Purchase Agreement

### Prepaid Forward Asset Purchase

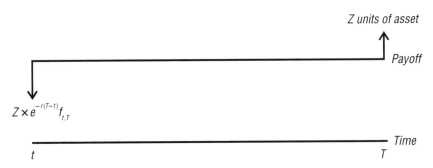

**FIGURE 5.1** Transaction Types by Timing of Asset Delivery and Cash Payment

currency. Forward contracts may also be cash-settled, in which case the cash-equivalent value of the underlying asset is remitted by the short (i.e., the seller of the asset for future delivery) to the long (i.e., the buyer of the asset for future delivery) rather than the hard asset itself. Cash settlement is popular when the economic function played by the contract depends more on the cash flows of the contract than its physical settlement; for example, many risk management applications do not require physical delivery.

In its most basic form, a forward contract negotiated between two parties on some date $t$ for delivery of $Z$ units of the underlying asset by the short to the long on future date $T > t$ has a payoff to the long at maturity of

$$\pi_T^l = Z(S_T - f_{t,T})$$

where $S_T$ is the spot price of the underlying asset at time $T$, and $f_{t,T}$ denotes the fixed price per unit negotiated at time $t$ that the long must pay the short at time $T$ to receive the $Z$ units of the asset.

If the contract is physically settled, the long pays $Z \times f_{t,T}$ to the short in cash and the short delivers $Z$ units of the asset to the long. The asset delivered has a current market price of $S_T$ per unit and thus is worth that amount. In an otherwise equivalent cash-settled forward, the short remits a cash payment of $Z \times f_{t,T}$ to the long instead of delivering physical assets with the same value.

Like many derivatives, forward contracts are known as *zero net supply* assets; that is, for every long there is a corresponding short. To verify this, recognize that the payoff to the short in the same forward just described is:

$$\pi_T^s = Z(f_{t,T} - S_T)$$

The seller in the contract—the short—thus receives $f_{t,T}$ per unit for an asset whose value at the time of sale is $S_T$. Clearly,

$$\pi_T^l + \pi_T^s = 0$$

## Example: A Simple Forward Currency Purchase Agreement

As an example of a forward contract, consider an agreement that requires the long to purchase 1,480,000 Swiss francs with U.S. dollars for the fixed total purchase price of US$1,000,000. The fixed purchase price can be expressed in terms of $f_{t,T} \times Z$ by noting that the size of the contract, $Z$, is the amount to be delivered, or CHF1,480,000. The fixed purchase price is thus CHF1.48/US$, or, equivalently $f_{t,T}$ = US$0.6757/CHF. The payoff of such a forward contract is shown in Figure 5.2 from the perspective of the long.

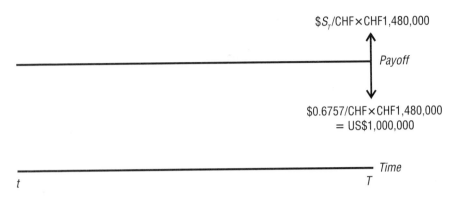

**FIGURE 5.2**  Swiss Franc Forward Purchase Contract

Note that the value of the contract to the long (i.e., the franc purchaser) on delivery date $T$ still depends on what the actual dollar price of francs is on date $T$. If $S_T = $ US\$0.67/CHF, then the buyer must still remit US\$1,000,000 in return for receiving CHF1,480,000. But the francs now have a market value at that time of US\$991,600. (Just imagine the CHF1,480,000 purchased at the fixed price of US\$1,000,000 is immediately converted back into dollars at $S_T=$US\$0.67/CHF.) So, the franc buyer is paying US\$1,000,000 for a fixed amount of francs that are now worth only US\$991,600 at time $T$.

Figure 5.3 shows an otherwise identical Swiss franc forward purchase agreement assuming that the length of the contract is one year and that the dollar interest rate is 5 percent per annum. Instead of delivering 1,000,000 U.S. dollars at time $T$ and receiving CHF1,480,000 at time $T$, the long now delivers the *present value* of US\$1,000,000 at time $t$—or US\$952,381—and

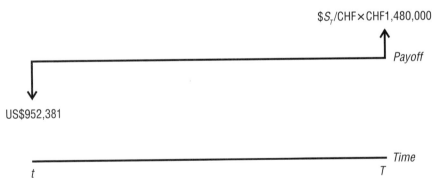

**FIGURE 5.3**  Prepaid Swiss Franc Forward Purchase Contract

receives CHF1,480,000 at time $T$. The contract is essentially the same as the traditional forward shown in Figure 5.2 except for the timing of the cash flow by the long.

## EARLY ANTECEDENTS OF DERIVATIVES

It is no easy task to find documented examples of early uses of derivatives. The problem was not their lack of usage or popularity, but rather that derivatives as we now know them were historically considered much more instruments of *commerce* than instruments of *finance*.

In this section, we consider two examples to illustrate the very early origins of derivatives activity—the first involving a traditional forward contract, and the second a prepaid forward.

## THE ORIGIN OF TRADITIONAL FORWARD CONTRACTING: BABYLONIAN GRAIN LENDING

Perhaps the earliest recorded commercial uses of derivatives occurred in the commodity lending activities of ancient Babylonia in the time from around 1900 B.C. to 1600 B.C. Like many other activities of the Mesopotamian era, banking in ancient Babylon was predominantly centered around sanctuaries and temples. These religious institutions were involved in financial activities such as extending credit, asset and project finance, and intermediating merchant transactions. Jastrow (1911) likens Mesopotamian temples to modern "national banks," not only because of their financial undertakings but also because they engaged in those activities with official backing from the authorities.

Although the Babylonian economy was both pecuniary and real, most banking activities of the temples in that era involved commodity finance. Like all banks, Babylonian temples had to fund their loans. In the case of commodity lending, funding the loan meant acquiring the asset to be loaned out— hopefully at a lower rate than charged on the loan. In that connection, most of the assets were actually acquired by the temples *at no cost*. They came in the form of tithes to the gods "deposited at" the temples. Individual tithes would not have been adequate to support the volume of commodity lending in which Mesopotamian temples engaged, but municipalities' tithes of that era were often very substantial.

The Temple of Šamaš (Ebabbara or Bit-Uri) at Sippar—a shrine to Šamaš, the sun god and lord of justice and righteousness—was perhaps *the* dominant "banking institution" for much of the Mesopotamian period (Bromberg, 1942). When the grain and livestock received by the Temple of Šamaš first began to exceed storage capacity, the temple began to provide merchant services. An active market for the spot purchase and sale of grains and livestock arose in which the Temple of Šamaš was the dealer or primary intermediary.

Acting as the Babylonian equivalent of a "market maker" in grains, however, was not enough to solve the storage problems that were becoming increasingly costly for the Temple of Šamaš. Fortunately, there was no shortage of demand for commodity finance. Specifically, farmers in the region needed access to physical commodities before their own harvests came in, both to feed the families and workers and to sell for cash. To meet that demand, the Temple of Šamaš began an aggressive asset lending program.

Commodity loans made by the temples were considered repayable to the god for whom the temple was erected. A loan of grain from the Temple of Šamaš was thus repayable to Šamaš. As an example, the following is text translated from a loan tablet that documents a loan made by the Temple of Šamaš to Minutum around the time of Sin-muballit, the father of Hammurabi:

> *10* gur *of grain—at the rate of 1/5th* gur *per* gur—*Minutum has borrowed from Šamaš. At harvest time he shall return it.*
> *3 witnesses. Undated.* (Bromberg, 1942, p. 80)

The phrase "at the rate of 1/5th *gur* per *gur*" means that for every unit of barley borrowed by Minutum from the Temple of Šamaš, Minutum shall return that unit *plus 20 percent*. This thus represents a "commodity interest rate," or the rate Minutum must pay to borrow grain until harvest time when the grain is repayable. (See Chapter 8.)

Loan tablets of this sort were extremely common during the whole of the First Babylonian Dynasty, dating from 1894 B.C. to 1595 B.C. Up to the time of Hammurabi, the commodity interest rate on grain seemed to remain at around 20 percent. In the famous legal Code of Hammurabi, a maximum commodity interest rate of $33\frac{1}{3}$ percent per year was stipulated (Bromberg, 1942).

Chapters 8 and 9 discuss in great detail the relations between physical commodity loans and forward markets, but suffice it for now simply to assert that loans of commodities essentially *are* forward contracts by another name. To see that, recognize that borrowing one *gur* of barley today and agreeing to repay 1.2 *gur* of barley on a future date is economically equivalent to purchasing one *gur* of barley today in the spot market and simultaneously entering into a forward contract to sell 1.2 *gur* of barley in the future.

If commodity loans are viewed as the equivalents of forward contracts, then their use during the Mesopotamian period can only have represented the beginning. It is difficult to imagine periods of history in which *either* prenegotiated purchases or sales of grain in the future or loans of grain (or money collateralized by a coming grain harvest) were not common. In a real sense, derivatives thus entrenched themselves into the trading and merchandising process four millennia ago and have not left the scene since.

## Prepaid Forwards in Sixth Century Islamic Finance

Thanks largely to the Enron scandal, the use of prepaid forwards has been subjected to significant scrutiny in the past three years. The public policy concern seems to be that firms like Enron can go short prepaid forwards to generate up-front cash that is accounted for as operating cash flow rather than long-term indebtedness. Indeed, many have alleged that prepaid commodity forwards are really just bank loans in disguise. Bockus, Northcut, and Zmijewski (2003) and Culp and Kavanagh (2003) explore these claims in detail and emphasize that whether or not Enron abused these transactions, they can play an important risk transfer function in the financial system.

Historical facts, moreover, do not support assertions that prepaid forwards are somehow inherently connected with unlawful or illegal activities. On the contrary, as this next early documented example of prepaid forwards shows,[4] prepaids were often the only form of derivatives transactions on which the authorities did *not* frown!

*Shariah* (literally "a path to life-giving water") refers to the Islamic legal tradition.[5] *Shariah* as a whole comes from the *Koran*, messages from the life of the prophet Mohammed (called *sunnah*), and narrations or explanations about the life of the prophet Mohammed (called *hadith*). One of the most famous principles of *Shariah* is the prohibition on *riba*, or usury. Specifically, the extension of money credit is not allowed when it is for the purpose of generating income from interest charged.

*Shariah* also prohibits entering into transactions involving *gharar*, or risk in the sense that Knight used the term (see Chapter 2). Any transaction involving the future exchange of an asset thus is permissible only if there is no uncertainty about the future value of the asset to be exchanged. At face value, *Shariah* thus prohibits traditional forward contracts, as well as many other types of derivatives.

There are some important exceptions to the principles just set forth. A major principle underlying Islamic finance is the notion of entrepreneurship. Instead of extending credit on fixed-interest terms, Muslims are encouraged to take equity investments in which they share the profits, losses, and risks of a venture with the managers and other partners. An extension of credit in which the principal is at risk thus is permissible under *Shariah*, provided it does not violate the charge against speculation or contracts involving *gharar*.

A second major exception to the prohibition on extensions of credit is called *salam* and is defined as a sale in which the specific goods are contractually promised to a buyer for future delivery in exchange for a price paid in full up front (i.e., a prepaid forward). There are several specific characteristics that a transaction must have to qualify as *salam*, but none are substantively different from the conditions associated with any contemporary prepaid forward contract.

*Salam* was explicitly intended to govern applications like project and trade finance. As an example of the former, suppose a farmer needs money to finance the growth of his crops and to feed his family and laborers but lacks funds because the crops have not yet been harvested and sold. *Salam* would enable a buyer to pay for some or all of the farmer's crop in advance of the crop coming in and in return for a promise of a future crop delivery.[6] As an example of the latter, traders seeking export financing could use *salam* to presell their wares. The funds obtained up front would then be used to cover transportation expenses to ensure final delivery of the presold asset, usually abroad.

Thanks to the permissibility of *salam*, project and trade finance in Muslim countries was possible as early as the sixth century, despite clear prohibitions on usury in Islamic finance. In other words, prepaid forwards were a legitimate derivatives market response to the need for trade and project financing in a culture that prohibited profiteering from extensions of credit.

## THE MEDICI BANK

Anecdotal examples of derivatives usage like the two in the prior section abound. For our next historical example,[7] we want to turn to a period—perhaps the first?—in which the widespread use of derivatives began to evolve away from customized individual contracts and into more standardized financial products. The derivatives we examine in this section are again prepaid forward contracts.

Many people regard the early development of derivatives as being in the commodities sector. Indeed, any time two merchants preagreed on the price for the future exchange of silk, tea, oil, spices, and the like, we can consider the transaction a forward contract. But the first real forward *market* that we are about to explore was not a commodity forward, but rather a *financial* forward—a contract based on currencies, to be precise.

### The Medieval Christian Church and the Cambium

The principal driving force for the origin of prepaid forwards in medieval Europe was yet again a religious prohibition on usury. Unlike the *Shariah*, however, the medieval Judeo-Christian Church did not prohibit transactions involving risk or uncertainty. Indeed, the presence of risk in a transaction was what made it *legal* under medieval Christian canons.

Banking and international trade were inextricably connected in the Middle Ages. This interconnection arose primarily from the structure of international trading in medieval Europe, which up to the mid-1300s consisted mainly of periodic regional fairs at which merchants from various lands exchanged their wares. A merchant in, say, Florence wishing to sell his wares in Champagne needed to purchase his goods in Florence with local florins. The goods were then transported to the fair in Champagne where they were resold for domestic currency.

Correspondent and foreign bank branches did not maintain funds outside their home locations until the fifteenth century. Prior to then, merchants had little choice but to convert their foreign currency revenues back into their home currency. More problematic, merchants had somehow to finance the "float" on their merchandise (i.e., the principal cost of goods purchased for resale abroad). Today, such merchants would simply post their merchandise as collateral and borrow from a bank through a trade credit facility. But in medieval Europe, the Church's prohibitions on usury encompassed straight trade credit. Specifically, usurious lending was defined as charging interest on a money loan in which the only risk to the lender was *credit risk*. If the transaction was subject to *exchange risk* (i.e., the risk of losses arising from foreign exchange conversions) then the usury prohibitions did not apply.

A *cambium* was the combination of an exchange transaction (i.e., a transaction in foreign exchange) with a commercial transaction, and the word derives from the word *cambi*, a credit extended to legitimate merchants as a type of investment in trade. To avoid the usury restrictions, the documentation underlying cambium contracts often even went so far as to include various declarations that both parties affirmed to be using the cambium to facilitate commercial exchange (De Roover, 1948).

In short, the basic cambium involved the payment of funds in one currency and location at a fixed amount (e.g., X florins in Florence) in exchange for the subsequent repayment of funds at a later date in a different currency and in a different place at a fixed amount (e.g., Y groats in Amsterdam). By borrowing locally, merchants could finance the purchase of the goods they would take abroad to the medieval fairs, then using the foreign currency revenues from those sales to repay the trade loan.

The traditional cambium thus functioned in the same manner as the Swiss franc forward sale agreement shown in Figure 5.2. Because local currency exchange rates did fluctuate, the merchants and bank were both exposed to the risk of changes in the spot rate of currency exchange. A merchant selling reals for florins, for example, obtained the florins required to trade at the Florence fair, but faced the risk that his florin revenues would convert back into fewer reals than he began with. And conversely for the bank. But this was enough for the Church to consider the transaction one that included both *credit* and *exchange* risk, and thus not a usurious instrument.

For the bulk of the fourteenth century, cambiums were essentially a standard feature of the merchant trade. Two types were popularly used during this period. The first were ordinary cambiums in which payment was due unconditionally. The second type, called the *cambium nauticum*, was specifically intended to facilitate maritime commerce. Performance on a cambium nauticum was conditional on acts of God and men-of-war and did not have to be repaid if the galley whose transportation was being financed never reached port. But unlike the ordinary cambium, the cambium nauticum required the borrower to post commodities (e.g., alum and ginger) as collateral that could be assumed by the borrower in the event the galley never arrived (De Roover, 1948).

Most early cambiums were called contracts "in notarial form," which meant that a notary had to affirm that the parties exchanging payments at the end of the transaction were the same as (or were the authorized agents of) the original parties to the deal. Not unlike modern swap and forward documentation, the notarial form also included numerous promises and pledges and warranties. The fair of Champagne was one of the largest medieval fairs but was dominated by a few small families, some of whom were fairly nefarious sorts. Mainly for this reason, the need for the extreme legal caution and detail found in cambium documents was justified to most merchants at the time.

The ordinary cambium and cambium nauticum in notarial form began to vanish in the late fourteenth century. The former declined in popularity mainly because of the decline in the fair of Champagne. As fairs and trade migrated to larger cities like London and Bruges, those cities became financial centers, and with their rise came the emergence of counting houses and correspondent banking. As merchants became able to maintain foreign currency balances at these establishments, the need for notarial cambiums declined. Similarly, the cambium nauticum vanished from the commercial marketplace primarily because of the development of *bottomry*—now known as maritime insurance—as an organized industry and a more efficient means of risk transfer than the cumbersome notarial documents (De Roover, 1948; Outreville, 1998).

## From the Cambium to Bills of Exchange

With competition for trade finance arising from counting houses and insurance providers, the banking community responded. Instead of customized, cumbersome, bilateral contracts filled with warranties and promises to pay, cambiums were replaced with much more standardized and simpler bearer certificates that contained unambiguous instructions to pay the bearer on demand. This was also consistent with a shift in priorities away from concerns over legal safeguards—many of which vanished with the wane of the Champagne fair—to the desire for greater expediency. The result was the financial instrument called the *lettera di pagamento* or *lettera di cambio*, which eventually became known as *bills of exchange.*

A bill of exchange was purchased by the lender in one currency and was repayable upon presentation to its issuer in another currency and at another location. The tenor of a typical bill of exchange depended on the *usance* period, or the average time for a merchant to travel between the two cities. Between London and Venice, for example, the usance period was three months, whereas between Venice and Bruges usance was only two months. In addition to specifying the period over which the bill could be redeemed, bills of exchange also clearly stated the fixed price for subsequent currency conversion and the quantity to be converted.

The basic process by which bills of exchange evolved into an organized and legal trade credit market is illustrated in Figure 5.4. A cambium almost always involved four parties. The deliverer/remitter purchased a bill for its stated local currency price from the taker/drawer in the domestic market. The deliver/remitter then gave this bill to its agent abroad, called the payee. In turn, the taker/drawer used the funds to acquire its wares in the domestic market and transport them to the specified location abroad for sale in the foreign currency. The bill of exchange could later be presented by the payee to the payer, an agent or correspondent of the taker/drawer, for repayment of the specified amount of foreign currency. Figure 5.4 indicates the relation between the two original parties in the exchange of the bill for domestic currency to their agents or correspondents with dotted lines.

It may help to consider an actual example.[8] Figure 5.5 reproduces the original language on the front and back sides of an actual bill of exchange originated in Venice on July 20, 1463, and written in the Venetian dialect.

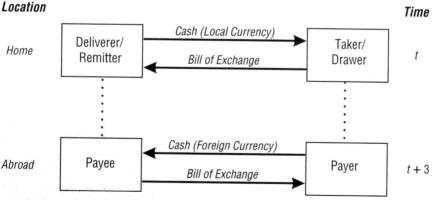

**FIGURE 5.4** A Medieval Exchange Transaction

> ### Front Side
>
> *YHS 1463 a dì 20 lujo in Vinexia*
> *[Ducati] 500*
> *Pegate per questa prima a uxo a Ser Girardo Chanixani ducati zinquezento a*
> *sterlini 47 per ducato per altretanti qui da ser Pierfrancesco di medizi e conpagni.*
> *Cristo vi guardi.*
>                    *Bartolomeo Zorzi e Ieronimo Michiel*
>
>
> ### Reverse Side
>
>                 *Dominis Francesco Giorgio e Petro Morozino*
> *Prima*                    *Londra*

**FIGURE 5.5**    Bill of Exchange Drafted in Venice, July 20, 1463

Figure 5.6 illustrates the contemplated exchange transaction or cambium graphically, putting the proper names into the locations outlined on Figure 5.4. Specifically, the two parties in Venice were the Medici Bank (remitter/deliverer) and the firm Bartolomeo Zorzi (Giorgi) e Geronimo Michiel was the taker/drawer. The payer in London was the correspondent of the drawer, the firm Francesco Giorgi e Piero Morosini, and the London payee was the London agent of the Medici Bank, Gherardo Canigiani.

Note in Figures 5.5 and 5.6 that the bill had a face value of 500 ducats and called for the future delivery of £97 18s. 4d. sterling. More specifically,

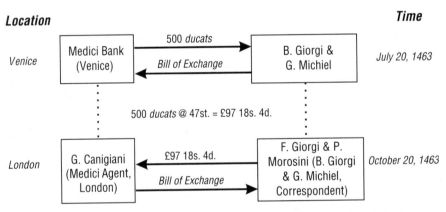

**FIGURE 5.6**    Actual Medieval Exchange Transaction, Medici Bank Bill of Exchange, Venice, July 20, 1463

the bill called for the payment to the Medici Bank agent in London of 500 ducats at the fixed exchange rate of 47st./ducat, which worked out to be £97 18s. 4d. in English currency equivalent at that time.

This is, of course, a classic prepaid forward contract on foreign exchange, quite like the one we saw in Figure 5.2. More accurately, from the Medici Bank's perspective this is a prepaid forward purchase of sterling for ducats with a trade date of July 20, 1463, a settlement date of October 20, 1463, an underlying quantity of $Z = 500$ ducats, and a specified fixed forward purchase price of $f_{t,T} = 47$ st./ducat. As Figure 5.7 illustrates for more obvious comparison to Figure 5.2, the transaction from the merchant's perspective is a prepaid forward sale of sterling for ducats.

This example makes clear then how bills of exchange—prepaid forwards by another name—were a lawful and legitimate solution to the need for trade credit in a medieval European culture whose dominant religion prohibited credit instruments. Because the lender was at risk from exchange rate changes, the transaction was simply not considered a loan.

How the transaction depicted in Figure 5.7 facilitates trade finance should now be fairly clear. A Venetian merchant sells a bill of exchange to a financier like the Medici Bank to obtain ducats, buys his wares in the local market, transports them to London, and sells the goods for sterling. The merchant is then presented the bill of exchange by the Medici Bank's London agent that requires a repayment from the merchant in sterling. In this manner, the merchant has avoided having to float the purchase price for the goods being transported to London for resale.

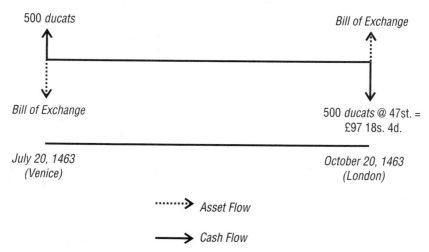

**FIGURE 5.7** Real Exchange Transaction from the Merchant Perspective

Like any other forward contract, the cambium subjected both counterparties to the risk of exchange rate fluctuations. Indeed, this very risk was what made the transaction permissible and nonusurious to the Church. The merchant is a borrower of ducats over the usance period and thus is a *forward seller* of a fixed amount of ducats for sterling at a fixed price. The merchant thus is *short* the ducat. The lender—the Medici Bank—is *long* the ducats as a forward purchaser of ducats at a fixed sterling price. Figure 5.8 illustrates the risk exposure of the forward contract from the Medici Bank's perspective. If the market exchange rate of a ducat is 47 st., the bank just breaks even on the exchange transaction. If the market price of a ducat has risen to, say, 48 st. per ducat, then the bank has made a profit. The bank receives 500 ducats that have a market price of 48 st. each but has paid only 47 st. per ducat to acquire the currency.

### From Off-Exchange to On-Exchange

The obvious difference between the preceding transaction and a traditional prepaid forward contract is the bill of exchange itself. In many ways, bills of exchange in their early applications resembled the pro forma master agree-

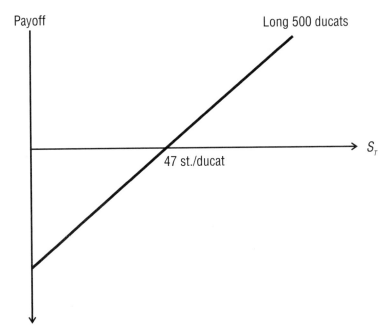

**FIGURE 5.8**   Payoff on Exchange Transaction (Medici Bank Perspective)

ments now used to document most privately negotiated derivatives transactions. And like modern-day derivatives documentation, bills of exchange were neither negotiable nor discountable. But as their use proliferated, bills of exchange did eventually become something that modern privately negotiated derivatives are not—*fungible.*[9]

Highly organized markets for the trading of bills of exchange emerged in cities like Bruges and Venice, and trading in bills of exchange became sufficiently active that the bills of exchange market actually began to drive the monetary policies of the major European trading nations![10] The Medici Bank became a very reliable dealer in bills of exchange; it made quotes on both sides of the market, offering to buy or to sell bills of exchange, in numerous cities.

As the number of correspondents, branches, and agents of the Medici Bank empire proliferated throughout the fourteenth and fifteenth centuries, the published quotes by the bank on various prices of foreign currency became *the* central source of information about the emerging global foreign exchange market. Commercial letters referencing Medici Bank exchange rate quotes often contained the phrase *stare sugli avisi*, which meant the same thing as to operate on an organized financial exchange.[11]

Eventually, bills of exchange did become listed items on organized European exchanges (i.e., bourses). In a real sense, the migration of the prepaid forward market evidenced in notarial cambiums onto organized exchanges for more standardized, liquid, and fungible bills of exchange was quite probably the first major documented example of the commoditization process. Nevertheless, even with an active dealer market and the posting of standardized contract quotes on local exchanges, these were still essentially forward contracts. It was not until much later in history that what we know as the *futures* contract emerged.

## EVOLUTION OF ORGANIZED FUTURES MARKETS, CHICAGO STYLE

Traditional forward contracts were—and still are—bilaterally negotiated between the long and the short. As a result, all the terms in a typical forward could be specified fully by the trading counterparties. But as the previous section suggests, the demand for customization often gave way to the demand for expediency. Accordingly, examples of increasingly standardized derivatives like bills of exchange can be found in several different places from the fifteenth to the nineteenth century. Standardization, for example, occurred in terms like location. Quotes for the exchange of currency dispatched from London to Bruges became easily standardized, with the associated bills fungible by virtue of being essentially similar to bearer bonds.

But standardization stopped there. In particular, the essential features of a futures market—the irrelevance of the counterparty's identity and the periodic resettlement of cash obligations—were still missing from the exchange-traded bill of exchange.

The real birth of futures as an active exchange-traded standardized alternative to forwards occurred in the inland port village of Chicago. The Village of Chicago was incorporated in 1837, and its tremendously rapid growth was due almost entirely to its location and function as a grain terminal for the United States' primary farming region. Not only was the city ideally located in the heart of the grain-producing Midwest, but it was an active inland port with access to numerous shipping lanes primarily on the Great Lakes transportation system.

In the early 1800s, farmers, packers, and millers regularly traveled to Chicago to buy and sell grain and livestock in spot markets (i.e., without contracting for future delivery) or in crude forward contracts negotiated in smoke-filled rooms with merchants that undoubtedly were Al Capone's ancestors. These merchants proved to be a significant credit risk for farmers, especially given that the wildly volatile weather in Chicago (some things never change) gave rise to huge supply and demand fluctuations and massive price swings. By the time a farmer brought his grain to Chicago, he often found no one there willing to buy it. After production gluts, farmers would often dump their grain on the streets of Chicago when they could not find buyers.

Although early forward contracts in the United States addressed merchants' concerns about ensuring that there were buyers and sellers for commodities, credit risk remained a serious problem. Petzel (1989) reports an Illinois folklore story of a farmer who, before his harvest, sold his crop forward to a grain merchant in Chicago. The entire grain harvest was huge that year. When the time came for the farmer to sell his grain, the price had fallen well below the agreed-upon purchase price in the forward contract. The merchant who had agreed to buy the grain then saw that he could buy it more cheaply elsewhere at current prices and reneged on the forward contract. Legend has it that the farmer walked up to the merchant and said, "I have a wagon of grain and a shotgun with me. Which should I unload?"

To deal with these problems, a group of 82 local businessmen formed the Chicago Board of Trade (CBOT) in 1848 for the purpose of trading commodities in a more centralized and organized arena. The primary intention of the CBOT was to provide a centralized location known in advance for buyers and sellers to negotiate forward contracts. The belief was that merchants who wanted to transact on the CBOT season after season would know the location to which all the merchants were going and would not risk their reputations among those other merchants by failing to perform on forward contracts negotiated on the CBOT.

In 1865, the CBOT went one step further and listed the first "exchange-traded" derivatives contracts in the United States. Designed to be close cousins to forward contracts, these CBOT contracts were called *futures* contracts. They were still bilateral agreements, but the essential difference was that the CBOT "listed" contracts that had certain standardized elements, thus eliminating the need for buyers and sellers to negotiate anything in the contract except the price at which a subsequent exchange would be made.

In 1874, another group of agricultural dealers formed the Chicago Produce Exchange to trade butter, eggs, poultry, and other perishable products. In 1898, the butter and egg dealers split off to form the Chicago Butter and Egg Board, which was again reorganized to allow futures trading in 1919. When it was reorganized, its name was changed to the Chicago Mercantile Exchange (CME).

Although exchange-traded derivatives developed at about the same time throughout the world, the Chicago exchanges set the standard for the success of exchange-traded derivatives. In part, this success traces to the Chicago exchanges' recognition that if exchange-traded derivatives were to succeed, they had to be different from—and at least to some people preferable to—customized, off-exchange forward contracts.

## The Benefits of Standardization

The Chicago exchanges sought to offer an attractive product different from off-exchange forward contracts. One way was to exploit the benefits of standardization. The role of an organized exchange was, and still is, primarily to list a contract by predefining its elements of standardization. Those standardized components of a futures contract include the definition of an underlying asset, the amount of the asset to be bought or sold, the date on which the exchange will occur, and the method of delivery and/or payment. The CME currently lists a futures contract on frozen pork bellies, for example, that allows a buyer to purchase 40,000 pounds of cut and trimmed frozen bellies. The pork belly contracts allow buyers to purchase for delivery in February, March, May, July, and August of each calendar year. A contract thus can be entered in September for the purchase of pork bellies the following August.

Organized futures exchanges also maintain a set of rules that buyers and sellers must obey in entering into the derivatives contracts that the exchange lists. Some of these rules address the following issues: trading hours, the particular forum in which trading must occur, price quotation styles, "tick" sizes, limits on how high or low a price can be quoted, the quality of product that must be accepted by a purchaser and delivered by a seller, the location and time of delivery, and so on. Perhaps the most important rules are those pertaining to the forum of trading. The Chicago exchanges, for example, utilize an "open outcry" trading forum in which buyers and sellers gather together in a "pit" and literally shout prices at one another. Other exchanges use different trading forums. At the other extreme, for example, are electronic exchanges such as GLOBEX that require all trading to be done over a set of interlinked computers. Whatever the forum, because it is specified as part of the rules an exchange provides, the forum's details (including any centralized location for trading) are known in advance.

The only nonstandard component of a futures contract is its price, which is set by buyers and sellers. This system of standardization and rule setting is regarded by many derivatives users as highly beneficial. It facilitates the speed with which trading occurs by eliminating the need for counterparties to negotiate anything other than price. Standardization thus also lowers transaction costs.

Today, the standardization and low transaction costs of futures markets make them natural arenas for "price discovery." As futures markets underwent the process of commoditization over time, their liquidity and depth grew, thus making those markets the ones in which most information is first incorporated into observed financial asset prices.

### The Benefits of Anonymity

Exchange-traded derivatives have two other features not shared with their off-exchange, customized-contract predecessors. First, margin is required by all derivatives exchanges today, which means that a trader must post a performance bond before engaging in a transaction. Second, derivatives exchanges utilize what is known as "multilateral clearing and settlement." Chapter 6 discusses the mechanics and details of how this process really works today, but some commentary on the evolution of these features of exchange markets is useful at this juncture, mainly because they help define an important benefit of exchange trading vis-à-vis private contracting—the "anonymity" benefit.

Wishing to mitigate the potential for farmers to show up with loaded weapons to enforce their contracts, members of the Chicago exchanges began informally collecting performance bonds from one another in the late 1800s. If one party refused to honor his contract, he forfeited his performance bond. This system of margin, as it came to be known, helped mitigate some of the credit risk concerns of buyers and sellers; the exchanges thus attracted merchants who had previously contracted only with forwards.

The farmer/merchant example illustrates what might be called "walkaway" or "don't know" risk—a credit risk relating to the willingness of counterparties to honor their commitments. The Chicago traders also perceived another form of credit risk, which pertains to counterparties' *ability* to make good on contracts. Margin arose in large part to manage walkaway risk, but that did not always take care of those situations in which a merchant simply did not have the money to pay up. Traders were quick to recognize that the risk of nonpayment on a single, small amount of money was lower than the nonpayment risk on two large sums of money. The risk that one trader, for example, would fail to come up with $1,000 was lower than the risk that either of two traders would fail to come up with $50,000 and $49,000, respectively. Also, it cost less to write one check than two. Pairs of traders on the exchange floors thus began to reach informal agreements whereby *net* rather than gross cash flows were exchanged. This process of reducing the amount of cash flows at risk between individual traders is known as "bilateral netting."

In the 1860s and 1870s, netting began to occur among more than just two traders because the contracts traded on the exchanges were standardized. Groups of traders in the same commodities formed "rings" in which financial obligations were netted multilaterally among all ring members. Traders then simplified matters even further by having everyone pay some money into a common ring fund before trading started each day. At the end of the day, traders took back out the net of what was due them.[12]

By the early 1880s, the CBOT rings had grown beyond specific commodities to the whole exchange. Every exchange member paid into a common fund and received his net cash flow at the end of the day. This arrangement was formalized, and the clearinghouse of the CBOT—often called the Board of Trade Clearing Corporation (BOTCC)—was set up in 1883.

When clearinghouses started to develop in the 1880s, the Chicago exchanges began to merge the settlement risk management function of the clearinghouse with the walkaway risk management function of the margin system. Specifically, clearinghouses began interjecting themselves as the counterparty to all transactions. Previously, if Party A entered into a futures contract to purchase soybeans from Party B, her contract would be with B. With the creation of clearinghouses, exchange members recognized the benefit of having the *legal* contract be between each trader and the clearinghouse. Immediately after A negotiates the contract with B and they agree on a price, a legal contract is established that commits A to purchase soybeans *from the clearinghouse* and commits B to sell soybeans *to the clearinghouse*. A and B still set the price in their negotiations, but after that their legal obligations are to the clearinghouse.

The clearinghouse system, still in existence today, provides a major attraction for some market participants when compared to off-exchange contracting: Every exchange-traded derivatives contract has the same default and settlement risks, equal to that the risk the exchange clearinghouse itself defaults. Exchange-traded derivatives users thus *do not really care who their actual counterparty is.* This benefit of exchange trading, typically referred to as "trading anonymity," reduces transaction costs by lowering the costs traders must incur to search for creditworthy counterparties. Not all market participants place a high value on lower search costs. Some firms, for example, might prefer to deal in the off-exchange market with counterparties they have known and trusted in numerous previous relationships. Other market participants, however, who are concerned about search costs and credit risk, often find exchange-traded derivatives appealing.

Standardization coupled with the clearinghouse system makes "offsetting" possible, which greatly enhances the operational efficiency and financial integrity of most futures clearinghouses. Offsetting a position simply entails reversing the purchase of a commodity in the future by selling the same contract. The prices for the purchase and sale may be different, but because the contracts are standardized, the two contracts together remove any obligation of a trader to make (or take) delivery to (or from) the clearinghouse. In a customized, off-exchange forward contract, by contrast, a counterparty can be released from its obligation only by negotiating an "unwind" of the contract with the *original* counterparty. Because all exchange-traded derivatives are contracts with the clearinghouse, a trader can reverse any obligation to buy by finding any other counterparty on the exchange who is willing to buy. The second transaction need not be negotiated with the same party involved in the first transaction, because both transactions are in fact legal contracts with the clearinghouse.

Offsetting not only improves liquidity on futures exchanges. It also enables an exchange clearinghouse to step in and offset a trader's positions the moment that her creditworthiness is called into question. Over time, futures exchanges have greatly refined the clearinghouse system in order to mitigate credit risk. Instead of merely *allowing* traders to post performance bonds with each other, the exchanges quickly adopted margin as a *requirement* for exchange trading. Today, *initial* or *original* margin is required of each trader before any trade is made. If the counterparty to the clearinghouse cannot honor a losing obligation, the posted performance bond is applied to the loss. In the rare event that a loss exceeds the initial margin, the clearinghouse members jointly bear the cost of the default.

Exchanges also now engage in a practice known as "settling up" or "marking to market." At least twice daily, much as they did in the 1800s, the clearinghouses tabulate the net position of all accounts and mark them to current market prices. Net winners may withdraw their profits, which come from the margin posted by the net losers of the day. If losers wish to maintain their positions in the market, the clearinghouse compares the new level in their margin account to a *maintenance* margin level. The maintenance level is often lower than the initial margin level. If a loser has lost so much that the end-of-day value of his performance bond is below that maintenance level, the clearinghouse demands the deposit of *variation* margin to bring the value of his performance bond up to the initial margin level. If the loser fails to meet this "margin call" by the next morning, his position is offset by the clearinghouse.

The effect of this daily settling up is the renegotiation of all futures contracts every day by adjusting margin accounts to reflect *current* prices. This ensures that at the end of every trading day, only those traders who can afford to make additional losses tomorrow are left in the market, and thus the chance of default is reduced significantly. If a default does occur, the loss is limited to the amount the price has moved since the previous mark-to-market period.

## OVER-THE-COUNTER DERIVATIVES AND THE SWAP MARKET TODAY

Apart from forward contracts and their exchange-traded futures counterparts, two other popular basic types of derivatives have evolved over time. "Swaps" are essentially multiple forward contracts snapped together and marketed as a single financial product. Instead of negotiating a fixed price for the delivery of a single amount of, say, wheat in the future, a swap allows a firm to negotiate a single fixed price for the delivery of a specified amount of wheat on *several* dates in the future—for example, once a month for a year, or once a quarter for two years. The most popular types of swaps are cash-settled and based on interest rates.

The remaining type of derivatives contract—the option—is fundamentally different from futures, forwards, and swaps because it creates a *right* and not an *obligation* for its purchaser. The buyer of (or long in) a *call* option has the right but not the obligation to purchase the underlying asset on or perhaps even before some specified future date at a fixed price negotiated in advance. The call option seller or writer must honor that obligation if the buyer "exercises" her right to buy the underlying at the fixed price. Similarly, the writer or seller of a *put* option must honor any decision by the buyer or long to exercise her right (but not obligation) to *sell* the underlying asset on or before a specified future date at a fixed price. Like other derivatives, options are available on a wide range of underlying assets (e.g., commodities, currencies, bonds, equities), but also may be cash-settled.

Like forwards, options also underwent the commoditization process in the late 1800s and early 1900s, gradually moving from customized off-exchange contracts toward more standardized exchange-traded products. Unfortunately, options ran afoul of the state antigambling laws mentioned earlier and thus were delisted in the 1930s. Options on futures did not return until October 1, 1985 (Petzel, 1989).

As commoditization occurred and innovative derivatives gravitated toward organized markets in the 1800s and early 1900s, the demand for more customized privately negotiated off-exchange contracts remained. Some of the reasons for this can be attributed to an ongoing demand by some institutions for more customized solutions than were available in standardized listed products. But in other cases, just as Merton's financial-innovation spiral predicts, the evolution of one innovation from bilateral and opaque transacting to transparent market trading often itself spawns changes in the structure of financial markets and institutions that in turn engender new customized bilaterally negotiated innovations.

In the early 1990s, bilateral privately negotiated derivatives—generally known as over-the-counter (OTC) derivatives—began to undergo their own process of commoditization with the development of the so-called "swap market." Actually encompassing all types of OTC derivatives, the term *swap market* is somewhat misleading, as was the use of the term *swap dealer* to describe the active intermediaries who first populated this market. Nevertheless, this was the term.

An important aspect of the commoditization process in OTC derivatives was the evolution of transactions away from user-to-user toward an explicitly intermediated dealer market. Before the 1990s,[13] one party in an OTC derivatives transaction had to find another party with a demand for the opposite side of the contract. A farmer wishing to protect herself from falling prices, for example, had to find a counterparty with a desire for a contract providing protection from *rising* prices (e.g., a miller). In the era when users of off-exchange derivatives had to find their own counterparties, both counterparties were principals in the transaction.

Typical swap and OTC derivatives transactions are now negotiated with one party to the contract functioning as a dealer. Such a firm functions as an intermediary with the purpose of entering into virtually any transaction, generally on either side (buy or sell) of the contract. Dealers thus transact with end users so that users do not need to identify a counterparty with a demand for the opposite side of the contract to enter that contract. Dealers thus can provide customized transaction services while dramatically reducing the cost of searching for counterparties in off-exchange contracting.

As OTC derivatives activity exploded in the 1990s, OTC derivatives markets began to look more and more like exchange-traded derivatives markets. Products were increasingly governed by pro forma standardized documents called "master agreements" that led to more and more product standardization—not at all dissimilar from the migration of the cambium into the *lettera di cambio* and bills of exchange. Dealers supplied liquidity, and transaction costs fell. Transactions began to be periodically cash-settled. About the only two major distinctions between active OTC derivatives markets and their exchange-traded equivalents by the turn of the twentieth century was the absence of organized clearinghouses in the former, and the absence of an organized set of trading rules.

Given its lack of explicit rules defining a "market," the forum for negotiating OTC derivatives is best characterized as the world of faxes and phones and e-mails. There are no closing times or opening bells, and there are comparatively few restrictions on the degree to which a user can still customize a transaction if she wants to. Otherwise, the OTC derivatives market is very much a market in the classical sense, absent a trading floor.

Just as the financial-innovation spiral predicts, of course, innovation begets changes in market structure that in turn beget innovation. In this case, the staggeringly rapid growth in OTC derivatives also likely influenced a shift in the structure of exchange-traded transactions. In particular, the advance of technology together with the visible success of highly liquid OTC derivatives markets without trading floors led most of the exchange-traded derivatives world to abandon the historical trading floor concept and move toward fully electronic organized exchanges. At the same time, exchange-traded products became increasingly wider in variety and easier to customize. In short, the two worlds began to converge.

## DETERMINANTS OF A SUCCESSFUL EXCHANGE-TRADED DERIVATIVES CONTRACT

Despite some obvious and strong convergence, privately negotiated derivatives remain the dominant form of derivatives activity. One reason surely must be the cost associated with managing and operating an organized derivatives exchange, which immediately gives rise to the question of when the benefits of those exchange-traded contracts are justified. Clearly, they *are* justified in many cases, as the huge historical success and strong current demand for futures attests. Nevertheless, the majority of futures contracts fail less than 10 years after they are introduced (Carlton, 1984). Given the costs of listing new contracts for organized exchanges, the characteristics of a successful exchange-traded futures contract is of central importance to exchanges. The revolution in OTC derivatives, moreover, has increased the cost of being wrong in this decision and forced even more attention on the issue of what distinguishes a successful exchange-traded derivatives contract from a comparable OTC contract.

Although the final arbiter of the success or failure of a contract is the market, history and empirical observation do provide some useful guidelines for when users are most likely to value exchange trading versus the more opaque world of OTC derivatives trading. The next few sections briefly explore the characteristics shared by most of the truly successful exchange-traded derivatives around the world.[14] Note that some of these characteristics are required to justify the demand for the derivatives contract *in general*, whereas others support the *relative* demand for exchange-traded vis-à-vis OTC derivatives.

## Volatility in Price or Quantity

Exchange-traded derivatives are fundamentally *trading markets*. They include firms that are seeking to engage in derivatives for risk transfer purposes (i.e., hedgers) as well as firms that are participating for another reason. Some firms—"day traders" or "scalpers"—maintain a presence in the futures market in an effort to benefit from supplying temporary liquidity in the market. Others take outright positions in one or more contracts in an effort to try to make money (i.e., speculators). But in both of these latter cases, the market must be moving in order to be interesting. With too little volatility, the cost of maintaining a market presence is hard to justify, and trading becomes significantly less interesting.

Volatility is also essential to attract hedgers. For this group, either price or quantity volatility can attract firms seeking to exploit the risk transfer features of derivatives. Without volatility in at least one of the two, however, the benefits of risk transfer will be too low relative to the transaction costs of trading.

## Contract Design

Unlike traditional insurance, derivatives are not indemnity contracts. This means that derivatives do not reimburse firms for actual economic losses they might sustain. Nevertheless, a successful futures contract will be designed and standardized to maximize the correlation between cash flows on the contracts and potential losses at would-be hedgers.

Consider a futures contract based on wheat, and suppose the exchange listing the contract is considering two different standardized definitions of the type of wheat that can be delivered by the short when the contract matures. One possibility is to define the underlying wheat asset very narrowly—for example, No. 2 red spring wheat delivered at a Midwestern U.S. grain elevator. Another option being considered is to allow the short to deliver any wheat at all at any grain elevator in the world. The choice the exchange makes will dictate the *price* of the asset on which the futures contract is based. A Midwestern U.S. farmer might clearly prefer the former, but that same contract would attract little interest among European farmers growing a different type of wheat entirely, plus facing the potential costs of transportation from the United States. The world contract, by contrast, would pose some risk of the same transportation cost issue for *all* would-be hedgers. Similarly, the correlation between changes in some average of world wheat prices and any individual farmer's crop might well be too low to be interesting *for anyone*.

Despite what you might think, successful contracts like the "world wheat" contract just described do exist. The issue for an exchange is very much a trade-off. On the one hand, the contract should be broadly enough defined that it attracts a large population of potential users. On the other hand, the contract should not be so broadly defined that either the transaction costs are potentially prohibitive or the price of the asset underlying the contract has a low correlation to the potential losses of a large number of would-be users.

Other issues are also important in contract design, such as tick size and minimum price fluctuation. As later chapters will make clearer, a contract with a tick size and minimum price move that are too big will not fluctuate enough to allow hedgers to match their actual assets at risk with a futures position. But a contract with a tick size and minimum price fluctuation that is too small will impose unnecessarily high transaction costs on users who must frequently rebalance their positions.

## Market Structure

In general, the larger the number of firms in the industry producing or selling the asset on which a futures contract is based, the better is the chance for success of that futures contract. A greater number of firms obviously means a larger number of potential users of the contract. But perhaps even more importantly, a diffuse and less vertically integrated industry for the underlying asset makes the information produced by the futures market relatively more valuable. Because futures are a natural arena for price discovery, monopolists may consider the information produced by the futures market to be harmful to their goal of preserving market power.

## Adequate Hedge Load

The "hedge load" of a market is defined as the proportion of traders in that market willing to take positions opposite to the hedgers in the market. In some markets, the hedge load is served naturally by the presence of both long and short hedgers—for example, farmers hedging their crop sales short against price declines may be across from millers hedging their crop purchases long against price spikes. Alternatively, a reasonable proportion of scalpers and speculators will also help ensure an adequate hedge load.

## Information about the Underlying

Successful futures contracts require frequent and reliable releases of information about the underlying asset. Without regular high-quality information releases, people will not revise their expectations about future prices, and price volatility will be lower than required to justify the costs of market participation. In short, trading markets require information, or else there will be no trading. And with no trading, exchange-traded markets lose all of their liquidity advantages to otherwise equivalent OTC products.

As an example, consider the futures contract on the U.S. consumer price index (CPI) introduced by the Coffee, Sugar, and Cocoa Exchange (CSCE) in 1985. Most hedgers wanted to be long with the futures to protect themselves against increases in inflation. Unfortunately, updates to the CPI were too infrequent to attract speculators. The hedge load thus proved inadequate, and the contract did not last (Petzel, 1989).

## NOTES

1. Referring to derivatives as a form of "financing" in a post-Enron era usually leads people to conclude that derivatives are debt in disguise. Chapters 7 to 10 should put an end to that erroneous way of thinking. See also Culp and Kavanagh (2003).
2. Tracing the origins of derivatives with any historical accuracy is a nearly impossible task because of the sheer number of commercial contracts that have resembled or been forms of derivatives over time. Instead, we focus on a handful of interesting specific cases.
3. In practice, the "trade date" may be the date on which the terms of the transaction are *confirmed* rather than first negotiated. We will get into this in Chapter 6.
4. I am very grateful to Navaid Abidi from my spring 2003 investments course at the University of Chicago both for pointing out this early application of derivatives and for providing capable research assistance. Most of the information in this section is based on two useful Web sites: Al Rajhi Banking & Investment Corp.'s "Principles of Islamic Banking" at www.alrahjibank.com.sa and Mufti Taq Usmani's "Forward Sales and Manufacturing Contracts: Salam and Istisna" at www.albalagh.net.
5. *Shariah* is essentially Islamic law, whereas *fiqh* (literally "understanding") is Islamic jurisprudence.
6. One of the conditions of *salam* is that it may not be based on a specific asset that is subject to destruction or degregation. A farmer thus cannot precontract to sell the specific crop from a specific field, but can enter into an agreement to sell a specified amount and quality of comparable grain instead.
7. The use of derivatives in medieval Europe is discussed in great detail by De Roover (1948, 1963), from which most of the historical facts presented in this section are drawn. I am extremely grateful to John Cochrane for introducing me to these books, which are easily two of the most fascinating financial history books available today.
8. See De Roover (1963), pp. 111–114.

9. Modern derivatives must be "unwound" by obtaining permission of the counterparty to the transaction and cannot be traded on a secondary market.
10. De Roover (1948) provides an interesting account of this.
11. De Roover (1963), p. 122.
12. For good discussions of the ring system, see Hardy (1923) and Williams (1986).
13. Dealers arguably arose in very simple currency derivatives markets in the late 1970s.
14. See Carlton (1984) and Petzel (1989) for a discussion of some of these characteristics in more detail. See also Culp (1996).

# CHAPTER 6

# Derivatives Trading, Clearance, and Settlement

The "transaction chain" in a modern-day derivatives contract consists of three components: trading, clearing or clearance, and settlement. The transaction chain for derivatives depends strongly on whether the transaction is OTC or exchange traded. As already noted, these two worlds have converged in many aspects of *product design*, but they still differ significantly in terms of what we call *market microstructure*, or the institutional features of the transaction chain. In some cases the distinctions in market microstructure are enough to change certain users' preference for undertaking a transaction.

## TRADING

The trading process typically includes the design of derivatives contracts, order placement and order taking, order execution, trade matching, and confirmation.[1] In OTC derivatives markets, trading remains largely decentralized and limited mainly to direct negotiation with dealers until a contract is in place. End users generally select their preferred dealer either by reputation or existing customer relations. In some cases, end users will shop for the best price on a deal, either perusing automatic quotation systems like Reuters and Telerate for the best indicative quote or making use of OTC derivatives brokers. In the case of electronic price bulletin boards, however, prices quoted by dealers are only *representative*. The price a specific end user gets quoted on a specific transaction depends ultimately on direct negotiation with the dealer.

Providers of organized trading markets in derivatives used to be synonymous with *exchanges*. Now the two terms are different, and providers of trading markets include more than just the classical organized exchanges like the Chicago Mercantile Exchange (CME) or Eurex. In particular, the derivatives trading world now includes Internet-based business-to-business (B2B) verticals and virtual exchanges (e.g., OnExchange, Altra Energy, and the former EnronOnline), automatic trading systems (ATSs) (e.g., the Blackbird platform for swap trading), and electronic communication networks (ECNs) and automatic order matching systems (e.g., Instinet and NexTrade). Whereas exchanges tend to remain relatively integrated across all aspects of trading, most of these other participants usually focus instead purely on order matching. In particular, these entities do not generally engage in product design, either partnering with an exchange for product listing (e.g., CheMatch and the CME with benzene futures) or providing a trading venue for customized OTC transactions (e.g., Blackbird). In other words, B2Bs, ATSs, and ECNs tend to focus solely on order matching.

Numerous different market structures now exist for matching shorts and longs or buyers and sellers. Especially in Chicago, the CME and CBOT still cling tenaciously to the original open-outcry pit trading system, but have also introduced electronic trading systems as well. The universe of electronic trading systems around the world can differ substantially and include electronic auctions and reverse auctions, electronic bulletin boards, and electronic limit-order books or matching algorithms. Many exchanges have chosen to develop their own proprietary technologies for trading, whereas others have procured off-the-shelf systems from the market. Two exchanges have become major providers of their own trading systems to the rest of the world: OM and Euronext/LIFFE.

Another important distinction in various market microstructures for derivatives trading is based on different definitions of *liquidity provision*. In pure OTC markets, liquidity is provided by swap dealers who generally stand ready to go long or short on any given deal. But this is a role they play purely voluntarily. Nothing obligates dealers to maintain a continuous market presence.

Ironically, open-outcry trading is probably the closest to OTC derivatives dealing in this regard. No individual or firm is given either special privileges or responsibilities for liquidity provision. Liquidity simply comes from the interactions of numerous longs and shorts, speculators, hedgers, and day traders alike.

In alternative market structures, the role of the liquidity provider is more formalized. In an electronic bulletin board market (e.g., EnronOnline before it closed down in late 2001), the "market" is essentially a series of prices posted by the sponsor of the market. Prices are simply those prices at which the sponsor itself will buy or sell, and the sponsor may choose to change or revoke those prices at any time. Liquidity in such a market thus is limited completely by the ability and willingness of the market sponsor to post and update prices.

Liquidity in many ATSs, by contrast, often comes either from designated market makers or from an automatic limit-order book. The former are firms that are designated as formal liquidity providers. In return for getting certain special privileges (e.g., all other trades must transact through them), they are typically obligated to maintain continuous two-sided (i.e., buy and sell) quotes at all times, even during periods of market instability.

In an automatic limit-order book, multiple participants enter not just buy and sell orders, but the maximum price they would be willing to pay to buy an asset or minimum acceptable to sell it (or, equivalently, to go long or short) for a specified quantity. In other words, market participants thus submit more of a *schedule* than just periodically entering the market to buy or sell. The agglomeration of multiple buy and sell orders for different quantities and prices creates liquidity at more than just the current quoted price.

## CLEARANCE AND NETTING SCHEMES[2]

Once a trade is confirmed, it creates either of two types of "settlement obligation(s)" for the counterparties to undertake on the settlement date: asset-for-funds; or funds-for-funds. The former involves the exchange of a nonmoney asset (e.g., wheat) for funds, whereas the latter represents an exchange of funds for funds. Physically settled derivatives fall into the former category, whereas cash-settled derivatives create the latter type of settlement obligations. Note that funds settlement is required in *all* derivatives, whereas asset settlement is involved only for transactions that settle by physical delivery if held to maturity.

After the terms of a transaction are confirmed by the two parties to the transaction, the *computation of clearing balances* occurs. For now, ignore the possibility that a third party computes these balances and just assume the two original parties to a transaction compute the required clearing balances themselves.

In a single transaction, the computation of clearing balances is just the establishment of the legal obligation(s) created by the transaction. In a single-currency funds transfer, the computation of clearing balances merely represents the determination that one bank will transfer some amount of funds denominated in a particular currency to another bank. In a multicurrency funds-for-funds exchange, the clearing balance consists of *two* obligations—the transfer of some amount of funds in one currency from one bank to another, and the transfer of some quantity of a different currency from the counterparty bank to the first bank. In a funds-for-assets exchange, the computation of clearing balances consists of the final determination that some number of securities will be exchanged for a specified cash payment.

In practice, banks, brokers, and other institutions frequently have multiple obligations to one another. These obligations can include all three types of transactions—funds transfers, multicurrency funds-for-funds exchanges, and funds-for-assets exchanges. The computation of clearing balances thus depends in practice on the netting scheme in place in a particular settlement system. *Netting* is defined by the Bank for International Settlements (BIS) as "an agreed offsetting of mutual positions or obligations by trading partners or participants in a system." Netting schemes may be either bilateral or multilateral and may apply to asset transfer obligations, funds transfer obligations, or both.

Certain types of transactions cannot be netted. If Bank A and Bank B agree in one transaction to exchange euros for dollars and agree in a second transaction to exchange Japanese yen for Swiss francs, no fewer than four funds transfers will be required to achieve final settlement. Consequently, the computation of clearing balances will simply involve the computation of the sizes of the four transfer obligations created by the two original transactions. Similarly, shares of one security cannot be netted against shares of a different security. Payments *in the same currency* and transfers *of the same asset*, however, *can* be netted, and, in practice, often *are* netted.

In general, there are four different types of netting schemes: position netting, binding payments netting, novation, and closeout netting. For the most part, OTC derivatives are distinguished from exchange-traded derivatives by the fact that only the fourth type of netting scheme is ever really used for OTC derivatives. Exchange-traded derivatives, by contrast, generally involve one of the first three types of netting schemes, as well as the fourth.

## Position Netting

Position netting is a form of offset in which payment or asset transfer obligations may be lumped into a single net transfer. In bilateral *payment* position netting, two single-currency funds transfer obligations are netted into a single amount—for example, if A owes B $10 and B owes A $1, payment position netting lets A pay B $9. Similarly, bilateral *contract* position netting is the netting of two asset transfer obligations. If A owes B three shares of XYZ stock and B owes A 10 shares of XYZ stock, for example, contract position netting lets B transfer the net of seven shares of stock to A.[3] In position netting, the underlying contractual obligations between two parties do not change. Payments or security transfers are "bulked," mainly to reduce the number of settlement instructions required.

## Binding Payments Netting

Binding payments netting is bilateral netting only of funds transfers. If two parties have two securities obligations with one another, for example, binding payments netting involves a formal agreement between the parties to exchange only one net cash flow to discharge their two gross payment obligations. The formal agreement to exchange one net cash flow rather than two gross cash flows constitutes a new, legally binding contract for one payment. The creation of that contract discharges the original gross payment obligations in full. Bilateral payment netting thus changes the actual legal obligation to transfer funds. Binding payments netting reduces the credit exposures of same-currency funds transfers but does not affect the gross transfers—whether securities transfers or funds transfers in a different currency—required on the other side of the original transactions.

## Novation

Netting by novation is the replacement of two existing payment and delivery contracts with a single payment and delivery contract that subsumes the obligations of both the original contracts. To illustrate, consider first two separate transactions *without* netting by novation. The first transaction is a forward contract negotiated in September between Mahler and Bach that requires Mahler to purchase 1,000 ounces of gold from Bach for $450/oz. (or for $450,000 total) in December. Then suppose in October that Mahler and Bach enter into a new contract, this time for Bach to purchase 800 ounces of gold from Mahler at $500/oz. (or for $400,000 total) in December. Without any netting, the two contracts give rise to four settlement obligations in December: asset-for-funds on the September transaction, and asset-for-funds on the October transaction.

Now suppose novation is allowed. The same two transactions executed in September and October now give rise to only two settlement obligations in December: one asset and one funds. The novated contract requires Mahler to purchase 200 ounces (1,000 ounces purchased in the September deal minus 800 ounces sold on the October deal) of gold from Bach in December for a total of $50,000 ($450,000 owed to Bach on the September contract minus $400,000 payable by Bach on the October contract).

Netting by novation occurs on an ongoing basis, so that each new contract between two parties fully subsumes the previous contract between those two parties. Because the previous contract will also have been novated, a single contract is outstanding at any time between two parties that represents the total security and/or net funds transfer obligations between the two firms. In other words, when the new contract is established by novation, the obligations on all previous contracts are legally discharged. In our example, this means that Mahler and Bach have a single contract in place in September for Mahler to buy 1,000 ounces of gold from Bach in December for $450,000. When the new transaction is negotiated in October, the prior contract is rolled up, resulting in a single new contract requiring Mahler to purchase 200 ounces of gold from Bach in December for $50,000.

## Closeout Netting

The final type of netting scheme—the only one that applies to both OTC and exchange-traded derivatives—is called closeout netting, or netting that applies in the event of a default by one of the counterparties. These netting schemes are the most controversial, because local insolvency laws in various countries often affect the enforceability of such arrangements. When closeout netting is not enforceable following an insolvency of one counterparty, "cherry picking" can result. For example, suppose Broker Godesberg has purchased one share of XYZ stock from Broker Bonn for $10 and has sold one share of XYZ stock to Broker Bonn for $12. The security transfer obligation nets to zero, and Broker Bonn owes Broker Godesberg $2 net on the funds side. If closeout netting is not enforceable, Broker Bonn (or its receiver) may attempt to avoid the netting scheme in insolvency by demanding the $10 gross payment on the first transaction while refusing (or having no funds with which) to pay the $12 gross payment owed on the second transaction.

## FINAL SETTLEMENT FOR ASSET TRANSFERS

*Final settlement* occurs when all the settlement obligations created by a derivatives transaction are fully discharged. An asset-for-funds transfer reaches final settlement only when both the title of ownership of the asset is actually transferred (in a legally enforceable manner) from the short to the long *and* when the required funds are actually transferred from the buyer to the seller. For derivatives transactions, asset settlement and funds settlement are generally accomplished in different ways.

An asset transfer achieves final settlement when the transfer of title of ownership from the seller (short) to the buyer (long) is both irrevocable and final. In both OTC and exchange-traded derivatives markets, asset settlement finality depends on the type of asset and the role played by any designated settlement agent, or an organization appointed to ensure that the asset changes hands at the right time and "is really there." This may include verifying the proper quality of the asset (e.g., the wheat delivered in a forward has enough protein to satisfy the contract terms, the oil does not have too much sulfur, the bond has the right maturity and coupon range, etc.).

If the asset underlying a derivatives transaction is a physical commodity, final settlement generally occurs through some designated third party. For OTC derivatives, this is usually a logistics firm of some kind—for example, an oil transportation company paid to transport oil from the short to the long.[4] For exchange-traded derivatives, the designated clearinghouse organization (CHO) generally maintains a warehousing facility of its own or one that is operated for the CHO under contract by a third party, and this warehouse facility ensures that the final asset transfer occurs. In many cases, commodity futures can satisfy final settlement by the exchange of a warehouse receipt.

If the asset underlying a derivatives transaction is a security, final settlement must be achieved by the local national central securities depository (CSD) that is responsible for custody and transfers of ownership. Following the Big Bang in 1986, most industrialized countries have dematerialized securities (especially equities) so that the CSD can effectuate changes in ownership by making a notation in a book-entry securities ownership recording and tracking system. Otherwise, the registrar and custodian for the security must certify that the security has changed hands.

Local CSDs often differ for stocks and bonds. In the United States, for example, equity ownership records are tracked and transfers are facilitated by the Depository Trust Clearing Corporation (DTCC). Government bond ownership, by contrast, is tracked and changed by the record-keeping system of the Federal Reserve (Fed).

Final asset settlement on OTC derivatives on securities usually means direct communication between the counterparties and the CSDs. In exchange-traded derivatives, by contrast, the CHO of the exchange generally must coordinate the final transfer with the CSDs. How this works depends very much on the role played by the CHO itself.

CHOs in exchange-traded derivatives can act in any of three different capacities. *Infrastructure providers* are CHOs that play a purely operational role in facilitating the final settlement of both assets and funds. BrokerTEC, for example, is an automated trading system for bonds that facilitates trading, but is only an infrastructure provider for settlements. Final transfer of ownership of bonds traded through BrokerTEC must occur through the Federal Reserve's book-entry system for tracking and changing government bond ownership.

A second type of CHO is a *delivery versus payment* (DVP) agent that ensures no funds transfer occurs until the asset transfer has occurred and vice versa. Like the infrastructure provider, this is generally a coordination role in which the CHO does not issue instructions for a funds transfer until the asset transfer can be confirmed or vice versa. In some cases, escrow accounts are set up to facilitate the DVP process. If a securities sale is initiated and the buyer ends up not having the funds to pay for the security, the securities sale can simply be reversed or released from escrow by the DVP agent.

The DVP principle helps mitigate settlement risk, sometimes known as Herstatt risk because of the settlement losses that occurred following the failure of Bankhaus Herstatt on June 26, 1974. Bankhaus Herstatt was ordered into liquidation during the banking day but *after* the close of the German payments system. (See the next section on funds transfer finality.) Before the closure of the bank was announced, however, several firms that had transacted with Herstatt in spot and maturing forward currency transactions had already submitted irrevocable payment instructions to transfer deutsche marks to Herstatt in anticipation of receiving dollars from Herstatt later that day in New York. When Herstatt closed, however, the New York branch of Bankhaus Herstatt immediately suspended all dollar payments. In consequence, Herstatt's counterparty banks lost the full value of the deutsche mark payments already made and never received the dollars. The presence of a DVP agent eliminates this type of credit risk, provided the DVP does its job properly.

Finally, the CHO for exchange-traded derivatives can—and most often does—play the role of central counterparty (CCP). As noted in Chapter 1, this involves the CHO's actually becoming the legal counterparty to each trade, so that what is originally a funds-for-assets settlement obligation pair between two traders becomes a single funds settlement obligation and a single asset settlement obligation of the CCP. The CCP generally provides full trade guarantees to its participants. This not only addresses Herstatt risk, but also now protects traders from replacement cost risk—the risk that a default by the long (or short) the original contract to be replaced at a higher (or lower) price than the original contract.

Final asset settlement in CCP systems may be accomplished by the CCP itself or by the trading participants under the CCP's guidance. As an example of the former, the short in a maturing bond futures contract would issue instructions to the Fed to transfer the bond directly to the account of the CCP. The CCP would then transfer ownership of the bond to one of the longs.

Alternatively, many CCPs engage in a matching process when a physically settled contract matures. In this process, each long is randomly matched to a short, and final settlement of the asset then occurs directly between the two parties. The CCP is still in this case acting as trade guarantor, so a failure by the short to deliver would simply result in the CCP matching the long to a new short, or the CCP would make the long whole directly.

## FINAL SETTLEMENT FOR FUNDS TRANSFERS

Most major countries of the world have "bank-centric" payment systems. That means that in order to achieve final and irrevocable settlement, a funds transfer must be conducted through a bank. In OTC derivatives, counterparties settle funds transfers directly through their nominated bankers. In exchange-traded derivatives, things are a bit more complex. Let's first explore how finality in a funds transfer is achieved, and we then examine how this process works in exchange-traded derivatives activity.

## Irrevocable and Final Funds Transfers[5]

Any funds transfer contains two components—the transfer of information and the final transfer of funds between two banks. The funds transfer process is initiated when one bank issues a payment order or instruction to the other bank. The transmission of a payment order essentially amounts to an electronic request for payment. The bank that sends the initiating payment request message is called the *payee* and the bank receiving the request for payment is the *payer*.

Most modern payment systems are credit transfer systems. This means that both the payment messages *and* the funds move from the payer to the payee. After the initial request for payment from the payee, all messages thus are sent by the payer and received by the payee. These messages are typically electronic and consist of verifications of the transaction, identification authentications, reconciliations of payment instructions, and so forth.

The information exchange between two banks pertains only to the *instructions* for the funds transfer. The funds transfer itself is usually accomplished electronically and is independent of the information exchanges. Specifically, a funds transfer is said to have achieved final settlement when two conditions are met: The funds transfer is *irrevocable*, and the funds transfer is *final*. Revocability concerns the capacity of the payer or, in some cases, a third party to rescind payment after a payment instruction has been issued. Any funds transfer that can be rescinded is known as a *revocable transfer*, whereas *irrevocable transfers* are irreversible by any party once initiated.

In general, finality in a funds transfer is can be achieved in any of four ways.

### Transfers of Central Bank Money

Commercial banks in virtually all countries around the world maintain balances with the central bank. These balances are held in "nostro" accounts, meaning that the funds are on deposit with the central bank but still belong to the commercial bank. Finality in funds transfers is usually achieved through debits and credits to banks' nostro accounts with the central bank. Specifically, a funds transfer is final when the nostro account of the payer with the central bank has been debited and the nostro account of the payee with the central bank has been credited. So, finality in a funds transfer occurs when central bank money has been used to settle the transaction.

Finality achieved through the transfer of central bank money is usually important only when some risk is perceived that one of the counterparties to a transaction will fail. If central bank money has been used to settle a funds transfer, the failure of the payee would not affect the payer. With other methods of funds transfers, complications can arise—a payee may end up with a claim on the failed payer rather than with hard cash. Nevertheless, finality achieved through central bank money transfers is not always a necessary ingredient to funds transfers. Indeed, because many central banks do not pay interest on reserve deposits, banks often do not maintain enough funds with the central bank to discharge all their payment obligations through central bank money transfers. So, even though debits and credits to banks' nostro accounts at the central bank are the only means by which finality can be assured in a funds transfer, other means of funds transfers *are* routinely used, as described next.

### Bilateral Transfers Between Banks' Nostro and Vostro Accounts

When a bank maintains a deposit with another bank in a nostro account, the *depositing* bank is called the nostro bank. From the perspective of the bank accepting the deposit, the funds on deposit are held in what is called a *vostro* account and the bank taking the deposit is the vostro bank. So, if Bank A deposits funds at Bank B, Bank A is the nostro bank and Bank B is the vostro bank. The deposit is a nostro deposit for Bank A and a vostro deposit for Bank B.[6] Nostro and vostro deposits may arise either from transactions between the banks (e.g., money market transactions) or from transactions by banks on behalf of nonbank customers (e.g., the settlement of securities transactions).

We have already explained that funds transfers can be effected by banks through transfers between their nostro accounts with the central bank. In that case, the central bank is the only relevant vostro bank. In addition, funds transfers can be effected by *direct* debits and credits to banks' nostro and vostro accounts arising from bilateral interbank funds transfer obligations. Suppose, for example, that Bank N maintains a nostro account with Bank V with a current balance of $100. Then suppose that a nonbank customer of Bank V instructs Bank V to transfer $50 to Bank N—say, to settle a security purchase made by a broker who maintains a settlement account at Bank N. Rather than transferring central bank balances, the banks may simply agree that Bank V will *credit* the vostro account held for Bank N with $50. To Bank N, the value of its nostro account has risen by $50, and this represents a tangible balance sheet asset. If Bank N wishes to withdraw those funds permanently, a central bank balance transfer still will be required, but banks are quite often willing just to settle their transactions only using these sorts of book-entry debits and credits to nostro and vostro accounts *with one another* for operational simplicity, especially when the payer is a creditworthy institution.

### Transfers of Correspondent or Settlement Bank Balances

Not every bank has a nostro and/or vostro relationship with every other bank. Yet, virtually all banks do maintain relationships with *correspondent banks*, or third-party banks whose primary services include the intermediation of interbank funds transfers.

If Bank A and Bank B do not have deposits with one another and do not wish to settle the transaction using their central bank reserve balances, they can settle the funds transfer through their common correspondent bank.[7] Bank B will issue a payment order to Correspondent Bank C instructing Bank C to debit $100 from Bank B's nostro account held by Bank C and then to credit Bank A with $100. To effect the transfer, Bank C will debit its vostro account held for Bank B by $100 and credit its vostro account held for Bank A by the same amount.

## Large-Value Transfer Systems and Clearinghouses

Banks not only have relationships with one another and with the central bank, but they also often have relationships with the equivalent of a funds CHO known as a *large-value transfer system* (LVTS).[8]

LVTSs support all interbank payments and thus comprise the backbone of any national payments system. All major funds transfers occur through LVTSs in the industrialized countries of the world. In essence, an LVTS acts as a central counterparty for funds, standing in between individual banks and the central bank. Members settle their transactions with one another through the LVTS and the LVTS then links these individual settlements with final settlements discharged in central bank money. LVTSs are quite often provided and maintained by the central bank itself to facilitate transfers in nostro account balances of its members. For this reason, however, participation in LVTSs is usually restricted to institutions that do indeed maintain reserve balances with the central bank (i.e., to banks).

## Characteristics of Large-Value Transfer Systems

LVTSs are distinguished from one another by three primary features: the netting scheme, the clearance scheme, and the extension of intraday credit by the central bank.

### Netting Schemes

When a bank engages in a funds transfer on behalf of a customer, that bank is said to be operating as a *settlement bank* for that customer. Between settlement banking and their own interbank activities, commercial banks tend to have numerous single-currency transactions with one another through the course of a day. Clearance and settlement in national payments systems can occur on either a *net* or a *gross* basis to address those multiple funds transfer instructions.

In a gross settlement LVTS, all funds transfers are settled separately and independently. In a net settlement LVTS, by contrast, funds transfers are based on the *net* payables and receivables of a bank—either to other banks or to the central bank. A *bilateral* net settlement system involves separate debits and credits of a bank's nostro account with the central bank *for each bank with which the original bank has transacted.* If Bank A has 50 transfers with Bank B resulting in a $10 *net* debit to Bank B, and has 13 transfers with Bank C resulting in a *net* credit with Bank C of $5, in a bilateral netting system the debit with Bank A would be settled with a $10 debit to Bank A's nostro account at the central bank and a $10 credit to Bank B's nostro account, and the credit with Bank C would be settled by a $5 debit to Bank C's nostro account and a $5 credit to Bank A's nostro account.

In a *multilateral* net settlement system, the central bank or LVTS computes the *net-net* obligation of each bank (i.e., the net debit or credit of each bank *to the central bank* based on the net of all its net debits and net credits to other banks). In our example, Bank A's transactions with both Bank B and Bank C would result in a net debit to Bank A's nostro account at the central bank—only one funds transfer, as compared to two in the case of bilateral netting. Virtually all net settlement LVTSs operating in industrialized countries rely on multilateral net settlement with the central bank.

### Clearance Schemes

LVTSs are either *batched* or *continuous*, depending on the frequency and timing of final funds transfers in the system. Batched settlement systems are LVTSs in which funds transfers occur only at designated times during the day. An end-of-day funds settlement system, for example, is a batched settlement system in which all funds transfers are processed in some predefined order at the end of the processing day. In such systems, like the Bank of England's system, payment messages may be transmitted throughout the day and on a transaction-by-transaction basis, but final settlement is achieved only at discrete settlement intervals. A continuous settlement system, by contrast, is a payments mechanism that can achieve the finality of funds transfers in real time throughout the day.

In practice, batched settlement systems may be either gross or net settlement systems. Continuous settlement systems, however, are never net settlement systems. When considering both netting and the timing of settlement, three possible payment systems thus emerge—batched gross settlement, batched net settlement, and real-time gross settlement (RTGS).

### Daylight Overdrafts

An intraday loan is an extension of credit to a bank with a duration of a few hours—perhaps even just a few minutes. The extension of intraday credit by the central bank in a payments system can occur when a bank does not have adequate funds in its nostro account with the central bank to honor a payment order when that order is confirmed. In that case, the payer may incur a "daylight overdraft," or a payment obligation in excess of available funds constituting a loan from the payment system provider (i.e., the central bank) to the payer bank. Suppose, for example, that Bank A instructs the central bank to remit a $1 million payment to Bank B by debiting its nostro account and crediting the $1 million to the nostro account of Bank B. Suppose further that Bank A has only $600,000 on deposit with the central bank at the time the payment instruction is issued. In some systems, the central bank will allow the payment to occur by effectively extending Bank A a $400,000 loan to cover its overdraft.

In an LVTS for which intraday credit is extended by the central bank, the expectation is that any daylight overdrafts will be rectified by the end of the processing day. If not, LVTS providers typically impose heavy penalties on banks with net overnight debit positions in their nostro accounts with the central bank. When intraday credit is extended to banks in RTGS systems, in particular, the central bank usually charges interest on daylight overdrafts, at rates that often are subsidized.

## Finality of Funds in Exchange-Traded Derivatives

Exchange-traded derivatives involve funds transfer obligations that rely heavily on a system of designated settlement banks, where all participants in the exchange CHO have at least one settlement bank. In addition, the CHO itself maintains accounts with at least one settlement bank to discharge *its* obligations.

Most organized derivatives exchanges rely on a prudential margin system with both initial and maintenance margin requirements. Initial margin is set by the exchange at a level designed to absorb an extremely high percentage (e.g., 99.9 percent) of all anticipated price changes in a given contract between mark-to-market intervals. Trading participants must post this margin as a type of performance bond prior to entering into a futures contract.

As explained earlier, all futures positions are marked to current market prices at least twice daily on most exchanges. If this results in a gain, the designated settlement bank of the CHO issues instructions to transfer funds into the trader's account. Traders often maintain accounts with the same bank acting as the CHO's settlement bank, as well as a separate settlement bank account from which they conduct their primary banking business. Profits from trading are automatically transferred into the trader's designated settlement account, but the trader may then decide whether to transfer the funds *again* into its primary banking account.

If a mark-to-market revaluation results in a loss, the CHO debits the funds from the trading participant's designated settlement bank and credits those funds to the settlement bank of the CHO.

A second type of margin requirement, called "maintenance," specifies a minimum level below which a trading firm's margin account may not fall for a given open position. (Recall that initial margin applied to new positions only.) Once the account reaches that maintenance level, the firm is required to deposit additional funds into its settlement account to bring the level of the account back up to the *initial* margin level. Suppose, for example, that initial margin on a given contract is $15,000 and that the maintenance margin level is $9,000. If prices move against the trader on the first day and impose a $5,000 loss, the CHO debits $5,000 from the trader's settlement account, which now is left with only $10,000. If on the next day another $2,000 loss occurs, the CHO again debits the $2,000 from the trader's settlement account. Now the new account balance is $8,000, which is below the $9,000 maintenance level. The member thus receives a "margin call" and must deposit an additional $7,000 to bring her account back up to the $15,000 initial margin level. Otherwise, the CHO can declare the trader in default and liquidate her open positions.

In some cases, traders can petition for special margin requirements. CHOs often set margin differently for hedgers and speculators, for example. And conversely, CHOs generally have the ability to ask for additional margin—even intraday—if they so much as suspect the trader may not have the funds to cover his next mark-to-market payment obligation.

The flow of funds arising from periodic marking to market is called the pay/collect. A deposit of additional funds that occurs when a trader's margin account falls below the maintenance level is called *variation margin*. Note carefully that initial margin and maintenance margin are *levels*, whereas variation margin is the *cash flow* that occurs when current account funds fall below the required maintenance level.

Depending on the particular CHO, flows of funds for pay/collects, initial margin deposits, and variation margin may involve different final settlement methods. CHOs often require variation margin and pay/collects to occur in cash, and the settlement banks of the trading members are sometimes asked to guarantee intraday credit risk on those flows of funds. If a settlement bank informs a CHO that funds are there to meet a pay/collect but the funds actually are not there, the bank may well be on the hook to the CHO. Initial margin, by contrast, can often be deposited in the form of assets other than cash, and the settlement bank plays no part in this process except to notify the CHO when the required funds or assets have been transferred.

Notice that it does not really matter whether a contract is physically or cash settled from a funds transfer standpoint. Thanks to the margin and pay/collect system, funds flow *all the time* to reflect the changing value of a futures position. By the time a contract matures, the only funds transfer obligation is the last trading period's pay/collect. The rest of the price the long must pay the short will already have been distributed over time through the daily pay/collect process.

## RECENT ISSUES IN CLEARING AND SETTLEMENT[9]

The demand for clearing and settlement services is a *derived* demand. Clearing and settlement have no value without a financial transaction to clear and settle. Accordingly, several recent developments in the world of trading have had a strong impact on the clearing landscape.

One such development has been the heightened degree of integrated cash and derivatives market product coverage by exchanges, especially in Europe. Globalization and the integration of world capital markets, increased demands by institutional investors trading across national borders and product lines to lower their transaction costs and to exploit portfolio-based cross-margining across like products on different exchanges, and rising user interest in one-stop shopping have all led to a recent wave of strategic alliances, electronic linkages, and consolidations designed largely to provide users with a more comprehensive set of cash market and derivatives products in the same trading platform. As exchanges have grown in size to accommodate these new market demands, the relative size and capacity of clearinghouses capable of clearing, settling, and guaranteeing trades in those markets has also been forced to grow accordingly.

With the disintermediation of the financial transaction supply chain at the trading end, not surprising has been the disintermediation of that supply chain at the other end(namely, the provision of clearing and settlement services as an independent business line. Some new exchanges have kept to the historical norm of creating a captive clearinghouse. BrokerTec Clearing Company LLC, for example, is essentially captive to BrokerTec Futures Exchange. But most new exchanges and exchangelike organizations have chosen instead to focus on trading and rely on outsourced clearing and settlement.

One of the first exchanges to outsource its clearing and settlement function was the Australian Derivatives Exchange (ADX), which had arranged to clear through the Australian Stock Exchange's Options Clearing House. Merchants' Exchange chose a similar path and opted to focus on providing the best trading platform possible (mainly in the near future for structured oil and gas transactions) and outsourcing its clearing and settlement to the Board of Trade Clearing Corporation. Similarly, B2Bs and other exchangelike organizations often rely on existing clearinghouses to handle their clearing and settlements. CheMatch, for example, lists benzene futures for trading that are cleared and settled through the clearinghouse division of the Chicago Mercantile Exchange.

Another example is the clearing of OTC markets that exists around pure exchange markets. Such markets can be cleared by existing clearinghouses that clear the exchange market that has a connection with the OTC market. Examples of this are the tailor-made clearing services offered by Stockholms-börsen and OM London Exchange, both part of OM.

Complicating matters greatly is the "freedom to clear" movement that arose in late 2002, largely at the behest of the Futures Industry Association (FIA) in the United States. The FIA took the aggressive position that vertical integration across trading, clearing, and settlement was a "tie-in sale" and a violation of antitrust law, a position echoed by the InterContinental Exchange (ICE) in a lawsuit filed in January 2003 against the New York Mercantile Exchange (NYMEX). The FIA, ICE, and others argue that exchange ownership of a clearinghouse should not include the right to force members to use that clearinghouse, lest the exchange exert its market power to charge excessively for clearing and settlement services. Exchanges respond that not only is vertical integration efficient, but allowing traders to clear the same product at more than one CHO would be intractably complex from an operational standpoint.

## Business Models for Clearing and Settlement

Two essentially distinct business models have evolved alongside one another in the world of clearing and settlement provided by CCPs, and both have been successful. The first is the traditional captive model, in which a clearinghouse CCP that was designed primarily to serve a single exchange market decides to offer outsourced clearing on a selective basis. The second clearing business model is the independent clearinghouse and CCP model, in which *all* clearing is outsourced—the clearinghouse has no "primary market" customer.

### The Captive Model: Deutsche Börse Group

The captive model is well-illustrated by Deutsche Börse Group, an exchange organization that has expanded dramatically across product lines for both trading and clearing/settlement. The cash trading markets run by Deutsche Börse include the FWB Frankfurter Wertpapierbörse (the Frankfurt Stock Exchange) and the New Europe Exchange (NEWEX), founded in 2000 to operate the segment for the regulated unofficial market on FWB in about 150 stocks on Central and East European companies. NEWEX is 50 percent owned by the Deutsche Börse and 50 percent owned by the Wiener Börse.

Eurex is the Deutsche Börse's derivatives exchange, formed in December 1996 as a joint venture of Deutsche Börse AG and Swiss Exchange and formalized in 1998 with the merger of the DTB Deutsche Terminbörse and SOFFEX

(Swiss Options and Financial Futures Exchange). The European Energy Exchange (EEX), 52 percent owned by 48 energy companies from 10 countries and 48 percent owned by Eurex, is an electricity trading exchange. Derivatives began trading there on March 1, 2001, following the commencement of trading for over-the-counter spot electricity contracts on August 8, 2000. On March 1, 2002, the EEX merged with the Leipzig Power Exchange (LPX).

Clearing and settlements for all Deutsche Börse constituent exchanges occur through captive clearinghouses. Cash transactions (including the financial side of spot EEX electricity contracts) are cleared and settled through Clearstream, created in January 2000 by the merger of Cedel International and Deutsche Börse Clearing AG. The recent acceptance of a tender offer by Cedel shareholders from Deutsche Börse has resulted in full integration and ownership of Clearstream International into the Deutsche Börse organization. All derivatives clearing and settlement is done through Eurex Clearing AG, a wholly owned subsidiary of Eurex.

Figure 6.1 summarizes the Deutsche Börse organization structure, where rectangles indicate exchanges, hexagons indicate CHOs, and ovals indicate co-owners of Deutsche Börse affiliates. Unbroken lines denote ownership stakes, and broken-line arrows denote clearing and settlement relations between the exchanges and the two CHOs owned by Deutsche Börse.

As the diagram shows, Deutsche Börse has aggressively pursued an integration strategy in which its own exchanges clear and settle through clearing organizations owned and operated by Deutsche Börse. This does not mean that Deutsche Börse clearing affiliates eschew clearing for hire. On the contrary, Clearstream International is still a dominant settlement agent for

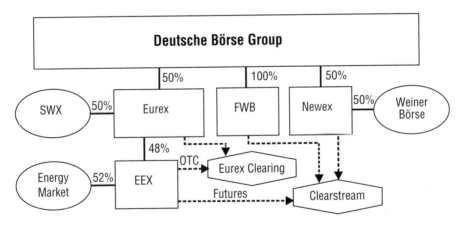

**FIGURE 6.1**   Deutsche Börse and the Captive Clearing Model

cross-border cash market transactions conducted outside the Deutsche Börse organization.

### Independent Model: London Clearing House

When a CHO has a separate and distinct ownership and management structure from the constituent exchanges whose trades are cleared and guaranteed by the CHO, the clearinghouse is independent. Although the participating exchanges often have a portion of share ownership, the independent CHO is characterized by a management that has its own objectives—objectives that may well be distinct from the management goals of the exchanges routing order flow through the CHO. In essence, an independent clearinghouse is a CHO that provides *only* outsourced clearing services; no single exchange is the dominant sponsor, owner, manager, or user of the clearinghouse.

London Clearing House (LCH) is perhaps the oldest example of a highly successful independent CHO. Its structure is depicted in Figure 6.2, where rectangles indicate exchanges clearing through LCH, ovals represent other exchanges, and hexagons represent the different clearing divisions of LCH.

Known originally as the London Produce Clearing House and later as the International Commodities Clearing House, LCH has been providing independent clearing and settlement services since 1888. In 1981, LCH began to clear transactions on the International Petroleum Exchange (IPE). In 1982, LCH began to act as central counterparty for trades done on the London International Financial Futures and Options Exchange (LIFFE). And in 1987, LCH added the London Metal Exchange (LME) to its list of constituent futures markets.

LCH has cleared cash equities since September 1995 when LCH began to act as central counterparty to Tradepoint Stock Exchange in London. Tradepoint has subsequently been renamed Virt-X, with ownership now shared by

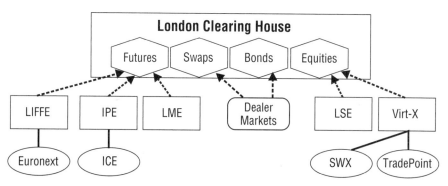

**FIGURE 6.2**  London Clearing House and the Independent Model

the old Tradepoint and the Swiss Exchange. Since February 26, 2001, LCH has also cleared transactions conducted on the London Stock Exchange (LSE) through its automatic order book. Since 1999, LCH has acted as central counterparty to certain off-exchange products as well, including single-currency interest rate swaps (LCH SwapClear) and repurchase agreements (LCH RepoClear). The clearing of cash bonds was added to RepoClear in 2000.

In the contemplated merger between LCH and Clearnet, press reports suggest that a new holding company would assume control of both clearinghouses and that in the process the stake of Euronext would move from 80 percent of Clearnet to a minority shareholding in the new entity. At present, Euronext is more similar to Deutsche Börse than to LCH—that is, it is primarily an exchange organization that also owns a clearing and settlement function. In March 2000, Euronext became a horizontally integrated pan-European cash and derivatives exchange through the merger of the Paris Bourse with the Amsterdam and Brussels exchanges. In late 2001, Euronext expanded its derivatives market coverage through an aggressive acquisition of the LIFFE.

The Banque Centrale de Compensation SA—better known as Clearnet SA—was first established in 1969 to clear contracts traded on the commodity exchanges of Paris. In 1986, the Marché à Terme d'Instruments Financiers (MATIF) was formed to become the primary French financial futures exchange, clearing its trades through its own clearinghouse, La Chambre de Compensation des Instruments Financiers. In 1988, MATIF merged with the local Paris commodity exchanges—as well as those in Lille and Le Havre—and took over the Banque Centrale de Compensation, which retained responsibility for commodities clearing. Clearnet assumed clearing and settlement responsibilities for all Euronext markets by February 2001. Clearnet currently provides Euronext with clearing and settlement services mainly for equities, futures, and options.

## Recent Changes to Both Models

As this manuscript was going to press, recent events have created some important changes to both of the above examples. First, the planned merger between LCH and Clearnet discussed earlier has now been approved and formalized. LCH and Clearnet will continue to operate as separate clearinghouses (with separate margin, clearing, and default funds and separate risk management) but will be owned by the new LCH, Clearnet joint venture holding company. A groupwide risk management function has been established that will evaluate risk exposures across the clearinghouses, including credit exposure concentrations to specific firms active in both clearinghouses.

The second major development has been the announcement that Eurex will open a U.S. exchange and will use the Clearing Corporation (CCorp.)—

formerly the BOTCC—as its clearinghouse. The opening of Eurex U.S. is subject to regulatory approval, and trading is expected to commence sometime in 2004.

Members of CCorp. voted in October 2003 to become the designated clearinghouse for the U.S. operation of Eurex. This shift in the business focus of CCorp. followed a decision by the CME and CBOT earlier in 2003 to pursue a common clearing arrangement, with all clearing on the two exchanges to be done through the CME clearinghouse division, thus eliminating the traditional role of the BOTCC.

CCorp. has not simply changed its exchange affiliation from the BOTCC to the Eurex. On the contrary, CCorp. has adopted a new structure that represents a major move toward more independence in clearing—especially noteworthy given the prior reliance by Deutsche Börse only on captive clearing organizations. Under its new structure, CCorp. "owners" and "users" can now be completely independent of one another. CCorp. is fully demutualized, and CCorp. stock can be freely transferred to anyone. Participants in the clearinghouse that happen to own CCorp. stock can pledge that stock to the clearing guaranty fund, but are not required to do so. Importantly, users of the clearinghouse *need not own stock* in CCorp. The new structure thus completely separates the equity capital of CCorp. from the guaranty fund that backs the clearinghouse as cover in the event of a participant's default. In this sense, the structure of CCorp. not only is a novel development for the industry as a whole, but also represents a major move by the Deutsche Börse toward the independent clearing business model.

## Issues in Choosing the Right Business Model for Clearing and Settlement

As the alternative business models for clearing and settlement have begun to receive more attention, some concerns have developed over the benefits and costs of a captive clearinghouse structure vis-à-vis the more independent LCH-like structure. The "freedom to clear" debate has badly exacerbated these concerns (although perhaps without merit). Some of these specific issues are discussed next.

### Favoritism and Bias

A major concern expressed by many market participants in a world where outsourced clearing is becoming increasingly common is the fear that a CHO may be biased toward its dominant exchange customers. This concern is arguably greater for those CHOs that remain captive of one major exchange or group of exchanges but nevertheless provide outsourced clearing on a selective basis to outsiders. A captive CHO, for example, might be tempted to approve new contracts much faster for its primary exchange affiliate than for its outsourcing customers. This would seem to argue then for a fully independent clearinghouse solution.

Financial exchanges and CHOs were historically operated as mutual or membership organizations in which shareholders were also the major users. Under this structure, there really was no market for corporate control in which shareholders of an inefficiently operated exchange could be bought out by outside investors seeking to improve the exchange's bottom line. As a result, exchanges often introduced new products that failed within a few years of their listing, overinvested in infrastructure, and underinvested in strategic R&D.

A growing constituency of "upstairs" or off-exchange market participants that had little or no governance role in cooperative mutual exchange structures, moreover, began to express concerns of bias that the old mutual structures had given disproportionate control to smaller or more specialized members vis-à-vis members controlling large blocks of trading volume. The result over the past decade has been a dramatic increase in the abandonment of the mutual organizational structure for a share capital structure in which owners, trading participants, and management may well be three distinct groups. The trend was started with the demutualization of the Paris, Madrid, and Frankfurt stock exchanges in 1988, 1989, and 1991, respectively, and has been followed by nearly all securities and derivatives exchanges in North America and Europe, as well as a few in Asia and Latin America. (OM was actually founded as a private company in 1984 and thus remains the oldest significant nonmutual exchange structure.)

In some cases, demutualization has turned a pure membership cooperative into a closely held firm in which share ownership is distributed in a manner much like the original membership distribution. LCH, for example, is a limited liability company whose owners are its constituent futures exchanges and the members of LCH. In other cases, there is little or no overlap between owners of the exchange and its users. Clearing Bank Hannover, for example, is owned primarily by several German banks and provides clearing services for transactions in the German over-the-counter wholesale power market—a market in which the clearing bank's owners do not materially participate. In still other cases, demutualization has been accompanied by public listing of shares, as is the case with Deutsche Börse.

Perhaps the most important result of demutualization has been the shift in management focus away from *user satisfaction* toward *shareholder value*. Among other things, this has led to increased attention to new product viability, as well as a search by different organizations for where their comparative advantage truly lies.

To the extent that captive CHOs can reduce their costs and further exploit their comparative advantages in clearing and settlements by providing outsourced clearing to exchangelike organizations, demutualization provides a powerful reason *not* to worry about bias and favoritism. Quite simply, bias against certain customers is bad business that will quickly lead to very negative reputation effects for the CHO practicing such discrimination.

To the extent a CHO is providing clearing, settlement, and related services as a business, a failure to provide those services to *any* customer could raise serious questions about the integrity of the clearinghouse for *all* customers. Whether or not the CHO is captive or independent thus is secondary, provided the CHO is being operated as a commercial enterprise.

## Market Power

As the FIA and others maintain, the captive model can also give the owning exchange market power over trading participants when it comes to setting clearing and settlement fees. Interestingly, however, they do not support the independent model, either. Even under the independent model, every exchange-traded derivatives transaction is still cleared by only *one* CHO. What the FIA seems to support is a choice for traders across *multiple* clearinghouses.

Apart from the almost complete lack of evidence supporting the FIA's market power concerns, the operational risks and transaction costs of forcing CHOs to clear products by unaffiliated exchanges would be huge. Arguments about the captive model versus the independent model may have some merit, but proposals that would result in one product's being cleared at several CHOs are unlikely to garner much support.

## Loss-Sharing Rules Following a Default

A CHO that provides full central counterparty services not only acts as central counterparty for operational purposes, but also typically provides trade guarantees to cover the replacement cost of defaults by trading/clearing participants. In derivatives markets, the use of margin and periodic resettlement has long been the primary mechanism by which CHOs help ensure that funds are adequate to cover most reasonable default-related losses without tapping into some mutualized default fund or the equity of the CHO itself. As markets have horizontally integrated, "futures-style" margining is now increasingly being applied to cash market clearing, as well. OM uses futures-style margining for JIWAY equities, for example, as does LCH for the LSE equities that it clears.

Should the margin on deposit by a clearing participant be inadequate to cover losses arising from the failure of that firm to meet its clearing obligations, a CHO must maintain access to additional funds to cover those losses. Such default funds often include a mixture of mutualized pay-ins or guarantees provided by other clearing participants, external insurance and guarantees, internally allocated CHO funds, and, ultimately, the equity of the clearinghouse.

In a captive or dominant exchange-based clearing model, the funds available to cover default-related losses are generally provided by the same participants that use both the exchange and its clearinghouse. But as captive CHOs begin to provide clearing on an outsourced basis, the question of priority arises concerning the application of default funds. And for independent clearinghouses, avoiding cross-subsidies across different markets can pose an even greater challenge.

When a clearinghouse expands its clearing services into a new product market, the CHO must decide how to apportion losses arising from potential defaults on the new product market. Default funds across the old and new markets may, of course, be segregated by market. Because this eliminates most of the efficiency gains of horizontal integration across clearing products, however, segregation is generally eschewed for handling new clearing markets in favor of integrating the new market into an existing albeit larger common default fund. But this creates a potential cross-subsidy problem for the old clearing members, especially when the risks of the new market are large relative to the old ones.

One solution to this problem that does not have the inefficiencies of outright segregated default funds is for each clearing member's required deposit to a mutualized default fund to be based on the risk of the markets that member clears. In the event of a loss, *all* funds are still available to cover losses arising in *any* market, but at least the *ex ante* funding of the default cushion is based on the marginal risk of any new markets cleared. This is the approach taken by LCH.

More recently, LCH has taken an additional step to help ensure the ongoing integrity of its default funds, even in the face of expansions into new markets. Namely, LCH recently instituted a change that *directly* ties the level of its default fund to a highly conservative "stress testing" model. LCH has in place strict internal policies that allow the clearinghouse to call for additional contributions to the default fund from LCH members if the fund ever falls below the amount required to cover the default of its largest participant plus some "collateral damage" (i.e., the failure of a few smaller firms at the same time) during a severe market stress scenario. In this manner, regardless of how LCH expands into new markets, the adequacy of the default fund will be driven by the stress testing model.

Unlike LCH, OM's clearing and settlement functions are primarily captive to OM's exchanges and markets—primarily the Stockholmsbörsen; the OM London Exchange (OMLX), including JIWAY; and a few others. OM also engages in outsourced clearing and settlement services. In addition to the examples already given, OM also acts as a provider of technical solutions for central clearing and settlement services (e.g., Athens Stock Exchange, BOTCC, Hong Kong Exchanges and Clearing, Korea Futures Exchange, Nord Pool, SFE Corporation, and Vienna Stock Exchange). For the exchanges that OM actually guarantees, OM uses a model to determine the size and adequacy of its clearing funds and to help evaluate its market expansion decisions. Based on its RIVA/OMSII margining algorithm, OM has developed a model called "Riva Capital-at-Risk" or RCaR, a capital-at-risk calculation that resembles risk-adjusted return on capital (RAROC). Incorporating both market and credit risk, RCaR helps OM's management judge the adequacy of its default funds *and* the risks of assuming a new clearing business *ex ante*.

The innovations of LCH and OM in explicitly linking clearing risk and the capital structure of the CHOs is not only prudent and novel, but highly likely to become de rigueur in an increasingly horizontally integrated market. Note, however, that the successful implementation of such models by both an independent and a captive CHO suggests again that independence itself may not be the deciding factor in how the CHO operates.

### Prudential Risk Management

Although the provision of trade guarantees is a critical function played by the CHO in most markets, it is not strictly necessary for default guarantees to be provided by the same organization that provides clearance and settlement services on a purely operational basis. Settlement organizations that perform mainly delivery versus payment (DVP) services, for example, usually do not act as CCP for the markets they settle and thus do not provide trade guarantees. Euroclear's settlement services, for instance, are essentially purely DVP, with any performance guarantees provided by settlement banks.

When the CHO does not bear the cost of a default by a participant to which it has "leased" clearing and settlement services, some contend that the CHO's incentives to engage in prudential risk management are attenuated. The Danish derivatives clearinghouse Futop—a part of the Copenhagen Stock Exchange—has outsourced, for example, most of its clearing services to Stockholmsbörsen (part of OM), but not the trade guarantee. Because market participants considered risk management at Futop to be so closely related to the provision of trade guarantees, risk management responsibilities were retained by Futop along with the trade guarantee.

Even if a CHO does not have its own funds at risk in a default situation, the reputation of the CHO is still very much at risk if the CHO has defined part of its mandate to be the provision of risk management services. Thanks to demutualization, the highly negative commercial consequences of a risk management failure should provide more than adequate incentive to the CHO to be as unbiased as possible in functioning as an outsourced risk man-

ager. Again, the independence of the CHO does not appear to make much of
a difference.

### Diversification versus Concentration

The optimal degree of consolidation across clearinghouse structures within
any one country or across national borders is hotly contested. On the one
hand, brokers and other users of trading and clearing organizations argue ve-
hemently that further consolidations in clearing are not only beneficial but inevitable, given the need for market participants to reduce their expenditures
on maintaining multiple exchange and CHO relations, reduce their costs of
margining and credit risk management, and the like. And indeed, provided
the CHO has adequate risk management processes and capital backing to
guarantee performance on the transactions it attracts, the well-known benefits of routing more order flow through a multilateral netting scheme should,
in principle, lead to a more stable financial system.

On the other hand, if the CHO becomes so large that it guarantees virtually all of the transactions in a region, the result is a concentration of credit
risk of *all* market participants to that CHO. If the CHO lacks the risk management processes or depth of capital backing to deliver on its guarantee, the
net result is a riskier and more fragile financial architecture. This is essentially
the concern expressed originally for foreign exchange clearing by the Bank for
International Settlements (BIS) in 1990.

Now often generalized to *all* multilateral clearinghouses, the "Lam-
falussy standards" set forth in the 1990 BIS report create very specific requirements for cross-border netting and clearing schemes to receive central
bank approval, both in the host country where such a clearinghouse might
be domiciled as well as by international banking regulators approving
memberships by organizations under their jurisdiction in such a "super
clearinghouse." The fundamental concern of regulators is that the more
transactions are guaranteed by a single market clearing participant, the
more risk that the failure of that participant would create a catastrophic
systemic meltdown due to the concentration of credit risk in that entity.
Consolidation thus has both benefits *and* risks, and it is unclear where the
resulting optimum lies.

Proponents of larger and more comprehensive product coverage in a single CHO tend to favor the independent CHO model, mainly because an independent CHO is not as constrained in the products it can clear. A captive
CHO, by contrast, can only offer expanded product coverage first through
the expansion of the exchange and trading side of the market. To the extent
that captive CHOs and exchanges can achieve greater horizontal integration
in clearing without full consolidation, however, independence becomes less
important. If most of the benefits of consolidation can be achieved, for exam-

ple, through nonconsolidation measures like common banking or cross-product netting agreements, then the captive and independent models appear to be on close to equal footing.

## REVISITING THE DISTINCTIONS BETWEEN OTC AND EXCHANGE-TRADED DERIVATIVES

As noted earlier in this chapter, the distinctions between OTC and exchange-traded derivatives *product* worlds have eroded over the past several decades. But as should now be obvious, the *market structures* are significantly different. A major implication of these differences concerns the management by derivatives users of the credit risk they bear.

Exchange-traded derivatives seek to make derivatives trading anonymous by replacing counterparty credit risk with credit risk to the CCP. As long as the CCP makes good on its guarantees, the identity of the counterparty with whom you initially contracted does not matter from a credit standpoint. The CCP, in turn, bears *all* the credit risk in a given product market. This explains why such conservative measures as twice-daily marking to market and a generally conservative margining system are so important in exchange-traded derivatives. Apart from the time-tested margin and pay/collect system, CHOs also frequently take additional steps to control their own credit exposures to possible participant defaults. Some of these measures include maintaining a default fund to cover losses in excess of margin on deposit, acquiring synthetic capital or insurance to top up that default fund, engaging in regular prudential stress tests of the default fund, and enforcing minimum financial (including capital) requirements.

Now consider the almost complete absence of central clearing and settlement in OTC derivatives. That does not mean, however, that OTC derivatives are rife with credit risk. On the contrary, OTC derivatives dealers and users alike manage their counterparty risk using several other methods.

Closeout netting intended to prevent "cherry picking," for example, limits the amount at risk in the event of an insolvency. Similarly, the credit exposure of an OTC transaction can also be reduced through contractual requirements for periodic cash resettlement. By marking assets to their current replacement costs at regular intervals, a nondefaulting firm can never lose more than the *change* in the replacement cost of the contract since the last mark-to-market date.

Early termination and acceleration triggers are further examples of exposure management in OTC derivatives. Price triggers in derivatives, for example, allow the transaction to be terminated if the underlying asset price rises and/or falls by a specified amount. This guarantees that either party can get out of the transaction if it reaches a maximum tolerable credit exposure. Call and put provisions in bonds can serve a similar purpose.

Early termination and acceleration triggers can also be linked directly to indicators of credit quality. Some contracts terminate automatically, for example, in the event of a credit rating downgrade by one of the parties. Similarly, "cross-default" provisions in derivatives commonly allow for early termination by a firm if its counterparty misses a single required payment on *any* of its obligations with the firm. In some cases, cross-default provisions even allow a firm to terminate a derivatives contract early if its counterparty defaults on *any* obligation *to any firm*.

## SETTLEMENT LAGS

One major reason for learning the settlement details in derivatives is to manage the inevitable delays that the settlement process can introduce. In virtually all derivatives transactions involving a funds or asset transfer, the transaction chain is not instantaneous, and these delays need to be addressed.

Three calendar dates are of interest for a typical forward contract: trade, value, and settlement. The trade date $t$ is the date on which two parties agree to the terms of the future exchange of funds for funds or funds for assets. The value date is the date on which the net present value of the contract is realized. And the settlement date is the date on which the funds and/or assets to be transferred pursuant to the contract achieve finality and irrevocability.

Consider, for example, a forward contract on a commodity such as wheat whose terminal payoff to the long is as we saw earlier:

$$z_T = Z(S_T - f_{t,T})$$

The trade date for this transaction—date $t$—is the date on which the terms of the transaction are defined, such as the amount of the commodity $Z$ underlying the contract, the exact time and location for delivery, minimum quality requirements for what is deliverable, and so forth. The fixed purchase price $f_{t,T}$ is also set on date $t$.

The value date for this forward—date $T$—is the date on which the contract matures and the settlement process is initiated. *Assuming no credit risk*, this is also the date on which the value of the contract to the long and short are known. As the above equation shows, this value depends on the time $T$ realization of the price of the underlying asset, $S_T$. On any date prior to $T$ this spot price is still unknown, thus making the final value of the contract unknown.

Finally, the settlement date is the date on which cash and the underlying commodity change hands. This particular wheat forward might allow the short two days after maturity to deliver the required wheat, so that settlement would occur at $T + 2$.[10] As long as the short eventually delivers, this settlement lag is generally not presumed to affect the value of the contract because the long has "effective ownership" of the asset as of date $T$. In other words, the long can resell the wheat at $S_T$ and *also* take two days to deliver it, thus allowing the long to lock in $S_T$ before actually taking ownership of the wheat.[11]

To take another example, consider a cash-settled equity option contract negotiated on date $t$ with a maturity date of $T$. The value date is either the date of any early exercise (denoted $E$) or the maturity date $T$. Because settlement occurs in funds, it depends on the LVTS in which the option is being redeemed. If both buyer and seller are in the United States, for example, $T + 1$ settlement is likely, and same-day settlement on $T$ is even a possibility.

Now consider an otherwise identical option on equity that is settled in equity shares. In this case, the trade date is $t$, the value date is the early exercise date $E$ or expiration date $T$, and the settlement date is either $E + 3$ or $T + 3$. This is because the settlement lag to clear and finally settle U.S. equities is currently three days.

An important concept that will recur several times in book text is the notion of a *settled-in-arrears* transaction. A contract that is settled in arrears has the unusual feature that the value date precedes the settlement date by more than the amount of time in the settlement window. A certificate of deposit, for example, is settled in arrears. For a CD with a face value of $100 and an interest rate of 5 percent per annum that matures in 180 days, you would deposit $100 on trade date $t$. On that date, you already know that in 180 days your CD will allow you to withdraw $102.50. The value date thus is the same as the trade date, and the settlement date follows both by six months.

## NOTES

1. Sometimes matching and confirmation are part of clearing.
2. Most of this section is based on Culp and Neves (1999).
3. The distinctions between payment and contract position netting are discussed in Hanley, McCann, and Moser (1995).
4. In some commodity derivatives, the counterparties themselves act as settlement agents.
5. This section is based on Culp and Neves (1999) and Culp (2001).
6. This rather difficult terminology is explained in more detail and illustrated in Blommenstein and Summers (1994).
7. Even if the banks have different correspondent banks, the two correspondent banks can settle with one another using any of the available interbank funds transfer options.

8. Corresponding retail transfer systems like automated clearinghouses exist for small transactions.
9. This section is based on Culp (2002b).
10. Some derivatives incorporate the settlement lag into the maturity date, so that in this example settlements would be initiated on date $T - 2$ and date $T$ would be the value and settlement date. We will not assume this occurs in this book.
11. Mechanically this is a bit oversimplified, but it will suffice for our purposes here.

# PART TWO

# Derivatives Valuation and Asset Lending

# CHAPTER 7

# Principles of Derivatives Valuation

The price of any financial contract is the expected discounted present value of the future payoff on that contract and can be written most generally as

$$p_t = E_t(m_T z_T)$$

where $z_T$ is the payoff on the contract and $m_T$ is the factor used to discount that payoff back to the present. "Valuation" is the process by which we compute the price of a capital asset in this manner.

In this chapter, we will explore the fundamental principles of derivatives valuation. The approach we will take here is quite general and is equally relevant for all types of derivatives—both forwardlike and optionlike, and both OTC and exchange-traded. But before we get into the meat, let us consider briefly what the phrase *derivatives valuation* actually means—a question with an answer not as obvious as it might first appear.

## AT-MARKET VERSUS OFF-MARKET DERIVATIVES AND "DERIVATIVES VALUATION"

The phrases d*erivatives pricing* and *derivatives valuation* can be very confusing and misleading, especially when interpreted in the broader context of financial asset pricing more generally (e.g., as applied to stocks and bonds). The reason

---

This chapter is based heavily on Cochrane and Culp (2003). Cochrane is completely innocent of any errors or omissions that have crept into this version, which has been stylized to conform to this book.

is that what we are pricing depends on the type of transaction in question. With most assets, when we engage in "asset pricing" that means we are looking for the discounted expected payoff of the contract. Not so with all types of derivatives.

Derivatives transactions are said to be either "at-market" or "off-market." By market convention, an at-market derivatives transaction is defined as any derivatives contract that has a *true price of zero* on its trade date. At-market derivatives are easy to spot because they involve no initial cash payment from the long to the short or vice versa.[1] Examples include traditional forwards and futures contracts and many types of swaps. Off-market derivatives, by contrast, do involve an initial payment by one counterparty to the other of an amount equal to the price of the contract—its expected discounted payoff. Off-market derivatives include options, prepaid forwards, and certain traditional forwards and swaps that are deliberately negotiated "off" the current market price.

In general, "asset pricing" is all about solving for discounted expected payoff to get a price. For at-market derivatives, however, the task of "pricing" is instead the task of solving for the fixed rate or price that equates the discounted expected payoff *to zero*. Consider a forward purchase contract that requires the short to deliver one unit of some asset on date $T$ (then worth $S_T$ per unit) in exchange for receiving a cash payment on date $T$ of $f_{t,T}$ per unit. The terminal payoff to the long in the forward thus is

$$\pi_T^1 = (S_T - f_{t,T})$$

If this forward contract is at-market, then "pricing the forward" does not have much substance or meaning. By convention, the price of this at-market forward, like all other at-market derivatives, is zero; that is,

$$E_t[m_T(S_T - f_{t,T})] = 0$$

We thus *already know the price* on trade date $t$. What we *don't* know on trade date $t$ is the fixed purchase price $f_{t,T}$ that equates the initial expected discounted payoff to zero. In this context, the phrase "derivatives pricing" thus very misleadingly refers to the determination of the fixed purchase price $f_{t,T}$ that equates the discounted expected payoff to zero.

The same basic principle applies to any at-market derivatives transaction. Consider, for example, a plain-vanilla interest rate swap in which the "long" makes a fixed payment of $K$ and receives a variable payment of $R_j$ on every date $j = t + 1, \ldots, N$, where both $K$ and $R$ are computed as a fraction (appropriately compounded) of some fixed notional principal amount. If the swap is at-market so that its true initial price is zero, "pricing the swap" means finding the fixed rate $K$ that satisfies

$$\sum_{j=t+1}^{N} E_t\Big[m_j(R_j - K)\Big] = 0$$

Some derivatives contracts are off-market by design. Examples include options and prepaid forwards. Options are off-market because the short is assuming a potentially unlimited liability in exchange for a single fixed premium payment, and the long is making that payment in exchange for a *limited-liability* transaction from her perspective. So, the initial cash flow from the short to the long represents the payment of a premium equal to the expected discounted payoff on the option. A European call option, for example, has an initial price of

$$c_t = E_t(m_T c_T) = E_t\{m_T[\max(0, S_T - K)]\}$$

where the fixed strike price $K$ is predefined and we are left to solve for the true price $c_t$.

Still other derivatives are *normally* at-market but can be customized into off-market deals if the counterparties have a reason for doing so. Suppose, for example, that a firm has outstanding debt with a 6 percent annual coupon and wants to use derivatives to swap that fixed-rate liability into a floating-rate liability. It may well be the case that at the time of the deal, the swap rate that prices an at-market swap to zero is not precisely 6 percent. The firm could still do the at-market swap, receiving whatever the current fixed rate on an at-market swap is. Or the firm could choose to do an off-market swap with a prespecified fixed rate of exactly 6 percent to match the fixed rate on the debt. In this case, the net present value (NPV) of the swap is not zero, and the party perceiving the deal to have a negative net present value at a fixed rate of 6 percent will demand a payment equal to the true NPV of the swap.

The net present value of an off-market derivatives transaction *plus the initial cash flow* will, of course, be zero so that you are indifferent to the two transactions in a present value sense. Suppose the current market fixed swap rate is $K^*$, so that

$$\sum_{j=t+1}^{N} E_t\Big[m_j(R_j - K^*)\Big] = 0$$

Now consider an off-market swap rate $K' < K^*$. The true price of the swap with fixed rate $K'$ will be

$$p_t = \sum_{j=t+1}^{N} E_t\Big[m_j(R_j - K')\Big]$$

which is positive from the standpoint of the fixed-rate payer. In order for the floating-rate payer to agree to the deal, she will demand an initial cash payment of $p_t$. From the perspective of the fixed-rate payer, the expected discounted present value of the off-market swap *plus the initial cash payment* is just

$$\sum_{j=t+1}^{N} E_t\Big[m_j(R_j - K')\Big] - p_t = 0$$

Similarly, from the perspective of the floating-rate payer,

$$\sum_{j=t+1}^{N} E_t\Big[m_j(K' - R_j)\Big] + p_t = 0$$

So, both parties are indifferent to the at-market or off-market swap in a present value sense. Why do them then? One obvious reason is that the timing of cash flows is different, and this can matter to some firms (Culp, 2001, 2002a).

Our purpose here, however, is merely to be clear about what we are doing when we say we are applying the principles of "asset pricing" to derivatives. For at-market derivatives, "pricing" means finding the fixed rate or price specified in the contract on the trade date that equates the true initial price of the contract to zero. For off-market derivatives, "pricing" requires actually computing the expected discounted payoff of the contract as of the trade date for a *given* fixed rate or price.

## ABSOLUTE VERSUS RELATIVE PRICING

The mechanics of pricing at-market and off-market derivatives may be different, but the hard work and the fundamental principles of finance come into play in the two approaches in the same way. Namely, the name of the game is defining the discount factor $m$ that we use to discount the payoff inside the expectation. Once we have defined $m$, we either solve a known payoff function for its expected discounted present value (i.e., true price) or we set the expected discounted present value of an unknown payoff function equal to zero and solve for the unknown. The discounting is the holy grail.

There are two fundamental and polar approaches to applying the central idea that price is discounted expected payoff: *absolute* and *relative* asset pricing. In *absolute* pricing, we value a bundle of cash flows (dividends, coupons and principle, option payoffs, firm profits, etc.) based on its exposure to fundamental sources of macroeconomic risk. Equivalently, we find a discount factor by thinking about what macroeconomic states are of particular concern to investors. The Capital Asset Pricing Model (CAPM) is a paradigm example of this approach. Virtually all such models are based on some notion of general equilibrium in order to use aggregate rather than individual risks, or to substitute an easily measured index such as the market return (in the case of CAPM) for poorly measured consumption. They are therefore often called equilibrium asset-pricing models.

In *relative* pricing, by contrast, we ask what we can learn about one asset's value given the prices of some other assets. We do not ask from where the prices of the other assets came, and we use as little information about macroeconomic risk factors as possible. Instead, we use these other prices to "replicate" the cash flows of the asset to be priced. Buying the target asset and selling the replicating portfolio is, in principle, riskless, so we can value the target asset by riskless discounting of the *net* payoffs of the target asset and hedge portfolio. Modigliani and Miller (1958) pioneered this approach in valuing a firm given prices for its equity and debt, and Black and Scholes (1973) famously used this approach to value options and corporate liabilities given stock and bond prices.

Absolute pricing offers generality—it can be applied to anything—at the cost of precision in many applications. Relative pricing offers simplicity and tractability—it can be done easily, at least to a first approximation—at the cost of often limited practical applicability.[2] Most good applications do not use one extreme or the other, but rather a blend of absolute and relative approaches appropriate for the problem at hand. Even the most die-hard applications of the CAPM, for example, usually take the market risk premium as given. Conversely, most realistic option pricing exercises implicitly use some absolute pricing model to characterize pesky "market prices of risk" that cannot be perfectly hedged.

Chapter 8 deals with the dominant relative pricing model for forwards and forwardlike derivatives. For the remainder of this chapter, we will focus instead on *absolute* or *equilibrium* pricing models. Although we ultimately want to see how these work for pricing derivatives, we need to begin first with some more general background on the pricing of capital assets in the most general terms possible.

## ECONOMIC INTUITION FOR VALUING UNCERTAIN CASH FLOW STREAMS

The basic objective of asset pricing is to determine the value of any stream of uncertain cash flows. Consider an asset with a single cash flow or payoff $z_{t+1}$ at time $t + 1$. (This payoff can be the price at $t + 1$ plus any dividend, so we have not abandoned the real world.) We find the value of this payoff by asking what the stream is worth to an investor.[3] The answer is:

$$p_t = E_t\left[\xi \frac{u_c(c_{t+1})}{u_c(c_t)} z_{t+1}\right] \tag{7.1}$$

where $\xi$ is the investor's pure rate of time preference, $E_t[\cdot]$ denotes an expected value conditional on information available at time $t$, and $u_c(c_t)$ is the benefit to the investor of a small additional unit of consumption received at time period $t$ (i.e., the "marginal utility" of time $t$ consumption).

This is the basic equation underlying all of asset pricing—the fundamental value equation (FVE)—so it is worth understanding carefully. (A mathematical derivation appears in Appendix 2.) Investors do not value money directly. The theory adopts a more sophisticated approach and recognizes that the pleasure or "utility" of the consumption that money can buy is what really matters. That is why $u_c$ and $\xi$ enter equation (7.1). Specifically, people value money more if it comes sooner, and if it comes in bad times when they really need it rather than good times when they are already doing well. A $\xi$ slightly less than one and a marginal utility function $u_c$ that declines as $c$ increases capture these important considerations. If the economist's "utility function" sounds strange, just think of $u_c(c_t)$ as an index of " bad times," or a measure of how painful it is to give up a dollar at date $t$.

Equation (7.1) then describes the investor's optimal portfolio decision as marginal cost of investment equals marginal benefit. The true cost of an extra dollar invested is the price of the asset $p_t$ (how many dollars the investor had to give up) times the value of a dollar (utility cost to the investor) $u_c(c_t)$ at time $t$. The true benefit is the expectation $E_t$ of the dollar payoff $z_{t+1}$ times the value of a dollar $u_c(c_{t+1})$ at time $t + 1$, times $\xi$, which discounts future value (utility) back to time $t$.

The logic of equation (7.1) is often confused. Equation (7.1) is usually used to describe a market "in equilibrium," *after* the investor has reached his or her optimum portfolio. But to get to that optimum, the investor had to know the price $p_t$. What's going on? In watching a market in equilibrium, we are like scientists, watching over the market in white lab coats and trying to understand what it does. Equation (7.1) holds once the investor has found the optimal portfolio, but it does not describe causes on the right and effects on the left. If we observe consumption and payoff, we can use this equation to determine what the price must be. If we observe consumption and prices (a common case), we can use the equation to learn what the expected payoff (e.g., expected return in the case of stocks) must be. If we observe price, consumption, and payoff (the entire distribution of payoffs, mind you, not just how it happened to come out a few times), then we can use equation (7.1) to decide that the world really does make sense after all.

We can also use equation (7.1) to think the value of payoff $z_{t+1}$ to an investor who has *not* yet bought any—that is, who has not found the optimum portfolio or when the market is "out of equilibrium." This interpretation is especially important in thinking about the potential value of securities that have not been created or are not traded or in giving portfolio advice. Now the value $p_t$ need not correspond to the market price (there might not be one), and the investor need not know what the price is. Still, we can compute the value of a *small incremental investment* in this uncertain cash flow to *this particular investor* by equation (7.1). If there is a market price, and the value to the investor is greater than that price, we can recommend a buy. Similarly, we can compare our private valuation with market prices of derivatives to evaluate the desirability and cost of various hedging opportunities.[4]

## THE FUNDAMENTAL VALUE EQUATION

We commonly split the fundamental value equation (7.1) into two parts, one that expresses price as an expected discounted payoff

$$p_t = E_t[m_{t+1} \, z_{t+1}] \tag{7.2}$$

and one that relates the stochastic discount factor $m_{t+1}$ to the *intertemporal marginal rate of substitution* (IMRS), the rate at which the investor is willing to substitute one unit of consumption now for one unit of consumption later:

$$m_{t+1} = \xi \frac{u_c(c_{t+1})}{u_c(c_t)} \tag{7.3}$$

The term $m_{t+1}$ is called a *stochastic discount factor* by analogy with simple present value rules. We are used to discounting a payoff by some discount factor or required gross rate of return $R$—if $z_{t+1}$ is known:

$$p_t = \frac{1}{R} z_{t+1}$$

The term $m_{t+1}$ acts exactly as such a discount factor in equation (7.2). The discount factor $m_{t+1}$ is *stochastic* because nobody at time $t$ knows what consumption will be at time $t + 1$ (whether $t + 1$ will be a good or bad time), and hence nobody knows what $u_c(c_{t+1})$ will turn out to be. It is random, in the same way stock returns are random.

This randomness of the discount factor is crucial. As the index of good and bad times, the stochastic discount factor is high if time $t + 1$ turns out to be a bad time (i.e., consumption is low). Assets that pay off well in bad times are particularly valuable, and equation (7.2) will give them an appropriately high price.

In finance, we commonly do not think too much about consumption and utility functions. The stochastic discount factor remains an index of bad times (strictly speaking, *growth* in bad times). Finance theorists tend to think directly about discount factor models in which data such as the market return are used as indicators of bad versus good times.

## The Fundamental Valuation Equation in Different Guises

The stochastic discount factor representation of the fundamental value equation in (7.2) can be expressed in a number of different and equivalent ways, depending on the nature of the particular financial problem being solved and the history and traditions of different fields. (As usual, unification came after the fact.)

If we use required returns to value a project or compute a capital budget, we typically use a different, risk-adjusted required return for each project. The beauty of equation (7.1) or (7.2) is that the *same* discount factor can be used for *all* assets, simply by putting it inside the expectation—$m$ is a *universal* discount factor. Capital budgeting thus can be undertaken using (7.2) directly. For a project that costs $I_t$ in initial investment and generates $X_{t+1}$ in revenue at time $t + 1$, the usual net present value criterion tells us to undertake the investment if its value is greater than its cost,

$$E_t[m_{t+1} X_{t+1}] \geq I_t$$

In applications to stocks and portfolios, it is often convenient to think about rates of return rather than prices. To do so, we divide both sides of (7.2) by $p_t$ (or recognize that a return is a payoff with price equal to one):

$$1 = E_t[m_{t+1} R_{t+1}] \tag{7.4}$$

where $R_{t+1}$ is the gross return on the asset ($z_{t+1}$ divided by $p_t$). Thus, simply use "return" for the payoff $z$ and one for price to apply the equation to stocks and portfolio problems. Similarly, if we want to work with returns in excess of the risk-free rate $R_t^e = R_{t+1} - R^f$ then (7.4) becomes[5]

$$0 = E_t[m_{t+1} R_{t+1}^e] \qquad (7.4)'$$

In equity analysis, we have gotten used to a slight transformation of equation (7.4)'. Using an $i$ superscript to remind us that there are many assets, writing out the definition of covariance $E(mr^i) = E(m)E(r^i) + \text{cov}(m,r^i)$ and the definition of a regression coefficient $\beta_i = \text{cov}(m,r^i)/\text{var}(m)$ and then defining $\lambda = -\text{var}(m)/E(m)$, we can write (7.4)' in classic form as

$$E_t(r^i) = \beta_i \lambda \qquad (7.4)''$$

The expected excess return of each asset should be proportional to its beta. (Note that we use a capital $R$ to represent gross return and a small $r$ to represent net return, such that $R = 1 + r$.)

This is not the CAPM—it is *perfectly general*. The beta here is calculated relative to the discount factor, not the market return. All the assumptions of the CAPM (or other models) come in substituting the market portfolio return or some other index for the discount factor.

As we saw at the beginning of the chapter, to determine the fixed price in an at-market forward purchase contract, we look for the fixed price that equates the initial expected discounted present value of the payoff to zero:[6]

$$E_t[m_{t+1}(S_{t+1} - f_{t,T})] = 0 \Rightarrow f_{t,T} = E_t[S_{t+1}] + \text{cov}_t(m_{t+1},S_{t+1})R^f$$

In other words, the forward price is the expected future spot price of the asset to be purchased at time $t + 1$ plus a term that reflects how the discount factor covaries with the underlying spot price—as we shall see later, a "systematic risk premium." The second term is grossed up by the risk-free rate to reflect the fact that the terms of the contract are set at time $t$ but the contract is settled at time $t + 1$.

In option pricing and fixed income applications, the discount factor $m_{t+1}$ is often used to define a set of "risk-neutral probabilities." Equation (7.2) is written simply as

$$p_t = \frac{1}{R^f} E_t^*[z_{t+1}]$$

where the * reminds us to take the expectation with an artificial set of probabilities that are scaled by $m_{t+1}$. Either we can use the discount factor to make good payments in bad states more important in determining the price, or we can boost up the probabilities of those states to the same effect. Risk aversion is the same thing as overestimating the probability of bad events.

All these formulations are just different ways of writing the same thing. Continuous-time asset pricing models also all reduce to the analogue to equation (7.2) in continuous time.[7]

## UNDERSTANDING SYSTEMATIC RISK

Asset pricing is about risk and reward. Identifying risks and assessing the premium one earns for bearing risks are the central questions for asset pricing, and the point of theory is to provide necessary quantitative tools to answer these questions. Risk managers tend to classify risk as market, credit, liquidity, operational, or legal risk. Portfolio managers tend to think of market risk and the risks associated with certain styles such as size, value, and growth, as well as risks associated with industry and country portfolios.

Financial economists tend instead to distinguish between "systematic" and "idiosyncratic" risk. And of course, not all risk is bad—you earn a premium over risk-free interest rates only by taking on some risk! What risks should we pay attention to? And how are these concepts related?

### Systematic versus Idiosyncratic Risk

A central and classic idea in asset pricing is that only systematic risk generates a premium. Idiosyncratic risks are "not priced," meaning that you earn no more than the interest rate for holding them. That is why we employ risk managers to get rid of idiosyncratic risks.[8] Plausible, but a theory proves its worth by helping us to understand what "systematic" and "idiosyncratic" mean in this context.

By using the definition of covariance $E(mz) = E(m)E(z) + \text{cov}(m,z)$ we can rewrite the fundamental value equation (7.2) as

$$p_t = \frac{E_t[z_{t+1}]}{R^f} + \text{cov}(m_{t+1}, z_{t+1}) \qquad (7.5)$$

This equation says that asset prices are equal to the expected cash flow discounted at the risk-free rate, plus a risk premium. The risk premium depends on the *covariance* of the payoff with the discount factor. This covariance is typically a negative number, so most assets have a lower price than otherwise (or a higher average return) as compensation for risk.

Here's why. Recall that the discount factor is an indicator of *bad* times. Most assets pay off well in *good* times. Thus, most asset returns and payoffs covary negatively with the discount factor. The converse case drives home the intuition. Insurance is a terrible investment. The average return is negative—you pay more in premiums than what you receive, on average, in settlements. Yet people willingly buy insurance. Why? Because insurance pays off well in bad times—just as the house stops smoldering, here comes a check in the mail. The value of insurance is *higher* than predicted by the standard present value formula, because the covariance term is *positive*. Financial assets are "anti-insurance," and it is this feature—and *only* this feature—that generates a risk premium and allows risky assets to pay more than the interest rate.

Equation (7.5) has a dramatic implication: A risk may be very large in the sense of having a high *variance*, but if it is uncorrelated with the discount factor, its *covariance* is zero, and it generates no premium. Its price is just the expected payoff discounted at the risk-free rate. *The volatility of the asset's cash flow per se is completely irrelevant to its risk premium.*

To see why a little more carefully, consider an investor who adds a small fraction $\psi$ of the asset to her portfolio. Her consumption at time $t + 1$ is now $c_{t+1} + \psi z_{t+1}$. As always, the investor cares about the variance of consumption and the variance of the utility that consumption generates, not any characteristics of single assets that, in a portfolio, determine the wealth from which she draws consumption. For a small asset purchase, the variance of the investor's new time $t + 1$ consumption is:

$$\mathrm{Var}(c_{t+1}) + 2\psi\mathrm{cov}(c_{t+1}, z_{t+1}) + \psi^2\mathrm{var}(z_{t+1})$$

The covariance with consumption, and hence with marginal utility $m$, enters with a coefficient $\psi$, while the variance is a second-order effect. For a small (marginal) investment $\psi$, the covariance of the cash flows on the asset with consumption is much more important to how buying the asset affects consumption—what investors care about in the end—than does the volatility of the asset's cash flows.

Now we can really understand and precisely define "systematic" versus "idiosyncratic" risk. *The systematic part of any risk is that part that is perfectly correlated with the discount factor.* It is the part that generates a risk premium. The idiosyncratic part of any risk is that part that is uncorrelated with the discount factor. It generates no premium.

We can divide any payoff into systematic and idiosyncratic components by simply running a regression of the payoff on the discount factor:

$$z_{t+1} = \beta m_{t+1} + \varepsilon_{t+1} \tag{7.6}$$

Payoff = Systematic part + Idiosyncratic part

Regression residuals $\varepsilon_{t+1}$ are, by construction, uncorrelated with the right-hand variable.

Once again, this modern version of the theory is perfectly general. Systematic means correlated with the investor's marginal utility—*period*. This is true no matter what asset pricing model—no matter what specification of the discount factor—is correct. The CAPM, for example, is one special case of the general theory. It specifies that the discount factor is linearly related to the market return $m_{t+1} = a - br_{t+1}$ (more on this later). Hence, it defines systematic risk for every asset by regressions of returns on the market portfolio return.

In many portfolio management applications, "systematic" and "diversifiable" components are defined with multiple regressions on style portfolios, including size, book to market value, and industry groupings as well as the market portfolio. Implicitly, these definitions correspond to models that the discount factor is a function of these portfolio groupings. These specifications are fine, but they are special cases and they reflect lots of hidden assumptions. Other specifications may be useful.

### When Variance Does Matter

The proposition that variance does not matter for risk premiums does not mean you ought to ignore variance in setting up your portfolio. Again, equations (7.2) and (7.5) refer only to *marginal* valuations. That perspective is appropriate *after* the investor has already set up an optimal portfolio, or for deciding which asset to *start* buying. For very little portfolio changes, covariance matters more than variance.

For big asset purchases and sales of the sort one considers while setting up the optimal portfolio to begin with, however, variance can matter a lot. If an investor buys a big bit of a payoff, the variance *will* start to affect the properties of consumption, marginal utility, and hence the investor's discount factor. So, by all means *do* consider variance in making the big changes required to set up a portfolio!

## DIVERSIFICATION, HEDGING, AND SPECIAL INVESTORS

We often think of idiosyncratic risks as those risks that affect a particular security only, leaving all others untouched. Such idiosyncratic risks include firm-specific risks like operational and liquidity risk, as well as those components of market and credit risk that are unique to the firm in question. This is a good approximation in many cases, but understanding the correct definition we can quickly see how it is only an approximation.

A risk that moves many securities, but is uncorrelated with the discount factor, is also idiosyncratic. The market as a whole is built of individual securities, so each idiosyncratic risk is in fact a small part of the total risk. Many apparently firm-specific risks—a drop in sales, an accounting fiasco—also hit many other firms in the market, and thus *become* "market risks." We often call idiosyncratic risks "diversifiable" because they largely disappear in well-diversified portfolios. This, too, is a good approximation, but specific to the CAPM world that the market portfolio return captures the discount factor and thus defines systematic risk.

A good counterexample for all these cases is to think of an investor who must hold a large part of some risk. Consider, for example, the owner of a business who must hold a large amount of one company's stock. Risks correlated with the business or company stock will be systematic for this investor, albeit not necessarily for the market as a whole. The investor thus must require a premium to hold such risks, even though the market as a whole would not require such a premium. The CAPM is an appropriate cost of capital for investment decisions only if the investor holds the market portfolio, and thus his or her discount factor depends only on the market portfolio. For the vast majority of investors, this is not the case.

Although idiosyncratic risk does not generally matter for pricing, it is not necessarily easy to avoid it. Much of the art of risk management and corporate finance consists of just how to shed oneself of idiosyncratic or residual, nonpriced, risk. The fact that risk managers focus on market, credit, liquidity, operational, or legal risk rather than systematic versus unsystematic reflects the different techniques needed to hedge different varieties of idiosyncratic risk. Risk managers, however, need to understand the real distinction between systematic and idiosyncratic so that they do not hedge good risks, ones that bring rewards, as well.

There are a few circumstances, moreover, in which idiosyncratic risk *does* matter for asset pricing. Most of these circumstances involve some form of "market incompleteness," such as institutional restrictions on the portfolio decisions of certain special investors, the nonmarketability of financial claims, or the nonparticipation by some firms in financial markets. These sources of market incompleteness are frequently ignored for simplicity when pricing traditional securities, but they are often very important considerations in pricing futures, forwards, and swaps.

Specifically, following Keynes (1923), users of derivatives often worry about a "speculative risk premium" above and beyond the systematic risk premium. Often depicted as a kind of insurance payment by hedgers to their risk transfer counterparties, a speculative risk premium is essentially an additional risk premium for certain idiosyncratic risks. We return to this issue explicitly in Chapter 11. For the remainder of this chapter, we make the more traditional assumption that systematic risk is the only risk that matters to investors in the pricing of all assets, including derivatives.

## THE CAPM AND CCAPM

A critical question for practical application remains: What data do we use for the discount factor $m$? The search to populate $m$ with actual data has led to the many "named" asset pricing models. All of these models are just special cases of the fundamental value equation. They add additional structure, usually from simple general equilibrium modeling, to substitute some other variable for consumption in the discount factor or IMRS.

### The Consumption CAPM

Armed with our presentation of the theory so far, the simple obvious approach is to assume some reasonable utility function (power or quadratic forms are popular), use the easily available aggregate consumption data, and apply pricing formulas (7.2) or (7.5) directly. This is the famous approach of Lucas (1978) and Hansen and Singleton (1982).

A little less directly, but more popular in finance, we can linearly approximate the discount factor as a function of consumption:

$$m_{t+1} \approx a - \gamma \Delta c_{t+1}$$

where $\Delta c_{t+1}$ denotes consumption growth and $\gamma$ is a constant of proportionality.[9] This specification for the discount factor together with our fundamental value equation (7.2) is equivalent to the statement more popular in finance in terms of average returns and betas:

$$E(r^i) = r^f + \beta_{i,\Delta c} \lambda_{\Delta c} \tag{7.7}$$

where $E(r^i)$ denotes the average return on the $i^{\text{th}}$ asset, $\beta_{i,\Delta c}$ is the regression beta of the asset return on consumption growth, and $\lambda_{\Delta c}$ is a market risk premium. Equation (7.7) predicts that assets with higher consumption betas will have higher average returns, with the market risk premium as constant of proportionality. This is the form of Breeden's (1979) famous statement of the Consumption Capital Asset Pricing Model (CCAPM).

The basic idea is really natural. We need an indicator of bad and good times. If you really want to know how people feel, don't listen to them whine; watch where they go out to dinner. Consumption reveals everything we need to know about current wealth, future wealth, investment opportunities, and so on. Compared to many of the models discussed later, the CCAPM in all its simplicity avoids the theoretical problems associated with restrictive and unrealistic assumptions. (Historically, the CCAPM came last, in order to repair those problems.)

Although a complete answer to most absolute asset pricing questions in principle, this consumption-based approach does not (yet) work well in practice. As one might imagine from even a rudimentary experience with the data, running regressions of returns on the government's consumption growth numbers does not reveal much. Instead, financial economists use a wide variety of tricks of the trade that, while requiring heroic assumptions to derive them as perfect truth, nonetheless have great intuitive appeal and have performed well in a variety of applications. At heart, they all involve substituting or proxying some other variables for hard-to-measure consumption.

## The CAPM

The simplest and probably still the most popular model is the single-factor CAPM developed by Sharpe (1964) and Lintner (1965), and later extended by Black (1972). In the usual statement of the CAPM, the expected return of asset $j$ is higher as its beta is higher, with the expected return on the market portfolio as a constant of proportionality:

$$E(r^j) = r^f + \beta_j[E(r^m) - r^f] \tag{7.8}$$

where $r^j$ and $r^m$ denote one-period arithmetic returns on asset $j$ and the market, $r^f$ denotes the risk-free interest rate, and $\beta_j$ is the regression coefficient of the return on the market, or

$$\beta_j = \frac{\text{cov}(r^j, r^m)}{\text{var}(r^m)}$$

The CAPM is *mathematically identical* to a specification of the discount factor linear in the market return, rather than linear in consumption growth:

$$m_{t+1} = a - br^m_{t+1} \tag{7.9}$$

where $a$ and $b$ are free parameters that can be determined by the risk-free rate and market premium, which are taken as given values in equation (7.8). See equation (7.4″) to make the connection between (7.8) and a discount factor.

The CAPM was a huge empirical success for a generation. Categories of assets have now been identified, however, whose average returns bear no relation to betas calculated against traditional proxy indexes for the market portfolio. Efforts to find theoretically purer proxies for the market portfolio of world invested wealth (Roll, 1977) have not helped. In addition, the betas calculated against several new risk factors apart from the market have been empirically shown to help explain why some average returns are higher than others. Prominent examples include the "small firm" and "value" effects (Banz, 1981; Fama and French, 1993).

The CAPM discount factor model is a sensible approximation. When the market tanks, most people are unhappy! But it is clearly only an approximation. To derive the CAPM formally, you need to state assumptions under which a linear function of the market return is a *completely sufficient* indicator of good and bad times. The essence of the various formal derivations of the CAPM is to get every investor's consumption growth to depend only on the market return.[10]

The CAPM (and all following models) is not an *alternative* to the consumption-based model; it is a *special case*. Now, consumption surely goes down when the market return goes down, but, in the real world, other things matter as well. For the CAPM to hold, people cannot think that market fluctuations are temporary, and hence ignore a bad day and go out to dinner anyway. Instead, we must have returns that are independent over time. People cannot have jobs, houses, cars, businesses, or other sources of income that sustain them through market crashes, or these other things will start to matter to consumption and the discount factor. In addition, all investors in a CAPM world must hold the same portfolio of assets—the market portfolio.

Having seen how the sausage is made, we should be surprised, if anything, that the CAPM lasted as long as it did. We should not be surprised that it ultimately proved a first approximation.

## MULTIFACTOR MODELS

*Linear factor models* dominate empirical asset pricing in the post-CAPM world. Linear factor pricing models measure the discount factor (i.e., specify indexes of bad times) with a model of the form

$$m_{t+1} = \beta \frac{u_c(c_{t+1})}{u_c(c_t)} = a + b_1 f_{t+1}^1 + b_2 f_{t+1}^2 + \cdots + b_N f_{t+1}^N \qquad (7.10)$$

where $a, b_1, \ldots, b_N$ are free parameters and where $f^j$ is the $j$th "risk factor."

What exactly does one use for factors $f_{t+1}$? In general, factor models look for variables that are plausible proxies for aggregate consumption or marginal utility growth (measures of whether times are getting better or worse). This is just like the CAPM, with additional indicators of good and bad times.

## ICAPM

Merton's (1973) multifactor Intertemporal Capital Asset Pricing Model (ICAPM) was the first theoretical implementation of this idea. The ICAPM recognizes that investors care about the market return, so that is the first risk factor. The extra factors are innovations to "state variables" that describe an investor's consumption-portfolio decision. Other things being equal, investors prefer assets that pay off well when there is bad news that *future* returns will be lousy. Such assets provide insurance; they help to reduce the risk of long-term investments. Covariance with this kind of news thus will drive risk premiums as well as the market return.

In the traditional statement of the model, corresponding to the expected-return statement of the CAPM in (7.8),

$$E(r^j) - r^f = \gamma \operatorname{cov}(r^j, r^m) + \lambda_z \operatorname{cov}(r^j, \Delta z)$$

where $\gamma$ and $\lambda_z$ are constants (the same for all assets), $r^m$ denotes the market (wealth) return, and $\Delta z$ indicates the news or the return on a "factor-mimicking portfolio" of returns correlated with that news.[11] Technically, this model generalizes the CAPM assumption that the market return is independent over time.

Equivalently, for a given value of the market return, investors will feel poorer and will lower consumption if there is bad news about subsequent investment opportunities.[12] News about subsequent returns thus should drive our discount factor, as well as current market returns.

The ICAPM does not tell us the precise *identity* of the state variables, and, as a result, it is only after 30 years of theoretical fame that the ICAPM has received its first serious tests—tests that do not just cite it as inspiration for ad hoc multifactor models, but actually check whether the factors do forecast returns as the theory says they should (Ferson and Harvey, 1999). It is not yet common in applications.

One of the most popular current multifactor models is the Fama-French three-factor model (Fama and French, 1993, 1996). The Fama-French model includes the market portfolio, a portfolio of small minus big stocks (SMB), and a portfolio of high book/market minus low book/market stocks (HML). In expected return language, average returns on all assets are linearly related to their regression betas on these three portfolios. In discount factor language, the discount factor is a linear function of these three portfolios, as the CAPM discount factor is a linear function of the market return.

This model is popular because the betas on the additional factors *do* explain the variation of average returns across the size and book-to-market portfolios, and market betas do not. The model is not a tautology. Size and book-to-market sorted portfolios do not have to move together, and move more as their average returns rise. Size and book-to-market betas also explain the variation of average returns across additional portfolio sorts, beyond those that they were constructed to explain (Fama and French, 1996). This kind of more general good performance is the hallmark of an empirically useful model.

The open question for the Fama-French model is: "What are the additional sources of risk about which investors are *economically* concerned?" It is well and good to say that investors fear "value" risk uncorrelated with the market, but why? Put another way, the sales talk for value portfolios is that, since other investors are so afraid of this risk, you, the remaining mean-variance investor, should load up on the "value" portfolio that provides high reward for small market beta. Fine, but if the *average* investor is really scared of this value risk, maybe you should be, too. If value risk turns out to be risk of poor performance during a financial crisis, for example, are you sure you want to take that risk? To answer this question, we really need to understand what fundamental macroeconomic risks are behind the value effect, not just understand a set of mimicking portfolios that capture them for empirical work.

An empirical counterpart to this worry is that the Fama-French model found its limitations as well. Namely, average returns on "momentum" portfolios go in the *opposite* direction from that predicted by Fama-French betas (Fama and French, 1996). This can be cured by adding a fourth momentum factor, the return on a portfolio long recent winners and short recent losers. For all purposes except performance attribution (where it is exactly the right thing to do), however, this fix smells of such ad-hockery that nobody wants to take it seriously. We do not want to add a new factor for every anomaly. On the other hand, multifactor models used in many industry applications suffer no such compunction and proudly use 50 or 60 portfolios as factors, picked purely on the basis of in-sample empirical performance.

## Macroeconomic Multifactor Models

The alternative to finding essentially ad hoc portfolio factors that perform well for a given sample is to sit back and think about risk factors that make sense given the fundamental economic intuition. What variables are good indicators of bad versus good times for a large number of investors? The market return obviously still belongs. Following ICAPM intuition, variables that forecast future investment opportunities such as price-earnings ratios, the level of interest rates, and so on, make sense. Indicators of recessions may belong as well, such as proprietary and labor income, the value of housing or other nonmarketed assets, business investment, and so forth. The CAPM and ICAPM exclude these variables (i.e., they derive relations in which the discount factor is *only* a function of the market return and state variables) by presuming that investors have no jobs or other assets; they simply live off their portfolios of financial assets. Because investors *do* have jobs and other assets, bad times for these will spill over into market premiums.

With this intuition, a wide variety of asset pricing models have been used that tie average returns to macroeconomic risks. The grandfather of all of these is the Chen, Roll, and Ross (1986) multifactor model. They used interest rates, industrial production, inflation, and bond spreads to measure bad times in the discount factor. More recently, multifactor models have used macroeconomic risk factors such as labor income (Jagannathan and Wang, 1996) and investment growth (Cochrane, 1991a, 1996) to explain expected stock returns.

*Conditional* factor models in which factors at time $t + 1$ are scaled by information variables at time $t$ are also now increasingly popular ways to allow betas and factor risk premiums to vary over time—see Cochrane (1996) and Lettau and Ludvigson (2001).

All the special cases of the fundamental value equation that we have discussed so far impose the simplifying but very unrealistic assumption that markets are "complete"—that is, investors have insured or hedged away all personal risks, and the only risks that affect their IMRS are aggregate, marketwide, or economywide risks. This, too, is obviously an extreme simplification, so it is worth seeing if removing the simplification works. Duffie and Constantinides (1996), for example, investigate a model in which the *cross-sectional* dispersion of labor income growth matters. Given that the *overall* income is what it is, it is a "bad time" if there is a lot of cross-sectional risk— you might get very rich, but you might also get very poor.

In addition, researchers such as Pastor and Stambaugh (2001) are finally documenting the importance of liquidity. Once dismissed as an institutional friction that is assumed away in complete markets, it seems that assets paying off poorly in times of poor market liquidity must pay higher average returns—that is to say, the discount factor is affected by liquidity. The marginal utility of a dollar, delivered in the middle of a market meltdown such as after the 1998 Russian bond default and Long-Term Capital Management (LTCM) collapse, may well have been very high.

## Current State of Affairs—Better Than It Looks

Unfortunately, no single empirical representation wins, and the quest for a simple, reliable, and commonly accepted implementation of the fundamental value equation continues. Models that are theoretically purer or that work over a wider range of applications tend to do worse in any given application and sample than models that are motivated by a specific application and sample. The "right" model, even if we had it, would take a long time to emerge relative to the large number of spurious fish in each pond.

This survey looks maddeningly tangled, with a long (and yet woefully incomplete!) list of approaches. But this appearance hides an exciting common theoretical and empirical consensus that has emerged from all this work: In addition to the market return specified by the CAPM, there are a few additional important dimensions of risk that drive premiums in asset markets. If you take on assets with high betas on these risks, you will get higher returns on average, but these assets will all collapse together at times that many investors find very inconvenient. Those times are something related to recessions—when people's job prospects are risky, wages are doing poorly, investment and new business formation are at a standstill—and something else related to financial distress, poor market liquidity, and the like—when a dollar in your pocket or an easily liquidatable investment with a high price would be particularly convenient. The empirical approaches mentioned earlier really only disagree about which particular data series to use to construct the best indicators of these two kinds of bad times unrelated to overall market returns.

## FIXED INCOME AND COMMODITIES

The models used to price fixed income assets, commodities, and derivatives often simply amount to fairly ad hoc discount factor models. Consider first the factor models or affine models that dominate bond pricing, following Vasicek (1977), Brennan and Schwartz (1979), and Cox, Ingersoll, and Ross (1985). In principle, valuing a bond is easier than valuing other securities, because the payoff is fixed. A one-year discount bond that pays one dollar for sure in one year has a value today of simply

$$p_t^{(1)} = E_t[m_{t+1}] \tag{7.11}$$

where the superscript denotes maturity. To generate a bond pricing model, you write down some model for the discount factor and then take expectations.

What makes bond pricing interesting and technically challenging is the presence of many maturities. For example, you can think of a two-period bond as a security whose payoff is a one-period bond, or as a two-period security directly. Its price is

$$p_t^{(2)} = E_t[m_{t+1}p_{t+1}^{(1)}] = E_t[m_{t+1}m_{t+2}] \tag{7.12}$$

Pursuing the first equality in equation (7.12), you can see an interesting recursion developing, leading to differential equations for prices (across maturity). Pursuing the second equality, you can see interesting expectations or integrals to take.

Still, we need a discount factor model to value bonds, so bond pricing models all come down to discount factor models. The simplest example with which to show this point concretely is the discrete-time Vasicek model.[13] We write the following time series model for the discount factor:

$$\ln(m_{t+1}) = -z_t + \varepsilon_{t+1}$$
$$z_{t+1} = (1 - \phi)\mu + \phi z_t + \delta_{t+1}$$

where $\phi$ and $\mu$ are parameters and $\varepsilon$ and $\delta$ are shock/error terms. We then find the prices and yields of one- and two-period bonds from the fundamental value equation, (7.11), and equation (7.12).[14] The result is a one-factor model for yields:

$$y_t^{(1)} = (1 - \phi)\mu_y + y_{t-1}^{(1)} + \delta_{t+1}$$

$$y_t^{(2)} = const. + \frac{1}{2}(1 + \phi)y_t^{(1)} + \frac{1}{2}cov(\delta, \varepsilon)$$

The short rate $y_t^{(1)}$ evolves on its own as an autoregressive (AR) process. The two-period bond yield, and all other yields, are then linear functions of the one-year yield. All yields move in lockstep. Two-factor and multifactor models work the same way. For example, the Brennan and Schwartz (1979) two-factor model has a long rate as well as a short rate moving autonomously and then all other yields following as functions of these two.

This model is *not* composed of an AR(1) for the short rate plus "arbitrage." The fly in the ointment is the third term in the last equation—$cov(\delta, \varepsilon)$. This is the "market price of interest rate risk." It is the covariance of interest rate shocks with the discount factor. From our old friend (7.5), we recognize it as the risk premium that an asset must pay whose payoff goes up and down with the interest rate. As this term varies, the two-year bond yield can take on any value. Term structure models typically just estimate this term as a free parameter—the models pick this term to fit bond yields as well as possible.

That's fine as far as it goes, but it does not obviate what we are doing here. Just as before, $cov(\delta, \varepsilon)$ specifies the systematic part of interest rate risk. It specifies whether the marginal utility of consumption is higher or lower when interest rates rise unexpectedly. It specifies whether higher interest rates correspond to good times or bad times, and how much so. Term structure models are no more immune from assumptions about consumption, macroeconomic risks, and so forth than anywhere else. Current term structure models are much like financial multifactor models discussed in the preceding section. The discount factor depends on rather arbitrary portfolio returns, selected for empirical fit (in sample) rather than even armchair theorizing about good and bad states.

Often, the discount factor modeling is implicit in a transformation to "risk-neutral probabilities." Recall that we can write the fundamental value equation as

$$p_t = E_t[m_{t+1} z_{t+1}] = \frac{1}{R^f} E_t^*[z_{t+1}]$$

where the * indicates a expectation under altered risk-neutral probabilities. The transformation from $E_t$ to $E_t^*$ is called a "change of measure," and $m_{t+1}$ is the transformation function. Algebraic manipulations can be much easier after the change of measure, but the economic content and implicit discount factor modeling are not changed. Exactly the same information must go into forming the change of measure that goes into specifying the discount factor or market price of risk. In the same way, bond price authors often do not present the discount factor, but go directly to assumptions about the market price of risk, which we have labeled cov($\delta,\varepsilon$).

Similarly, the Gibson and Schwartz (1990) model for valuing long-term oil derivatives is based on oil price movements and changes in the convenience yield. Their model requires a "market price of oil price risk" and the "market price of convenience yield risk." These parameters are usually estimated to make the model fit well. Again, they are equivalent to specifying a discount factor.

## ARBITRAGE AND NEAR-ARBITRAGE PRICING

So far, we have discussed only "absolute" pricing methods. These methods specify a discount factor that can in principle price any asset, using only fundamental information (i.e., the source of aggregate risks). In many applications, that is a far more powerful tool than is called for. Usually, we do not need to value every asset, we only want to value one asset; and we are happy to use the information about the prices of similar assets in order to do so. In this case a *relative* pricing approach is useful. To find the value of a McDonald's hamburger, absolute pricing starts thinking about how much it costs to feed a cow. Relative pricing looks at the price of a hamburger at Burger King. For many purposes, such as deciding where to eat, this is good enough. In finance, option valuation and corporate finance (the use of comparable investments to determine required rates of return) are the prime applications of relative pricing methods.

The central question is, as always, how to construct a discount factor. The relative pricing approach uses information from *other* asset prices in order to construct a discount factor useful for pricing a given asset.

## Arbitrage Pricing

"Arbitrage pricing" is the purest case of relative pricing, as it makes the least assumptions about investors, utility functions, and so forth in specifying the discount factor. When it works, this approach neatly cuts short the endless discussion over what are the true risk factors, market price of risk, and so on. Black-Scholes option pricing is the canonical example. The Black-Scholes formula expresses the option price given the stock and bond prices.

The only assumption we need to derive an arbitrage pricing relation such as the Black-Scholes formula is that there is *some* discount factor that generates the price of the focus asset (option) and the basis assets (stock, bond). As long as there is some discount factor, then the Law of One Price must hold:[15] Two ways of generating the same payoff must have the same value. If payoffs $x$, $y$, $z$ are related by $z = x + y$, then their prices must obey $p(z) = p(x) + p(y)$.[16] The key insight in the Black-Scholes formula is that you can dynamically hedge an option with a stock and a bond. The payoff of the option is the same as the payoff of the hedge portfolio. Hence, the price of the option must be the same as the value of the hedge portfolio. (Arbitrage pricing should really be called "Law of One Price pricing," and probably would be if the latter were not so ugly a name.)

Another way to look at the same thing paves the way for more complex relative pricing. Because the existence of *any* discount factor implies the Law of One Price, *any* discount factor that prices the basis assets (stock and bond) must give the same result for the focus asset (option). Following this insight, we can price options by simply constructing any discount factor that prices the stock and bond. This task is easy. For example, once you know $p_t$, the choice

$$m^*_{t+1} = z'_{t+1} E_t(z_{t+1} z'_{t+1})^{-1} p_t$$

does a pretty good job of satisfying $p_t = E_t(z_{t+1} m^*_{t+1})$! (The primes denote transpose and allow for vectors of prices and payoffs in the formula.) Then we can simply use the discount factor $m^*$ to value the option.[17]

The discount factor $m^*$ is not unique. There are many discount factors that price the stock and bond. For example, a new discount factor $m_{t+1} = m^*_{t+1} + \varepsilon_{t+1}$ where $\varepsilon_{t+1}$ is any random variable uncorrelated with payoffs $E_t(\varepsilon_{t+1} z_{t+1}) = 0$ will do. But with arbitrage pricing it does not matter which one you use. They all give the same option value.

Arbitrage pricing is still technically challenging, because these trivial-sounding statements hold at every point in time, and you have to chain it all back from expiration to find the actual option price. This means solving a differential equation or an integral. But technical challenges are a lot easier to solve than economic challenges—finding the right absolute asset pricing model.

You can see the attraction of arbitrage pricing. Rather than learn about discount factors from macroeconomics, introspection, philosophy, or over-simplified economic theories, we can simply construct useful discount factors from available assets and use them to price derivatives. Put another way, every asset pricing model posits that there is *some* discount factor, so implications that derive from the mere existence of a discount factor are common to every asset pricing model; we do not have to choose which asset pricing model to use if all discount factors give the same answer. Arbitrage pricing seems so pure that option pricing theorists, financial engineers, and risk managers often sneer at the models we have presented.

Arbitrage pricing, however, is not completely assumption-free. It assumes that there is *some* discount factor. In turn, this assumption requires that there is at least one unconstrained investor out there forming an optimal portfolio. We need to know nothing about the utility function and consumption stream (i.e., what states of nature the investor fears)—we will learn all we need to know about that from stock and bond prices—but we do need something. The Law of One Price is routinely violated in retail stores (the price of a 32-ounce bottle of ketchup is *not* twice the price of a 16-ounce bottle), so it does reflect some assumptions. It is not a law of nature.

Much more seriously, application of relative pricing techniques to real-world problems is not nearly as straightforward as the Black-Scholes example suggests. The lost car keys are usually not right under the streetlight. In practically every interesting application, even a textbook-perfect hedge is exposed to *some* risk arising from institutional frictions, transaction costs, illiquidity, and so forth. More often, there is no textbook-perfect hedge, due to nonmarketed risks such as changing volatility, shifting interest rates, asset specific liquidity premiums, nonmarketed fundamental securities, and so on. And when there is no way to *perfectly* replicate the payoff of the focus asset with some portfolio of other assets, there is no way to perfectly "arbitrage price" the focus asset. The premiums for market prices of the unavoidable basis risks will matter. Different, and apparently arbitrary, choices among the many discount factors that price hedge assets (different choices of $\varepsilon$ in $m = m^* + \varepsilon$) produce different valuations for the derivatives. We cannot avoid the questions: "How big are the extra risks?" and "What is the premium for those extra risks?"

At this point, we could simply return to the beginning and look to answer these questions using some implementation of the fundamental value equation. But we usually want to avoid an extended discussion of CAPM versus ICAPM and consumption in every little application. Many option pricing exercises leave "market price of risk" assumptions as free parameters, as we discussed earlier for term structure and commodity models. But in many cases, the market price of risk assumptions matter a lot, and pulling them out of thin air is very unsatisfactory. Instead, we can add a little absolute information to winnow down the range of possible discount factors, while still using the information in hedge assets (stock and bond) as much as possible. This works because in most options pricing applications, the residual or tracking error risks are small. It takes only a little discount factor economics to make sure that small residuals have small effects on values.

### Arbitrage Bounds

What can we say about discount factors? The weakest thing we can say in general (beyond existence) is that investors always like more over less.[18] Marginal utility is positive, and this implies that the discount factor is positive. Keep in mind that the discount factor is random, so "positive" means "positive in every state of the world at time $t + 1$, no matter what happens."

As the existence of a discount factor implies the Law of One Price, a positive discount factor has a nice portfolio interpretation: the "Principle of No Arbitrage." If a payoff $z$ cannot be negative and might be positive, then it gets a positive price. (Multiplying two positive things in $E_t(m_{t+1}z_{t+1})$ and taking the average, we must get a positive result. In finance terminology, this stronger property is called *arbitrage*. Colloquial use of *arbitrage* usually refers to the Law of One Price.)

Positive discount factors lead to "arbitrage bounds" on option prices when we cannot completely hedge the option payoff. We solve the problem: "What are the largest and smallest option prices we can generate, searching over all positive discount factors that price stocks and bonds?" More formally, we solve

$$\max_{\{m_{t+1}\}} E_t(m_{t+1}z_{t+1}^{option})$$

$$s.t. \quad p_t^{stock} = E_t(m_{t+1}z_{t+1}^{stock})$$

$$s.t. \quad p_t^{bond} = E_t(m_{t+1}z_{t+1}^{bond}) \qquad (7.13)$$

$$s.t. \quad m_{t+1} > 0$$

Most textbooks solve this problem more simply for a simple European call option. For example, we note that the call option payoff is always positive, so its price must always be positive. In more complex situations, this discount factor search (a linear program) is the only way to make sure you have not forgotten some clever dominating portfolio, and it can provide useful arbitrage bounds even in dynamic applications. (See Ritchken, 1985.)

## BEYOND ARBITRAGE: A LITTLE BIT OF ABSOLUTE PRICING GOES A LONG WAY

Alas, arbitrage bounds are too wide for many applications. They still allow us to generate weird option prices, because there are weird positive discount factors that nonetheless price the stock and bond. For example, we generate the lower arbitrage bound on a European call option $C(t) > 0$ by imagining a discount factor arbitrarily close to zero anytime the option finishes in-the-money. Now, we are all happy when the stock market goes up, but are we so wildly happy that more money has become *worthless*? Surely we can sensibly restrict the discount factor more than that without getting back into the messy model business.

Following this insight, a number of approaches suggest how to use a *little* absolute pricing even in traditional relative pricing situations in order to at least bound the effects of unhedgeable residual risks. Equivalently, we can combine information about the discount factor from basis assets (stock, bond) whose prices we do not want to question with relatively weak but hence robust information about the discount factor available from economic theory and practical experience in many markets.

### Arbitrage Pricing Theory

Ross's (1976b) Arbitrage Pricing Theory (APT) is the first such mixture of a little absolute pricing into a fundamentally relative-pricing problem. His APT is also a second source of inspiration for the factors in multifactor models.

Ross pointed out that many portfolios of stocks can be reasonably approximated as linear combinations of the return on a few basic or factor portfolios. In equations, we can run a regression of the focus portfolio on factor portfolios:

$$r_{t+1}^i = a + \beta_1^i f_{t+1}^1 + \beta_2^i f_{t+1}^2 + \ldots + \varepsilon_{t+1}^i$$

and the error term will be small. For example, most of the thousands of mutual funds' returns can be quite well approximated once we know the funds' styles in terms of market, size, value, and a few industry groupings. If the actual, *ex post*, returns on these portfolios can be approximated in this way, it stands to reason that the expected returns can also be so approximated. If not, one could buy the focus portfolio, short the right-hand side combination of the factor portfolio returns, and earn a high return with little risk. As a result we derive a multifactor representation in which average returns depend on the betas on the factor portfolios.

$$E(r_{t+1}^i) = r^f + \beta_1^i \lambda_1 + \beta_2^i \lambda_2 + \ldots \tag{7.14}$$

Equivalently, a discount factor that is a linear function of the factor returns will do a good job of pricing the focus portfolios. Of course, like any relative pricing approach, the APT's applicability is limited. You cannot apply it to assets whose returns are poorly approximated by the returns of the few basic portfolios—assets with large residuals $\varepsilon_{t+1}^i$.

Unfortunately, if you are willing to say nothing at all about absolute pricing (utility functions, risk aversion, macroeconomic states, etc.), then *any* residual risk $\varepsilon_{t+1}^i$ can have an *arbitrarily* large price or risk premium, and the hoped-for APT approximation can be arbitrarily wrong. With any error, the Law of One Price alone says nothing about the focus portfolio. For stock portfolios, arbitrage (positive discount factors) does not help, as no portfolio of stocks does better than another portfolio *always*.

Ross realized a way out of this dilemma. If the risk premium associated with a residual $\varepsilon_{t+1}^i$ were very large, it would be very attractive investment in terms of its Sharpe ratio (ratio of mean return to standard deviation). A high Sharpe ratio is not an arbitrage opportunity or a violation of the Law of One Price, but extremely high Sharpe ratios are nonetheless unlikely to persist. If we rule out very high Sharpe ratios *in addition to* the Law of One Price and Principle of No Arbitrage, we do obtain a well-behaved approximate APT. Small errors $\varepsilon_{t+1}^i$ now must mean small risk premiums, so equation (7.14) will hold as a good approximation.

Ruling out high Sharpe ratios is another little bit of absolute pricing. It is equivalent to the assumption that discount factors are not too *volatile*. Precisely, Hansen and Jagannathan (1991) show that the maximum possible Sharpe ratio attained by all assets priced by a particular discount factor is given by[19]

$$\sigma(m) = \frac{1}{R^f} \max_{\{Rs.t.1=E(mR)\}} \left\{ \frac{E(R) - R^f}{\sigma(R)} \right\}$$

Limiting volatility is an additional but plausible and mild restriction on marginal utility. Does marginal utility growth—growth in the pleasure we get from an extra dollar's consumption—really vary by more than, say, 50 percent per year? The historical market Sharpe ratio is 0.5 (8 percent mean, 16 percent standard deviation), so even such a high bound on discount factor volatility is enough to restrict market prices of risk to CAPM values.

In more economic terms, the volatility of the discount factor is given by the volatility of consumption growth times the risk aversion coefficient. If we know that at least one marginal investor's consumption growth varies less than, say, 5 percent per year, and risk aversion is sensible—say, less than 10—then we know that the discount factor varies by less than 0.5 per year, and the maximum Sharpe ratio should be less than 0.5. Equivalently, we might be willing to assume traders will take any Sharpe ratio more than twice the Sharpe ratio of the market as a whole and impose that maximum Sharpe ratio in evaluating the premium for residual risks.

## Derivatives Valuation Bounds

Cochrane and Saá-Requejo (2000) apply Ross's idea to option pricing, when either market frictions (e.g., you cannot trade continuously) or nonmarketer risks (e.g., stochastic volatility or interest rates) break simple arbitrage pricing and require us to evaluate market prices of risks. Cochrane and Saá-Requejo find that the upper and lower bounds on option prices (searching over all discount factors that price stocks and bonds) are positive *and* have limited volatility. This amounts to adding an additional restriction to arbitrage bound equation (7.13):

$$\max_{\{m_{t+1}\}} E_t(m_{t+1} z_{t+1}^{option})$$

$$s.t. \quad p_t^{stock} = E_t(m_{t+1} z_{t+1}^{stock})$$

$$s.t. \quad p_t^{bond} = E_t(m_{t+1} z_{t+1}^{bond}) \qquad (7.15)$$

$$s.t. \quad m_{t+1} > 0$$

$$s.t. \quad \sigma(m) \leq R^f h$$

The last restriction is the novelty over arbitrage bounds. $h$ is the upper limit on discount factor volatility; the extra assumption is that investors would want to take any bet with a Sharpe ratio greater than $h$. Cochrane and Saá-Requejo (2000) find that the resulting bounds on option prices are much tighter than the arbitrage bounds that result from ignoring the last term—the bounds that result from arbitrary assignment of the market price of residual risk.

For option pricing, both positive discount factors and a limit on discount factor volatility are important. So far, the discount factor interpretation has been a matter of aesthetics. You could solve problems (for example) imposing a positive discount factor or by checking that all positive payoffs had positive prices. The restrictions in equation (7.15) have no pure portfolio interpretation. The only way to put all these ideas together is to add restrictions on the discount factor, tightening the bounds on option pricing. They have to be posed and solved with discount factor methods.

This is only the beginning. Bernardo and Ledoit (2000) add the restriction that discount factors cannot be too small or too large, $a \leq m \leq b$. This is a sensible tightening of the arbitrage restriction $m \geq 0$. It also produces usefully tight option pricing bounds. Constantinides and Zariphopoulou (1999) consider the sensible restriction that higher index values must make investors happier. The discount factor $m$ thus must be a monotonically decreasing function of the stock index. The beauty of a discount factor framework is that it is easy to add all these restrictions and more together.

## NOTES

1. Do not confuse the absence of an initial *payment* with the absence of all cash or asset flows. If one party is required to post a bond with the counterparty as collateral, for example, a "cash flow" will occur on the trade date. But this is not a payment—the collateral belongs to the party that posts it and is merely pledged to the counterparty to cover prospective events of default.
2. Culp (2003d) explores the relative-pricing approach.
3. The discussion here and in the next two sections is adapted from Cochrane (2001).
4. As a matter of theory, this really works only for investors. Corporations do not have utility functions and thus engage in a different type of analysis of hedging opportunities—see Culp (2001, 2002a).
5. Derivation: For any two returns $r^j$ and $r^k$, $E_t[m_{t+1}(r^j - r^k)] = E_t[m_{t+1}r^j] - E_t[m_{t+1}r^k] = 0$, where $r^k = r^f$ is a special case.
6. Derivation: Note that $R^f = 1/E(m)$ and $E(mP) = E(m)E(P) + \text{cov}(m,P)$ and solve.
7. See, for example, Ross (1976b) and Cox, Ross, and Rubinstein (1979). Cochrane (2001) discusses the relations between discrete-time and continuous-time formulations of the problem and how to implement discount factors in continuous time.
8. Alternatively, that is why investors diversify their holdings to get rid of these risks on their own. See Culp (2002b).
9. The parameter g can be interpreted as the degree of risk aversion.
10. Cochrane (2001) shows different derivations of the CAPM under alternative assumptions and provides a comparison of the multiple approaches.

11. Usually, $z$ is a vector of multiple state variables and factor-mimicking portfolios.

12. Technically, this statement requires a risk aversion coefficient greater than one, but that is the usual case.

13. This treatment is adapted from Campbell, Lo, and MacKinlay (1992).

14. Derivation: The price and yield of a one-period bond are

$$p_t^{(1)} = E_t[m_{t+1}] = E_t\left[e^{\ln(m_{t+1})}\right] = E_t\left[e^{-x_t + \varepsilon_{t+1}}\right] = e^{-x_t + \frac{1}{2}\sigma_\varepsilon^2}$$

$$y_t^{(1)} = -\ln(p_t) = x_t - \frac{1}{2}\sigma_\varepsilon^2$$

With an adjustment to the constant $\mu$, the state variable $x$ thus is the short rate $y_t^{(1)}$. Things get more interesting with a two-year bond:

$$y_t^{(2)} = -\frac{1}{2}\ln E_t[m_{t+1}m_{t+2}] = -\frac{1}{2}\ln E_t\left[e^{-x_t - x_{t+1} + \varepsilon_{t+1} + \varepsilon_{t+2}}\right]$$

$$= -\frac{1}{2}\ln E_t\left[e^{-(1+\phi)x_t - (1-\phi)\mu - \delta_{t+1} + \varepsilon_{t+1} + \varepsilon_{t+2}}\right]$$

$$y_t^{(2)} = \frac{1}{2}(1+\phi)x_t + \frac{1}{2}(1-\phi)\mu + \frac{1}{2}\mathrm{cov}(\delta,\varepsilon) - \frac{1}{4}\sigma_\delta^2 - \frac{1}{2}\sigma_\varepsilon^2$$

$$y_t^{(2)} = \frac{1}{2}(1-\phi)\mu + \frac{1}{2}(1+\phi)y_t^{(1)} + \frac{1}{2}\mathrm{cov}(\delta,\varepsilon) - \frac{1}{4}\left\{\sigma_\delta^2 + (1-\phi)(\sigma_\varepsilon^2)\right\}$$

15. The converse statement is one of the most famous founding theorems of finance. If the Law of One Price holds, then there exists a discount factor. See Ross (1976b), Harrison and Kreps (1979), and Hansen and Richard (1987).

16. Proof: $E[m(x + y)] = E(mx) + E(my)$.

17. See Cochrane (2001) for the algebra.

18. You can always burn or give away what you do not want, so less is never preferred to more.

19. Proof: $0 = E[m(r - r^f)] = E(m)\,E(r - r^f) + \sigma(m)\sigma(\sigma r \sigma(r)\rho(m,r)$

$$E(m)\frac{E(r - r^f)}{\sigma(r)\rho(m,r)} = \sigma(m)$$

Correlations are less than one.

# CHAPTER 8

# Own Rates of Interest
# and the Cost of Carry Model

**H**aving thoroughly explored the proper use of *absolute* pricing techniques for derivatives, we now turn to *relative* pricing. In this chapter we focus on relative pricing *for forward-based derivatives*, and we do this for two reasons. The first is that your prior exposure to the relative pricing of options through methods like the Black-Scholes-Merton and binomial models is probably fairly significant, and there is no sense in being repetitive. The second and more important reason is that the economics underlying the particular relative valuation approach discussed here are precisely those forces that give derivatives their power to facilitate intertemporal risk transfer. Knowing the pricing relations between forward-based derivatives and their underlying asset markets is an essential part of understanding the role of these markets in risk shifting over time.

Our specific focus here is on the famed *cost of carry* model of forward-based derivatives. The model is based on the idea that the price of an asset for delivery in the future should be equal to its current spot price plus the cost of carrying it over time. To derive this precise relation and to appreciate its economic significance, we begin by revisiting a principle that was briefly asserted when we explored Babylonian banking in Chapter 5—namely, that forwards are essentially *asset loan markets*. As such, the relation between prices of the same asset for immediate and for deferred delivery imply a type of "interest rate" for borrowing or lending the asset over time. This rate on any given asset has been called the *natural*, *own*, and *commodity* interest rate, dating back to Sraffa (1932a,b), Keynes (1936), and Hicks (1939), respectively. Whatever you wish to call it, this rate *is* the cost of carry on which the pricing model of the same name is based.

This is almost certainly not the first time you have seen the cost of carry model. Most textbooks, however, tend to emphasize the model as a relative valuation approach prima facie without exploring where the model came from *or* the important correspondence between the cost of carrying an asset over time and the own interest rate on that asset. Our discussion here, in contrast to what you may have seen, will place a primary emphasis on these two dimensions of the cost of carry model. So, even if you have seen the model before, it is not likely you will have seen it discussed from the perspective adopted here.

## DERIVATIVES, ASSET LENDING, AND OWN RATES OF INTEREST

Capital theory is the branch of economic analysis (both micro- and macro-) that attempts to explain capital as a factor of production. Modern neoclassical economic theory tends to treat capital theory as a basic staple of the economic diet, with derivatives falling into the theoretical paradigm closer to dessert. Ironically, the connection between the two was of much greater importance to the classical and early neoclassical economists writing around the turn of the nineteenth century than it seems to be today. To a handful of those early economists, in fact, capital theory and the theory of forward markets were basically *the same problem*.

The "price" of capital is an "interest rate," and an interest rate in turn is essentially the rate of exchange between the present and the future (Böhm-Bawerk, 1890, 1891; Cassell, 1903; Fisher, 1907, 1930). The relations between interest rates, savings, investment, money demand, and economic output have been among the most contentiously debated issues in the history of economic thought. In particular, capital theory lies at the center of the intellectual maelstrom concerning the determinants of inflation and unemployment.

Beginning with Marshall (1894), Pigou (1923), Keynes (1923), and Fisher (1925), the so-called *quantity theory of money* was advanced to explain the relation of inflation to money demand and supply (viewed from either a cash balances or velocity of circulation perspective)—the idea that, as Friedman would later quip, "inflation is always and everywhere a monetary phenomenon." Wicksell (1898, 1906) in turn introduced the notion of a credit system and reinforced the earlier Ricardian idea that in a credit system, the demand for loans is dependent on the rate of interest, which in turn depends on profitability of real investment. Keynes (1936) then took Wicksell's notion and wandered off from the pure quantity theory—which he himself had helped develop in his *Treatise on Money* in 1930—in the meandering and confused direction of his famous Phillips-curve-like trade-off between inflation, unemployment, and output. In a sense, debates over capital theory and the theory of interest essentially sparked the decades-long Monetarists versus Keynesians argument.

In the early days of debate over capital theory, forward markets played a central role. Specifically, most of the economists writing at the beginning of the twentieth century recognized fully well that *any* market explicitly producing a price for the purchase or sale of an asset in the future will invariably have an interest rate component. Hicks (1939, p. 141) puts it most directly: "Any exchange of present goods or services for a promise to deliver goods or services in the future has the economic character of a loan."

More specifically and more importantly for our purposes, forward transactions *can always be reduced to or replicated by a spot transaction plus an explicit loan of some kind* (Sraffa, 1932a; Keynes, 1923, 1936; Hicks, 1939, 1989; Kaldor, 1939; Working, 1948, 1949b; Telser, 1986; Williams, 1986). And this certainly does not need to be limited to physical commodities—it is equally true for financial assets like stocks and bonds. Accordingly, "Where forward markets exist, rates of interest . . . are always implicitly established." (Hicks, 1939, p. 141)

Knowing where these interest rates came from in the history of economic thought tells us a lot, including the determinants of these rate's and their relation to the cost of carry model. It is instructive, moreover, to review the emergence of this concept chronologically as well, to reinforce why the idea of separate interest rates for all assets is important, especially given how little attention is paid to this notion in modern economics and finance curricula.

## Sraffa and Natural Rates of Interest

Pierro Sraffa may not be as widely recognized as Keynes or Marshall, but he certainly was a prominent figure in the intellectual development of twentieth-century economics. He is unfamiliar to many—like Knight (see Chapters 2 and 3)—because he actually wrote relatively little. Also like Knight, a significant amount of his influence came through his impact on others. And again like Knight, his influence on others often went well beyond "economic science." Sraffa apparently played a significant role, for example, in helping Antonio Gramsci and Ludwig Wittgenstein develop and hone certain of their philosophical views.[1]

In his economic writings, Sraffa was intensely critical of the neoclassical paradigm in general and the marginalist revolution (see Appendix 1). Sraffa (1926), for example, points out—quite correctly—a fundamental logical flaw in Marshall's "law of non-proportional returns" that leads to the traditional U-shaped average cost curve with increasing returns to scale followed by decreasing returns to scale as production rises. Sraffa (1926) reminded people that decreasing returns arise from changes in the proportions of factors of production, whereas increasing returns during expanded production arise from the division of labor. They cannot simply be "put on the same table" like Marshall tried to do with the U-shaped average cost curve. Roncaglia (2000, p. 16) argues that following Sraffa, economists "may say that the analytic construct of the Marshallian tradition can only be made to square with the canons of logical coherence through unrealistic *ad hoc* hypotheses—hardly a sound basis for a framework designed for general interpretive application."

Sraffa is perhaps best known for having compiled and edited the collected *Works and Correspondences of David Ricardo* for Cambridge University Press and for his controversial own text *Production of Commodities by Means of Commodities* (1960). The two projects were closely related. In his 1960 treatise, Sraffa essentially recommends a return to the classical Ricardian paradigm. Following Smith (1776), Ricardo (1817), and Marx (1859), he specifically advocated a return to the assumption (belief?) that all industries earn an equal rate of profit and that the only real question for the economic system is how capital is distributed among those industries.

Recall from our discussion in Chapter 2 (and see Appendix 1) that the marginalist perspective made a significant advance beyond this earlier thinking by arguing for marginality-based production optimality—that is, the idea that firms pursuing profit maximization will be led to choose an output level where the marginal cost of production equals the marginal revenue, which in a competitive market is the demand curve. This was an important advance in part because it allowed for the role of the firm to become an important feature of the economic system. But also recall from Chapter 2 that this is what got us into the "firms cannot make money except through imperfect competition" world of which Knight was so critical. In his own way, Sraffa's arguments against the marginalists in general—and especially Marshall—were not far removed from Knight's. A primary criticism Sraffa leveled against Marshall, for example, was his assumption of a "representative firm," which Sraffa, like Knight, strongly believed essentially "assumed away" a lot of the interesting problems in production theory.

Unlike Knight, however, Sraffa took his crusade against the marginalists fairly personally. Within just a few of months of the 1931 publication of F. A. Hayek's *Prices and Production*, Sraffa had already penned and published a bitter and scathing critique of Hayek's capital theory—see Sraffa (1932a). Hayek's theory was an expansion of Böhm-Bawerk (1890, 1891) and Wicksell (1898, 1906) and hence was deeply rooted in the marginalist tradition. But Sraffa rejected Hayek's interpretation—especially the parts concerning Wicksell—and argued for the alternative view presented by John Maynard Keynes in his *Treatise on Money* (1930a,b).[2] At the core of their dispute was their interpretation of Wicksell's contention that some "natural" rate of interest exists that is determined by largely exogenous factors, and that in an economy with both money and credit the "bank rate" in the loan market for funds should be set equal to the natural interest rate—a notion that Hayek accepted and Sraffa did not.

Sraffa argued that when forward and spot prices on *any* assets are not the same, multiple natural interest rates exist. These rates, he argued further, could be explained only by a disequilibrium in which saving exceeds investment. Because of the multiplicity of these natural interest rates, Sraffa believed Wicksell's argument about how the bank rate on loanable funds should be set was nonsensical:

> *If money did not exist, and loans were made in terms of all sorts of commodities, there would be a single rate which satisfies the conditions of equilibrium, but there might be at any moment as many "natural" rates of interest as there are commodities, though they would not be "equilibrium" rates. . . . .In order to realize this we need not stretch our imagination and think of an organized loan market as savages bartering deer for beavers. Loans are currently made in the present world in terms of every commodity for which there is a forward market. (Sraffa, 1932a, pp. 49–50, emphasis added)*

Sraffa defines this natural rate of interest *for any asset on which there is a forward market* as:

$$S_t r_{t,T} + (S_t - f_{t,T})$$

which can easily be expressed as a rate by dividing each term by the spot price:[3]

$$x_{t,T} = r_{t,T} + \frac{S_t - f_{t,T}}{S_t} \tag{8.1}$$

Equation (8.1) is what we shall call the *natural rate of interest* on an asset.

Equation (8.1) says that the natural interest rate for a given asset is equal to the rate at which the price will change over time purely to reflect the time value of money $(r_{t,T})$ plus the premium or minus the discount of the spot price vis-à-vis the price of the asset for delivery at time $T$.

If we assume for a moment that the time $t$ forward purchase price is an unbiased predictor of the time $T$ spot price (a topic to which we will return in Chapter 12), equation (8.2) can be rearranged slightly to express the natural rate as a function of the expected price change of the asset:

$$x_{t,T} = r_{t,T} - \frac{E_t(S_T) - S_t}{S_t} \tag{8.2}$$

The *real* natural rate of interest on an asset thus should equal the nominal money interest rate minus the expected price change of the asset. This is analogous to the definition of a real money interest rate in the sense of the Fisher (1925) equation—the nominal money rate is equal to the real rate plus the expected change in the price level. Here, the nominal natural rate of interest is equal to the real natural rate of interest $x_{t,T}$ plus the expected change in the price level of this specific asset (Telser, 1986).

The economic intuition behind Sraffian natural interest rates is straightforward when you recognize the fundamental equivalence between forward markets and asset borrowing or lending. Sraffa (1932a) explained, "When a cotton spinner borrows a sum of money for three months and uses the proceeds to spot purchase a quantity of raw cotton which he simultaneously sells three months forward, he is actually 'borrowing cotton' for that period." (Sraffa, 1932a, p. 50) The first component of equation (8.1) is just the interest burden associated with borrowing the funds to make the spot purchase, and the second component completes the commodity loan by reflecting the cost of a spot purchase and simultaneous forward sale.

To be a little more explicit about how this works, consider a forward contract for the purchase and delivery of one bale of cotton one year hence. Suppose the one-year money interest rate is 5 percent. If the spot price for one bale of cotton is £100 and the quoted forward price is £107, the simultaneous spot sale and forward purchase will result in a minus 7 percent "return." The total commodity interest rate, however, will also need to reflect the fact that £100 will buy £105 for forward delivery because the present is at a 5 percent money discount to the future. So, the natural interest rate on cotton must be minus 2 percent per annum. If you interpret this as borrowing cotton for a year, this means that the borrower of one bale of cotton for one year will actually *get paid* £2 rather than have to make any kind of interest payment on the commodity loan. Table 8.1 confirms this £2 profit by looking at the specific components of the cotton borrowing operation.

The only real reason for Sraffa's introducing this natural interest rate point—and it never appears in his other writings in a meaningful way—was to criticize Hayek's interpretation of Wicksell by arguing that the bank lending rate cannot be set equal to the natural rate when there are as many natural rates as there are assets with forward markets. Hayek responded that "there might, at any moment, be as many 'natural interest rates' as there are commodities, *all* of which would be *equilibrium rates*." (Hayek, 1932, p. 245) To Hayek, the existence of all these natural rates was perfectly reasonable. But Sraffa again replied, "The only meaning (if it be a meaning) I can attach to this is that [Hayek's] maxim of policy now requires that the money rate should be equal to all these divergent natural rates." Hayek did not re-

**TABLE 8.1** The One-Year Borrowing Rate for Cotton

|  | *t* | *T* |
|---|---|---|
| *Money Loan:* | | |
| Borrow | £100 | — |
| Repay principal and interest | — | –£105 |
| *Commodity Market Operations:* | | |
| Purchase cotton spot | –£100 | — |
| Sell cotton forward | — | £107 |
| Net | 0 | £2 |

spond to this immediately, leaving things to seem like Sraffa was the victor in this particular exchange.

Because he was not focused on the role played by multiple natural interest rates and believed those rates to be disequilibrium phenomena, Sraffa never made any effort to explain the *determinants* of these multiple asset-specific natural rates of interest. Although the Sraffian natural interest rate is essentially the first expression of the cost of carry model—and we will see that a bit later if it's not already obvious to you—he appears to have been so preoccupied with his Hayek debate that he was utterly oblivious to the concept he had identified.

## Keynes and Own Rates of Interest

The importance of the Sraffian natural rate of interest was *not* lost on Lord Keynes. Himself a close friend of Sraffa's, Keynes found the insight both central at its face value as well as formative to his own theory of money interest rates, credit, and capital. Perhaps more than any other economist, Keynes rested his theory of interest rates strongly on his belief in the function of forward markets as loan markets.

Presumably wishing to avoid confusion with what classical Ricardians called the "natural" rate, Keynes (1933) referred to Sraffian natural rates on assets for which forward markets exist as *own rates of interest* for those assets. He argued that the own interest rate could be expressed either in terms of the asset or in terms of money—essentially a distinction between the *real* and *nominal* own rate of interest, respectively. The nominal own interest rate—the own rate in terms of money—was what Keynes (1933) defined very generally as the *marginal efficiency of capital*. This concept played a pivotal role in his *General Theory* of the workings of a macroeconomic system.

Keynes defined the *real* own interest rate as

$$x_{t,T} = q_{t,T} - c_{t,T} + l_{t,T} \tag{8.3}$$

and the *nominal* own interest rate as[4]

$$x_{t,T} + a_{t,T} = q_{t,T} - c_{t,T} + l_{t,T} + \frac{E_t(S_T) - S_t}{S_t} \tag{8.4}$$

where $q$ is the asset yield, $c$ is the physical cost of storage, $l$ is the asset's liquidity premium, and $r$ is the money rate of interest—all of which are to be defined in more detail shortly. Following Keynes, we also use the variable $a_{t,T}$ to define the conditional expected change in the asset price (spot) from $t$ to $T$. Hicks (1939) later referred to the own interest rate as the *commodity interest rate*, although we will stick to Keynes's terminology to remind ourselves that this relation applies to financial assets as well as physical commodities.

Keynes did not draw an easy connection between his version of the own interest rate and the money interest rate. As is seen in Chapter 10, Keynes simply believed that money was a special case of equations (8.3) and (8.4). For our purposes, however, we will find it useful to relate the Keynesian own interest rate and Sraffian natural interest rate to express the expected return on the asset in terms of both the money interest rate and the real own interest rate. Again assuming unbiased forward prices, we can combine equations (8.2) and (8.3) and rewrite the result in terms of the expected change in the asset price:

$$a_{t,T} = r_{t,T} - x_{t,T} = r_{t,T} - q_{t,T} + c_{t,T} - l_{t,T} \tag{8.4}$$

So, the expected price change of the asset is equal to the nominal money rate of interest minus the real own rate of interest on the asset. The expected return on asset ownership thus must be high enough to compensate the asset owner for the cost of storage plus the time value of money. But that expected return is then reduced by the benefit of asset ownership, which is the asset yield and liquidity premium. If the real own rate of interest is positive and greater than the money interest rate so that there is a *net gain* associated with asset ownership, the price of the asset will decline over the ownership period to reflect this. We return to this subject in Chapter 9.

Neither Keynes nor Sraffa gave explicit attention to whether the own rate of interest and its components might be stochastic (i.e., vary randomly over time) or to whether all market participants perceive and have access to exactly the same own rate for a given commodity. Because the money interest rate less the own rate is equal to the expected price change and we have every reason to believe the expected price change is stochastic, it is reasonable to assume that at least one of the components of the own rate of interest (and perhaps the money interest rate) is stochastic. But for now, we shall assume that the own rate of interest is both nonstochastic and homogeneous across firms. We relax these assumptions later in this chapter, but for now we concentrate on the simplest formulation of this model.

Unlike Sraffa, Keynes *did* give thought to what the own interest rate *included*. Let us consider those components of the nominal own interest rate in turn.

### Asset Yield

The first term in the real own interest rate, $q_{t,T}$, is the yield on the physical asset itself. Keynes described the term as reflecting the benefit to the asset owner of "assisting some process of production or supplying services to a consumer." (Keynes, 1936, p. 225)

The yield on a given asset represents essentially any benefit conveyed to the owner of record of the actual asset except for the liquidity premium (see later section). Just as the yield is *earned* by an asset owner or borrower, the yield is *forgone* by an asset lender or purchaser of an asset for future delivery.

Many assets on which derivatives are based have yields that are either observable or close to observable. The yield on a unit of foreign currency is the foreign currency deposit rate that can be earned by holders of the currency. The yield on an interest-bearing security is the coupon income as a proportion of the security's price. Dividends paid to equity share owners as a proportion of the share price define the dividend yield. Although that dividend yield can in principle be changed unexpectedly, it is unusual to see significant variation in dividend yields on individual securities—at least over relatively short periods of time. Dividends thus are generally treated as known and observable.

The yield on physical commodity ownership is a much more slippery concept. It is not explicitly observable and does not correspond to an actual cash flow per se. Instead, holders of commodities earn an implicit *convenience yield*, a concept developed by Keynes (1923), Kaldor (1939), Working (1948, 1949b), Brennan (1958), and Telser (1958). The convenience yield is essentially the value that a market participant derives from physical storage, primarily to help avoid inventory stock-outs.

We discuss the convenience yield in more detail later in this chapter and again in Chapters 9 and 11. For now, it is probably easiest if you think of it as little more than an "implicit dividend" earned at a constant rate any time the commodity is on hand to avoid an inventory depletion.

### Cost of Storage

The second component of the own interest rate is the cost of physical storage of the asset, $c_{t,T}$. For physical assets like commodities, the cost of storage includes allocated rent or space costs, warehousing and transportation fees, insurance, and the like. This term quite literally reflects all the *logistical* costs of moving an asset over time through storage.

Assets that have a known and observable yield are generally financial assets and are precisely those same assets that tend to have a negligible cost of storage. Consider, for example, securities likes equity and government bonds. Following the "Big Bang" in 1986, most global securities markets began the dematerialization process. As a result, stock certificates and government bonds in most industrialized countries exist only in electronic form. Purchases and sales are effected through registrar notations in an electronic book specifically designed to track security ownership.

Even when a financial asset is not fully dematerialized, the asset does not really "decay" over time as storage costs mount. At best, you might expect to see a small custodial fee, but this is generally fairly trivial.

### Asset Liquidity Yield or Premium

The component $l_{t,T}$ of the own rate of interest is a measure of the convenience of the "power of disposal over an asset during a period" (Keynes, 1933, p. 226). In other words, $l_{t,T}$ represents a liquidity premium on the asset, where a higher and positive $l_{t,T}$ is a benefit to the actual asset owner and indicates a greater degree to which the asset can be sold without significant price disruption in the market.

Like the convenience yield on physical assets, the liquidity premium does not show up as an explicitly identifiable cash flow. Again like the convenience yield, it will affect *prices* and hence *returns*—that is, it *does* compensate the asset owner somehow, but not through a payment or some other explicit mechanism.

Because of Keynes's general preoccupation in the *General Theory* with liquidity, this term is often ignored in modern applications of own interest rates—some of which we will see shortly in this chapter. But there is no good reason to ignore this term. In fact, there is a good reason to believe that for financial assets in particular, a liquidity premium may in fact exist on instruments of at least certain maturities and credit qualities. Chapter 10 revisits the liquidity premium in more detail.

## THE COST OF CARRY MODEL

Keynes concludes the following:

> *It follows that the total return expected from the ownership of an asset over a period is equal to its yield* minus *its carrying cost* plus *its liquidity-premium*, i.e. *to q – c + l. That is to say, q – c + l is the own-rate of inter-*

*est of any commodity, where q, c and l are measured in terms of itself as the standard. (Keynes, 1936, p. 226)*

By "total return expected from the ownership of an asset," Keynes literally means the benefits that accrue during the ownership period. Be careful here. This is *not* the expected *price* return in the sense of Chapter 7 and, in fact, does not *include* the expected capital appreciation or depreciation of the asset.

If this total expected return on asset ownership is nonstochastic and the same for all firms, then the price of the asset for future delivery must be at a discount to the price of the asset for immediate delivery to reflect this expected return that is *forgone* when a market participant opts to delay her purchase of the asset. Taking into account this factor plus the money rate of interest leads us to the *cost of carry model* in is most basic form.

## BASIC FORMULATION OF THE MODEL

Comparing equations (8.1), (8.2), and (8.4), we can now rewrite the proportional discount of the forward purchase price to the spot price as a function of the nominal and real own rates of interest for the asset:

$$\frac{S_t - f_{t,T}}{S_t} + r_{t,T} = x_{t,T} = q_{t,T} - c_{t,T} + l_{t,T}$$

$$\frac{S_t - f_{t,T}}{S_t} = y_{t,T} = q_{t,T} - c_{t,T} + l_{t,T} - r_{t,T} \tag{8.5}$$

where we have defined $y_{t,T}$ as the real own interest rate less the nominal money interest rate for reasons to become clear shortly. All else equal, the forward price will be at a greater discount to the spot price (or a smaller premium) the higher the yield on the underlying asset, the higher the liquidity premium on the underlying asset, and the lower the physical cost of storage. Rearranging (8.5), we get:

$$f_{t,T} = S_t(1 + r_{t,T} - x_{t,T})$$
$$f_{t,T} = S_t(1 - y_{t,T}) \tag{8.6}$$

Equation (8.6) tells us that, all else being equal, the forward purchase price must be at a premium to the spot price to reflect the time value of money *less* the real own interest rate for that commodity expressed in terms of the asset. Alternatively, the forward percentage premium over the spot price is exactly equal to *minus* the nominal own rate of interest.

We can express this in terms of the components of the own rate more usefully:

$$f_{t,T} = S_t(1 + r_{t,T} - q_{t,T} + c_{t,T} - l_{t,T}) \qquad (8.7)$$

The relation between the current spot price and the forward price shown in equation (8.7) is the most elemental form of the cost of carry model of forward purchase prices. It tell us that the forward purchase price must equal the spot purchase price plus cost of carrying the asset across time from the spot market to delivery into the forward contract. The *cost of carry* is $-y_{t,T} = r_{t,T} - q_{t,T} + c_{t,T} - l_{t,T}$. The *real cost of carry* is the cost of carrying the asset over time *excluding* the money interest or capital cost—that is, the negative of the real own rate of interest, or $-x_{t,T} = -q_{t,T} + c_{t,T} - l_{t,T}$. These are, of course, expressed as rates, but can easily be shown as *total* carrying costs by multiplying through the spot price.

To preview a discussion to which we return in some depth in Chapter 10, the cost of carry model is also often written as:

$$f_{t,T} = S_t(1 + r_{t,T} - q_{t,T} + c_{t,T} - l_{t,T}) = S_t(1 + b_{t,T}) \qquad (8.8)$$

where $b_{t,T}$ in (8.8) is called the *basis* or *calendar basis* prevailing from time $t$ to time $T$. The basis from time $t$ to $T$ is just another way of writing the cost of carry and is defined as the money interest rate less the real own interest rate.

### The Law of One Price and Arbitrage

Although the intuition behind the cost of carry expression for forward purchase prices shown in equation (8.6) is appealing, we have done nothing to show why this *must* be the forward price in an efficient capital market. Specifically, if we really believe that derivatives are economically equivalent to asset loan markets, we need to show that equivalence. Without it, the function derivatives play in intertemporal risk transfer would be greatly diminished.

As noted in Chapter 7, as long as there is *some* stochastic discount factor, then the Law of One Price (LOOP) must hold: Two ways of generating the same payoff must have the same value. If three different payoffs occurring at the same time denoted $x$, $y$, and $z$ are related by $x + y = z$, then their current prices must obey $P_x + P_y = P_z$. We can use the LOOP to "prove" that the cost of carry expression for forward purchase prices is "correct" both in absolute terms (i.e., in the sense of Chapter 7) and in relative terms. Not only is this instructive in understanding how market participants actually undertake certain kinds of arbitrage transactions, but validating the cost of carry model in several different ways also will help us develop a deeper understanding for the economic function of derivatives as risk transfer instruments.

Recall, moreover, that throughout this section we continue to assume that market participants have homogeneous expectations, that all market participants face the same own interest rate for a given commodity (e.g., storage costs are equal across firms), and that both the nominal interest rate and the own interest rate are nonstochastic.

When you first encountered the cost of carry model in your first course on derivatives, you probably "proved" or "derived" the model using relative valuation—the standard replicating portfolio approach in which a portfolio that replicates the payoff of the forward is formed. Knowing that the true price of the forward contract is zero if the contract is at-market on trade date $t$, the fixed forward purchase price can be solved by equating the payoff of the forward with the payoff on the replicating portfolio. The LOOP then guarantees that the resulting forward purchase price is "the right price."

This particular application of the LOOP is an application of relative pricing methods because the transactions undertaken to ensure that the cost of carry relation governs the relation between the spot price, forward purchase price, and cost of carry involve the actual process of (or sometimes the credible threat of) arbitraging *traded financial instruments* or *market exposures*. We call this valuation by replication because we can actually engage in transactions that *exactly* replicate the cash flows of the position to be valued; there is no residual risk with which to contend as discussed in Chapter 7.

Replicating the cost of carry model can be done in several different ways in the context of relative pricing. The only difference between the methods is the markets and products used to replicate the forward contract's payoffs. We consider the most common alternatives in the following subsections.

### Physical Storage and Forwards

We have already seen that the combination of borrowing money to buy the asset and selling it forward is equivalent to borrowing the asset itself. Now let us examine another "equivalence proposition"—namely, that going long a forward contract is economically equivalent to borrowing money to buy the underlying asset and then storing it over time. The latter set of operations replicates the payoffs of a long forward exactly, or, as some say, *synthesizes* the forward payoff. As a result, going long a forward is frequently called *synthetic storage* or *synthetic ownership* of the underlying asset—you have synthesized the payoff of buying and storing the asset when you use a forward without actually having to buy and store the asset.

To keep things simple, the forward contract in question is based on an underlying asset that pays a single dividend on date $t + k$ and requires its owner to pay a single storage cost on the same date $t + k$. If we wish to repli-

**TABLE 8.2**  Replication of Forward Purchase with Physical Storage

|  | $t$ | $t+k$ | $T$ |
|---|---|---|---|
| **Buy and Hold Asset + Borrow Money** | | | |
| *Money Loan:* | | | |
| Borrow to purchase asset | $S_t$ | — | $-S_t(1 + r_{t,T})$ |
| Borrow to pay storage costs | — | $C$ | $-C(1 + r_{t+k,T})$ |
| Invest dividends | — | $-Q$ | $Q(1 + r_{t+k,T})$ |
| *Buy and Hold Stock:* | | | |
| Buy asset | $-S_t$ | — | $S_T$ |
| Pay storage costs | — | $-C$ | — |
| Earn dividend/distribution | — | $Q$ | — |
| Net | $0$ | $0$ | $S_T - S_t(1 + r_{t,T}) - (C - Q)(1 + r_{t+k,T})$ |
| | | | |
| **Long Forward** | | | |
| Net | $0$ | — | $S_T - f_{t,T}$ |

cate the cash flows of the forward contract, we begin by borrowing $S_t$ to finance our purchase of the underlying asset, which we hold until date $T$, when it is worth $S_T$. The interim cash flows, $C$ and $Q$, occur at time $t + k$. To finance the storage costs, we borrow $C$ from time $t + k$ to $T$. We invest the dividend over the same period of time. For this example, assume there is a single prevailing interest rate used for financing, investment, and discounting known cash flows, and that is the riskless rate.

Table 8.2 shows the net effects of all these operations. You can see clearly from the net of the two strategies that both yield one unit of the asset at time $T$ worth $S_T$, both involve a zero net outlay, and both have the same risk (i.e., fluctuations in $S_T$). The two strategies must yield the same *final payoff*. So,

$$f_{t,T} = S_t(1 + r_{t,T}) + (C - Q)(1 + r_{t+k,T}) \qquad (8.9)$$

Now define

$$x_{t,T} = \frac{(Q - C)(1 + r_{t+k,T})}{S_t} \qquad (8.10)$$

and substitute (8.10) into (8.9):

$$f_{t,T} = S_t(1 + r_{t,T} - x_{t,T}) \qquad (8.11)$$

which is the cost of carry model in (8.6) exactly. In other words, if the quoted price at time $t$ for the delivery of one unit of the underlying asset at time $T$ is not equal to $f_{t,T}$ in (8.11), a riskless arbitrage opportunity exists.

The forward price implied by the replication strategy—that is, the theoretical forward price in (8.11)—is sometimes called the *synthetic forward price*. The strategies that firms can undertake to exploit observed deviations between the quoted forward purchase price and the synthetic forward price depend on the direction of the "mispricing." Let $f^*$ denote the forward price implied by the replicating strategy in Table 8.2 of borrowing funds to purchase the asset at time $t$ and storing the asset through time $T$, and suppose the actual quoted forward price $f$ is greater than $f^*$. In that case, you would undertake precisely the replicating strategy in Table 8.2 and simultaneously sell the asset forward for $f$. This is known as *cash-and-carry arbitrage*. If $f$ is below $f^*$, then you want to buy the asset for future delivery using the underpriced forward and simultaneously sell the asset (short) for immediate delivery and lend the proceeds. This called *reverse cash-and-carry arbitrage*.

### Repurchase Agreements, Asset Loans, and Forwards

We already asserted that selling an asset now and simultaneously going long a forward to buy the asset back later is equivalent to borrowing the commodity. When explicit asset loan markets exist, the market prices of those loans represent observable equivalents to the own interest rate that is implied by the spot-forward price relation. Gold, for example, is frequently borrowed and lent in a physical asset loan market with an observable *commodity leasing rate* that directly corresponds to the own rate of interest. In such cases, arbitraging observed price differences across economically equivalent positions is relatively straightforward.

Asset borrowing and lending is also often accomplished using *repurchase agreements* and *reverse repurchase agreements* (called *repos* and *reverses*, respectively), especially for financial assets. A repo is a transaction in which the asset is sold spot on trade date $t$ and repurchased on date $T$ at a price fixed on the trade date $t$.

Repos function like collateralized money loans, where the underlying asset is given to the counterparty in exchange for cash at the beginning of the transaction and, at the end of the transaction, the cash is repaid plus interest and the asset returned to its original owner. A repo is economically equivalent to simultaneously selling the asset spot and purchasing it forward.

Repos on liquid financial assets like Treasury securities are quite common. And for some commodities, physical asset loans are also accomplished using repos. The repo rate—the interest rate on the money loan—is reflected as a premium in the fixed repurchase price. If the asset is initially sold for $S_t$ and repurchased for $f_{t,T}$ on date $T$, the multiperiod repo rate $\rho_{t,T}$ is defined as:[5]

$$\frac{f_{t,T}}{S_t} - 1 = \rho_{t,T}$$

When the repo market is observable and relatively liquid, the observed repo rate should be equivalent to the cost of carry for an asset. In other words, the rate charged on a cash loan secured by some underlying asset held as collateral by the money lender should be equal to the money lending rate less the own rate of interest. Otherwise, arbitrage could be undertaken to exploit the difference.

A cash-and-carry strategy in which an arbitrageur buys the asset for immediate delivery and simultaneously sells the asset forward is economically equivalent to and thus can be replicated by a reverse repo. Table 8.3 shows this.

Note in Table 8.3 that unlike most replication strategies, both the cash-and-carry and the reverse have an initial cost of $S_t$. But because this cost is *the same* for both strategies—that is, the initial asset purchase must be funded in both cases—the terminal payoff must be the same. Arbitrage will occur unless:

$$f_{t,T} = S_t e^{\rho(T-t)} \Rightarrow \rho = r - q + c - l = r - x$$

In practice, the initial outlay of these two equivalent strategies does not matter. If we wanted to actually *exploit* an arbitrage opportunity arising from a violation of the above equality, one strategy could be used to finance the other. Suppose in particular that

$$f_{t,T} > S_t e^{\rho(T-t)}$$

**TABLE 8.3**   Cash-and-Carry and a Reverse Repo

|                                             | $t$     | $T$                       |
|---------------------------------------------|---------|---------------------------|
| **Original Portfolio**                      |         |                           |
| *Cash-and-Carry:*                           |         |                           |
|    Buy the asset for immediate delivery | $-S_t$ | —                         |
|    Short the forward          | —       | $f_{t,T} - S_T$           |
| Net                                         | $-S_t$  | $f_{t,T} - S_T$           |
|                                             |         |                           |
| **Replicating Portfolio**                   |         |                           |
| *Reverse Repo:*                             |         |                           |
|    Buy the asset for immediate delivery | $-S_t$ | —                         |
|    Resell the asset           | —       | $S_t e^{\rho(T-t)} - S_T$ |
| Net                                         | $-S_t$  | $S_t e^{\rho(T-t)} - S_T$ |

As Panel (a) of Table 8.4 illustrates, the arbitrage involves a forward sale at $f_{t,T}$ combined with a spot market purchase of the asset and a repo. Instead of just borrowing from a bank as in our earlier example, however, the arbitrageur now finances the spot market purchase *with the repo*. The sale of the asset today with an agreement to repurchase it on date $T$ generates cash at time $t$ to cover the time $t$ asset purchase, assuming no settlement lags. Instead of borrowing from a bank and owing money interest on a loan plus earning the own rate to hold the asset over time, you have used the repo to borrow funds *and* lend the commodity. You are thus now borrowing at rate $\rho$ rather than at money rate $r$, but because you have sold the asset for the period, the borrowing rate $\rho$ is reduced by the own rate of interest now earned by the asset borrower for the period.

Panel (b) of Table 8.4 shows the opposite situation in which

$$f_{t,T} < S_t e^{\rho(T-t)}$$

Now a reverse cash-and-carry is hedged with a reverse repo to lock in the deviation between the repo rate and the own rate of interest reflected in the forward price. In this case, the sale of the asset on the spot market generates cash to finance the purchase of the asset in the reverse repo.

When repo markets exist and are relatively liquid and accessible, the resulting arbitrage keeps the own rate of interest reflected in the forward price and the reverse repo rate relatively closely in line. Notice that the repo rate itself is expressed as the rate charged on a money loan backed by the asset. So,

**TABLE 8.4**  Cash-and-Carry Arbitrage

| | $t$ | $T$ |
|---|---|---|
| **Panel (a): $f_{t,T} > S_t e^{\rho(T-t)}$** | | |
| *Cash-and-Carry:* | | |
| Buy the asset for immediate delivery | $-S_t$ | — |
| Short the forward | — | $f_{t,T} - S_T$ |
| Repo | $S_t$ | $S_T - S_t e^{\rho(T-t)}$ |
| Net | — | $f_{t,T} - S_t e^{\rho(T-t)} > 0$ |
| **Panel (b): $f_{t,T} < S_t e^{\rho(T-t)}$** | | |
| *Reverse Cash-and-Carry:* | | |
| Sell the asset for immediate delivery | $S_t$ | — |
| Long the forward | — | $S_T - f_{t,T}$ |
| Reverse Repo | $-S_t$ | $S_t e^{\rho(T-t)} - S_T$ |
| Net | — | $S_t e^{\rho(T-t)} - f_{t,T} > 0$ |

a repo involves borrowing cash and lending the asset. Conversely, a *reverse repo* involves borrowing the asset and lending cash. The reverse repo rate thus is the asset borrowing/lending rate or nominal own rate of interest, and the repo rate is the negative of that nominal own rate.

## Implicit Own Interest Rates and Absolute Pricing

The cost of carry of an asset is often regarded as tautology. More specifically, the asset yield plus liquidity premium on an asset are frequently thought to be tautology *because they are not directly observable*. As such, many just define the asset yield plus liquidity premium as

$$\frac{f - S}{S} - r - c = q + l$$

In other words, the *unobservable* asset yield plus liquidity premium is often defined to be that part of the forward-spot relation that cannot be explained with other observed variables.

Sraffa, Keynes, and Hicks clearly had in mind the need for a forward market to exist in order to give the own interest rate concept meaning, and this perspective stoked the first of critics who maintain that cost of carry is tautology. In fact, the own rate of interest is essentially just the expected return on the commodity itself. Even if there is no forward market, the own rate of interest *still exists*. The problem is that we cannot directly observe it, nor can we execute clean cash-and-carry-like arbitrage transactions to ensure consistency between own rates implied by physical storage or repos and own rates explicitly reflected in the forward-spot price differential.

We can, of course, turn to absolute pricing methods to value *any payoff*, and that includes the value of a forward contract that cannot be priced by replication. Continue to assume as we have thus far that the components of the own rate of interest are nonstochastic and the same for all market participants.

### Expected Discounted Present Value

The time $T$ payoff on a long forward contract for the future delivery of one unit of underlying asset is:

$$z_T = S_T - f_{t,T} \tag{8.12}$$

If the forward is at-market as described in Chapter 7, its true price is zero. This implies no initial cash flow and that both parties must perceive the net present value of the contract to be zero at inception:

$$NPV_t(S_T - f_{t,T}) = 0 \qquad (8.13)$$

We can compute $PV_t[f_{t,T}]$ explicitly; because $f_{t,T}$ is not a random variable for which risk-adjusted discounting is required, we just deflate $f_{t,T}$ at the riskless rate. And because we are dealing with a presumed source of risk and not uncertainty, we know the counterparties will reach agreement eventually on the expected value calculations.

Recall from Chapter 7 and from your introductory finance courses that one of the most fundamental relations in finance is the following for an asset that has no interim cash flows:

$$PV_t(S_T) = S_t \qquad (8.14)$$

where $PV_t(S_T)$ denotes the expected present value of $S_T$ as of time $t$ using the appropriate discount rate. In other words, the present value today of the future price of a nondividend paying asset is equal to the current spot price. Importantly, we do not need to know the asset pricing model or stochastic discount factor as discussed in Chapter 7 in order for (8.14) to hold. *This is perfectly general.* If we wrote equation (8.14) out longhand, it would involve the stochastic discount factor from Chapter 7 to discount $S_T$. But we don't need to write it out longhand. We merely need to recognize that the notation *PV* indicates the *expected discounted present value.*

For an asset that pays a single dividend $Q$ at time $t + k$ and requires a single storage cost payment $C$ at time $t + j$, the analogue to equation (8.14) can be written as

$$PV_t(S_T) + PV_t(Q_{t+k}) - PV_t(C_{t+j}) = S_t \qquad (8.15)$$

(Assume no liquidity premium on this asset.) Simplifying (8.13) using (8.15) yields

$$f_{t,T} = S_t(1 + r_{t,T}) + C_{t+j}(1 + r_{t+j,T}) - Q_{t+k}(1 + r_{t+k,T}) \qquad (8.16)$$

Now define

$$q_{t,T} = \frac{Q_{t+k}(1 + r_{t+k,T})}{S_t} \quad \text{and} \quad c_{t,T} = \frac{C_{t+k}(1 + r_{t+k,T})}{S_t} \qquad (8.17)$$

Multiply *and* divide the second and third terms of (8.16) by $S_t$ and then substitute (8.17). This gives us the usual result for the forward purchase price with an assumed liquidity premium of zero on the asset:

$$f_{t,T} = S_t(1 + r_{t,T} - q_{t,T} + c_{t,T})$$                    (8.18)

Additional lump-sum storage costs and distributions can be added easily to (8.17). Our assumption of a single distribution and storage payment thus can be abandoned and generalized to multiple interim cash flows very easily.

So, we have shown that the expression of a forward purchase price as the current spot price times one plus the own rate of interest in money terms (i.e., the current spot price plus the net cost of carry) is not in fact merely a musing of Sraffa and Keynes. In fact, it is a direct implication of first principles in finance.

Our use of the present value operator was intended to keep the text simple. As noted, this is perfectly general notation. Nevertheless, readers wishing to verify that the net cost of carry expression for the forward price as the spot price times one plus the own interest rate in terms of money is a *direct implication* of the fundamental value equation may consult the brief proof in Appendix 3.

### Relevant Interest Rate

This derivation in the previous section on present values makes it clear that the interest rate determining the net cost of carry (both capital cost and discounting) is the *risk-free* interest rate. The replication strategy just discussed, however, clearly couched things in terms of borrowing and lending. If the risk-free rate is the relevant interest rate, these replication strategies will not yield exactly the same results in the real world.

As a general rule, the risk-free rate is the proper rate to use when computing the fair market value of $f_{t,T}$—that is the only rate that equates the net present value of the forward to zero at inception. But when thinking about actually doing an arbitrage to exploit pricing deviations or using the forward as an alternative to actual ownership of the asset, care must be taken to account for differences in real corporate borrowing and lending rates vis-à-vis the discount rate.

## THE COST OF CARRYING SOME SPECIFIC ASSETS

We can, of course, express the economic idea behind the cost of carry model in quite a few different ways depending on the assumptions we want to make. We could assume, for example, that the components of the own interest rate are multiplicative rather than additive, as in Steele (2002).

Alternatively, it sometimes helps to consider the possibility that at least some of the components of the net cost of carry are paid or received as lump-sum amounts. To take the easiest case, suppose the underlying asset is a bond that pays a level coupon $K$ at every date $t + t_k$ over the period from $t$ to $T$, where $k$ denotes the $k$th coupon payment. We can then define our asset yield in terms of these lump sums as:

$$q_{t,T} = \frac{\sum_{k=1}^{N} K\left(1 + r_{t+t_k,T}\right)}{S_t}$$

where the numerator is the value of all the coupon payments expressed in time $T$ dollars. Because q itself is expressed as a rate in terms of the asset, we need to deflate the sum by $S_t$. The resulting forward purchase price is

$$f_{t,T} = S_t\left(1 + r_{t,T} + c_{t,T} - l_{t,T}\right) - \sum_{k=1}^{N} K\left(1 + r_{t,T}\right) \tag{8.19}$$

which can be further simplified to become exactly equation (8.2). As before, the forward discount to the spot price rises or becomes less negative as money interest rates and the liquidity premium rise, and conversely for increases in the coupon rate, the number of coupons, and the physical storage costs.

Any number of different ways to allow for compounding can also be incorporated into the model. The expression in (8.7) is probably the most complete and general, if only because all of the components of the own interest rate and that rate itself are expressed as multiperiod rates. And we can always get to (8.7) from annualized rates; for example, if $R_{t,T}$ is the simple annualized money interest rate expressed as a percentage for funds of maturity $(T - t)$ days, then

$$r_{t,T} = \frac{R_{t,T}}{100}\left(\frac{T-t}{DCB}\right)$$

easily gets us back to (8.7), where $DCB$ is the day-count basis for the quotation of $R_{t,T}$ (i.e., the length of the year assumed for annualization)—for example, 360 days for U.S. money market rates, 365 days for U.K. money market rates, and so on.

Finally, suppose we define $y$ as the own interest rate expressed as a constant continuously compounded and annualized rate, where the components $q$, $c$, and $l$ have similar meanings. Denoting the money interest rate $r$ on a continuously compounded annualized basis, the price of an asset for future delivery now is

$$f_{t,T} = S_t e^{y(T-t)} = S_t e^{(r+q-c+l)(T-t)} \qquad (8.20)$$

Now let us turn to see how the cost of carry model can be expressed for a few specific examples. Most of these should look familiar to you in formula form, but because we have developed the concepts here in a slightly different way, a brief review is prudent.

We will continue to assume a single interest rate prevails, and that is the risk-free rate. Despite the unrealism that adds to the replication strategies, the results are correct for valuation purposes. If you actually want to arbitrage an observed difference to these "fair values," be sure that substitution of *your own* borrowing and lending rates does not make the arbitrage opportunity vanish!

We will also assume that all of the components of the net cost of carry are known and nonstochastic over the life of the corresponding forward contract. Finally, we will continue to assume that the forward contracts are always for the future delivery of a single unit of the underlying asset, have the same value and settlement date, and have a time $T$ payoff of:

$$z_T = S_T - f_{t,T}$$

## A Stock with No Dividends

Consider a forward contract on a single share of non-dividend-paying common stock issued by Company Brando. The prices per share of the stock are $S_t$ and $S_T$ on dates $t$ and $T$, which respectively denote the trade and value dates of the forward contract.

The own interest rate on the share of Brando stock is likely to consist almost exclusively of the money interest rate. With no dividends, the yield on holding the stock is zero, and, as a stock, storage costs are negligible. And because the stock is a single share on a single firm, it is not likely that the asset conveys any unique liquidity benefits on holders. So, $x_{t,T} = 0$ (the real own rate of interest on the stock is zero), and we can conjecture that

$$f_{t,T} = S_t(1 + r_{t,T}) \qquad (8.21)$$

so that the forward price will differ from the spot price *only* to reflect the time value of money.

To verify this result, let's first consider the relative valuation approach. Because the asset has no yield, storage costs, or liquidity premium, the replication strategy is simple. At time $t$, a single share of stock is purchased for $S_t$ using funds that have just been borrowed for that purpose and that are repayable with interest at $T$. The stock is held and grows in value to $S_T$.

Table 8.5 compares the payoff on this investment strategy with the payoff on a long forward. The net payoffs on the two strategies both have the same initial cost and risk, and both leave you holding the asset at $T$. To preclude arbitrage, the forward purchase price thus must be exactly the form shown in equation (8.21).

We can also verify the result using absolute pricing directly. If the forward is at-market, the net present value of the expected discounted payoff must be zero at time $t$:

$$NPV_t(S_T - f_{t,T}) = 0 \qquad (8.22)$$

But the present value of the time $T$ price of a non-dividend-paying stock is just $S_t$, so equation (8.22) immediately simplifies to (8.20).

## A Stock Paying Known Lump-Sum Dividends or a Bond Paying Fixed Coupons

Now suppose Company Brando pays $N$ dividends between dates $t$ and $T$, each of which is fixed and denoted by $Q_{t+t_k}$. The present value of all the dividends can be expressed as:

$$\sum_{k=1}^{N} \frac{Q_{t+t_k}}{1 + r_{t,t+t_k}}$$

We can express all the dividends paid as a dividend rate between $t$ and $T$ by summing the values of these dividends when paid and assuming each is in-

**TABLE 8.5** Replicating the Forward Purchase of a Stock That Pays No Dividends

|  | $t$ | $T$ |
|---|---|---|
| **Buy and Hold Stock + Borrow Money** | | |
| *Money Loan:* | | |
|    Borrow dollars | $S_t$ | — |
|    Repay dollars and interest | — | $-S_t(1 + r_{t,T})$ |
| **Buy and Hold Stock:** | | |
|    Buy stock | $-S_t$ | $S_T$ |
| Net | $0$ | $S_T - S_t(1 + r_{t,T})$ |
| | | |
| **Long Forward** | | |
| Net | $0$ | $S_T - f_{t,T}$ |

vested from the time it is received until $T$, and then deflating that total by the initial spot price:

$$q_{t,T} = \frac{\sum_{k=1}^{N} Q_{t+t_k}\left(1 + r_{t+t_k,T}\right)}{S_t} \tag{8.23}$$

Note that the formulation is perfectly equivalent to a bond that pays level coupons periodically.

As in the non-dividend-paying stock case, it seems reasonable to assume a zero storage cost. For simplicity, we also again assume a zero liquidity benefit. So, the real own interest rate on this asset is $x_{t,T} = q_{t,T}$ and we can conjecture that the forward purchase price is:

$$f_{t,T} = S_t(1 + r_{t,T} - q_{r,T}) \tag{8.24}$$

To verify our conjecture, consider an investment strategy in which you borrow cash to finance the immediate purchase of the asset, as before. You earn the dividends or coupons when they are paid and invest them until date $T$. Table 8.6 compares the payoff on this strategy with the payoff at $T$ on a long forward.

From Table 8.6, we see that the two strategies will be economically equivalent if and only if the forward purchase price is given by equation (8.24), just as we conjectured. You can also easily verify on your own that the present value method yields the same result.

**TABLE 8.6** Replicating the Forward Purchase of a Stock That Pays Fixed Dividends

|  | $t$ | $T$ |
| --- | --- | --- |
| **Buy and Hold Asset + Borrow Money** | | |
| *Money Loan:* | | |
| Borrow dollars | $S_t$ | — |
| Repay dollars and interest | — | $-S_t(1 + r_{t,T})$ |
| *Buy and Hold Stock/Bond:* | | |
| Buy stock | $-S_t$ | $S_T$ |
| Invest dividends/coupons as they are received | ... | $S_t q_{t,T}$ |
| Net | 0 | $S_T - S_t(1 + r_{t,T} - q_{t,T})$ |
| | | |
| **Long Forward** | | |
| Net | 0 | $S_T - f_{t,T}$ |

## Bond Earning a Continuous Proportional Liquidity Premium

Now suppose we consider a forward contract on a coupon bond. Highly liquid bonds are often used for liquidity management purposes in the so-called repo market. Assume this gives rise to a liquidity premium, l.

Let us assume in this example that all these rates are continuously compounded and annualized, so that the nominal own rate is $r - x = r - q - l$. We can conjecture that the forward purchase price should be:

$$f_{t,T} = S_t e^{(r-q-l)(T-t)} \tag{8.25}$$

For the replication strategy, we want to do things a little differently than before given our assumption here about continuous compounding. First, suppose we assume that the interest paid to bondholders is continuously reinvested in the bonds over the period from $t$ to $T$. In that case, one dollar of outstanding bonds will grow to $e^{q(T-t)}$ dollars by time T, all else equal. If we only invest $e^{-q(T-t)}$ in the bonds at time $t$ and then continuously reinvest coupon income, our investment will grow to exactly one dollar by time $T$: $e^{-q(T-t)} \times e^{q(T-t)} = 1$.

The logic is even more straightforward when considering the liquidity premium. Because it is reflected in the price of the bond but is not ever explicitly "earned," we do not need to worry about continuous reinvestment assumptions. We can thus again reduce what we borrow and invest by $e^{-l(T-t)}$ initially because we know the liquidity premium will make the bond price rise at a rate reflecting the liquidity benefit of holding the bond.

So, we borrow $S_t e^{-(q+l)(T-t)}$ and use the proceeds to buy the equivalent amount of bonds. We continuously reinvest the coupon income over the life of the forward and repay the loan at maturity. Table 8.7 shows the resulting payoff of the strategy compared to the forward. Given the equivalence of the two strategies, to preclude arbitrage it must be the case that the forward purchase price conforms to equation (8.25).

## Foreign Exchange

If the asset in question is a foreign currency, the one trick is to keep our notation straight. If we are buying the foreign currency with the domestic currency, then the "underlying price" is the domestic currency price of a unit of

**TABLE 8.7**  Replicating the Forward Purchase of a Bond with a Liquidity Premium

|  | $t$ | $T$ |
|---|---|---|
| **Buy and Hold Bonds + Borrow Money** | | |
| *Money Loan:* | | |
|   Borrow dollars | $S_t e^{-(q+l)(T-t)}$ | — |
|   Repay dollars and interest | — | $S_t e^{-(q+l)(T-t)}$ |
| *Buy and Hold Bonds:* | | |
|   Buy bonds and continuously reinvest | | |
|     coupon income | $-S_t e^{-(q+l)(T-t)}$ | $S_T$ |
| Net | $0$ | $S_T - S_t e^{-(q+l)(T-t)}$ |
| **Long Forward** | | |
| Net | $0$ | $S_T - f_{t,T}$ |

foreign currency. For example, a forward purchase agreement on Swiss francs denominated in dollars has an underlying spot price of $S_t$, where this reflects the dollar price of a franc.

Knowing that the contract is dollar-based, what is the rate at which we must borrow funds to finance a spot purchase of francs if we engaged in a buy and hold replication strategy? Clearly, the answer is the dollar interest rate. Similarly, what we forego in this case is the interest payable on a *Swiss franc*–denominated deposit. We can assume no storage costs, and, although there may well be a liquidity premium associated with holding cash, it is not likely that liquidity premium will be any higher holding *francs* as cash than *dollars* as cash. The liquidity premium for the franc thus is presumed to be reflected in the two money interest rates, and the real own interest rate on Swiss francs thus is $x = q$, again assuming continuously compounded annualized rates. The net cost of carry thus is $r - x = r - q$, and the forward purchase price should be:

$$f_{t,T} = S_t e^{(r-q)(T-t)} \tag{8.26}$$

Our replication strategy is now a bit more complex because we have to switch from one asset into another and back again. We know we need to borrow dollars in order to buy Swiss francs with dollars. We also know that once we convert to francs, we will invest whatever that amount is in franc-denominated deposits to earn the franc interest until time $T$. In particular, if we bor-

**TABLE 8.8** Replicating the Forward Purchase of Swiss Francs with U.S. Dollars

|  | $t$ | $T$ |
|---|---|---|
| **Buy and Hold Foreign Currency + Borrow Money** | | |
| *Dollars:* | | |
| Borrow dollars | $S_t e^{-q(T-t)}$ | $-S_t e^{(r-q)(T-t)}$ |
| *Swiss francs:* | | |
| Convert dollars into francs and invest at franc rate | $e^{-q(T-t)}$ | 1 |
| *Dollars:* | | |
| Convert francs back into dollars | — | $S_T$ |
| Net | 0 | $S_T - S_t e^{(r-q)(T-t)}$ |
| | | |
| **Long Forward** | | |
| Net | 0 | $S_T - f_{t,T}$ |

row $S_t e^{-q(T-t)}$, then that amount converts into exactly $e^{-q(T-t)}$ francs which will grow into one franc by time $T$. Converting one franc back into dollars at the time $T$ dollar price of francs yields exactly $S_T$ dollars. On top of that, we then repay our dollar loan. Table 8.8 compares the cash flows on this strategy to a long forward on Swiss francs.

The forward price of a franc purchased with dollars that precludes arbitrage with the interest rate markets thus is given by equation (8.26). This is also the continuously compounded formulation of what we call *covered interest parity*.

## Equity Indexes and Other Cash-Settled Products

Consider a forward on an index of $N$ stocks whose current value is $I_t$. The forward purchase price $f_{t,T}$ to be paid at time $t$ entitles the long to a cash payment equal to $I_T$, or the value of the underlying stock index at time $T$. The contract thus is *cash-settled*, which immediately tells us that the underlying involves no storage costs. The "underlying" is not the stocks in the index, but the *cash equivalent* of the stocks in the index. Because the forward allows the long and short to hold a payoff perfectly correlated with the index of stocks without having to tie up funds in all $N$ stocks, the liquidity premium could be fairly significant. This is the case on all cash-settled futures and forwards.

Denote the multiperiod fixed proportional dividend yield on the index as $q_{t,T}$ and liquidity premium as $l_{t,T}$. Recall from the bond example that the liquidity premium is not earned, but does affect prices and the expected growth rate in prices. So, we can borrow $I_t(1 + l_{t,T})^{-1}$ and buy all the stocks in the index. As dividends are received, invest them until time $T$. You can easily verify that we get the expected result:

$$f_{t,T} = I_t(1 + r_{t,T} - q_{t,T} - l_{t,T})$$  (8.27)

## Commodities

For our final illustration of cost of carry forward pricing, consider a storable physical commodity (wheat, corn, gold, oil, etc.) and assume that the commodity is continuously stored in some amount over the period from $t$ to $T$.[6] The holder of that commodity earns an implicit convenience yield of $q_{t,T}$ for keeping the commodity in storage, but incurs storage costs at the rate $c_{t,T}$. Assume that all firms face the same storage cost and earn the same convenience yield. Assume further no liquidity premium, so that the real own interest rate on the commodity is $x_{t,T} = q_{t,T} - c_{t,T}$. We conjecture that the price of one unit of this commodity for time $T$ delivery will be:

$$f_{t,T} = S_t(1 + r_{t,T} - q_{t,T} + c_{t,T})$$  (8.28)

The replication strategy is straight buy-and-hold—borrow $S_t$ and buy the commodity, earning the convenience yield and paying the storage costs over time. Table 8.9 shows the payoff from this strategy and the forward purchase.

**TABLE 8.9**  Replicating the Forward Purchase of a Storable Commodity

|  | $t$ | $T$ |
|---|---|---|
| **Buy and Store Commodity + Borrow Money** | | |
| *Money Loan:* | | |
| Borrow dollars | $S_t$ | — |
| Repay dollars and interest | — | $-S_t(1 + r_{t,T})$ |
| *Buy and Store Commodity:* | | |
| Buy asset | $-S_t$ | $S_T$ |
| Pay storage costs | . . . | $-S_t c_{t,T}$ |
| Earn implicit convenience yield | . . . | $S_t q_{t,T}$ |
| Net | 0 | $S_T - S_t(1 + r_{t,T} - q_{t,T} + c_{t,T})$ |
| | | |
| **Long Forward** | | |
| Net | 0 | $S_T - f_{t,T}$ |

Not surprisingly, the strategies are economically equivalent if $f_{t,T}$ is given by equation (8.28).


## THE COST OF CARRY WHEN THE OWN INTEREST RATE IS STOCHASTIC

We now consider a slightly different variant of the cost of carry model. Specifically, we now allow for the possibility that the own rate is stochastic.


### Derivatives on Financial Assets Subject to Liquidity Shocks

To keep the discussion tractable, suppose that the asset in question is financial. Physical storage costs can be presumed trivial, and the asset yield can be presumed known and nonstochastic (e.g., coupons paid to bondholders over the period from $t$ to $T$). We can further assume that the money interest rate is the risk-free rate and that all firms can borrow and lend at this rate. This leaves us with the liquidity premium, which we now allow to be stochastic. For further concreteness, suppose the liquidity premium is expressed as a time $T$ random variable $L_T$, where we can define the liquidity premium "rate" as $l_T = L_T / S_t$.

If the true price of an at-market forward must be zero at inception, then:

$$E_t\big[m_T(S_T - f_{t,T})\big] = 0$$
$$\Rightarrow f_{t,T} = R^f E_t\big[m_T S_T\big] \tag{8.29}$$

We can also use the fundamental value equation (FVE) to express the current price of the asset as the expected discounted present value of the terminal price *plus liquidity premium*:

$$S_t = E_t[m_T(S_T + L_T)] \tag{8.30}$$

which we can rewrite as

$$S_t = E_t[m_T S_T] + \frac{E_t[L_T]}{R^f} + \text{cov}(L_T, m_T) \tag{8.31}$$

The forward price thus can now be written by substituting (8.31) into (8.29):

$$f_{t,T} = S_t(1 + r_{t,T}) - E_t[L_T] - (1 + r_{t,T})\text{cov}(L_T, m_T) \qquad (8.32)$$

or, in a much friendlier and more familiar fashion,

$$f_{t,T} = S_t(1 + r_{t,T}) - E_t[l_T]) + \lambda \qquad (8.33)$$

so that the forward price is just the *expected* own interest rate plus a risk premium, which in this case is equal to:

$$\lambda = -(1 + r_{t,T})\text{cov}(L_T, m_T)$$

If the liquidity shock is positively correlated with the discount factor, this implies that the liquidity benefit of owning the *physical asset* is higher during bad times. The forward price must fall to compensate the derivatives user for choosing a forward purchase rather than a spot purchase plus physical storage.

Because the components of the own interest rate are additive, equation (8.33) can easily be generalized for any other component of the cost of carry that might be stochastic, such as the convenience yield on a physical asset. In general,

$$\begin{aligned} f_{t,T} &= S_t(1 + E_t[b_{t,T}]) + \lambda \\ f_{t,T} &= S_t(1 - E_t[y_{t,T}]) + \lambda \end{aligned} \qquad (8.34)$$

Equation (8.34) cannot be arbitraged risklessly through some strategy like cash-and-carry. As noted in Chapter 7, however, the LOOP still governs even risky assets. The practical distinction is that arbitrage in this case is no longer a riskless proposition. If the discount factor is not properly measured and identified, for example, a firm could be conducting an arbitrage transaction that is in fact simply a misdirected result of the wrong specification for $m$.

## Alternative Interpretation of the Convenience Yield

If we assume that the only source of randomness in the own interest rate is the convenience yield on physical commodities, then an alternative interpretation can prove quite useful in considering the relations between spot and forward markets for the asset and the market for storage. In particular, the convenience yield is usually viewed as an implicit dividend that is either continuously earned over the storage period or accrues in some lump sum.

A more interesting way to view the convenience yield, however, is as an *option on the physical commodity*. Recall that the convenience yield had value primarily because of the precautionary demand for storage. The lower the aggregate inventory, the higher the convenience yield—and the greater the option's value.

If the convenience yield is viewed as an option allowing its holder to shift the asset from storage into the current market, then the price for that option should be additive to the other components of the cost of carry model. Litzenberger and Rabinowitz (1992) provide an argument along similar lines for the value of immediate access to inventory in the oil market.

## HETEROGENEOUS FIRMS AND OWN RATES OF INTEREST

We thus far have assumed that all of the components of the own rate of interest for a given asset—the money rate of interest, the cost of physical storage, the asset yield, and the liquidity premium—do not differ across firms. For derivatives on financial assets, this might be a plausible assumption given the triviality of storage costs and the fact that asset yields are usually explicit monetary distributions. Because firms do not have anything akin to a "marginal utility of wealth," a dollar coupon paid to one firm has the same value as a dollar coupon paid to another firm.

Physical assets and their derivatives, however, are frequently associated with cross-sectional variations in the cost of carry. We begin this section by considering where these firm-specific variations come from, and then consider the impact of heterogeneity on the own rate of interest reflected in the forward purchase price of an asset.

### Where Does the Own Rate of Interest Come From?

In our foregoing discussion, we paid relatively little attention to the issue of "what drives what." As explained in Chapters 7 and 8, relative pricing is essentially a partial equilibrium approach in which we take the prices from certain explicit and implicit markets *as given* and then derive a price for the "target" asset such that the LOOP holds.

In fact, for many assets the nominal own rate of interest—which we have argued is essentially the expected return on the asset underlying the corresponding spot and forward contracts assuming no risk premium—is best viewed as the price of a separate asset or financial activity. Specifically, the own rate of interest is essentially the *price of storage*, and, accordingly, will be driven by firm-specific considerations *in the storage market*. The following subsections consider how each component of the own rate may be affected by these idiosyncratic considerations.

### Nominal Money Rate of Interest

From our discussion of absolute pricing and the cost of carry model earlier in this chapter and in Chapter 7, we know that the correct interest rate to use when expressing cost of carry pricing using the FVE is the risk-free rate. But we also know that this is *not* the relevant rate when considering the cash-and-carry arbitrage process that keeps prices across related spot and derivatives markets in line. We need instead to take into account the actual borrowing and lending rates faced by firms that are conducting arbitrage between the spot and forward markets for the asset and the physical storage market.

### Liquidity Premium

Much of the *General Theory* by Keynes was an effort to construct an elaborate explanation for the workings of the economic system. Keynes intended the interpretation of the liquidity premium in the own rate of interest to be a liquidity premium determined in a general competitive equilibrium across all assets, each of which has its own liquidity premium—including money itself. Indeed, for Keynes, money was *unique* because of its liquidity premium: "But it is an essential difference between money and all (or most) other assets that in the case of money its liquidity-premium much exceeds its carrying cost, whereas in the case of other assets their carrying cost much exceeds their liquidity-premium." (Keynes, 1936, p. 227)

Many of the theories advanced by Lord Keynes prior to 1930 gained widespread and lasting acceptance. The notions he advanced in the *General Theory*, however, met with relatively significant criticism and generated years of contentious debate. Ultimately, many of the ideas proposed by Keynes in his *General Theory* have been abandoned because of the lack of empirical support and in some cases just theoretical flaws and inconsistencies.

The tendency of many economists has been to throw the proverbial baby out with the bathwater when it comes to the ideas expressed in the *General Theory*. But we have already seen the fallacy of this approach. We certainly are *not* prepared, for example, to dispense with own interest rates and the cost of carry model just because they were first meaningfully developed in Keynes' *General Theory*. And so it is true for the liquidity premium.

Virtually all contemporary discussions of the cost of carry model ignore the liquidity premium. Yet, it is perfectly intuitive and reasonable to assume that this sort of variable might be of real importance for at least some types of assets on which forwards may be based. Like the asset yield, this premium is *sacrificed* for users of derivatives engaged in synthetic ownership or asset lending.

If a liquidity premium for certain types of assets does exist in a manner that affects the own rates of interest and costs of carry for those assets—and there is good reason to believe it does—then it must emerge from some equilibrium that is far beyond the scope of our analysis here. As noted, the determination of equilibrium liquidity premiums was the backbone of the monetary portions of Keynes' entire *General Theory*, so far be it for us to take on such a grand task here. Accordingly, we shall take the admittedly cowardly approach of simply continuing to assume that if it exists, the liquidity premium is an exogenous constant and is identical across firms for a given asset. Perhaps we can address the nature of this variable more earnestly in future research.

### Physical Cost of Storage

Storage costs for physical assets include warehousing fees, transportation costs into authorized delivery points, insurance, and the like. In general, storage costs will be zero for cash-settled derivatives, negligible for physically settled derivatives on financial assets, and fairly significant *but stable* on commodity derivatives. In other words, the cost of physical storage does not generally exhibit significant *time series* variation.

Cross-sectional variability in the cost of storage, however, is an entirely different matter altogether. Evidently, not all firms will have the ability and infrastructure to store all assets as a part of their main businesses. Those that do not may turn to logistics firms and other supply chain managers, or firms whose primary business *is* the provision of storage and often also transportation services. But those logistics firms, together with those market participants that can undertake storage, can be expected to have very different cost schedules for storing physical inventory. We return later to how equilibrium in the market for physical storage across firms with heterogeneous storage costs and capacities affects the own rate of interest and the relation between forward and spot prices for the asset being stored.

### Convenience Yield

Working (1962) argued that there are four reasons why people and firms store physical commodities. First, the "transactional" demand for storage leads some firms to store products to avoid the transaction costs of getting rid of them. People store pennies for this reason—the benefit of getting rid of five pennies for a nickel is surely smaller than waiting until you have 100 or even 1,000 pennies saved up.

Second, firms sometimes have a "pure storage" motive for storage, as Working calls it. This simply means that storage is required for a purely physical reason usually having to do with some production process. Some auto manufacturers let every car leave their assembly lines, for example, with at least *some* gasoline in the tank. In order for this to be possible, they must store some gasoline near the assembly lines. And so forth.

A third motivation for storage is speculative—people store an asset in anticipation of an increase in its value. This is the classical rationale for hiding money under a mattress—or, better still, for buying gold bullion. Gold has virtually no appreciable use in any major production process, but people hold on to it as a store of value and in the hope that its value will rise.

Finally and most importantly, Working characterizes the "precautionary demand" for storage. Firms sometimes have a precautionary demand for storage not because of *current* production needs—that is the "pure storage" rationale for inventory—but because of *unanticipated shocks to future* production needs. To put it in terms developed in Chapter 1, precautionary storage is one of the mechanisms of a market economy for ensuring consistency in plans when short-term consumption and production deviate. This can result in an inventory stock-out, which can be very costly. Imagine an airline having to ground its fleet because of a temporary shortage in deicing fluid! Or Fratelli Rosetti having to close down its Geneva store for a week because it ran out of shoes.

The distinctions between these four motivations for physical inventory holdings are not always clear. Fratelli Rosetti needs *some* shoes on hand in Geneva to keep its store open. But the company might choose to inventory more than it needs for the current week's sales to avoid having to turn customers away next week later because of a problem with its shipping agent. The shoes it needs to open the store and sell this week is a pure storage motive for inventory, whereas keeping enough shoes to last another week is precautionary.

The convenience yield of an asset is driven almost entirely by the "demand for immediacy" based on the precautionary demand for storage. The convenience yield cannot be negative and remains very close to zero when a large amount of the commodity is in storage. Plenty of the commodity is on hand to assure producers and intermediaries that a future stock-out will not occur given reasonable demand and supply conditions. On the other hand, as inventories start to decline, it becomes harder for firms to ensure the consistency of short-term plans by just tapping into the storage market. Accordingly, the convenience yield of each additional unit of the commodity rises as aggregate stocks of the stored asset fall. Figure 8.1 illustrates this relation.

Every producer with a precautionary demand for the storage of the asset faces a relation like the one depicted in Figure 8.1, but the exact shape of the curve facing each firm may differ. As long as the precautionary demand for storage exists, the convenience yield will rise as inventory falls for all firms, and in most cases it will do so at an increasing rate. But the precise properties

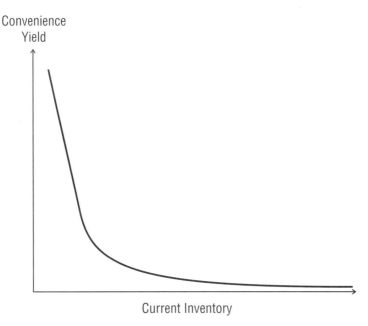

**FIGURE 8.1**  The Demand for Immediacy

of the curve are particular to the firm in question and depend on a variety of factors (e.g., how costly a stock-out would be, how much inventory is required to avoid a stock-out, the ability of the firm to borrow from the inventory of other firms, etc.).

## Equilibrium in Storage Markets[7]

The asset market (both for immediate and for future delivery) and the storage market are sufficiently interconnected that it makes sense to consider these markets as being in some type of *simultaneous* or *general equilibrium*. True, we can take the real own rate of interest as exogenous (i.e., take the price of storage as given) and then compute the fair forward purchase price consistent with that own rate of interest and the current spot price. Or we can define the real own rate of interest as simply the proportional discount of the forward price to the spot price plus the money interest rate, thus taking forward and spot prices as exogenous and given. But neither of these perspectives is entirely satisfactory from a theoretical or practical standpoint. If we had to choose, we would surely want to consider equilibrium in the market for immediate delivery of the asset and storage of the asset—the latter of which is essentially the expected return on the asset—and then derive the forward price as a function of those variables. But even then, we need to know more about how the market for storage clears.

As a base case, let us first consider a situation in which the notion of a Marshallian long-run equilibrium (see Appendix 1) is well defined, and let us set aside both risk and uncertainty for the time being by assuming nonstochastic components of the cost of carry. Under these assumptions, a competitive long-run Marshallian equilibrium in the storage market will leave us with a salvageable version of the cost of carry model. To see how this process works, suppose the competitive quoted forward purchase price is:

$$f_{t,T}^o = S_t(1 + r_{t,T} - q_{t,T} + c_{t,T}^o - l_{t,T})$$

where $c_{t,T}^o$ denotes any arbitrary cost of storage.

A firm for which $c_{t,T} < c_{t,T}^o$ can earn positive *short-run* economic profits by going short the forward at the quoted price $f^o$ and simultaneously buying and storing the commodity, earning exactly $c_{t,T}^o - c_{t,T}$ from the operation. As long as the firm is not capacity constrained, it will continue to short the forward, buy the asset, and store until the forward price falls to $f_{t,T} = S_t(1 + r_{t,T} - q_{t,T} + c_{t,T} - l_{t,T})$ or until the firm reaches a point where expanding its storage is either no longer possible (e.g., a capacity constraint) or not sensible (i.e., the firm reaches its minimum average cost so that further storage would lead to decreasing returns).

Even if the firm in question stops storing before the selling pressure in the forward market is sufficient to drive the quoted forward price to $f_{t,T}$, as long as *any* firm has a storage cost below the cost reflected in the forward price, this process will continue. The forward market sales and additional physical asset storage cycle will end only when the forward price is:

$$f_{t,T}^* = S_t(1 + r_{t,T} - q_{t,T} + c_{t,T}^* - l_{t,T})$$

where $c_{t,T}^*$ denotes the *marginal* cost of storage for the *marginal storer* from $t$ to $T$. This marginal entrant earns exactly zero economic profits since its own cost of carry is equal to the cost of carry reflected in the forward price.

Things work in the other direction for any firms where $c_{t,T} > c_{t,T}^o$. Those firms will go *long* the forward and short the asset, effectively loaning the commodity. Again, entry occurs until the forward price finally reflects the marginal storage cost of the marginal storer.

In the short run, the own interest rate or cost of carry reflects the marginal cost of storing an incremental unit of the commodity for the marginal storer. In the long run, the cost of storage reflected in the forward price will also correspond to the minimum point on a traditional U-shaped industry long-run average cost curve. Suppose all firms have $c^*$ below this minimum long-run average cost of storage. In this case, at least one firm will expand its storage activities until marginal cost rises to minimum average cost and equals the marginal price of the cost of carry, and the new $c^*$ will also be reflected in the forward price.

The same adjustment mechanism works to bring the spot-forward price relation in line with the price of storage when any of the other components of the cost of carry diverge between the physical storage market and the synthetic storage market *implied by* the forward-spot relation. The most likely candidate of these other components to vary across firms is the convenience yield on physical assets, given the strong possibility that the demand for immediacy will differ by firm. Ultimately, the same process as that described earlier will occur until the convenience yield reflected in the forward price is the convenience yield of the marginal storer.

In fact, a much more realistic way of viewing the adjustment process is to consider the own rate of interest as the price of storage and then simply consider equilibrium *in the storage market*. That enables us to take into account relations across these variables. A firm with a high demand for immediacy but capacity constraints in storage, for example, will have a different optimal storage decision than a firm with a low demand for immediacy and declining average storage costs. Firms participating in the physical storage market will identify their storage optimum given the price of synthetic storage reflected in forward prices, and conversely. A long-run simultaneous equilibrium in the asset market and storage market will eventually clear when the marginal asset lending rate is equalized across both markets.

Things get a lot more complicated when we assume that the own rate of interest is both heterogeneous across firms *and* stochastic. We also end up with a messier situation when we relax the unrealistic assumption of a long-run Marshallian equilibrium and allow for the possibility of long-run profits arising from Krightian uncertainty. For various reasons that will become clear later, we postpone a discussion of these scenarios until Chapter 12.

## A SUMMARY OF TERMINOLOGY

We have introduced a lot of new concepts and terminology in this chapter, all of which are summarized in Table 8.10 so that we can keep track of the concepts and terms we have developed.

**TABLE 8.10**  Terminology in the Cost of Carry Model

| Term | Notation | Concept | = |
|---|---|---|---|
| Interest rate | $r_{t,T}$ | Asset funding cost or money interest rate | — |
| Asset/convenience yield | $q_{t,T}$ | Distributions to asset owners or benefit of physical asset being on-hand | — |
| Cost of storage | $c_{t,T}$ | Physical storage cost | — |
| Asset liquidity premium | $l_{t,T}$ | Liquidity benefit of asset ownership | — |
| Real own rate of interest | $x_{t,T}$ | Implied rate at which asset can be lent over time | $q_{t,T} - c_{t,T} + l_{t,T}$ |
| Nominal own rate of interest | $y_{t,T}$ | Implied rate at which asset can be lent over time | $q_{t,T} - c_{t,T} + l_{t,T} - r_{t,T}$ $= x_{t,T} - r_{t,T}$ |
| Real cost of carry | $-x_{t,T}$ | Cost of carrying the asset over time (excluding funding or capital cost) | $c_{t,T} - q_{t,T} - l_{t,T}$ |
| Nominal cost of carry | $r_{t,T} - x_{t,T}$ | Total cost of carrying the asset over time | $r_{t,T} + c_{t,T} - q_{t,T} - l_{t,T}$ |
| Basis/calendar basis | $b_{t,T}$ | Real cost of carry | $-y_{t,T}$ $= r_{t,T} + c_{t,T} - q_{t,T} - l_{t,T}$ $= b_{t,T}$ $= -y_{t,T}$ |
| Asset repo rate | $\rho_{t,T}$ | Explicit rate at which asset can be borrowed over time | |

# NOTES

1. Sraffa was, for example, virtually one of the only people that Wittgenstein explicitly thanked and acknowledged in the preface to his *Philosophical Investigations*. See Roncaglia (2000) for an interesting account of some of these interactions.

2. Typical of the vitriol in some of these Sraffian exchanges, Hayek—normally quite detached but not at all bashful—responded to Sraffa's article with a reply that was as critical of Sraffa as Sraffa had been of him. At one point, Hayek (1932, p. 249) argues, "I venture to believe that Mr. Keynes would fully agree with me in refuting Mr. Sraffa's suggestion. . . . That Mr. Sraffa should have made such a suggestion, indeed, seems to me only to in-

dicate the new and rather unexpected fact that he has understood Mr. Keynes' theory even less than he has my own." But Sraffa and Keynes were close friends, and Sraffa would not let Hayek have the last word. At Sraffa's insistence and with Hayek's permission, a footnote was inserted after the quote above that read as follows: "With Prof. Hayek's permission I should like to say that, to the best of my comprehension, Mr. Sraffa has understood my theory accurately.—J. M. Keynes" (Hayek, 1932, p. 249)

3. Keynes (1936) gives the most complete treatment of own interest rates, and we will stick broadly to his notation.

4. We have taken some small liberties with notation but basically stick to Keynes's definitions here.

5. Repos and reverses often involve "haircuts" in which the actual cash paid for the initial sale of the asset is below $S_t$ to reflect the credit risk of the cash borrower. We will ignore this for the purpose of maintaining clarity in our discussion and examples.

6. French (1986) explains the importance of the continuous storage assumption.

7. Much of this section is based on an analysis developed in Culp and Hanke (2003).

# CHAPTER 9

# The Supply of Storage and the Term Structure of Forward Prices

In the preceding chapter, we developed the idea that every asset—financial and physical—has an own rate of interest that represents the price of moving that asset over time. This price of storage is the bridge connecting the price of an asset for immediate delivery to its price for future delivery. Thanks to the Law of One Price, the own rate of interest on an asset is equivalent to the asset's lending rate. The own rate charged by an asset lender to a borrower, moreover, is essentially the negative of the cost of carrying that asset over time.

In order to develop the intuition of the pricing model, we confined our attention in Chapter 8 to a single holding period from $t$ to $T$. In this chapter, we begin by generalizing the own interest rate concept to multiple periods. We examine the economic forces that lead to simultaneous equilibrium and market clearing in intertemporal storage markets and asset markets themselves. We then turn to look at the economic function and interpretation of a series of own interest rates on a single asset prevailing at the same time but for different future delivery dates—the so-called term structure of own interest rates, with which is associated the *term structure of futures or forward prices*.

## THE SUPPLY OF STORAGE

In this section, we consider in more detail the mechanics of the storage market and how the own rate of interest as a price of storage helps "clear" this market. We will focus first on analyzing the components of the own rate of interest that are directly tied to the amount of an asset in storage, and then turn to the process by which the market adjusts.

## Inventory Levels and the Own Rate of Interest

Recall from Chapter 8 and Figure 8.1 that the demand for immediacy resulting from many firms' precautionary demands for storage is considered to be the principal driver of the convenience yield. Similarly, unexpected shifts in the demand for immediacy generally account for much of the *variation* in the convenience yield, both cross-sectionally (i.e., across many firms) and over time.

Compared to the convenience yield, the other components of the cost of carry are relatively stable over time. Because financial assets usually pay explicit yields that are not related to underlying storage and inventory considerations, the yield component of the own rate of interest on financial assets is generally a lot less variable than the yield on physical asset ownership. And given the low volatility of the other components of the own rate, this implies that the own rate of interest is generally more volatile for commodities than for stocks, bonds, and other financial assets.

The liquidity premium, nominal interest rate, and physical cost of storage, moreover, generally do not change much as the level of current inventory changes.[1] The relation between current inventory levels and the nominal own rate of interest over some defined time period from $t$ to $T$ is shown in Figure 9.1,

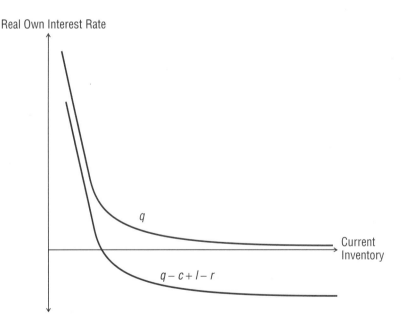

**FIGURE 9.1** The Supply of Storage

assuming a negligible liquidity premium for simplicity. The assumption that nothing but the convenience yield depends on storage essentially means that the inclusion of the physical cost of carry, interest rate, and liquidity premium do little except shift the graph downward by a constant.

Figure 9.1 also reminds us—as did the numerical example we saw early in Chapter 8—that the nominal own rate may well be negative. When inventories are high and the demand for immediacy low, the convenience yield is low. With an assumed negligible liquidity premium, the physical and capital costs of storage more than swamp the asset yield, thus driving the own rate below zero. This implies that a firm will *get paid* to borrow a commodity, which is perfectly reasonable given that the benefit from borrowing the commodity is very low but storage costs remain positive.

The cost of carry from $t$ to $T$ is the negative of the nominal own rate of interest prevailing for the same time period. Figure 9.2 shows the supply of storage from that perspective by indicating the relation between the cost of carry and the current level of inventory. Apart from showing the same basic relation as Figure 9.1 but from the opposite perspective, Figure 9.2 also depicts what we call the *full carry* for the storage period depicted on the graph (i.e., from $t$ to $T$). A full carry occurs when there is absolutely *no* benefit to owning the asset, and the price of storage from $t$ to $T$ is exclusively the cost of capital tied up plus the cost of physical storage. In this situation, the price of storage reflects full compensation of the storer for holding the asset. But as inventory shrinks, the convenience yield rises and the cost of carry declines, both at an increasing rate.

Notice also that there is no analogue to "full carry" when inventories shrink toward zero.[2] As we saw in Figure 9.1 when we first looked at the demand for immediacy and the precautionary demand for storage, inventories that get tighter and tighter cause convenience yields to rise at a faster and faster rate. Figure 9.2 confirms from a cost of carry perspective that the convenience yield can essentially grow without bound, thereby implying a cost of carry that can become extremely negative. But the converse is not true at high levels of inventory. Storage costs and nominal interest rates can be presumed to be bounded from above, and the convenience yield and liquidity premium cannot be negative by assumption. Accordingly, no matter how large current stocks of inventories grow, the cost of carry never exceeds the nominal interest rate plus the physical cost of storage.

A natural asymmetry is thus built into the storage market. When inventories decline, the own rate of interest rises more and more. Inventories never actually reach zero in this world, because the own rate simply becomes too high—the next section provides an explanation of the adjustment effects that guarantee this result. As inventories rise, however, the own rate of interest falls and becomes negative, but it can never exceed the physical and capital cost of storage.

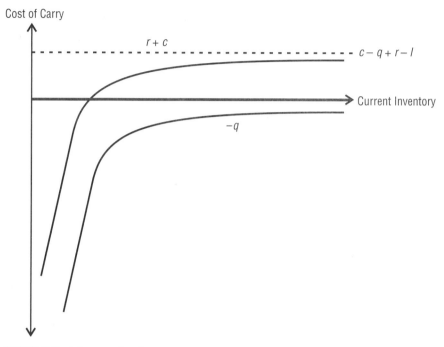

Cost of Carry

$r + c$

$c - q + r - l$

Current Inventory

$-q$

**FIGURE 9.2**  The Supply of Storage as a Function of the Cost of Carry

## Adjustments to Inventory Changes and the Supply of Storage

Figures 9.1 and 9.2 are "comparative static" representations. In other words, they represent the relations between inventory and the own interest rate or cost of carry as known, static functions. At any given point in time, we can use these figures to see what own rate or cost of carry is implied by a given amount of the asset held in storage, assuming everything else (here and in the background in other markets) is unchanged.

Although Figures 9.1 and 9.2 are not meant to facilitate a dynamic analysis of how the variables shown change over time, we can certainly use them in this manner if we just assume that the functional relations depicted *do not change* from one period to the next. In this case, these figures can be used to visualize the process by which equilibrium in the storage market is achieved.[3] Recall that we can interpret the own rate of interest as the rate charged on an asset loan or the expected nonprice return on holding the commodity. Alternatively, the real own interest rate or asset lending rate is the negative of the cost of carry. Accordingly, Figures 9.1 and 9.2 tell us that the higher current inventories are, the lower the benefit of holding the asset. In full carry, the "benefit" of holding the asset is actually negative—the lender of the asset would be willing to pay another firm to take the asset off his hands to avoid the physical and capital cost of storage. The amount the lender would be willing to pay, of course, is just equal to that forgone physical and capital storage cost, making the commodity lender indifferent to the loan or holding the asset in equilibrium.

As inventories shrink, the nominal own interest rate shifts from negative to positive and eventually becomes strongly positive when inventories approach depletion. What is the economic intuition behind this? Quite simply, each unitary decline in the quantity of the asset in storage results in an increasingly large jump in the convenience yield as firms become progressively more "nervous" about stock-outs. The less there is available to cover a stock-out, the more beneficial it is to have some of what is available in your possession. Or from a commodity loan perspective, the lower the quantity of an asset in storage, the harder it will be for firms with a precautionary demand for storage to satisfy shocks to current demand by asset borrowing and thus the more the borrowing rate will rise to clear the market.

A more useful way to consider how changes in inventory precipitate changes in the own rate of interest that in turn lead to changes in the storage decisions of market participants is to consider the relation between the own rate of interest and the *expected change in the price of the asset*. For now, we will skirt all issues related to a risk premium by simply examining the discounted expected percentage change in the asset price without regard to the specific discount factor used, and we will simply express this "all-in" discounted expected price change as $\Delta S_T / S_t$. Assuming a nonstochastic real own rate of interest, we can generalize equation (8.15)—or, for that matter, any of several different relevant equations in Chapter 8—to express the discounted expected percentage price change in the asset as:

$$\frac{\Delta S_T}{S_t} = r_{t,T} - x_{t,T} = r_{t,T} - q_{t,T} + c_{t,T} - l_{t,T} \tag{9.1}$$

The expression in (9.1) reminds us that the expected discounted price change of the asset will equal the cost of carry of the asset. Equivalently, the price of the asset is expected to *decline* (on a risk-adjusted and discounted basis) by an amount equal to what Keynes (1936, p. 226) called the "total return expected from the ownership of the asset" minus the nominal interest rate. So, the price of the asset is expected to decline by an amount that just offsets the benefits received over the period by owners of the asset less the costs they bear for asset ownership. If the costs of storing an asset exceed the benefits of storage, then the asset's price must be expected to rise by an equivalent amount.

Now let us see how the supply of storage fits into this picture, and to do so let us assume we are considering wheat as our asset. First suppose that current wheat inventories are high. In that case, the nominal own rate of interest will probably be negative—owners of the asset have to pay more in capital and physical storage costs than they receive in convenience yield and liquidity premium. But as equation (9.1) reminds us, the negative real own rate of interest implies that the price of wheat is expected to rise by just enough to compensate asset owners for wheat storage.

Now suppose a massive series of warehouse fires results in a substantial depletion of current wheat inventories. Suppose further that the next harvest is a long way off. In this case, we are likely to see a major and rapid increase in the convenience yield. The nominal own rate of interest on wheat will shift from negative to positive, and the cost of carry goes negative—it now *pays* to store wheat. From equation (9.1), the increase in the own wheat interest rate also implies that the price of wheat is now expected to decline over the storage period.

If we think about how all this works to help clear the market for storage, it makes remarkably good sense. The decline in current inventories that led to a drastic increase in the convenience yield precipitated a rise in the own rate of interest—in fact, a shift from a negative to positive own rate. Before the warehouse fires, the owner of wheat would have been willing to pay something in order to lend his wheat for the period. But now that the convenience yield has made the little remaining wheat in storage so much more valuable, the asset lending rate shifts from negative to positive, and the wheat owner will now charge another firm for borrowing wheat.

You can think of this from both the wheat borrower's and lender's perspectives. If you are a wheat borrower, that means you probably do not have enough wheat in your own elevators to cover a stock-out and thus are willing to pay a fairly substantial amount to borrow wheat and avoid such a stock-out. If you are a wheat lender, you are forgoing the ability to cover a stock-out with whatever you lend, and the less there is available in aggregate storage the more you will charge in order to sacrifice that buffer stock.

The relation between own rates and expected price changes also makes sense. When the inventory shock caused a significant increase in the convenience yield, the strong increase in the own rate of interest caused the expected price change of wheat to move from positive to negative. That means that it now costs something to hold wheat. With an expected price decline, firms will have a strong incentive to sell wheat at the current relatively high spot price rather than wait and sell it later at a lower price. And this is precisely what we would hope to see. Because current inventories are low, the price of storage changes to prod firms to sell their wheat today when it is relatively badly needed in order to satisfy current precautionary storage and spot market demands. Depriving the market of your wheat by storing it will penalize you in the form of an expected decline in the nominal value of your inventory. True, you get the benefit of knowing that wheat is in storage to cover a possible stock-out, but you pay for that in the form of a depreciating wheat stock.

## THE FORWARD-SPOT RELATION AND THE SUPPLY OF STORAGE

Examining the way the market for storage responds to inventory changes in terms of the own rate of interest and expected price changes has been instructive, but we want to go further. Now we want to see how these economic forces affect the forward-spot price relation, or the *basis* as we defined the term in Chapter 8. As explained in Chapter 8, the own rate of interest is perhaps best interpreted as the equilibrium price of storage. But thanks to the Law of One Price, we know (either by synthetic replication or application of the FVE) that the price of an asset for immediate delivery and the price of that asset for future delivery must be related to one another by the cost of carry or own rate of interest for that asset.

Considering inventory shocks in terms of the observed forward-spot differential is more powerful than looking at the impact of shocks on the own rate or the expected change in the asset price. As noted, the own rate is a market price—the price of storage. And it also corresponds to the asset lending rate and, if the market exists, the reverse repo rate. In this sense, the market does respond to changes in scarcity with changes in price. But looking only at an expected price change is more limited. To exploit that, you must buy and store the asset. Looking at things in terms of the forward purchase price instead introduces yet another market price into the picture *and* provides another mechanism by which the market can adjust to inventory and other shocks.

Assuming the LOOP holds and the cost of carry model is in force, Figure 9.3 now shows the relation between inventory levels and the cost of carry (i.e., the negative nominal own rate of interest). The only difference from the earlier figures is that these relations are now expressed in terms of what they imply for the forward-spot proportional price differential.

As in Figure 9.2, the full carry line is again shown in Figure 9.3. Assuming as we have that the nominal interest rate and physical storage cost do not depend on current inventory levels, the price of an asset for time $T$ delivery cannot exceed the price of the asset for immediate delivery by more than the physical and capital costs of storage. As the liquidity premium and/or convenience yield rise, the forward purchase price falls. And as inventories get

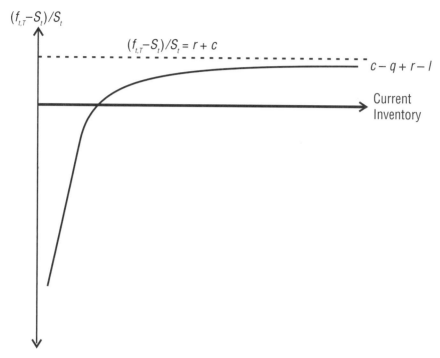

**FIGURE 9.3** The Supply of Storage and the Forward-Spot Price Relation

tighter and tighter, the forward purchase price eventually falls to a discount to the price of the asset for immediate delivery.

We can once again interpret this in the context of how the market for storage clears. When inventories are high and the convenience yield is low, the own rate of interest is low or negative and the cost of carry near full carry. The price of an asset for future delivery thus is at a premium to the spot price by exactly the cost of carrying the asset over time. But when inventories shrink and the convenience yield rises, the forward purchase price declines relative to the spot price.

When the forward purchase price is at a discount to the spot price, the market is essentially signaling a need for firms to sell their assets today rather than defer delivery of them. We can interpret this in terms of the convenience yield as a high demand for immediacy today and a low inventory of assets capable of satisfying that demand for immediacy. Firms thus must pay sellers a premium to induce them to part with their assets as quickly as possible, rather than delaying delivery into the future when the demand for immediacy might not be so strong.

## TERM STRUCTURE OF FORWARD/FUTURES PRICES

Our discussion in Chapter 8 and thus far in this chapter has been limited to a single storage period from $t$ to $T$. The role played by forwards and futures in intertemporal risk transfer and supply allocation, however, does not really become clear until we consider a series of forward purchase prices observed at the same point in time but for different future delivery dates. We refer to this array of forward/futures prices as the *term structure of forward/futures prices*.

### Term Structure Terminology

The fundamental role played by forward and futures markets in facilitating risk transfer across time rests on the existence of multiple own rates of interest corresponding to multiple future delivery dates. Together, this term structure of own interest rates is a powerful mechanism for rationing resource scarcity over time.

Let us fix a date $t$ as the present date and the trade date for the forward purchase agreements we wish to consider. We now allow for forward purchases on all dates $t + j$ up to the last date we wish to consider, date $T$. So, whereas we have been focused solely on the own rate of interest from $t$ to $T$, we now consider a series of nominal own interest rates $\{y_{t,t+1}, y_{t,t+2}, \ldots, y_{t,T}\}$ corresponding to contracts for the purchase of some underlying asset on dates $t + j$ up to $T$, or the series $\{f_{t,t+1}, f_{t,t+2}, \ldots, f_{t,T}\}$.

The relation between forward purchase prices at different maturities is often described with some very specific terminology. A market is said to be *in full carry* if

$$f_{t,t+j} = S_t(1 + r_{t,t+j} + c_{t,t+j}) \qquad \forall j \in \{j = 1, \ldots, T - t\}$$

In other words, a full carry market is a market in which the forward purchase price *each period* reflects the forward purchase price the *prior period* plus the one-period physical and capital cost of carry. The convenience yield and liquidity premium are thus zero at all maturities.

A market is said to be in *backwardation*—a term first given widespread acceptance by Keynes (1923, 1930b)—if the price of an asset for delivery in the near future is at a premium to the price of an asset for delivery in the distant future. Specifically, a market is said to be in *strong backwardation* if

$$f_{t,t+j} < f_{t,t+j-1} \qquad \forall j \in \{j = 1, \ldots, T - t\}$$

where $f_{t,t} = S_t$. This implies that the spot price is the maximum of all observed prices and that the forward purchase price declines for each successively more deferred delivery date. A market in *weak backwardation* or *local backwarda-*

*tion* exhibits this relation only across a handful of neighboring delivery dates. If the spot price of oil is $35 per barrel, for example, the oil market would be in strong backwardation if oil for delivery one to six months forward had forward delivery prices of $34, $33, $30, $25, $24, and $20. If the next six months of oil forward purchase prices were instead $34, $33, $40, $41, $42, and $42, then the market is no longer in strong backwardation. The oil market is in *weak* backwardation, however, for deliveries one and two months forward.

A market in which the price of an asset for future delivery is increasing for more deferred delivery dates is said to be in *contango*. In a manner analogous to the definition of backwardation, a market is in *strong contango* if

$$f_{t,t+j} > f_{t+j-1} \qquad \forall j \epsilon \{j = 1, \ldots, T - t\}$$

and is in *weak contango* for any two future delivery dates $t + j$ and $t + k$ where $k > j$ if

$$f_{t,t+j} > f_{t,t+k}$$

Figure 9.4 illustrates the various concepts graphically for three different assets. Broken lines represent backwardation, and solid lines represent con-

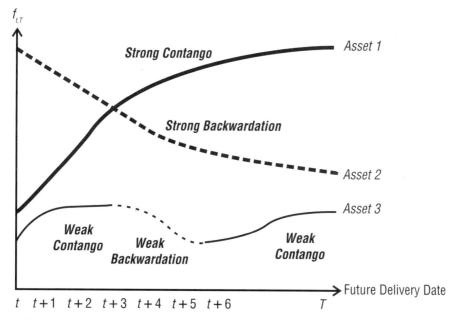

**FIGURE 9.4** Backwardation and Contango

tango. Asset 1 is in strong contago, whereas Asset 2 is in strong backwardation. The term structure of forward prices for Asset 3 rises, falls, and then rises again, indicating two periods of weak contango and one period (in the middle) of weak backwardation.

Figures 9.5 through 9.7 provide some concrete illustrations from actual markets using settlement prices for three futures contracts as of the close of trading on April 25, 2003. Figure 9.5 shows the light, sweet crude oil futures market on the New York Mercantile Exchange—not only in strong backwardation, but exceptionally so for the spot month when compared to the next available delivery date. In Figure 9.6, a market in strong contango is illustrated using settlement prices for rough rice futures traded on the Chicago Board of Trade. Finally, Figure 9.7 shows a market that exhibits weak backwardation and contango both over the maturities shown—specifically, the live cattle futures market on the Chicago Mercantile Exchange.

## Forward/Futures Term Structure and Supply of Storage

A market in contango is frequently also said be a *carry market*, whereas a market in backwardation is an *inverted market*. These are abbreviated versions of the more descriptive *carrying-charge market* and *inverse carrying-charge market*, respectively. Just like these latter terms suggest, a carrying-

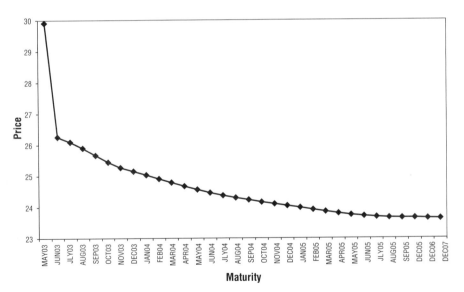

**FIGURE 9.5** Light, Sweet Crude Oil Futures, Settlement Prices on April 25, 2003, New York Mercantile Exchange

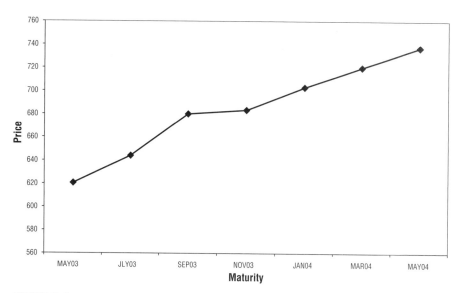

**FIGURE 9.6** Rough Rice Futures, Settlement Prices on April 25, 2003, Chicago Board of Trade

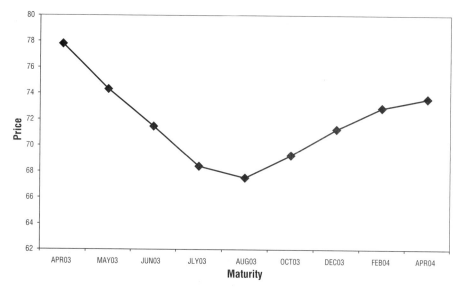

**FIGURE 9.7** Live Cattle Futures, Settlement Prices on April 25, 2003, Chicago Mercantile Exchange

charge market is an asset market for which the cost of carry is positive over time, whereas an inverse carrying-charge market has a negative cost of carry.

We can of course interpret this just as easily using a term structure of nominal own interest rates (being careful to annualize them for proper comparison). A graphic depicting the term structure of own rates of interest indicates the prevailing rates at which the asset can be borrowed or lent for the specific holding period indicated, and this represents (as always) the mirror image of the cost of carrying that asset over the indicated time period.

Now consider the economic meaning of these concepts in the context of the supply of storage discussion earlier in this chapter. In essence, the slope of the forward price term structure is an indication of the relative scarcity of the amount of an asset in the current market and in storage.

First consider a market in strong contango—possibly even full carry. In such a market, the price of the asset for successively deferred future delivery dates is higher by exactly the cost of storing the asset over the period. The corresponding own rate of interest is negative—if you want to lend the asset, you must pay the borrower to take it to cover the capital and physical storage costs. In terms of Figures 9.1 and 9.2, a market in contango is thus associated with plentiful current inventories.

Now consider a market like Asset 2 in Figure 9.4 that is in strong backwardation. In this case, the spot price is at a premium to all deferred forward purchase prices, indicating a positive real own rate of interest and a negative carrying cost. The market is signaling the need for the asset to be moved out of current inventory and sold in the current spot market. Firms that need the asset now must pay a premium to get it, either by borrowing the asset at a positive (and possibly quite high) own rate of interest or by buying it for a spot price that exceeds what the firm could pay to get the asset later. All of this clearly indicates low current inventories and a high convenience yield. Keynes (1930b, p. 143) describes the situation:

> If there are no redundant liquid stocks, the spot price may exceed the forward price (i.e., in the language of the market there is a "backwardation"). If there is a shortage of supply capable of being remedied in six months but not at once, then the spot price can rise above the forward price to an extent which is only limited by the unwillingness of the buyer to pay the higher spot price rather than postpone the date of his purchase.

The term structure of forward prices thus is an indicator of the current supply of storage. When inventories tighten, the convenience yield or marginal benefit of owning the asset rises, and it pays for firms owning the asset to sell it now or lend the asset out rather than store it. The market thus adjusts to the current inventory and demand for immediacy. And when inventories are plentiful, the convenience yield is low and there is no premium on taking the asset out of storage to meet current demand.

### Shocks to Demand and Supply

Many people become confused when first encountering the convenience yield because of confusions over demand and supply shocks. From the cost of carry model, we know that the forward purchase price is a function of the spot price. Shocks to supply and demand will affect that spot price. So, how can we tell when a shock to supply or demand will affect *only* the spot price versus when it will affect the own rate of interest *as well*?

French (1986) has carefully studied relations between spot and forward/futures prices and has shown that the impact of supply and demand shocks on spot prices and the spot-forward price relation depends primarily on the level of inventories *when the shock occurs*. If inventories are high, demand and supply shocks tend to impact the spot price and the futures price in much the same way. In other words, because the shock hits the spot price it *also* hits the futures price proportionately. But the convenience yield does not change much, and so the *relation* between the futures and spot price—the own rate of interest—remains nearly constant. But as inventories shrink, a shock to supply or demand impacts the spot price much more significantly than the futures price. This is the convenience yield responding to the level of inventories and acting as an adjustment mechanism for moving inventory across time.

## SUPPLY OF STORAGE FOR FINANCIAL ASSETS

What about financial assets for which the physical cost of storage is negligible and the convenience yield is replaced with an observable asset yield? Ignoring the liquidity premium, markets for such financial assets are either in backwardation or in contango based entirely on whether the asset yield is above or below the interest rate.

Recall from Chapter 8 that the cost of carry is the same as a repo rate, the rate paid to borrow funds in exchange for an asset loan. In the Treasury bond market, for example, the repo rate is the money interest rate less the coupon income on the bond being lent. Very rarely will the coupon income forgone by the bond lender/cash borrower exceed the money interest rate, implying that the Treasury bond forward market is virtually always in a carry.

When financial asset markets do switch from contango to backwardation or vice versa, the shift generally represents a fairly long-term change in the markets. Consider, for example, a stock index futures contract on the Standard & Poor's index of 500 stocks. Unless the dividend yield on the S&P 500 is less than the interest rate, the S&P 500 futures market should always be a carry market. And if it should switch to an inverted market because nominal money rates fall below dividend yields for some reason, the market probably will not snap back into contango very quickly given the slow speed at which corporate dividends are changed.

Consider another example of a forward contract to buy Swiss francs with euros. Whether the forward purchase price for francs is above or below the spot purchase price depends on the interest rate differential. The euro price of francs will be increasing over time only if the corresponding franc Eurodeposit rate is below the comparable rate on euro-denominated certificates of deposit. Indeed, the term structure of Swiss franc rates might well be upward sloping across all maturities and the euro-rate term structure downward sloping. But what matters is whether the Swiss franc rate is *above* or *below* the euro rate. Figure 9.8 shows an example of a situation when euro rates are steadily falling and Swiss franc rates are rising, but euro rates are still at a premium to franc rates at all maturities.

The reason that the slope of the term structure of forward prices for a financial asset like the Swiss franc does not change from positive to negative (or vice versa) very often should now be clear. In the currency example, a major shift in the relative term structure of interest rates would have to occur, implying a substantial change in the relative monetary policies of the coun-

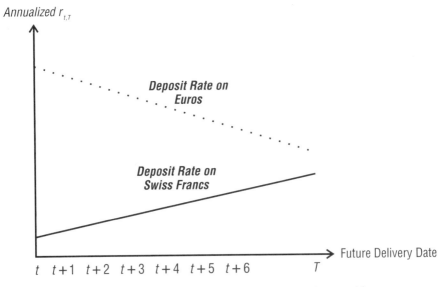

**FIGURE 9.8**   Swiss Franc and Euro Term Deposit Rates Consistent with a Contango Market for Forward Purchases of Swiss Francs with Euros

tries. Not only does this rarely happen overnight, but it also does not switch back and forth very often.

Look again at Figure 9.8 and note that the term structure of euro-denominated deposit rates is declining. What do you think that implies about forward contracts on euro-denominated deposits or rates? As you might guess, interest rate markets behave a bit differently than other markets, especially in the context of their term structures of forward prices.

## NOTES

1. Remember that the physical storage cost is the marginal cost for the marginal storer. Except for very low levels of inventory, this quantity is not likely to change much with the total amount in storage.
2. Also worth remembering from Chapter 8 is the assumption that inventory never actually reaches zero—at least *some* of the asset is continuously stored. French (1986) discusses the importance of this assumption.
3. This is admittedly a bit contradictory, if only because the usual interpretation of comparative statistics is one in which at least a partial equilibrium is already presumed to hold.

# CHAPTER 10

# The Term Structure
# of Interest Rates

Telser (1986) argues that money and futures are very similar for a number of reasons. We already saw in Chapter 5 that commodities can function as both a medium of exchange *and* a unit of account, and we saw in Chapter 8 that thanks to the convenience yield they also can function as a store of value. We then saw in Chapter 9 how forwards can be used to borrow and lend assets at their own rates of interest.

Not surprisingly, the term structure of money interest rates thus is essentially just the forward curve for money or capital—a special case of the term structure of forward prices applied the asset money (e.g., Keynes, 1930a,b, 1936). We see in this chapter how the term structure of interest rates can be viewed as a special case of the theory of supply of storage, and we review the implications of that perspective on the practical estimation of spot discount rate curves in the interbank market.

## CAPITAL THEORY

We must begin by returning to capital.[1] An interest rate, after all, is the price of capital—the price of time, as it were. Unfortunately, capital is a rather slippery term.

Historically, capital and labor are the two principal factors of production in an economy. In neoclassical macroeconomic theory, some production function is presumed to exist that describes the physical transformation of inputs like capital and labor into final products. Solow (1956) posits most generally that aggregate output $Y$ can be expressed as

$$Y = A_t f(K, L)$$

where $A_t$ captures "technical change," $K$ is capital, $L$ is labor, and the ubiquitous $f$ is a production function (Cobb-Douglas, constant elasticity of substitution, etc.).

Dating back to John Locke and Adam Smith, the value and meaning of the *labor* input to production as depicted by the preceding function has generally been well-understood. But *capital* is a different story entirely. The road to this "production function" view of how capital is related to output has been a long and rocky one—and, some would say, one that has taken us more than once in the wrong direction, if not also deposited us in the wrong place.[2]

## Adam Smith on Capital

As in much of economics, the earliest serious treatment of capital comes from Adam Smith. In his *Enquiry into the Nature and Causes of the Wealth of Nations* (1776), Smith depicted the capital stock of a country as including "fixed" and "circulating" capital; today the former includes plants, equipment, machines, and the like—largely things that did not exist in Smith's time—and the latter includes goods in the making, inventory, and other "goods in the pipeline." Both ultimately result in produced goods that in turn make consumption possible.

Smith's conception of capital owed much to the context in which he was writing—about an agrarian economy. To Smith, the "capital stock" was mainly circulating capital—and indeed was even vaguely synonymous with a harvest that might be used to feed laborers, feed animals used in other productive activities, and create seeds to be used for reinvestment in next year's crop. For Smith, capital thus was basically the same thing as "output" or "production."

In this sense, Smith's notion of capital was almost a "subsistence" notion—capital was the thing that sustained workers from one harvest to the next, and the main benefit to the owner of the capital was the ability it created to continue the employment of laborers. $A_t$ the same time, savings and accumulation were clearly important to Smith, who also believed that owners of capital did indeed earn a profit on their capital, one economic purpose of which was reinvestment that would continue and extend the division of labor. Smith's hypothesis about how capitalists earned a profit was an early instance of what was to become a significant question in the history of capital theory: What is it about capital exactly that makes it valuable and allows capitalists to earn a profit on it?

On this issue, Smith actually had two somewhat different—and somewhat contradictory—views. First, Smith simply asserts that capital creates value over and above the labor expended on the production of the capital good, and this surplus is the profit on capital. Second, Smith also seems to believe that the return on capital (i.e., "interest") is just a deduction made by capitalists from the value of the good defined by the value of labor expended on production of the good. In this sense, the return on capital kept as profit by the capitalist thus is really a return on labor, simply held back by the capitalist.

Not at all surprisingly, Smith's own apparently contradictory views of capital gave rise to decades of argument over what is meant by the term "capital." Some argue that capital is synonymous with a capital *stock* or a capital *good*, so capital is a physical thing. Others have argued that capital is itself a concept of productivity and value that results from but is not the same as the capital stock. Lachmann (1978) summarizes this latter perspective nicely:

> Beer barrels and blast furnaces, harbour installations and hotel room furniture are capital not by their physical properties but by virtue of their economic functions. Something is capital because the market, the consensus of entrepreneurial minds, regards it as capable of yielding an income.

Smith's two views of capital also spurred a century of debate on what gives capital its value. These conflicts over capital value are worth briefly reviewing.[3]

### Productivity and Use Theories of Capital

Smith's first view of capital became the basis for what would later be called "productivity theories" of capital. First developed by J. B. Say in 1803, productivity theories of capital argue that capital is productive in the sense that it is used to produce consumption goods that will satisfy *future* needs rather than *current* needs. Specifically, capital can be viewed as productive in four senses: It is required for the production of goods; it allows the production of more goods than could be produced without it; it facilitates the production of more value than would be created in its absence; and it has the capability of producing more value than it has in and of itself (Böhm-Bawerk, 1959).

Unfortunately, many of the early productivity theories offer no reason for *why* capital is productive in these four senses. Some seemed to conjecture that "from capital springs value" in an almost mystical way, providing little economic intuition for their reasoning. Others argued that capital was valuable simply because it allowed the owners of that capital to appropriate the wages of the labor *displaced* by the use of capital.

Thomas Malthus was perhaps the first to add teeth to the productivity theory of capital. In his *Principles of Political Economy* (1820), he argued that the value of capital itself was the value of *what was produced* with that capital.

From this notion sprang the "use theories" of capital, which embraced the concept that there is a causal link between the value of *products* and the value of the *production process* for those products. But whereas pure productivity theories posited a direct link between the value of goods produced and the value of production, use theories argued that the value of capital was also driven by the fact that the *use* of capital was sacrificed to a production process during the time in which the capital was sacrificed to production. In other words, use theories developed a notion of the value of capital assets based on their *opportunity costs*.

A major proponent of the use theory was Austrian economist Carl Menger. In his *Principles of Economics* (1871), he developed a notion of capital in which production is viewed as a sequential process. "Higher-order" goods (i.e., capital goods) are transformed into "lower-order" goods (i.e., consumption goods) in this process. Menger also believed that the value of production was *subjective* and could not be measured by objective criteria like labor input—which, as we shall see, is what labor theorists like Ricardo maintained. Menger (1871) states, "There is no necessary and direct connection between the value of a good and whether or in what quantities, labor or other goods of higher order were applied to its production." To Menger, the value of the capital stock was the sum of the subjective values of the consumption goods that would ultimately result (at different times) from the production process. And because production is time-consuming, the opportunity cost of not having those goods is the "use value" of capital.

## Labor Theory of Capital

David Ricardo's *Principles of Political Economy and Taxation* (1817) contains numerous insights that impact the study of economics even today. Owing admirably to John Locke's notion that the natural right is the right to self-ownership of one's labor, Ricardo attempted to develop a labor theory of capital. Unfortunately, it was not well developed.

In Smith's time, assuming that capital was relatively homogeneous was at least plausible. But as Hicks (1965) put it, by Ricardo's time "it was no longer tolerable, even as an approximation, to assume that all capital was circulating capital; nor that, even in a metaphysical sense, all capital was 'corn.' " Nevertheless, Ricardo was reluctant to let go of the notion that all capital was circulating capital. When it came to complex capital like machines, Ricardo simply believed that it was circulating "more slowly" than capital like corn.

To reduce all capital back to a homogeneous concept, Ricardo thus embraced the labor theory of value that all productive outputs could be measured based on the labor inputs required for the production. In this manner, the return on capital was just the return on labor involved in the capital production process. Whether that production process involved a pig or a machine was of little consequence. A corn harvest this year could have its input value measured based on the number of hours it took to bring the corn to harvest, much as in Smith. But to Ricardo, a machine in production for 10 years involved an expenditure of labor hours in each of the 10 years. Part of the machine got "used up" in each year.[4]

Ricardo then developed his concept of a "uniform rate of profit" on capital. Simply put, he argued that all capital goods tended to earn the same rate of return in the long run. The distribution of wealth in society and the flows of capital to different activities of differing productivity was a *result* of this tendency toward a uniform rate of profit.

The Ricardian labor theory of capital value was filled with flaws. Despite the obvious one—a uniform rate of profit does *not* exist and does *not* guide resource allocation (see Appendix 1)—the analysis was also a completely static one. Indeed, many of Menger's efforts to emphasize the importance of a "time structure of production" in the use theory were direct retaliatory responses to the completely static nature of the labor theory.

Despite its known logical flaws and clear empirical shortcomings, the labor theory of capital was eventually extended into a full argument that the value of capital was not simply the value of labor required to produce with capital, but was rather the value to capitalists of *exploiting* labor to produce with capital. This theory, of course, owes its origins to Karl Marx (*Das Kapital*, 1859).

## Contributions of Hicks

Hicks considered the capital stock to include a wide range of capital assets, including fixed and circulating capital or "goods in the pipeline." He embraced the productivity theorists' notion that the value of capital was not the value of the capital assets themselves, but rather the value of the goods produced by those capital assets. At the same time, however, he also emphasized the need to retain Menger's important insight that production is a *sequence* or *process* of inputs that give rise, in turn, to a sequence of outputs.

By combining a productivity theorist's view that the value of capital is driven by the value of what capital produces with a use theorist's view that the opportunity cost of capital over a sequence of a time must also impact the value of a capital production plan, Hicks was able to shed tremendous light on capital at the *micro*economic level. Perhaps most notably, Hicks provided a number of insights on capital investment decisions in which corporations evaluate whether to undertake investments in new production technologies to find new ways of transforming fixed and circulating capital into a sequence of outputs that ultimately become consumer goods.[5]

# THE RATE OF INTEREST

As the price of capital, the rate of interest is as contentiously debated as the nature of capital itself. In the neoclassical period, the biggest divergence in the interpretation and theory of the rate of interest can be found between Keynes and the neoclassical school. In the case of the interest rate, the neoclassical school also is fairly representative of the earlier classical theories on the rate of interest. But before we get to the real source of this disagreement, we can make some progress by defining a common ground that all dominant economic theories of the interest rate share.

## Common Features in Characterizing the Money Rate of Interest

A faithful survey of all the alternative theories of interest in the classical period would fill several books. E. von Böhm-Bawerk did just that up to 1890 and managed to fill *three* books. So, we make no effort here to present all the competing theories or marginal developments to the conventional wisdom. Instead, we can focus here on making the few statements with which most people would agree concerning the nature of interest rates.

The first is that interest rates reflect some pure rate of time preference (RTP). In the fundamental value equation of Chapter 7, we captured the RTP with the discount factor $\zeta$. The *pure* RTP—as in the classic formulation by Fisher (1907, 1930)—is not a function of the productivity of capital over time, but is quite literally the *price of time*—our impatience to consume today rather than tomorrow.

Second, observed money lending rates contain multiple components. We know that observed rates, for example, are nominal and thus can be decomposed into the real interest rate plus expected inflation (Fisher, 1925). The real interest rate then can be viewed as the RTP in its most basic form.

Third, the RTP is always nonnegative, so real interest rates must also be nonnegative. Here we must recognize that in order for this to be true, the RTP must essentially be the real *riskless* interest rate. In that case, the real interest rate is essentially the exchange rate for consumption today and consumption tomorrow. The reason this cannot be negative is that two-way arbitrage is not possible. Lachmann (1978, p. 78) explains:

> *The ultimate reason [that the real riskless interest rate cannot be negative] lies in the simple fact that stocks of goods can be carried forward in time, but not backwards. If present prices of future goods are higher than those of present goods, it is possible to convert the latter into the former unless the good is perishable or the cost of storing excessive; while future goods cannot be converted into present goods unless there are ample stocks not*

*otherwise needed which their holders are ready to reduce for considera-*
*tion. And as there are always a number of goods for which the cost of*
*storage would be small, money being one of them, a negative rate of in-*
*terest would be eliminated by a high demand for present goods which are*
*easy to store and a large supply of easily storable future goods, at least as*
*long as the stocks carried are covered by forward sales.*

Note this does not preclude backwardation in money rates. It merely precludes *negative* real rates.

Fourth, interest rates are not a return on capital. To go from an interest
rate to a return on capital requires a richer notion of capital theory, but virtually all such theories agree that return on capital as a factor of production
contains components above and beyond the RPT. In productivity- and use-
based theories of capital, for example, the return on capital is proportional to
the value of the wages or land displaced by capital—or, more generally, to the
opportunity cost of resources tied up in capital—or to the value of what is
produced with capital (Smith, 1776; Malthus, 1820; Menger, 1871). This will
contain compensation above and beyond the RTP, especially if the capitalist
faces risk and/or uncertainty.

Finally, any given observed money rate may reflect a risk premium to
compensate capitalists for bearing a specific risk. Interest on money loans
with a higher probability of default, for example, will generally be higher
than comparable riskless rates, all else equal.

We can consider the last two points together in the context of Knight. If
the only source of randomness for the capitalist is risk, then the nominal interest rate should include the real RTP plus an adjustment for expected inflation plus a risk premium that is essentially commonly perceived by all. In the
usual neoclassical fashion, profits on capital thus tend to zero in the long run.
Positive profits to the capitalist must come from some source of Knightian uncertainty.

## Classical and Neoclassical Conceptions of the Interest Rate

The neoclassical conception of the interest rate is totally consistent with the
neoclassical conception of equilibrium in general (see Appendix 1). Namely,
the market is presumed to be in equilibrium only when supply and demand
balance. The dynamic nature of capital itself is generally ignored by "tricking
the problem" with various stylized definitions of demand and supply that can
be reduced to a single time period for analysis. For example, Cassell (1903)
defined investment as "the demand for waiting" and savings as "the supply of
waiting" from which emerges his characterization of the rate of interest as the
equilibrium price of time.

In classical and neoclassical economics alike, the interest rate is essentially the rate that clears the capital market by equating the demand for investment with the supply of investment capital—usually savings or what is left over out of income that is not consumed. Marshall (1890) defined interest in terms of the *stock* of capital as "the price paid for the use of capital in any market [such that the interest rate] tends toward an equilibrium level such that the aggregate demand for capital in that market is equal to the aggregate stock forthcoming at that rate." Knight (1932) offers a typical comparable neoclassical definition of the interest rate in terms of *flow*: "[Equilibrium in the capital markets occurs at] such a rate of interest that savings flow into the market at precisely the same time-rate or speed as they flow into investment producing the same net rate of return as that which is paid savers for their use."

There are some important differences between the classical and neoclassical theories of interest, most of which do not warrant explicit attention here. One difference that does merit our attention, however, is the belief held by many neoclassical economists that aggregate savings need not equal aggregate investment. Classical economics, by contrast, adhered strictly to the belief that the two were necessarily equal, and this conviction was maintained even by Marshall in the early neoclassical tradition. The classical school essentially believed that income was a given and was perfectly interest inelastic. Savings thus was just the amount left over at the interest rate that equates the demand for investment capital with the constant proportion of income assumed to be saved known as the *marginal propensity to save* (the obverse of the *marginal propensity to consume*).

Neoclassical theorists—and Keynes—allowed instead for the possibility that the marginal propensity to save/consume is dependent on the level of income. This implies an upward sloping investment supply or savings curve, which is no longer consistent with the notion that the level of investment must equal the level of savings. They may differ because total income is different at different levels of the rate of interest.

The basic flaw often identified with classical and early neoclassical theories of interest is reminiscent of a common Austrian or Neo-Austrian criticism of the neoclassical paradigm—namely, the lack of explicit attention to *time*. As usual, the neoclassical equilibrium can be defined in Marshallian short- or long-run terms, but there is very little attention paid to the adjustment process between the two. Jumps from one steady state to the next—from a short-run equilibrium to a long-run equilibrium—are thought to bring about proper adjustments in interest rates, but it is unclear *just how*.

## Keynesian Liquidity Preference

In a very thoughtful summary on the theoretical debates over interest and capital theories, Davidson (2002) observes that the neoclassical assumption of instantaneous adjustment in the area of capital is simply an illustration of a model whose erroneous assumptions completely drive the end result. The neoclassical theory essentially assumes no settlement lags, that all transactions occur on the spot market, and that the investment/saving decision is a one-step decision.

Davidson (2002) argues that with a proper reading of Keynes—including not just the *General Theory* (1836) but also his *Treatise on Money* (1930a,b)—the use of current income is a *two-stage* process in which individuals first choose consumption and investment based mainly on their RTPs and then choose whether or not to invest in assets or to hold money. Keynes (1936) called this the *liquidity preference* decision.

The Keynesian framework is actually much more general than the traditional neoclassical view in which all investment is treated equally and there is no liquidity preference decision to be made. Thinking in terms of the own interest rate on assets developed in Chapter 8, the neoclassical analysis of the savings/investment decision essentially assumes that $l_{t,T}$ is equal to zero for all assets. With no liquidity premium to distinguish assets from one another, the decision to hold money or less liquid assets is largely irrelevant.

To Keynes, liquidity was not only relevant, it was the key. In the pure Keynesian world, the demand for liquid assets was driven by two fundamental and related considerations: the time-intensive nature of capital production processes and a belief in Knightian uncertainty. To Keynes, money as the only truly liquid asset is traced to its unique role as "a link between the present and the future." In classical and neoclassical economics, rational expectations tend to rule out Knightian uncertainty so that plans can be made consistently by all market participants based on expectations that are generally shared. But, as we have seen elsewhere in this book, Keynes shared Knight's view—and was later joined by Hicks—in arguing that the existence of uncertainty together with lags in production processes made long-term contracting impossible. Firms and individuals thus would place some premium on liquid assets—money—to resolve temporary inconsistencies in plans arising from uncertainty and inconsistent expectations.

In the context of our discussion in Appendix 1, Keynes' view was extraordinarily similar to the Austrian school and later to the neo-Austrian theory of capital developed by Hicks (1973). The fundamental basis for liquidity preference lies in uncertainty-induced disequilibrium and the role that money as a totally liquid and fungible asset can play in addressing that disequilibrium. Of course, we know at this point that derivatives markets can also play the same role as a substitute of sorts for money (Telser, 1986). But then, this also explains why the Keynesian view of interest rates is really just a special case of the own interest rate.

Specifically, Keynes believed that own interest rate on an asset was its *marginal efficiency of capital*. The marginal efficiency of capital, in turn, was defined by Keynes as the discount rate that equates the output from a productive asset to its "supply price" in present value terms. Supply price, in turn, is not necessarily the market price of the asset, but rather the price that would induce a manufacturer to produce one more unit. In more modern language, the Keynesian marginal efficiency of capital is the discount rate that equates the marginal net present value of a capital investment project to zero. Culp and Miller (1995c) derived a similar discount rate for commodity hedging programs but did not explicitly draw the connection to the Keynesian own rate of interest at the time.

In the Keynesian model, the schedule of own rates of interest on various assets represents the demand curve for loanable funds. Introducing a credit system—as in Wicksell (1898)—complicates things a little but does not change much, which is another attraction of the Keynesian theory *and* the reason, you will recall from Chapter 8, that Sraffa and Hayek argued about the own rate of interest in the first place. The *supply* of loanable funds in the Keynesian model is the key determinant of the rate of interest.

## Forward Curves and the Keynesian Model

Two situations merit further attention in the Keynesian theory. In the first, Knightian uncertainty pervades the market for loanable funds and there is no consensus on expected future interest rates. Forward contracts thus do not exist. In this situation, Keynes simply argues that the supply of loanable funds will be the funds left over from savings after subtracting the quantity of money held for liquidity preference, which he defines quite abstractly as merely

$$M = L(r)$$

where $M$ is the quantity of money, $r$ is the rate of interest, and $L$ is the "function of liquidity-preference" (Keynes, 1936).

We know at this point in the text, however, that Keynes was a great believer in forward markets. We have also seen that forward markets transform uncertainty into quantifiable risk and thus can eliminate some of the motives for holding cash money associated with the Keynesian theory—see also Telser (1986). Not surprisingly, then, the Keynesian notion of an interest rate in equilibrium is very much a by-product of own interest rates reflected from the forward prices of various assets, including money.

Recall from Chapter 8 that the money interest rate never explicitly entered the Keynesian definition of an own rate of interest. For Keynes, the real and nominal own rates of interest on any asset were

$$x_{t,T} = q_{t,T} - c_{t,T} + l_{t,T}$$

$$x_{t,T} + a_{t,T} = q_{t,T} - c_{t,T} + l_{t,T} + \frac{E_t(S_T) - S_t}{S_t} \qquad (10.1)$$

In the second equation, Keynes was simply saying that the real own rate of interest plus the expected price change in the asset was the nominal own rate of interest.

Although you may already have guessed where this is headed from Chapter 8, we can now close the loop and observe that the Keynesian equilibrium occurs *when the nominal own rate of interest on an asset equals the money rate of interest.* Replacing the *expected* price change in (10.1) with the proportional premium of the spot price over the spot price and assuming an unbiased forward price confirms this:

$$q_{t,T} - c_{t,T} + l_{t,T} + \frac{f_{t,T} - S_t}{S_t} \qquad (10.2)$$

which we know must equal $r_{t,T}$ to preclude arbitrage in equilibrium.

The adjustment process is simple enough. If the marginal efficiency of an asset is greater than the rate of interest, more of the asset will be produced. More of the asset means the marginal efficiency of the asset falls, until production stops just when the marginal efficiency of the asset equals the money interest rate. In other words, when $x_{t,T} + a_{t,T} > r_{t,T}$, production of the asset rises until the two quantities are equalized in equilibrium.

What variables drive the adjustment process? One possibility is the expected return on the asset. We assumed in (10.2) that the forward price was unbiased. As we will see in Chapter 12, Keynes did *not* assume this. So, in a Keynesian world, equation (10.1) *must* equal the money interest rate in equilibrium, but (10.2) might not. In other words, the marginal efficiency of the asset is defined as the real own rate plus the expected price change, which can rise or decline to restore equilibrium to the market.

Alternatively, the liquidity premium may adjust. In fact, it is this term that allows us to treat money as just a special case of the own rate of interest in the first place. As you might have guessed, Keynes literally defined money as an asset for which

$$x_{t,T} = l_{t,T}$$

In other words, money has no explicit or convenience yield that its holders earn and no physical costs of storage. Because money is also our unit of account, the expected return on money is equal to zero—i.e., the price level of money does not change *in real terms*. So, in equilibrium, money exhibits the following property:

$$x_{t,T} = l_{t,T} = r_{t,T} \qquad (10.3)$$

Equation (10.3) is really one of the most remarkable expressions in economics, whether or not you believe the broader Keynesian theory. In short, (10.3) provides a systematic linkage between money and all other assets, their own rates of interest, and the relations between their forward and spot prices. It is perhaps *the* central insight into how deeply the economics of derivatives permeate the basic operations of the economy.

## WHERE DO WE GET THESE RATES?

"Benchmark discount curves" are the term structures of *spot* interest rates—i.e., multiperiod rates prevailing from the current date through some date in the future—that are used to discount cash flows in a given risk class. The spot Treasury and agency curves have long been used as proxies for risk-free debt. Increasingly, the most prevalent discount curve used for risky but very high-quality debt is the spot interbank rate curve. But from where do these rates come? In other words, how do we go from the discussion we just had about equilibrium interest rates being a special case of the term structure of forward prices unless we have observed forward prices?

Most of the time, we *do* have observed interest rate derivatives prices from which to construct these curves.[6] In fact, forward-rate agreements and interest rate futures give us *direct* estimates of forward rates that correspond to equation (10.3). More commonly, however, we want to populate (10.3) with spot rates that are useful for discounting. Fortunately, interest rate derivatives are among the most actively traded in the world. Constructing spot rates from observed forward and swap rates requires a little work, but is quite a straightforward exercise.

### The Par Swap Curve

According to the Bank for International Settlements, of the $141.7 trillion in notional principal outstanding on all OTC derivatives at year-end 2002, $79.2 trillion were interest rate swaps. The most common type of interest rate swap is a plain-vanilla fixed-for-floating Eurodeposit rate swap—an OTC derivatives contract in which one party periodically makes fixed interest payments to another party in exchange for receiving a variable interest payment based on a Eurodeposit rate such as the London Interbank Offered Rate (LIBOR). The interest payments in such swaps are expressed as a proportion of some notional principal amount. On plain-vanilla rate swaps, the interest payments are denominated in the same currency, and the floating reference rate is usually the Eurodeposit or interbank rate for that currency—LIBOR for dollar swaps, EURIBOR for euro swaps, Eurosterling for pound-denominated swaps, and the like.

In a typical Eurodeposit rate swap, the particular floating rate that determines the amounts of the cash flows on the swap's floating leg usually depends on the settlement frequency of the swap. For most Eurodeposit rate swaps, cash flows occur semi-annually, and the floating leg thus is based on realizations of the 180-day Eurodeposit rate. Eurodeposit swaps, moreover, are based on Eurodeposit *offered* rates. A characteristic Eurodollar swap, for example, references six-month LIBOR—not L*IBID* (i.e., the London interbank *bid* rate). Eurodeposit rate swaps are settled in arrears, just like the Eurodeposits underlying them. (See Chapter 6.)

The fixed rate that determines the amount of all the fixed cash flows on the swap—called the *swap rate*—is set at the inception the contract. For an at-market swap, the swap rate is thus the fixed rate that equates the expected discounted NPV of the cash flows on the swap to zero on the trade date (Turnbull, 1987; Rendleman, 1992).

The swap rate typically quoted by a dealer is the "par" swap rate, or the yield to maturity of the swap. The determination of arbitrage-free fixed par swap rates is trivial in a perfect capital market. For simplicity, we also want to make the assumption that credit enhancements (e.g., collateral, guarantees, etc.) are used so that the credit risk reflected in the floating reference rate—generally AAA for Eurodeposit interbank rates—is the same as the credit-enhanced or effective credit quality of the swap counterparties. In that case, portfolios of securities always can be formed that are *perfect substitutes* for a swap. The Law of One Price and Principle of No Arbitrage then guarantee equivalence in the prices of the two portfolios, from which the fixed swap rate can be deduced—a typical application of relative pricing.

In a perfect capital market, the cash flows on a pay fixed/receive floating swap are identical to the cash flows on a portfolio of two bonds: a purchased floating-rate note (FRN) and issued level-coupon bond.[7] To guarantee that the swap has a zero initial NPV, the present value of the fixed leg of the swap (plus a hypothetical principal repayment) thus must equal the price of the FRN. Provided the credit risk of the FRN issuer has the same risk of default that is reflected in the reference interest rate, the FRN will reprice to par on each reset date—including the trade date.

So, for a swap with $m$ periods to maturity and a $1 nonamortizing notional principal amount, the annualized par swap rate $K_m$ satisfies

$$\sum_{j=1}^{m} \frac{K_m\left(\dfrac{d_{t+j-1,t+j}}{DCB}\right)}{\left[1+Z_{t,t+j}\left(\dfrac{d_{t,t+j}}{DCB}\right)\right]} + \frac{1}{\left[1+Z_{t,t+m}\left(\dfrac{d_{t,t+m}}{DCB}\right)\right]} = 1 \qquad (10.4)$$

where $Z_{t,t+j}$ is the zero-coupon discount rate applied to a cash flow occurring at time $t + j$. The left-hand side of equation (10.4) represents the NPV of the fixed leg of the swap, and the right-hand side is the price of the floating leg, which is the par value of the FRN.

The $K_m$ that satisfies equation (10.4) is called the *m-year par swap rate*, which is also the yield to maturity of the swap. Evident from equation (10.4) is that the arbitrage-free *m*-period par swap rate depends on the *m*-period spot discount rate curve, $\{Z_{t,t+1}, \ldots, _{t,t+m}\}$. Because we have assumed the credit quality of the swap counterparties is the same as the credit quality reflected in the floating reference rate, the spot discount curve is just the spot Eurodeposit curve.

## From Par to Zero Rates

The preceding discussion does not get us where we want to go. We just learned how to price a swap at inception, but that does not give us a term structure of spot interest rates. In fact, we needed those spot interest rates in order to price the swap. Not surprisingly, however, what is possible in one direction is possible in the other. We can always take a term structure of observed *par* swap rates and *back out* the spot discount rate curve.

To obtain a *zero-coupon swap rate*, we take the par swap curve as given and then reexpress those par swap rates as spot rates on hypothetical zero-coupon Eurodeposits at each maturity of interest. Let's work with a swap that has annual interest payments so that we can ignore day-count compounding for a moment. For a given *m*-year par swap rate $K_m$, the zero-coupon swap rates up to maturity m can be constructed from equation (10.4). To actually calculate the zero-coupon swap rates $\{Z_{t,t+1}, \ldots, Z_{t,t+m}\}$ requires a sequence of par swap rates up to the same maturity, $\{K_{t,t+1}, \ldots, K_{t+m}\}$. The zero-coupon swap curve is then derived in the same manner that the Treasury coupon yield curve can be "stripped." Specifically, that $K_1 = Z_1$ is obvious from (10.4), and zero-coupon rates of longer maturities can be deduced iteratively. Given annualized zero-coupon swap rates $Z_1, \ldots, Z_{n-1}$ and the annualized par swap rate $K_n$, for example, the *n*th zero-coupon swap rate is just

$$S_n = \left[ \frac{1 + K_n}{1 - \dfrac{K_n}{(1 + S_{n-1})^{n-1}} - \cdots - \dfrac{K_n}{(1 + S_1)}} \right]^{1/n} - 1 \qquad (10.5)$$

As equations (10.4) and (10.5) show, a sequence of $m$ par swap rates implies a unique sequence of $m$ zero-coupon swap rates corresponding to those swap rates. In other words, the expression of the rates is different, but the basic economic factors that affect the determination of the rates is fully reflected in *both* the par and zero-coupon rates.

### Blended Curves and Eurodollar Strips

Market convention is to use the most liquid instruments available at certain maturities to construct a zero-coupon spot term structure. In Eurodeposit markets, this generally involves using actual cash offered rates on Eurodeposits for short maturities (e.g., up to six months), using swaps for longer-dated maturities (e.g., from two to five years through the most deferred maturity), and using "Eurodollar futures strips" for the dates in between.

A Eurodollar futures contract is a futures contract on a hypothetical 90-day Eurodeposit. The quoted time $t$ futures price $F_{t,T}$ is defined as 100 minus the annualized percentage interest rate expected to prevail when the hypothetical certificate of deposit (CD) is issued on maturity date $T$. A current futures price of 98.5 on a contract with two months to maturity thus indicates a $2 \times 5$ forward rate of 1.5 percent per annum—that is, the three-month rate expected to prevail in two months, or the rate on a CD that will be issued in two months and that matures in five months. Denoting the expected forward rate implied by the futures contract corresponding to maturity $t + k$ as $R_{t+k}$, a $m$-period futures strip rate is calculated as:

$$Z_{t,t+m} = \left\{ \prod_{j=1}^{m} \left[ 1 + \left( \frac{R_{t+j-1,t+j}}{100} \right) \left( \frac{d_{t+j-1,t+j}}{DCB} \right) \right] \right\} \left( \frac{DCB}{d_{t,t+m}} \right) - 1 \qquad (10.6)$$

## NOTES

1. This brief section originally appeared as Appendix 1-1 in Culp (2002a).
2. For some excellent recent thoughts on capital that challenge the current thinking, see Garrison (2001).
3. The terminology for the various theories summarized is borrowed from Böhm-Bawerk (1959).

4. See Lewin (1999) for a further discussion of this issue, and especially how Ricardo's view of time compares to Menger's.
5. See Lewin (1999) for a discussion.
6. Culp (1997) explores methods of extracting rates when derivatives are not available at all desired maturities.
7. Swaps also may be viewed as portfolios of off-market, settled-in-arrears forward-rate agreements (FRAs). Indeed, FRAs themselves can be used directly to construct a term structure of forward rates, from which spot rates can be deduced. See, for example, Smith, Smithson, and Wakeman (1986, 1988).

# CHAPTER 11

# Basis Relations and Spreads

The *basis* is the difference between the prices of two assets, usually expressed as a proportion of the base asset price. We saw in Chapters 8 and 9 that the *calendar basis* represents the price of storage and is equal to the cost of carrying the asset over time—that is, the negative nominal own rate of interest. In this chapter, we develop the notion of the basis as the price of some kind of asset transformation in much more general terms. We then examine how different basis relations are frequently exploited with portfolios or combinations of derivatives known as *spreads*.

## BASIS AND THE COST OF CARRY MODEL

Assuming the Law of One Price (LOOP) holds and that simultaneous equilibrium exists in the various markets for spot and forward asset purchases, asset storage, asset lending, and asset repurchase agreements, the cost of carry model can take the following forms:

$$
\begin{aligned}
f_{t,T} &= S_t(1 + r_{t,T} - q_{t,T} + c_{t,T} - l_{t,T}) \\
&= S_t(1 + r_{t,T} - x_{t,T}) \\
&= S_t(1 - y_{t,T}) \\
&= S_t(1 + b_{t,T}) \\
&= S_t(1 + \rho_{t,T})
\end{aligned}
\tag{11.1}
$$

where we define $f_{t,T}$ as the price negotiated at time $t$ for the delivery of an asset at time $T$ and $S_t$ as the price of the asset for immediate delivery on the spot. For easy reference, recall the definitions of the other terms in equation (11.1):

$r_{t,T} =$  Nominal money rate of interest from $t$ to $T$
$q_{t,T} =$  Asset yield (explicit or convenience) from $t$ to $T$
$c_{t,T} =$  Physical cost of storage from $t$ to $T$
$l_{t,T} =$  Asset liquidity premium from $t$ to $T$
$x_{t,T} =$  Real own rate of interest from $t$ to $T = q_{t,T} - c_{t,T} + l_{t,T}$
$y_{t,T} =$  Nominal own rate of interest from $t$ to $T = x_{t,T} - r_{t,T}$
$b_{t,T} =$  Calendar basis or cost of carry from $t$ to $T = -y_{t,T}$
$\rho_{t,T} =$  Repo rate from $t$ to $T = b_{t,T}$

In equation (11.1), many of the terms linking the price of an asset for immediate and future delivery are explicit market prices—prices that reflect the equality of marginal cost and marginal revenue in some specific market or activity. The own rate of interest $y_{t,T}$ is the explicit market price of an asset loaned by one firm to another, which is equivalent to the explicit market price of storage. The repo rate $\rho_{t,T}$ is the explicit market price of a repurchase agreement on the asset (i.e., the rate on a cash loan collateralized with the asset).

When we use the term *basis*, however, we are generally referring to an *implicit price* that is defined literally by the relation of one explicit market price to another—in (11.1) by the relation of the forward and spot purchase prices. Although in equilibrium the basis is equivalent to several observable market prices, the basis itself generally has the connotation of being *endogenous* to the spot and forward prices.

In this context, the basis is a term that has much more general usage in derivatives than to refer to the cost of carry. In fact, the cost of carry is very specifically called the *calendar basis* because it represents the implicit price of time in holding an asset from $t$ to $T$. But there are many others kinds of basis relations in derivatives.

## Basis as a Transformation Function

Perhaps the best way to think about the basis in general terms is as a *transformation function*. In order to get an asset from some location today to the same location in the future, for example, the transformation function is the storage market, and the cost of that transformation is the cost of carry or the calendar basis. More generally, to transform the price of any payoff $x$ into the price of any payoff $y$, the transformation function $b$ may be used such that:

$$P_y = P_x(1 + b) \tag{11.2}$$

We use the form in equation (11.2) because of the ease of interpretation of $b$ as a "rate" and for comparability to the cost of carry model. Like the cost of carry model, however, we need not link $P_x$ and $P_y$ multiplicatively. If we define $b \equiv B/P_x$, then equation (11.2) also can be written as:

$$P_y = P_x + B \tag{11.2}'$$

Keeping in mind that the basis is essentially the residual term characterized by the two explicit prices, equations (11.2) and (11.2)' imply that:

$$b \equiv \frac{P_y - P_x}{P_x} \qquad B \equiv P_y - P_x$$

In some cases the basis will correspond to a market price, as in the case we have already examined of the calendar basis. The LOOP helps ensure that *ex ante* the basis and, for example, the repo rate are the same. On *ex post* terms we can verify this for some holding period $T - t$ by running an ordinary least squares regression over a time series:

$$b_{t,T} = \alpha + \beta \rho_{t,T} + \varepsilon_t$$

With no transaction costs, the LOOP should imply that the estimated values for $\alpha$ and $\beta$ are 0 and 1 with an $R^2$ of unity.

In other situations, the basis may represent an *implicit price*, or the price of some transformation that *could* be replicated but usually is not. If $P_x$ is the price of a Bulgari tie sold at the Bulgari store on North Michigan Avenue and $P_y$ is the price of an identical Bulgari tie sold six blocks south at Nieman's on Michigan Avenue, then the basis $b$ will represent the *price of transportation* six blocks along Michigan Avenue. It is highly unlikely that a specific market for transporting Bulgari ties between Nieman's and Bulgari exists, but if it did it would have a price equal to the basis. In this case, though, the mere *threat* of competition is likely to keep prices in line and the LOOP in effect.

## Common Basis Relations

As the last example just illustrated, basis transformations need not be limited to transformations over time. The *calendar basis* examined in Chapters 8 and 9 is a specific form of intertemporal transformation function, but time is neither unique nor in the case of many derivatives is time the *only* dimension of even the calendar basis problem.

Consider, for example, a market like natural gas where the "spot price" is a basic misnomer. In fact, there are numerous markets for the purchase of natural gas for immediate delivery on the spot. But these wellhead prices may not be equal to one another. Denote the spot price per Btu of natural gas at the Henry Hub pipeline delivery terminal as $S_{\text{Henry Hub},t}$ at time $t$, and denote the time $t$ spot price of natural gas sold at a San Angelo, Texas, wellhead as $S_{\text{San Angelo},t}$. Assume in the context of our discussion in Chapter 6 that spot transactions involve a settlement lag of two days, and that natural gas of exactly the same quality can be transported between Henry Hub and San Angelo in less than two days. In that case, the following basis relation exists:

$$B_{\text{Henry Hub-San Angelo},t} = P_{\text{Henry Hub},t} - P_{\text{San Angelo},t}$$

In other words, the basis represents the implicit price of transporting gas between Henry Hub and San Angelo. Those transportation costs will include pipeline fees, insurance, and the like.

Now imagine that the quality or purity of natural gas differs in the two locations. In that case the basis will reflect both transportation costs *and* the difference arising from heterogeneous quality grades. These two components of the basis are unlikely to be correlated, so we could write the basis additively in this example.

The most commonly observed basis relations include the following:

- *Calendar basis:* cost of moving the same asset across time.
- *Geographic or locational basis:* cost of moving the same asset across physical space.
- *Quality basis:* difference in the prices of two related assets in the same place at the same time arising from quality differences.
- *Input-output basis:* the cost of transforming an input into an output.

We have seen examples already of all but the last type of basis relation, and the last is essentially the cost of transforming one asset into another. The *crushing basis*, for example, is the cost of transforming soybeans into soybean meal and soybean oil.

Quite often the difference between two prices involves more than one basis relation. A typical forward purchase agreement on a commodity, for example, may specify the quality of the asset to be delivered very clearly, but at the same time may require delivery at a location other than the delivery terminal used by either or both counterparties to the trade. For example, a wheat forward might require the seller to transport wheat to the buyer's designated grain elevator. In this case the forward price will differ from the spot price by the cost of carrying the asset over time *and space*. The basis thus includes the price of storage *and* the price of transportation.

## Optionality in the Basis

Standardized exchange-traded derivatives often reflect a basis that differs from the actual basis faced by individual market participants. As discussed in

Chapter 8, *forward* purchase prices are generally driven to reflect those considerations by equilibrium in the underlying storage market and the supply chain. But in futures, sometimes the explicit nature of the basis defined in the contract gives rise to valuable options for either the short or the long, and the value of these options then becomes a component of the futures-spot basis relation.

A typical standardized futures contract often allows either the short or the long some flexibility in determining what quality asset to deliver and where to deliver it. Commodity futures, for example, generally specify a minimum quality level that can be used to satisfy the contract, but this minimum may still allow the short to choose among several deliverable grades.

When the short can select the quality of asset to deliver, the short possesses a valuable option contract called the *cheapest to deliver* option. An oil futures contract requires the short to provide oil with a maximum amount of sulfur. But if the oil produced by the seller is very low in sulfur, it may pay for the seller to acquire oil on the market with a little more sulfur that still can be used to satisfy the futures contract. Suppose that the oil owned by the short is worth $30 per barrel. If the cost of the higher-sulfur oil is only $29 per barrel and the cost of transporting it from its point of sale to the designated delivery location in the futures contract is less than $1 per barrel, then the cheaper oil will be purchased and delivered. The ability to select the lowest-cost deliverable alternative can be considered a type of "exchange option"—an option to exchange one asset for another. In this case, the price of oil for future delivery thus will equal the price of the high-quality oil for current delivery plus the cost of carrying that oil over time *plus* the value of the option to swap the high-quality oil for a lower-quality oil and transport it to market.

Now consider a different example related to the need for futures contracts to define only a few authorized physical delivery locations. If a farmer operates several grain elevators, one of which is discernibly closer to an authorized delivery point in a grain contract, for example, the farmer will opt to deliver the wheat that keeps the transportation costs to a minimum. Transportation costs priced into the futures contract, however, may only reflect the cost of delivery *at the specified delivery points*. In this case, the value of the option to the farmer to select a close delivery point may *not* be reflected in the basis—it depends entirely on whether that individual farmer is a large enough market player to influence the implicit price of transportation reflected in the basis.

Cheapest-to-deliver options are also not unique to futures on commodities. All that is required is that the contract involve physical delivery. The futures contract on the long-term U.S. government bond listed on the Chicago Board of Trade (CBOT), for example, is a futures contract on a *financial* asset that nevertheless calls for physical delivery. Specifically, the short may deliver any noncallable bond issued by the U.S. Treasury with at least 15 years remaining to maturity (or, if the bond is callable, with at least 15 years remaining to its first call date). The last trading day for a given contract is the eighth to the last business day of the contract month, and delivery can occur at any time during the contract month.

When a bond is delivered by the short in the CBOT long bond futures contract, the invoice price paid by the long is equal to the futures price times a "conversion factor" plus accrued interest. Because such a wide range of bonds can be delivered into the CBOT contract, the Board of Trade tries to equalize invoice prices across bonds by adjusting the quoted futures price with a conversion factor calculated as the approximate decimilized price at which the delivered bond would yield 8 percent to maturity or first call.

Even with the conversion factor applied to the invoice price, however, the short has at least two valuable options written by the long by virtue of the contract's standardized features—an option on *what* to deliver and an option on *when* to deliver it. These two broad options can be viewed as a combination of more specific options, some of which can be exercised before the last day of trading and others of which can be exercised only between the last trading day and the last delivery day. Burghardt and Belton (1994) provide a comprehensive and highly recommendable discussion of these and other options in the long bond futures contract.

## SPREADS

A concept closely related to the basis is known as a *spread*. A spread is the simultaneous execution of multiple derivatives contracts in order to explicitly trade the implicit market defined by the multiple positions. Spread trades are sometimes also called basis trades when they are intended to exploit a specific position in the basis. The most popular forms of spread trading are discussed next.

### Calendar or Interdelivery Spreads

The simultaneous execution of more than one derivatives transaction in an effort either to hedge or to speculate on a specific basis relation is known as both a *basis trade* and a *spread trade*. When everything about the contracts is the same except for the date on which the contracts mature and/or the date on which future delivery will occur, the resulting mixture of positions is known as a *calendar basis trade* or a *calendar spread*.

#### Calendar Basis Trades and Interdelivery (or Intramarket) Spreads
A spread involving two forwards or futures with the same contract terms and based on the same asset that differ only by maturity date is known as a *calen-*

*dar basis trade*, an *interdelivery spread*, or an *intramarket spread*. Such trades involve the simultaneous purchase and sale of the same asset on exactly the same terms (OTC) or on the same exchange market (exchange-traded) except for the delivery month, which differs across the two contracts. These spreads are undertaken to hedge or speculate on shifts in the term structure of forward/futures prices.

To take a simple example, consider a shipping firm—call it TransAtlantique—whose primary business involves purchasing coffee from producers in Brazil, transporting the commodities across the Atlantic, and selling the commodities in Europe. Suppose further that the next major coffee crop will come in six months from now, and the firm needs to allow another three months for shipping and processing. Also assume for now that the spot price of coffee in Brazil is perfectly correlated with the spot price of coffee in Europe at the same point in time.

Absent any hedging activities, TransAtlantique will be buying coffee at the spot price six months hence and selling at the spot price nine months hence. The firm's natural risk exposure thus is short six-month coffee and long nine-month coffee. TransAtlantique can be said to be long the calendar basis from $t + 6$ to $t + 9$. If $S_{t+6}$ falls and $S_{t+9}$ rises so that the basis widens or gets larger, TransAtlantique makes money. But if $S_{t+6}$ rises and $S_{t+9}$ falls—a so-called *tightening of the basis*—then the firm's margin shrinks.

Notice that TransAtlanique's exposure is to *relative* prices over time, not absolute swings in the whole market. If current coffee inventories are plentiful and medical researchers prove that coffee cures cancer, for example, the increased demand will put upward pressure on the current spot price but *not* on the calendar basis—see Chapter 9. The expected spot price will rise *at both maturities* by a comparable amount, and the higher purchase price in six months will be offset by higher sales revenues in a year (ignoring discounting). So, the risk exposure of TransAtlantique is quite literally to changes in the slope of the term structure (i.e., the calendar basis).

To manage its calendar basis risk, the firm could lock in its purchase price by entering into a forward purchase agreement at price $f_{t,t+6}$ for coffee to be delivered in Brazil six months hence. At the same time, TransAtlantique could prenegotiate its coffee sales to European manufacturers for the forward sale price of $f_{t+9}$. Instead of engaging in fixed-price contracts with its commercial counterparties, the firm could also continue to make its purchases and sales at the spot price and then enter into coffee futures or forwards separately.[1] Using forwards will deprive the firm of any gains if the calendar basis widens, of course, but it also successfully mitigates losses. In a real sense, a calendar basis trade for TransAtlantique accomplishes full *intertemporal relative price risk transfer*. In other words, TransAtlantique has hedged its exposure to changes in the own rate of interest on coffee from time $t + 6$ to $t + 9$.

In this example, TransAtlantique is long the shorter-maturity forward and short the longer-maturity derivatives contract. This is known as a *bull spread*. To manage the opposite calendar basis risk, a firm could use a *bear spread* in which the firm is short the closer maturity and long the more deferred contract.

Especially in exchange-traded derivatives markets, more complex calendar basis trades are also possible. If the term structure of futures prices exhibits a "hump" or a "gap," firms may wish to trade around this or hedge it using a spread called a *butterfly* that consists of two calendar basis trades *in opposite directions* with a common center delivery month. A bull spread from March to June and a bear spread from June to September, for example, is a trade that on net pays off when the calendar basis weakens between June and its neighboring maturities in March and September. A bear spread from March to June and a bull spread from June to September contemplates a strengthening of the June basis. Such strategies are especially popular in interest rate markets when specific maturities of interest-sensitive products are viewed as being out of line with the surrounding maturities, generally for liquidity reasons.

### Options Calendar Spreads

Whereas the term "calendar basis trade" generally refers to trades designed to hedge or speculate on shifts in the term structure of forward prices, the term "calendar spread" generally refers to options markets. An option *calendar spread* involves the simultaneous purchase and sale of two otherwise identical options with different maturity dates. Calendar spreads can be accomplished using either calls or puts and can involve a short or long position in either the short-dated or long-dated option.

You will recall from your first course on derivatives that options are decaying assets—the more time elapses, the less valuable the option contract is. The rate of decay in the value of an option as time passes is called its *theta*, and theta increases the closer an option gets to expiration. A typical calendar spread thus might consist, say, of selling a one-year call and buying a 15-month call. Figure 11.1 illustrates how the time value (i.e., total option value minus intrinsic/exercise value) of the spread increases as the shorter-dated option approaches its expiration date. Comparing two different time periods prior to the expiration of the first option, the spread S1 prevailing when the 15-month option has nine months to expiration and the 12-month option has six months to expiration is clearly much smaller than the spread S2 prevailing when the longer-dated option has six months remaining in its life and the shorter-dated option has three months before expiration. As expiration approaches, the shorter-dated option loses value increasingly faster than the longer-dated option, which benefits this particular spread trade.

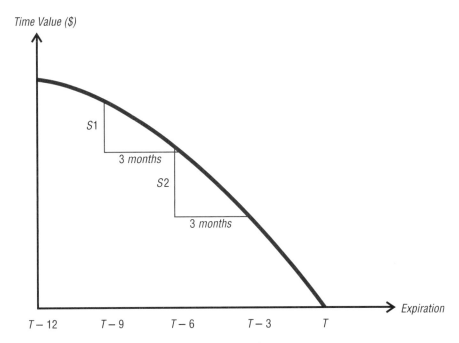

**FIGURE 11.1** A Typical Option Calendar Spread

## Intermarket Spreads

The simultaneous purchase of a derivatives contract in one market and sale of the same contract in another market is known as an *intermarket spread*. The only difference in the two contracts is the market on which they are executed or the market for the underlying deliverable asset. Although they may be combined with other spreads like calendar spreads, intermarket spreads in their purest form involve delivery on the same future date and thus are essentially designed to exploit a locational or quality basis, or to conduct arbitrage.

The term *market* in intermarket depends on whether the forward or futures contract is OTC or exchange-traded. In the former case, the "market" generally refers to the market for the underlying asset. Entering into a forward contract to buy Appalachian coal on December 1 for F.O.B. barge delivery on the Ohio River and simultaneously entering into a forward contract (perhaps with the same swap dealer) to sell Appalachian coal on December 1 for F.O.B. barge delivery on the Big Sandy River is an example of an interdelivery or intermarket OTC spread.

When dealing with exchange-traded derivatives, intermarket spreads involve the simultaneous purchase and sale of contracts that are essentially (although usually not exactly) the same except that they are listed on different exchanges. Intermarket spreads involving exchange-traded derivatives can be undertaken for several different reasons.

### Arbitrage

Intermarket spreads involving truly identical exchange-traded derivatives are often undertaken as arbitrage transactions. Nick Leeson, who achieved fame for establishing the runaway error account that eventually busted Barings Bank, was originally responsible, for example, with running an intermarket arbitrage book of futures on the Nikkei 225 stock index traded in Osaka and Singapore. Although not many futures contracts with *identical* terms are listed on multiple exchanges, many contracts with only small differences are listed in several places and lend themselves to this sort of trading.

### Quality Basis Hedging and Trading

When intermarket spreads involve contracts that are almost but not exactly the same, the spread is usually intended to hedge or establish a position in some quality or locational basis difference. Consider, for example, the wheat futures listed by the Kansas City Board of Trade (KCBT) and Chicago Board of Trade (CBOT). The contract specifications for the two virtually identical wheat futures are summarized in Table 11.1.

The main distinction between these otherwise very similar contracts is the distinct nature of the deliverable underlyings. The CBOT contract allows for the delivery at par of any of four classes of wheat—all No. 2 (a quality grade assigned by the U.S. Department of Agriculture reflecting variables such as

**TABLE 11.1**   Wheat Futures Contract Specifications, KCBT and CBOT

|  | KCBT | CBOT |
|---|---|---|
| Deliverable grades at par | No. 2 Hard Red Winter | No. 2 Hard Red Winter<br>No. 2 Soft Red<br>No. 2 Dark Northern Spring<br>No. 2 Northern Spring |
| Delivery amount | 5,000 bushels | 5,000 bushels |
| Delivery months | JLY, SEP, DEC, MAR, MAY | JLY, SEP, DEC, MAR, MAY |
| Trading hours | 9:30 A.M.–1:15 P.M. Central | 9:30 A.M.–1:15 P.M. Central |
| Minimum price | $.0025 ($11.50/contract) | $.0025 ($11.50/contract) |
| Daily price limit | ±$.30 from prior day's settle | ±$.30 from prior day's settle |
| Delivery points | Kansas City, Mo.–Kans.;<br>Hutchinson, Kans. | Chicago, Ill.;<br>St. Louis, Mo. |

damaged kernels, presence of foreign materials, etc.) but including four basic classes. The KCBT contract allows delivery at par of only one wheat class— No. 2 Hard Red Spring wheat. Both exchanges allow substitutions of different grades but assess a premium or discount accordingly.

Intermarket spreading across the two different wheat contracts could be pursued for any of several reasons. Consider, for example, the quality basis. Suppose a conglomerate that owns several grain elevators buys both No. 2 Hard Red Spring and Hard Red Winter and mills the wheat into flour that is sold at a constant markup to the price of the dominant quality grade, No. 2 Hard Red Spring. The price of the CBOT contract will reflect the cheapest to deliver of the four classes of wheat deliverable at par. Ignoring the transportation basis for the moment, it would be sensible for the elevator to hedge by going long the CBOT contract in the month the elevator makes its purchases and short the KCBT contract in the month the elevator plans to make delivery. The embedded calendar spread protects the elevator against shifts in the futures price term structure during the milling period, and the use of the CBOT contract provides protection for purchasing costs against a rise in *any* of the four deliverable classes. The short KCBT contract then hedges the producer against price declines on the flour sales.

Alternatively, consider the transportation basis. In the case of the CBOT contract, the transportation cost will be based on the average or marginal cost of getting grain to and from Chicago or St. Louis, whereas the KCBT contract will be based on Kansas City or Hutchinson delivery points. And in turn, the prices of the CBOT and KCBT contracts will differ based on the transportation cost between the two contracts' delivery points (assuming that No. 2 Hard Red Spring wheat is currently cheapest to deliver at the CBOT[2]).

Suppose the price of wheat for delivery next month in Chicago or St. Louis is 73 cents per bushel on the CBOT and is 76 cents per bushel on the KCBT for delivery in Kansas City or Hutchinson at a time when No. 2 Hard Red Spring wheat is the cheapest-to-deliver class on the CBOT. The implicit price of transportation between the two closest delivery points in the two contracts is 3 cents per bushel. If a conglomerated agricultural operation (e.g., Cargill) with elevators and mills near all the delivery points can either balance its inventory across elevators or actually transport wheat for, say, 1.75 cents per bushel, then the firm could go long the CBOT contract and simultaneously short the KCBT contract, earning as a profit the 1.25 cent per bushel difference between the transportation cost basis priced into the contracts and its own transportation costs.

For reasons already discussed in Chapter 8 concerning storage costs, the transportation costs reflected in the futures price will be the minimum average transportation cost, or the marginal transportation cost of the marginal storer. The same logic suggests that in equilibrium, the transportation basis reflected in the futures prices will eventually fall from 3 cents per bushel to

1.75 cents per bushel as the firm conducting the spread *becomes* the marginal participant in the transportation market. But until then, that firm is *infra*marginal and can profit from the difference. Add to this that uncertainty in the sense of Chapter 2 may influence the transportation market (e.g., only active firms know their true capacity and congestion points), and a small profit margin may persist over time that is never reflected in the basis.

### Relative Value Trades in Equities

Equity derivatives are very popular products for the use of intermarket spreads. Both speculators and hedgers use equity intermarket spreads involving futures with significant regularity, and the popularity of using equity swaps to accomplish the same results has become significantly higher even in the past five years.

A typical equity intermarket trade attempts to hedge or speculate on movements in one component of the equity market vis-à-vis another. A long S&P 500/short Russell 2000 trade, for example, is a trade that pays off when large-cap stocks outperform small-cap stocks. There are about as many relative value trading and hedging opportunities in equity derivatives as there are equity indexes.

## Intercommodity or Interasset Spreads

A simultaneous long and short position in derivatives based on slightly different but related underlyings is called an *intercommodity* or *interasset spread*. The forward delivery date is generally the same for both contracts, and these spreads are principally used to hedge or trade some quality basis relation. Interasset spreads may be executed using either OTC or exchange-traded contracts. Some of the more common forms of interasset spreads are discussed next.

### Seasonal Commodity Spreads

Relative value positions in derivatives based on different grains with common supply and demand characteristics are quite common in agricultural exchange-traded derivatives markets, in particular. These spreads generally are executed to manage risks associated with seasonality effects and deviations in normal seasonal patterns in different grain production cycles.

Probably the most frequently used intergrain seasonal spread is the wheat/corn spread. Wheat prices are generally at a premium to corn prices, so the spread is usually quoted as wheat minus corn to keep the basis positive (by convention). The spread tends to be low following the winter wheat harvest in May, June, and July and tends to be high following the corn harvest in September, October, and November. Figure 11.2 provides an example from 2002.

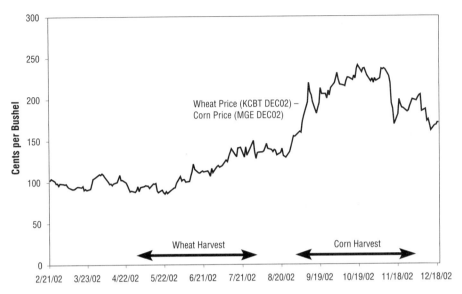

**FIGURE 11.2** The DEC02 Wheat/Corn Spread (2002)

To illustrate the risk transfer applications of such a spread, consider a U.S. farming cooperative producing most grains. Suppose the weather and crop forecasts for both wheat and corn are normal, so the basis is at normal levels given the two term structures of futures prices. But imagine that the firm is worried the weather forecast will be wrong—specifically, the cooperative worries that the corn harvest will be about as expected, but the wheat harvest will be much stronger than expected. The normal trend in the basis, as shown in Figure 11.2, is for the spread to decline up until summer and then rise going into the winter—a widening basis from June to December. But if the cooperative's fears are correct, the basis could easily tighten over this period as a strong wheat harvest prevents wheat prices from overtaking corn prices, as is the norm.

To transfer this kind of risk, a typical hedge might involve a short position in December wheat futures together with a long position in December corn futures, where both positions are established in, say, April. If the basis does indeed tighten, the cooperative has protected its revenues against the relative weakness in wheat prices.

### Input-Output or Commodity-Product Spreads

Another popular intercommodity spread involves the simultaneous execution of transactions designed to replicate the inputs and outputs of a production process or to hedge that production process by putting on the opposite spread. The most popular examples of these are the crush spread, the crack spread, the fractionation spread, and the spark spread.

**The Crush Spread.**[3]   The spread between soybeans and the two major products produced with soybeans—oil and meal—is known as *putting on the crush* or the *crush spread*. In the cash market, a 60-pound bag of soybeans can be crushed into 11 pounds of soybean oil, 44 pounds of 48 percent protein soybean meal, three pounds of hulls, and one pound of waste. If the hulls are not separated from the meal, the meal protein content falls to 44 percent.

The *gross processing margin* (GPM) allows producers to compare the input cost of beans with the output revenues of bean products. The GPM or "the crush" is:

$$GPM = 0.022S_m + 11S_o - S_b$$

where $S_m$ is the price (dollars per ton) of bean meal (48 percent protein), $S_o$ is the price (cents per pound) of bean oil, and $S_b$ is the price (dollars per bushel) of soybeans.

The *Board crush* is the same as the GPM calculation when applied to the soybean futures product complex traded on the CBOT. The Board crush may be traded in a 1:1:1 ratio, although the conversion factors and contract amounts suggest that a more precise version of the Board crush is a spread of 10:11:9 of beans to meal to oil.

A soybean processor concerned about rising input costs, for example, might go long 10 soybean futures contracts and simultaneously short 11 soybean meal and 9 soybean oil futures. In the event of a rise in soybean prices, the higher purchasing costs are offset with a gain on the bean futures. Similarly, a decline in the price of soybean meal or oil that attenuates the processor's revenues is offset by gains on the short futures positions. Such a hedge can be accomplished using contracts with the same delivery dates, although that exposes the processor to calendar basis risk arising from the time it takes to process beans into meal and oil. Instead, the processor could go long the soybean futures with a delivery date matched to the soybean purchase date and then hold the oil and meal futures until the end of the processing cycle, thus combining a calendar spread with the crush spread.

When the price of soybeans rises relative to the price of bean meal and oil, the GPM can occasionally become negative. In this case, processors may halt production. Alternatively, a *reverse crush* is a hedge consisting of short bean futures and long oil and meal futures that restores the viability of processing even during periods of negative GPMs. The reverse crush can also be called *synthetic processing* because the positions in the futures market replicate rather than hedge the processor's cash market position.

We saw in Chapters 8 and 9 that synthetic storage using derivatives is an important mechanism that helps keep the price of actual storage in line. If storage prices in the physical market go above marginal costs, then firms can store synthetically. The combined price pressure and decline in demand for physical storage would put downward pressure on storage prices until equilibrium is restored.

The reverse crush works the same way and reveals how inter*spatial* risk transfer using futures simultaneously acts as an important mechanism by which economic scarcity is rationed and equilibrium ensured. In other words, the combined effect of firms engaging in the reverse crush *and* slowing meal and oil production puts significant upward pressure on meal and oil prices relative to bean prices. Equilibrium will be restored when the GPM in the actual market and the GPM in the futures market are the same at the margin for the marginal processor.

**The Crack Spread.**   Another popular input-output margin is the *crack spread*, or the differential between crude oil as an input to the refining process and the refined products that are outputs of that process. In reality, there are several different crack spreads depending on the refined products in question.

The most popular crack spread involving derivatives is the *x:y:z* crack spread traded on the New York Mercantile Exchange (NYMEX) and OTC swap equivalents. The *x:y:z* refers to the ratio of NYMEX futures contracts— *x* barrels of crude oil, *y* barrels of gasoline, and *z* barrels of heating oil. Just as the crush spread is based on the GPM, the crack spread is driven by the *gross cracking margin* (GCM). The GCM is generally defined as:

$$GCM = 42(yS_{HU} + zS_{HO}) - xS_{CL}$$

where $S_{HU}$ is the price (dollars per gallon) of unleaded gasoline, $S_{HO}$ is the price (dollars per gallon) of heating oil, and $S_{CL}$ is the price (dollars per barrel) of crude oil—generally West Texas Intermediate (WTI) light, sweet crude. The 42 appears in the GCM computation to convert 42 gallons of gasoline or heating oil to the equivalent one barrel of oil.

The ratios chosen in the crack spread depend on the particular output of the refinery doing the hedging. One of the most popular ratios is the 3:2:1 crack spread, based on the premise that a refinery with a "diversified slate" has gasoline output that is generally double the refinery output of distillate fuel oil, which is the component of crude that includes diesel fuel and heating oil. Consider, for example, a refinery that plans to buy 90,000 barrels of crude in November on the spot market with the intention of refining the crude and selling 2,520,000 gallons of gasoline and 1,260,000 gallons of heating oil the following February. If the refinery is concerned about increasing crude costs relative to refined product prices (or declining heating oil and gasoline prices relative to crude purchase prices), the firm could transfer that risk to the futures market with a long 3:2:1 crack spread consisting of 90 long NYMEX crude futures expiring in November and simultaneously going short 30 NYMEX heating oil futures and 60 NYMEX gasoline futures for February expiration. (The NYMEX crude contract calls for delivery of 1,000 barrels of oil, and the gasoline and heating oil contracts call for the equivalent of 1,000 barrels, which is equivalent to 42,000 gallons.) The futures position then insulates the refinery from the market risk of an eroding GCM.

Note also that like the crush spread, this position is also a type of calendar spread. Given the lag in the refining period, the refinery's exposure is not simply to price levels, but to shifts in the term structure of the input-output basis, as well.

The crack spread is economically equivalent to the refining margin in the underlying physical industry. Accordingly, going short the crack spread is sometimes called *synthetic refining*. In other words, the crack spread transactions *hedge* an actual operating refinery, whereas the reverse crack spread *replicates* a theoretical refinery.

Ratios of other than 3:2:1 are also often undertaken in the crack spread. Simple 1:1 crack spreads between either light, sweet crude and heating oil or light, sweet crude and gasoline are also popular, especially for refineries with a more specialized production process. In fact, the NYMEX also lists *options* on the 1:1 crack spreads between crude and both gasoline and heating oil.

Whereas the crush spread in soybeans is primarily a futures market product, short-dated commodity swaps have become increasingly popular for managing the crack spread. These products are economically equivalent to the NYMEX products and often appeal to firms that are concerned with some other factor, such as risk of changes in the transportation or locational basis implicit in the standardized NYMEX contracts that can be solved through customization of the OTC products.

**Other Energy Spreads.** Energy markets generally involve the conversion of one form of energy into another and thus frequently involve spread risks for energy processors or intermediaries that can be hedged with derivatives spreads. The crack spread is the most common, but by no means the only energy input-output spread.

Another popular intercommodity input-output spread in energy markets is the spread between natural gas as an input for the production of propane, called the *fractionation* or *frac* spread. Natural gas processors again often turn to the NYMEX to hedge their propane extraction margins. NYMEX propane futures call for delivery of 42,000 gallons of propane and are quoted in cents per gallon, whereas NYMEX natural gas futures have an underlying of 10,000 mmBtu's (British thermal unit measures of heating) quoted in dollars per mmBtu. In gaseous form, one gallon of propane contains approximately 91,500 Btus, and 42,000 gallons of propane represent about 38 percent of the heating value of a 10,000 mmBtu natural gas contract. Accordingly, frac spreads are often traded in 3:1 or 5:2 ratios.

In the past few years, the *spark spread* has also become a very important market for energy companies seeking to transfer their exposure to rising natural gas prices relative to electricity produced from natural gas through combined-cycle gas turbines (CCGTs). Establishing simultaneous long and short positions in natural gas and electricity derivatives is a hedge for a CCGT generator, and the opposite short/long in natural gas/electricity is a synthetic generator.

### Financial Interasset Spreads

Interasset spreads are by no means unique to commodity derivatives. Common financial interasset spreads are designed to hedge or speculate on markets for essentially similar products that may differ along a specific risk or return dimension. Spreads involving interest rates with different maturities, credit qualities, or liquidity, for example, are very popular.

Interasset spreads involving financial derivatives are often relative value "plays" that are intended to hedge or speculate on relative value differences in asset classes (e.g., stocks versus bonds or bonds versus commodity indexes) or specific assets (e.g., U.S. stock market versus U.K. stock market). An often abused term in interasset spreading is the term *cross-hedging*, which generally refers to the use of an interasset spread as an effort to proxy hedge a position of some kind. Especially common in currencies, a typical cross-hedge might be for a U.S. dollar–based fund manager of European equities to hedge her exchange rate risk using only euro/dollar futures. This would be a true hedge for euro-denominated stocks, but if the portfolio also includes, say, Swiss franc–denominated stocks, the euro/dollar position would represent a proxy hedge of the true franc/dollar risk.

Also popular in foreign exchange derivatives are interasset spreads designed to synthesize a "cross-rate"—for example, combining a forward to buy Swiss francs with dollars together with a forward to buy dollars with yen in order to synthesize a single position whose value is based on relative movements in the franc/yen exchange rate.

Interasset spreads also are commonly observed in interest rate derivatives markets, where one of the most popular financial interasset spreads is the *Treasury-Eurodollar (TED) spread*. Generally traded using Treasury bill and Eurodollar futures traded on the Chicago Mercantile Exchange (CME), the TED spread is widely thought to be a good measure of interbank liquidity. The credit quality of both Treasury and Eurodeposit rates is generally very high and does not fluctuate significantly, but differential liquidity in these two markets can vary a lot. A bank concerned with the risk of having to borrow interbank during a period of financial crisis, for example, might use the TED spread as a hedge against liquidity-driven increases in short-term funding costs.

Other popular financial spreads include the *munis over bonds (MOB) spread* and the *notes over bonds (NOB) spread*. The MOB spread is driven mainly by credit and liquidity variables, whereas the NOB spread is primarily a calendar-basis trade at the long end of the term structure of interest rates. We return to many of these spreads in Part Three of the book.

## NOTES

1. Ignore quantity issues for now and assume the contracts are properly matched on a quantity basis.
2. Because four classes of wheat can be delivered at par into the CBOT contract, the price will always reflect the cheapest to deliver of these four classes.
3. The details of the crush spread presented here are based on CBOT (2003).

# Speculation and Hedging

# Speculation and the Speculative Risk Premium

**W**e saw in Chapter 3 that of Knight's four methods by which firms can control risk and uncertainty—retention, reduction, consolidation, and specialization—only the last involves the shifting of risk by the hedger to another firm. We divided potential counterparties to such risk transfer agreements into three categories: other hedgers with offsetting risk transfer demands; risk transfer specialists like swap dealers and insurance companies; and speculators.

A risk transfer specialist, you will recall, is a firm that essentially has some comparative advantage in intermediating risk transfer transactions like derivatives—for example, more equity capital and a high credit quality, a portfolio of exposures in which the idiosyncratic risks being transferred will be better diversified than if left where they began, the capacity to identify other hedgers with offsetting demands at relatively lower search costs, and so on. Speculators, on the other hand, we saw were firms and individuals with no natural offsetting risk exposure or capacity to consolidate that risk exposure. In conventional terms, speculators are outright position takers.

In this chapter, we explore the motivations for speculation in greater detail with a specific goal of examining the so-called "speculative risk premium" that we first encountered in Chapter 4. The speculative risk premium is a contentiously debated concept based on the belief by some that when speculators engage in at-market forward-based derivatives with hedgers, they demand a positive expected payoff to compensate them for the risk they are consenting to bear (over and above any systematic risk premium).

The theoretical and empirical quests both to defend and to debunk the speculative risk premium have endured for nearly a century. And to some extent, the issue remains unresolved. Nevertheless, this can significantly affect the cost of risk transfer and thus is an issue to which hedgers and derivatives participants must pay close attention.

## SPECULATION: MOTIVATIONS AND SOURCES
## OF EXPECTED PROFITS

We used a simple tool of neoclassical price theory—the Edgeworth Box—to show in Chapter 4 what hedgers must "pay" to engage in risk transfer. Outright purchases of limited-liability products with options- or insurance-like payoffs warrant the payment of a premium by the hedger in virtually all situations. The only real question is whether the premium is actuarially fair or loaded.

Things get more interesting with forward-based symmetric-payoff derivatives. If a hedger happens upon another hedger with an offsetting risk transfer demand, bilateral contracting at an actuarially fair price can still be Pareto efficient and thus can occur (we gave some examples that it routinely *does* occur). Entering into forward-based derivatives with a risk transfer specialist is essentially the same thing. The specialist is simply intermediating a Pareto efficient bilateral exchange to reduce search costs and credit risks. Risk transfer specialists rarely bear significant risk in their businesses, either relying on their own ability to consolidate and net down multiple exposures or turning to risk transfer markets themselves. Either way, "risk in" usually equals "risk out" for risk-transfer specialists.

Now we come to speculators. Here we have accepted the crude but conventional characterization of a speculator as a firm that engages in a risk transfer contract with no offsetting payoff. But we have been fairly dismissive and mysterious in our references to how speculators demand and receive compensation for playing this role. We promised in Chapters 3 and 4 to return to this issue, and here we are.

Evidently, the definition of speculation we have adopted is a highly unsatisfying one, especially when we try to draw an analytical or systematic distinction between speculators and risk transfer specialists. Connotatively, this distinction seems clear enough. A risk transfer specialist is a firm with some comparative advantage either in consolidating or managing risk or intermediating risk transfer agreements. Risk transfer specialists do not necessarily have any comparative advantage in risk *bearing*, and the behavior of risk transfer specialists is quite often to avoid significant risk exposures. Whether risk transfer specialists achieve risk reduction through consolidation, through compensation, or through risk transfer activities of their own (e.g., hedging or reinsurance), risk transfer specialists tend to run relative matched portfolios.

A speculator, on the other hand, usually has the connotation of a firm or individual who disagrees with a trading counterparty about the likelihood of a future event, thus giving rise to potential *ex ante* gains from trade. (Someone will, of course, experience a loss *ex post*.)

Despite the perception of an easily drawn distinction between risk transfer specialists and speculators, the reality of the distinction is much more ambiguous. Is a swap dealer "speculating" if it goes long the Japanese yen against the U.S. dollar for a day because it expects to find a customer that wants a short position a day later? Is an oil company that has a flat position in the market but goes long in anticipation of a short exposure that will arise tomorrow "speculating"? Is an insurance company that charges a fair price to provide life insurance but does not reinsure that line "speculating"?

Not only are these sorts of questions frustrating and essentially impossible to answer, they are largely irrelevant. The relevant question for firms engaged in risk transfer is how the identity and motivations of their counterparty in a risk transfer agreement affect the *cost* of risk transfer for the hedger. In other words, how do counterparties to risk transfer contracts like derivatives expected to get compensated for accepting these risks that the hedger is attempting to reduce?

In the following sections, we consider the motivations for speculation and the nature of speculators in more detail from two different perspectives. This is an important foundation for our exploration of the so-called "speculative risk premium" in the remainder of the chapter.

## Speculators as Risk-Bearing Specialists

Casual observers often refer to speculation as the process by which firms and individuals shift risk or uncertainty to speculators that are presumably "more willing" to bear that risk or uncertainty. Implicit in most people's connotative perceptions of speculation thus is someone who simply has a taste for loading up on risk or uncertainty. But this generally is *not* true. As Knight (1921, p. 255) says, "The mere specialization of uncertainty-bearing in the hands of persons most willing to assume the function is probably among the lesser rather than the greater sources of [profits for speculators as a class]."

The first characterization of speculators is as specialists in risk bearing. According to this notion, speculators are specialists in risk *bearing* but not necessarily specialists on risk. Although speculators may tolerate temporary increases in risk, they are not fundamentally more "willing" to suffer losses than the counterparties seeking to transfer risks to them. A key aspect of this view of speculators is that speculation *does result in increased risk for the speculator* and that speculators demand a risk premium—above and beyond any systematic risk premium—to bear this new risk.

Apart from the few notable exceptions like George Soros, few people would openly proclaim that their profession is "speculator," and fewer still would explain the economic function of their firm as "speculation." This is unfortunate, as it leads many to conclude speculation is mainly an ad hoc activity rather than an organized business. Speculators, so the logic goes, dart in and out of markets only when they have a specific (generally contrary) opinion but otherwise "create no value."

True, individuals and firms do make specific trading decisions—and sometimes do run a whole business—based on their perceived informational advantage. We will look at some examples of this. But for the most part, firms engage in speculation about uncertainty or risk not because they consistently disagree with their counterparties, but rather because they perceive themselves as being more efficient *risk consolidators*. In the context of the discussion in the prior section, a "speculator" thus is a risk transfer specialist *that does not reinsure or hedge all of the risk it accepts*. Informational advantage *may* play a role in this, but it need not. Knight explains:

> *The typical illustration to show the advantage of organized speculation to business at large is the use of the hedging contract. By this simple device the industrial producer is enabled to eliminate the chance of loss or gain due to changes in the value of materials used in his operations during the interval between the time he purchases them as raw materials and the time he disposes of them as finished product, "shifting" this risk to the professional speculator. It is manifest at once that even aside from any superior judgment or foresight or better information possessed by such a professional speculator, he gains an enormous advantage from the sheer magnitude or breadth of the scope of his operations. Where a single flour miller or cotton spinner would be in the market once, the speculator enters it hundreds or thousands of times, and his errors in judgment must show a correspondingly stronger tendency to cancel out and leave him a constant and predictable return on his operations. The same reasoning holds good for any method of specializing uncertainty-bearing. Specialization implies concentration, and concentration involves consolidation; and no matter how heterogeneous the "cases" the gains and losses neutralize each other in the aggregate to an extent increasing as the number of cases thrown together is larger. Specialization itself is primarily an application of the insurance principle; but, like large-scale enterprise, it grows up to meet uncertainty situations where, on account of the impossibility of objective definition and external control of the individual ventures or uncertainties, a "moral hazard" prevents insurance by an external agency or a loose association of venturers for this single purpose. (Knight, 1921, p. 256)*

When speculation is interpreted as *specialization in risk consolidation*, it becomes easier to imagine the speculator as engaged in a legitimate business enterprise. And this is especially true when considering the transfer of uncertainty rather than risk. To take an example, consider Lloyd's of London, an organized insurance company in which individuals or "Names" provide their personal capital to syndicates that accept small chunks of exposure to underwriting risks that are often considered "uninsurable." Examples include the risk to a Scottish whiskey distillery from the Loch Ness Monster, the risk that an expedition to the South Pole will be stranded in the ice, the risk that a court will decide against a corporation in a professional liability determination, and the like. Nevertheless, Lloyd's regularly underwrites exactly those sorts of policies—speculation not in the sense of superior information but in the sense of specialization in risk consolidation.

Similarly, consider a reinsurance company that underwrites the first $1 billion in claims payments made by a primary insurance carrier arising from a California earthquake. If the reinsurer itself purchases (i.e., "retrocedes") $1 billion in reinsurance, it is acting exclusively as a risk transfer specialist as defined in the prior section. But suppose the reinsurer only chooses to purchase reinsurance for losses in excess of $500 million up to $1 billion, the net impact of which is for the reinsurer to retain the first $500 million in loss exposure. Surely no one would argue this is because the reinsurer has "better information" about earthquake-related property losses incurred by another insurance company in the specific range of $0 to $500 million! No, the reinsurer is simply facilitating the "diffusion principle" for the primary insurer by providing risk transfer services. But, strictly speaking, the reinsurer is a speculator in every sense of the term.

Writing in the *Manchester Guardian Commercial*, Keynes (1923) provides a useful commentary of this perspective on speculators:

> *In most writings on this subject, great stress is laid on the service performed by the professional speculator in bringing about a harmony between short-period and long-period demand and supply, through his action in stimulating or retarding in good time the one or the other. This may be the case. But it presumes that the speculator is better informed on the average than the producers or consumers themselves. Which, speaking generally, is a rather dubious proposition. The most important function of the speculator in the great organized 'Futures' market is, I think, somewhat different. He is not so much a prophet (though it may be a belief in his own gifts of prophecy that tempts him into the business), as a risk-bearer . . . without paying the slightest attention to the prospects of the commodity he deals in or giving a thought to it, he may, one decade with another, earn substantial renumeration merely by running risks and allowing the results of one season to average with those of another: just as an insurance company makes profits. (Keynes, 1923, quoted in Rockwell, 1967, p. 574)*

As usual, Knight is quick to distinguish between speculation as the consolidation of *risk* versus the consolidation of *uncertainty*. When speculators function as specialists in true *risk bearing*, they are essentially exploiting a comparative advantage in their market position and charging for providing that service for which they have a comparative cost advantage. But just because speculators are the most efficient parties to hold a particular risk does not mean that the risk itself is reduced or changed by virtue of the transfer. When the two parties agree on the probabilistic nature of the risk, the price the speculators will demand fairly reflects the nature of the risk. This notion of speculation thus is consistent with the belief that speculators will demand a speculative risk premium for providing that service to hedgers.

When speculation is essentially the specialization in consolidation of uncertainty, however, it does have the effect of actually reducing uncertainty. Knight explains: "Most fundamental among these effects in reducing uncertainty is its conversion into a measured risk or elimination by grouping which is implied in the very fact of specialization" (Knight, 1921, p. 256). He continues:

> There is in this respect a fundamental difference between the speculator or promoter and the insurer, which must be kept clearly in view. The insurer knows more about the risk in a particular case—say of a building burning—but the real risk is no less because he assumes it in that particular case. His risk is less only because he assumes a large number. But the transfer of the "risk" of an error in judgment is a very different matter. The "insurer" (entrepreneur, speculator, or promoter) now substitutes his own judgment for the judgment of the man who is getting rid of the uncertainty through transferring it to the specialist. In so far as his knowledge and judgment are better, which they almost certainly will be from the mere fact that he is a specialist, the individual risk is less likely to become a loss, in addition to, the gain from grouping. There is better management, greater economy in the use of economic resources, as well as a mere transformation of uncertainty into certainty. The problem of meeting uncertainty thus passes inevitably into the general problem of management, of economic control. (Knight, 1921, pp. 258–259)

## Speculators as Information Specialists

A decidedly different perspective on speculation argues that speculators do not merely tolerate risk in order to perform a risk consolidation service for a fee, but in fact willingly assume risk in order to exploit a positive expected trading return on their private information or beliefs—to exploit a so-called "edge." Hicks (1939) was a strong proponent of this view of speculation:

> But it is the essence of speculation . . . that the speculator puts himself into a more risky position as the result of his forward trading—he need not have ventured into forward dealing at all, and would have been safer

*if he had not done so. . . . It will not be worth his while to undertake the risk if the prospective return is too small. (Hicks, 1939, p. 138)*

The role of speculators as informationally driven traders is often discussed in fairly vague and imprecise forms. But there are some very clear differences vis-à-vis the view of speculators as specialists in risk bearing. First, speculators may demand compensation from hedgers as some kind of speculative risk premium for providing risk transfer services, but this is not a necessary condition for information-based speculative trading. In this theory, the primary component of the expected returns to speculation comes from trading. Second, at least some portion of the total pool of speculators must perceive themselves as having (or actually have) a superior ability to forecast or anticipate prices. Finally, not all speculators are created equal. Whereas the speculator as a risk-bearing specialist depicts all speculators as akin to unhedged swap dealers or insurance companies, the view of speculators as information traders allows speculators as a group to be much more heterogeneous.

An important source of heterogeneity among speculators is whether or not any given speculator is correct in her presumption of having superior information. Working (1953a,b, 1960b, 1962) contended that speculators as a group included both "skilled" and "unskilled" members. The former are speculators with a *true* comparative informational advantage, whereas the latter *perceive* themselves as having such an advantage but in reality do not.

Black (1985) characterized two types of traders that he dubbed "news traders" and "noise traders." A news trader engages in transactions based on the arrival of new information, whereas a noise trader merely perceives the arrival of new information. A noise trader mistakes noise for news and trades accordingly. News traders, akin to Working's "skilled specialists," are generally correct in their beliefs about prices, whereas noise traders as the analogue to unskilled speculators are not.

Considerable attention has been paid in both industry and academia to the role of informational symmetries in explaining futures trading and other forms of derivatives and financial market activity. Lucas (1972) argued that informational asymmetries cannot persist in a rational expectations equilibrium because price aggregates disparate information and disperses it.[1] Lucas's view is reminiscent of Knight's (1921) argument that uncertainty cannot remain uncertainty once it has been turned into a price through trading, and is even more similar to Hayek's (1945) characterization of the price system.

Even stronger, though, are the famous "no trade theorems" of finance. These theorems hold that (1) differences in information may be incorporated into prices without inducing market participants to trade, and (2) market participants with the same prior beliefs will not trade with one another for purely informational reasons *even when information is asymmetric* (Rubinstein,

1975; Kreps, 1977; Milgrom and Stokey, 1982; Tirole, 1982; Hakansson, Kunkel, and Ohlson, 1982).

At the theoretical level, trading based on differences of opinion or information can be explained by market imperfections, transactional opacity, differences in prior beliefs that lead to different perceptions of the arrival of new information, and the existence of "speculation" (Jaffe and Winkler, 1976; Grossman, 1977, 1988; Danthine, 1978; Diamond and Verrecchia, 1981; Black, 1985; Morris, 1994).

A question frequently arises, however, as to whether more speculation is "good" or "bad" for hedgers. On the one hand, more speculators mean there is more liquidity and perhaps more potential counterparties for hedgers. On the other hand, if speculators have a destabilizing influence on prices and tend to drive markets away from their fundamental values, the additional liquidity is unconstructive.

Keynes was particularly skeptical of any speculation that did not fall into his conception of speculators as risk-bearing specialists. He believed that any speculators trading based on a presumed informational advantage were merely engaged in the unattractive "activity of forecasting the psychology of the market" (Keynes, 1936, p. 158). In other words, Keynes believed that all speculative activities necessarily involved the development of trading strategies purely intended to exploit perceived "herd mentality" or other purely behavioral drivers of trading in organized markets. As a result, Keynes was particularly chagrined by the proliferation of speculative activity in the U.S. stock market:

> *In one of the greatest investment markets in the world, namely, New York, the influence of speculation . . . is enormous. Even outside the field of finance, Americans are apt to be unduly interested in discovering what average opinion believes average opinion to be; and this national weakness finds its nemesis in the stock market. It is rare, one is told, for an American to invest, as many Englishmen still do, "for income"; and he will not readily purchase an investment except in the hope of capital appreciation. This is only another way of saying that, when he purchases an investment, the American is attaching his hopes, not so much to its prospective yield, as to a favourable change in the conventional basis of valuation, i.e. that he is . . . a speculator. (Keynes, 1936, p. 159)*

Keynes went so far as to argue that the participation of speculators in stock markets essentially invalidates their legitimate economic function:

> *When the capital development of a country becomes a byproduct of the activities of a casino, the job is likely to be ill-done. The measure of success attained by Wall Street, regarded as an institution of which the proper social purpose is to direct new investment into the most profitable*

*channels in terms of future yield, cannot be claimed as one of the out-standing triumphs of* laissez-faire *capitalism. (Keynes, 1936, p. 159)*

It would make little sense to deny that such speculation does occur routinely. Much technical analysis falls into this category. Consider, for example, a trader who takes a long position on soybeans not because he believes soybeans are fundamentally undervalued but because the market is about to reach a Fibonacci number or is concluding an Elliott Wave, thus leading *other investors* into the market to buy.

Applied to more traditional investment analysis, we might well refer to "market timing" as a speculative investment strategy of just this sort. The selection of a security to buy or sell may well be based on fundamental considerations, but the timing of when it is purchased or sold may be driven by just these sorts of nonmarket variables.

Others beside Keynes have assumed the mantra of criticizing speculation as having a destabilizing influence. The basic argument is that speculation based on asymmetric information relies on inconsistencies in plans and thus either must be eliminated in a rational expectations equilibrium or must eventually force markets to diverge from their true, fundamental values (e.g., Tirole, 1982; Hart and Kreps, 1986).

Nevertheless, the theoretical literature is also replete with examples of studies that show how speculation can be a stabilizing market influence—at least under certain conditions (e.g., Farrell, 1966; Danthine, 1978; Miller, 1997). The empirical evidence also supports the notion that derivatives markets in which speculation is allowed tend to be associated with lower price volatility in the underlying asset—see, for example, Hooker (1901), Gray (1967), Working (1958, 1960a, 1963), and Powers (1970).

The notion that speculators demand special compensation for their services is ambiguous when the interpretation of speculators as information specialists is adopted. Danthine (1978) argues, for example, that expected returns from trading are not enough and that a speculative risk premium is still required to induce informed speculators to share producers' risks. Other have argued, by contrast, that speculative profits on pure risk transfer are driven to zero in a competitive equilibrium and that profits by skilled speculators will just offset losses by unskilled speculators, thus abrogating the need for any payment by hedgers as a group to speculators as a group (Telser, 1958; Working, 1953a,b, 1960b, 1962).

## FORWARD PURCHASE PRICE BIAS AND RISK

Closely related to the speculative risk premium is the notion of "bias" in forward and futures prices. Specifically, the price of an asset for future delivery is said to be an unbiased estimate of the future spot price of that asset at time $t$ if[2]

$$f_{t,T} = E_t(S_T)$$

An unbiased estimate of a future spot price can also be interpreted as the market's best "guess," "prediction," or "forecast" today of what the spot price will be in the future. A downward biased forward price implies that $f_{t,T} <  E_t[S_T]$, and conversely for an upward biased forward price.

Forward price bias can be related back to the speculative risk premium by interpreting bias in terms of the expected payoffs on long and short forward positions, shown below respectively:

$$E_t\left[\pi_T^l\right] = Z\left(E_t[S_T] - f_{t,T}\right)$$
$$E_t\left[\pi_T^s\right] = Z\left(f_{t,T} - E_t[S_T]\right)$$

(12.1)

A downward biased forward price ($f_{t,T} < E_t[S_T]$) means that the long in a forward contract has a strictly positive expected payoff as of the trade date. Assuming both parties perceive the only randomness in the contract as a Knightian risk, the expected future price will be the same for both parties, in which case the short actually expects to lose money from the inception of a deal with a downward biased forward price. Why would a short voluntarily enter into a transaction with a negative expected payoff?

One possible reason that we have already analyzed is systematic risk. If the covariance between the stochastic discount factor and future spot price is negative, for example, the asset purchaser will be unwilling to commit on the trade date to a subsequent purchase of the asset at the expected future spot price. The most that the long will be willing to commit to pay in the future is the expected future spot price *minus* a risk premium reflecting the covariance of the future spot price with the stochastic discount factor. In other words, the expected payoff on the forward at maturity must be at least enough to compensate the long for the systematic risk that could affect the asset's price over the intervening period of time. Similarly, the negative expected value of the payoff to the short at maturity is the necessary additional price the short must pay to liquidate an asset whose payoffs vary inversely with our index of bad times.

The systematic risk premium is inherent to the underlying asset. Whether the purchase occurs on the spot market or in the future makes no difference; either way, the purchaser will demand some compensation for the risk that the asset pays off more only when the payoff is less valuable. This is the "anti-insurance" effect discussed in Chapter 7.

We cannot, of course, draw any general inferences about whether forward prices *in general* are upward biased, downward biased, or perhaps even *un*biased on the basis of the systematic risk premium alone. Ultimately, this is an empirical matter that depends solely on the sign of the covariance between the discount factor and the underlying spot price of the asset.

Thus far we have not seen anything new in this section. We have merely introduced the definition of bias and examined how the systematic risk premium is one possible explanation for why forward prices might be biased predictors of the future spot price. So that we can focus on the new material in this chapter, we now want to assume—for the time being—that the systematic risk premium is zero. Is there any other reason that a firm would voluntarily enter into an at-market forward or swap with a negative expected payoff at maturity? Yes—the so-called speculative risk premium.

## THEORY OF NORMAL BACKWARDATION

The first characterization of the speculative risk premium dates to Keynes (1923) and Hicks (1939). Despite early vehement efforts by Hardy (1923) and others to argue against the theory to which Keynes and later Hicks were wed, the Keynes/Hicks speculative risk premium was accepted as the conventional wisdom for many years after its first appearance. Indeed, not until Telser (1958) was the legitimacy of the Keynes/Hicks theory of a speculative risk premium seriously questioned.

The Keynes/Hicks speculative risk premium is based on the premise that risk transfer occurs mainly between hedgers as a group and speculators as a group. Specifically, demands for risk transfer by firms with a long exposure to the underlying asset price and hence a short derivatives position put downward pressure on forward/futures prices. This induces a downward bias in the forward price that translates into a negative expected forward payoff for the hedger shorts and a positive expected payoff for the counterparties that are long the forward. The speculative risk premium on any asset is the difference between the downward biased forward price and the expected spot price, representing compensation to speculators for assuming the price risk being shifted by the derivatives contract from the short hedger to the long speculator.

Let us examine this hypothesis a little more deliberately.

### Keynesian Theory of Normal Backwardation

The theory of normal backwardation for the speculative risk premium was originally developed by Lord Keynes in his *Treatise on Money: Volume II, The Applied Theory of Money* (1930b), written just before he first articulated the notion of own interest rates in the *General Theory*. The Keynesian theory rests on the critical assumption that those seeking to transfer their risks using derivatives are "producers." When he was writing, Keynes was focused mainly on agricultural markets in which he believed producers were farmers. Farmers were normally long the underlying asset (i.e., naturally benefiting from price increases or losing from price declines over the production period) and thus would normally hedge *by going short derivatives*.

Keynes further believed that opposite producers in the derivatives markets were speculators that would demand a risk premium to accept the price risk that producers were attempting to transfer away. To induce them to take on this risk, speculators—long the forward contract with the short producers/hedgers—would need to earn a positive expected return.

The theory of normal backwardation says that the speculative risk premium, if defined as the forward price less the expected spot price, should be *negative*:

$$\psi = f_{t,t+1} - E_t[S_{t+1}] < 0$$

Shorts thus expect to lose money on average. Conversely, long forward purchasers expect to *make* money on average. Think about the logic for a moment. If hedgers are on average long the asset and short the forwards and futures, then a negative expected payoff is the speculative risk premium or the positive expected profit the long speculators will demand to accept the transfer of risk.

The implication of the Keynesian theory is that forward and futures prices should be downward biased estimates of the future spot price. Keynes defined this downward bias in the forward price—that is, $f_{t,T} < E_t(S_T)$—as a *normal backwardation*. He explains:

> *It is not necessary that there should be an abnormal shortage of supply in order that a backwardation should be established. If supply and demand are balanced, the spot price must exceed the forward price by the amount which the producer is ready to sacrifice in order to "hedge" himself, i.e., to avoid the risk of price fluctuations during his production period. Thus in normal conditions the spot price exceeds the forward price, i.e., there is a backwardation. In other words, the normal supply price on the spot includes remuneration for the risk of price fluctuations during the period of production, whilst the forward price excludes this. (Keynes, 1930b, p. 143)*

From the preceding selected text, it might seem that Lord Keynes' theory of normal backwardation implies that the market should be in backwardation in the sense the term is defined in Chapter 9—in terms of *actual, observed* spot and forward purchase prices. And indeed, this passage frequently leads to confusion about what exactly the implication of the theory of normal backwardation is.

Further reading of this selection in Keynes' text, however, adds a significant amount of clarity to his theory. Now Lord Keynes is considering a carry market:

> *Indeed the existence of surplus stocks must cause the forward price to rise above the spot price, i.e. to establish, in the language of the market, a "contango"; and this contango must be equal to the cost of the warehouse, depreciation and interest charges of carrying the stocks. But the existence of a contango does not mean that a producer can hedge himself without paying the usual insurance against price changes. On the contrary, the additional element of uncertainty introduced by the existence of stocks and the additional supply of risk-bearing which they require mean that he must pay more than usual. In other words, the quoted forward price, though above the present spot price, must fall below the anticipated future spot price by at least the amount of the normal backwardation; and the present spot price, since it is lower than the quoted forward price, must be much lower than the anticipated future spot price. (Keynes, 1930b, p. 144)*

In other words, Keynes's conception of a normal backwardation is much more dependent on *anticipated prices* or *expectations* than might have seemed the case from the first passage quoted earlier. But this recent passage makes it very clear that to Keynes, the important implication of normal backwardation is that "the quoted forward price . . . must fall below the *anticipated future* spot price. . . ." (Keynes, 1930b, p. 144, emphasis added)

## Normal Backwardation and Expected Price Changes

The expected change in the spot price of an asset that is also available for purchase and sale in the forward market can be decomposed into two components: the cost of carry and the speculative risk premium. To see why, simply recognize that we can express the expected change in the spot price by using the Keynesian definition of the risk premium as a normal backwardation:

$$\frac{E[S_{t+1}] - S_t}{S_t} = \frac{f_{t,t+1} - \psi - S_t}{S_t} = \frac{f_{t,t+1} - S_t}{S_t} - \frac{\psi}{S_t} \qquad (12.2)$$

which can be rewritten as

$$\frac{E[S_{t+1}] - S_t}{S_t} = r - x + \omega \qquad (12.3)$$

where $\omega \equiv \psi/S_t$ is the speculative risk premium expressed as a proportion of the spot price. In other words, the price of the asset is expected to change by an amount equal to the cost of carry (i.e., the nominal interest rate less the real own interest rate) plus an insurance premium paid by the short hedgers to the long speculators.

This decomposition of the expected price change into these two components is especially clear when we examine the problem graphically. Figure 12.1 depicts a two-period spot and futures market for an asset in a state of normal backwardation at time $t$. The normal backwardation is immediately evident from the fact that $f_{t,t+1} < E[S_{t+1}]$. The current spot price is well above the futures price, moreover, indicating that the market is also in *market* backwardation.

The solid heavy line represents the expected movement of the spot price from $t$ to $t + 1$. Because the futures price must converge to the spot price at

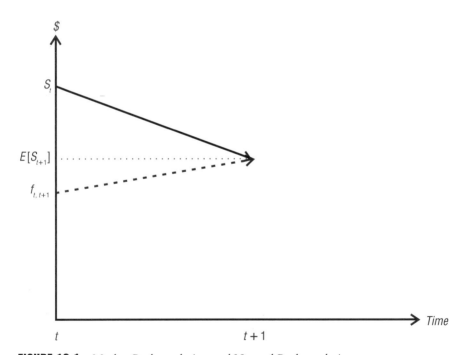

**FIGURE 12.1**   Market Backwardation and Normal Backwardation

expiration, the heavy broken line represents the expected movement of the forward price toward that same point.[3] The expected decline in the spot price includes the cost of carry (i.e., the *market* backwardation) *plus* the *normal* backwardation, or

$$E[S_{t+1}] - S_t = (f_{t,t+1} - S_t) + (E[S_{t+1}] - f_{t,t+1})$$

*Expected spot price change = Cost of carry*
*+ Normal backwardation premium*

Interpreted in terms of Figure 12.1, the market backwardation indicates a strong positive nominal own rate of interest. The spot price thus is expected to decline to induce firms to sell into the current market to cover the current relative inventory shortage. But acting in a countervailing direction is the premium paid to the speculative longs to compensate them for accepting the price risk transferred by the short hedgers. This attenuates the expected price decline by $\psi$. We could rewrite the expected price change in terms of all components more precisely as follows:

$$\frac{E[S_{t+1}] - S_t}{S_t} = r - q + c - l + \varpi \tag{12.4}$$

Although equation (12.4) and the foregoing discussion show that there is a clear relation among the expected total spot price change of an asset, market backwardation, and normal backwardation, caution must be exercised not to try to infer one type of backwardation from the other. As the earlier quotation from Lord Keynes reminds us and as Figure 12.2 plainly illustrates, normal backwardation can also exist for an asset in market contango.

As Figure 12.2 illustrates, the decomposition of the expected change in the spot price into the cost of carry plus a backwardation premium still works, and we still have

$$\frac{E[S_{t+1}] - S_t}{S_t} = r - q + c - l + \varpi$$

Unlike in the case of Figure 12.1, however, we now have a *positive* cost of carry, indicating an expected *increase* in the spot price from $S_t$ to $f_{t,t+1}$ to cover the excess of physical and capital storage costs over the convenience and liquidity yields. But on top of that, the spot price is expected to rise still further to provide an *additional* compensation to the long speculators for accepting risk transfer from the short hedger-producers.

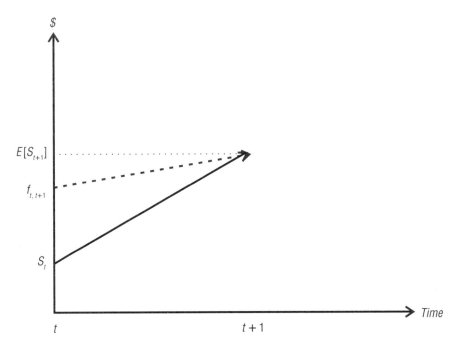

**FIGURE 12.2**   Market Contango and Normal Backwardation

## Hicksian Theory of Normal Backwardation

Hicks was an equally ardent proponent of the theory of normal backwardation, which he diligently attributed to Keynes in his *Value and Capital* (1939). Although the implications of the theory—downward biased forward prices and normal backwardation—are identical in the formulations by Keynes (1923) and Hicks (1939), their view of speculators is quite different. Exploring this difference is instructive and provides us with a useful additional perspective on the function of speculators.

Like Keynes, Hicks believed that hedgers were generally long the asset and thus short the hedge. Hicks thus believed that a derivatives market dominated by short hedgers would exhibit

> *a tendency for relative weakness on the demand side; a smaller proportion of planned purchases than of planned sales would be covered by forward contracts. But for this very reason forward markets rarely consist entirely of hedgers. The futures price (say, for one month's delivery) which would be made by the transactions of hedgers alone would be de-*

*termined by causes that have nothing to do with the causes ordinarily de-
termining market price; it would therefore be widely different from the
spot price which any sensible person would expect to rule in a month's
time, and would ordinarily be much below the expected price. Futures
prices are therefore nearly always made partly by* speculators, *who seek a
profit by buying futures when the futures price is below the spot price
they expect to rule on the corresponding date; their action tends to raise
the futures price to a more reasonable level. (Hicks, 1939, pp. 137–138)*

For Hicks, normal backwardation was not simply required so that
hedgers could transfer a risk premium to speculators. Instead, Hicks believed
that the very definition of a speculator is one who perceives the futures price
to be downward biased (i.e., below the expected spot price):

*[The speculator] will only be willing to go on buying futures so long as
the futures price remains definitely below the spot price he expects; for it
is the difference between these prices which he can expect to receive as a
return for his risk-bearing. (Hicks, 1939, p. 138)*

The difference between Keynesian and Hicksian normal backwardation
may seem subtle, especially because the two theories lead to the same implications for pricing and for the market. In fact, the two versions of the theory of
normal backwardation are remarkably different. Under the Keynesian theory,
speculators with no ability to forecast prices at all must be induced to take the
long side of derivatives opposite of short hedgers. The difference between the
forward price and the future spot price that everyone expects is the speculative risk premium. Under the Hicksian formulation, speculators *can* forecast
prices and believe them to be above current futures prices, given a presumed
preponderance of short hedgers in the market. The difference between the
forward price and the spot price *that speculators forecast* is simply the return
to accurate price forecasting that represents the return to speculation.

## Empirical Evidence

A test of the Keynes/Hicks theory of the speculative risk premium amounts to
a test of the hypothesis that most markets are in normal backwardation. Unfortunately, as we saw earlier in this chapter, we cannot simply look at the observed futures price term structure to answer that question because a market
can be simultaneously in normal backwardation and market contango. So
how do we test the hypothesis instead?

The primary testable implication of the Keynesian model of normal backwardation is that futures prices should on average rise toward expiration. Figures 12.1 and 12.2 help illustrate why. Because the model itself postulates

that the initial futures price is below the expected spot price, the futures price must rise on average over the life of the contract in order to reward the speculative longs.

The evidence does not support the Keynesian hypothesis of a risk premium that leads to a downward bias in futures prices. True, some studies in the tradition of Keynes and Hicks have purported to identify a price bias in futures that appears to support the Keynesian model; four early and often cited papers in support of Keynes are Houthakker (1957, 1959) and Cootner (1960a,b). But this evidence has been challenged—most would say successfully—by Telser (1958, 1960), Gray (1961, 1962), Dusak (1973), and Kolb (1992), among others. A common error that led some earlier researchers to identify what they thought was a Keynesian risk premium was small sample bias (in both commodities and length of time series). In some cases, moreover, authors mistook seasonality for a risk premium.

A common finding in most studies is that the proportion of hedgers that are net long or net short can sometimes make a difference in whether a futures price bias is observed. When the proportion of hedgers does not affect any observed price trend, the Keynesian and Hicksian theories of normal backwardation collapse under their own weight. But even if the proportion of hedgers that are net long or net short does matter, several findings support the notion of normal backwardation only when hedgers are net short.[4] This also is clear contradictory evidence to the theory as it was originally presented by Keynes, as well as Hicks.

## DEFICIENCIES WITH THE THEORY OF NORMAL BACKWARDATION

Recall the four Keynesian assumptions in order for normal backwardation to occur:

1. Hedgers are on average long the physical asset.
2. Because hedgers are on average long the physical asset, hedgers thus are on average short the futures contract.
3. Speculators are the counterparties to hedgers in the futures market as a group and are thus long futures on average.
4. Speculators require an insurance-like risk premium in order to accept the risk that hedgers are trying to avoid (Keynes) or have superior price forecasting abilities (Hicks).

Many scholars have argued over time, however, that any or all of these four assumptions might well be wrong (Telser, 1958). Let us take them one at a time.

## Natural Exposure of Hedgers

Is there any good reason to believe that hedgers should be long the physical asset on average? Of course not. This is an entirely empirical question. Keynes assumed that because *he* observed mostly natural longs in the markets, that must imply a general state of affairs consistent with his own anecdotal observation.

The folly of this reasoning is easy to see by considering the range of firms with natural short exposures to various assets. Any commercial *purchaser* of a commodity on the spot market, for example, is a natural short that may wish to hedge its price risk with a long derivatives position (e.g., grain elevators buying wheat and corn, airlines buying jet fuel, refineries buying crude oil, soybean crushers buying beans, electric utilities buying natural gas, etc.). And of course with financial assets, who can possibly tell whether a given company might be long or short interest rates, currencies, and the like?

## Types of Commercial Hedging

Even if we assume that most commercial participants are naturally long the underlying asset, there is no reason to believe this will translate into a position in the futures market that is on average short for commercial firms *as a group*. For any number of reasons, it is entirely possible that many of those firms with a natural long price exposure *will not fully or even partially hedge*. And if this is the case, then it is possible that the relatively smaller group of natural shorts could still be the dominant group of hedgers in the futures market.

In addition, the argument that a long natural exposure implies a short hedge is a vastly oversimplified view of the various types of hedging in which commercial enterprises are engaged. Apart from failing to give adequate consideration to firms with a natural long exposure that simply do not hedge all or even a big part of their position, this jump from a long asset exposure to a demand for short hedging presupposes a very stylized form of hedging. The discussion in Chapter 13 should put that notion to rest quickly.

## Nature of Counterparties to Risk Transfer

Continuing in our critical assessment of the four main Keynesian assumptions, we now come to the assumption that if firms with natural long exposures hedge by going short futures or forwards, the *counterparties* to those trades must be long speculators. Yet, we have already discussed at length in Chapters 3 and 4 that counterparties in a risk transfer transaction need not necessarily be playing "hot potato" with risk in which one party simply pays the other a price to accept a risk that it prefers to avoid. As a counterexample, a short hedger might very easily be on the other side of a long hedger—for example, a farmer hedging the risk of price declines with a grain elevator hedging the risk of price increases.

Remember that a major benefit of futures markets is anonymity and low search costs, thanks to standardization and the clearinghouse system. If a grain elevator and farmer are already dealing with one another and already know they have opposite risk exposure appetites, they might just decide to use a forward contract to lock in the physical grain sale in the first place, thus obviating the need for either to hedge. Or the two firms could merge, thus relying on the benefits of organizational diversification to address the two separate risks. But if the two parties cannot easily identify one another's risk profiles and tolerances, they may enter the anonymous world of futures trading and very possibly find themselves opposite one another in the trade. One can easily imagine a market in which long hedgers deal with short hedgers and long speculators deal with short speculators, in which case the Keynesian risk premium becomes unjustified.

The argument that hedgers "as a group" are opposite speculators "as a group" also ignores the inherently transactional nature of speculation and hedging. Both Keynes and Hardy seemed to believe that speculation was done only by professional speculators. Yet, if we think more along the lines of Knight and his definition of the entrepreneur as a speculator, we realize that speculation is essentially undertaken one risk and one deal at a time.

Classifying hedgers and speculators as opposing groups also ignores the fact that even in the context of a single transaction, there can be both "speculative" and "hedge" components. Consider a firm that plans to sell 10,000 barrels of oil from a tank farm to a refinery in three months. If that firm hedges by going long forwards and futures on 7,500 barrels of oil, then the Keynes/Hicks perspective suggests that a speculator must be on the other side of the transaction. But what about the remaining 2,500 barrels on which the oil company is speculating? Would the oil company demand a speculative risk premium as an extra profit margin on its 2,500 unhedged barrels in the same fashion as the speculators opposite the firm in the 7,500-barrel formal hedge? Our inability to answer that question in the framework of Keynes and Hicks illustrates a fairly fundamental logical flaw with their theory.

## Speculation and Prices

Even if a speculator is counterparty to a hedger, we have seen in Part One some reasons why not all speculators will demand an explicit risk premium that translates into price pressure and normal backwardation. As long as the risk in question is idiosyncratic, the hedger may be dealing with a firm that simply has a larger portfolio with lower costs of diversification (e.g., an insurance company).

If we interpret the speculative risk premium as a positive expected profit on the transaction, the assumption of homogeneous expectations becomes very important to justify the Keynesian theory. If both parties agree on everything underlying their expected value calculations, then the only way for the speculator to earn a positive profit is at the expense of the hedger. But with asymmetric information, this is no longer true.[5]

To take a simple case, suppose the hedger has been led to the market out of concern over *uncertainty* rather than risk. In this case, a speculator usually is thought to assume the uncertainty for a price, thereby turning it into a priced risk in the process. But because we are dealing with uncertainty, who is to say the price of the transfer of uncertainty from the hedger to the speculator will be positive? It may simply be the case that the two firms utterly disagree about the future direction of prices. If the speculator is searching for a firm simply for the purpose of betting on an uncertain outcome, the speculator may have no difficulty entering into the position without demanding a Keynesian-like risk premium. Indeed, the hard part for the speculator may well be finding a counterparty with an opposite exposure and view, in which case it is not inconceivable that the speculator would have to pay the hedger to induce it to enter into the betting transaction.

## ALTERNATIVE CHARACTERIZATIONS OF THE SPECULATIVE RISK PREMIUM

Given the poor empirical performance of the Keynes/Hicks model, considerable effort has been expended in an attempt to develop a more empirically robust theory of the speculative risk premium. In this section, several of the major theories are very briefly summarized.

### Keynes Revisited: The Hedging Pressure Theory

The *hedging pressure theory* of the speculative risk premium accepts the notion that speculators are counterparties to hedgers and demand a risk premium. But this theory does not assume which side of the market hedgers will be on. Hedgers are not presumed a priori to have a long natural price exposure nor to hedge that exposure by going short all the time. Instead, the *net* position of hedgers as a group may be long *or* short, and the speculative risk premium arises in response to that net hedging demand (McKinnon, 1967; Rolfo, 1980; Newbury and Stiglitz, 1983; Anderson and Danthine, 1983).

The hedging pressure theory is an essentially empirical theory. Whether forward prices are upward or downward biased depends on the asset market and the underlying composition of hedgers at any given time. Accordingly, one market might exhibit normal backwardation while another one exhibits normal contango. And if the complexion of hedgers changes over time from net short to net long (or vice versa), a market would switch from normal backwardation to normal contango (or vice versa).

The Keynesian model is not so much disproven by the hedging pressure hypothesis as it is a special case of the modern formulation of the hedging pressure theory—specifically, a special case in which hedgers are net short forwards/futures. But in the event that hedgers are net long, upward pressure on the forward price leads to upward biased forward prices and a positive expected payoff to *short* speculators.

This extension of the original theory is appealing because it allows pricing bias to differ cross-sectionally across different markets and over time. But the theory does still rely on the strong assumption that hedgers as a group are trading with speculators as a group, and that speculators are willing to engage in such trading only for compensation arising from price bias.

The empirical evidence for the modified or more general hedging pressure theory is mixed. In isolation, studies have indeed shown that observed biases in forward and futures prices are related to the net positions of hedgers in the market (Chang, 1985). At the same time, several studies that have looked in futures markets for patterns of how trades were matched by the type of trader and how speculators made money are at odds with the modified hedging pressure theory.

In general, long hedgers often match with short hedgers, and speculators as a class tend to trade among themselves. Speculators as a class tend to lose money over time on average. A minority group of speculators that may be called "skilled speculators" do exhibit positive average profits over time, but these profits are offset by losses from "unskilled speculators." Importantly, skilled speculators tend to make their profits off of "unskilled speculators" and not hedgers. This is strong evidence against the assumptions underlying the theory of normal backwardation. Most speculators, moreover, tend to remain in the market for fairly short periods of time. Those that last tend to be the skilled speculators that make positive average profits (Rockwell, 1967; Ross, 1975; Hartzmark, 1991). The typical characteristics of a "skilled speculator" include large size, an active role in both cash and futures markets, and relatively significant capitalization. Nevertheless, in the end it appears that even skilled speculators rarely improve on the profits associated with a random trading strategy when transaction costs are taken into account (Hartzmark, 1991).

## Hicks Revisited: The Market Balance Theory

Another alternative interpretation of the speculative risk premium in forward and futures markets is best embodied by Hardy (1923): "The market price, whatever it is, represents the balance of judgment of the trade, both speculative and non-speculative, as to the figure at which demand and supply will, during the next year or year and a half, be approximately equal" (Hardy, 1923, p. 23). This alternative explanation is thus often called the *market balance theory*. Merton Miller also refers to Hardy's view of the risk premium more generally as "the Chicago view" (Miller, 1997).

The market balance theory essentially holds that if a speculative risk premium exists, it either is zero on average or cannot be distinguished from zero statistically. The implications of the market balance theory are shown diagrammatically in Figure 12.3. Regardless of whether the own rate of interest is positive or negative and whether the term structure of actual forward prices exhibits market backwardation or contango, the forward/futures price thus is an unbiased predictor of future spot prices.[6] Long and short hedgers balance out with one another and with speculators as a group. Short-run pricing biases can be expected to appear every so often, but in the long run the speculative risk premium *does not exist*.

Whereas Keynes's theory of normal backwardation can be viewed as a special case of the hedging pressure theory, Hicks's theory of normal backwardation is more a special case of the market balance theory (although it is very rarely acknowledged as such). In Hicks's framework, a group of hedgers that are long the underlying go short derivatives to hedge, and this puts downward

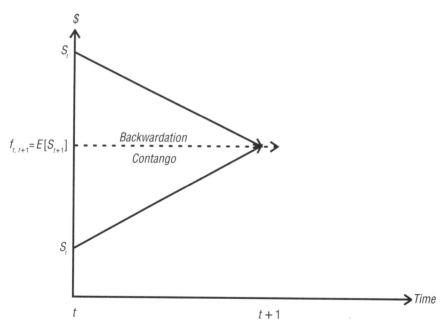

**FIGURE 12.3** The Market Balance Theory

pressure on forward prices. This, in turn, attracts speculators to the market with beliefs that the forward price is underpriced relative to the future expected spot price. This prevents the forward price from falling as much as it otherwise might, but some downward bias still persists. The market balance theory goes a step further and argues that this process continues to play itself out until the forward price is driven to near equality with the future spot price.

## SYSTEMATIC RISK REVISITED

We have assumed thus far in this chapter that the only source of pricing bias in forward-based derivatives will come from a speculative risk premium, if there is one. But we cannot simply ignore everything we learned in Chapter 7. In this section, we thus reconsider the risk premium for *systematic* risk and how that risk premium may be related to any speculative risk premium.

### Systematic Risk Premium

From the definition of a forward contract payoff and what we learned in Chapter 7, we can write the equilibrium forward purchase price in an at-market one-period forward as:

$$f_{t,t+1} = E_t[S_{t+1}] + R^f \text{cov}_t[m_{t+1}, S_{t+1}] \qquad (12.5)$$

The systematic risk of a forward purchase agreement thus is completely characterized by the covariance of the payoff on the asset with the stochastic discount factor. Because the forward price will be paid at time $t + 1$, $f_{t,t+1}$ and the other terms in equation (12.5) are all expressed in time $t + 1$ dollars. If we want the time $t$ dollar equivalent, equation (12.5) becomes just

$$PV_t[f_{t,t+1}] = \frac{E_t[S_{t+1}]}{R^f} + \text{cov}_t[m_{t+1}, S_{t+1}] \qquad (12.6)$$

Assuming no physical storage costs, liquidity premium, or convenience yield, we can use what we learned in Chapter 7 to rewrite equation (12.6) as:

$$S_t = PV_t[f_{t,t+1}] = \frac{E_t[S_{t+1}]}{R^f} + \text{cov}_t[m_{t+1}, S_{t+1}] \qquad (12.7)$$

In other words, as we saw in Chapter 8 in several guises, the spot purchase price is equal to the discounted present value of the forward purchase price, both of which can be expressed as the expected future spot price deflated at the riskless rate plus the systematic risk premium.

As the relation in equation (12.7) suggests, the systematic risk premium in a contract for the future delivery of an asset is essentially the same as the systematic risk premium on holding the asset itself—both are driven principally by the covariance of the asset price and the discount factor. Suppose, for example, that $cov_t[m_{t+1}, S_{t+1}]$ is negative, as is often the case for financial assets. As noted in Chapter 7, many financial assets pay off more highly in good states of the world and thus act as anti-insurance of sorts. The price of the asset today thus must be lower to compensate the long for tying up capital in an asset that pays off only when that payoff is relatively less valuable.

Looking back at equation (12.6), a negative covariance between the time $t + 1$ asset price and the stochastic discount factor also depresses the forward purchase price. Specifically, a negative covariance between the terminal asset price and discount factor gives rise to a systematic risk premium that causes a *downward bias* in the forward price—that is, $f_{t,t+1} < E_t[S_{t+1}]$. When the long in the forward stores the asset *synthetically*, a risk premium is still required to induce holding the asset. This risk premium comes in the form of a positive expected payoff that is just enough to compensate the long for the anti-insurance aspects of the forward contract.

Although we expect a negative covariance between purely financial assets like stocks and bonds with the intertemporal marginal rate of substitution, we have no such prior beliefs about the sign of the risk premium for real assets and derivatives on real assets. Some commodities, for example, are thought to be a good hedge against business cycle risk because they retain their value in recessions. In this case, we would expect the owners of such assets—whether through spot or forward purchases—to pay a higher price for the asset to reflect this insurance benefit (i.e., negative systematic risk premium). In the end, the sign of systematic risk premium is a completely empirical question.

## Empirical Evidence on Systematic Risk in Derivatives

Not surprisingly, empirical tests of various formulations of asset pricing models have yielded diverse results for estimates of systematic risk premiums in derivatives. Equally unsurprising is that the results differ by commodity or asset. Dusak (1973) estimated zero betas and thus deduced the absence of a systematic risk premium for wheat, corn, and soybeans. Bessembinder (1992) found similar results for wheat and corn but a strong negative systematic risk premium on soybeans. Breeden (1982) found little or no systematic risk evident in grain products, but a strong positive systematic risk premium on metals derivatives. Bessembinder's (1992) results for metals were comparable, although Bodie and Rosansky (1980) found negative risk premiums on metals and Fama and French (1988) found no risk premium on metals. Most studies agree that financial assets that tend to have positive betas also tend to show positive systematic risk premiums in the derivatives markets based on those assets.

Many other papers have been written that attempt to estimate the systematic risk premium for derivatives. About the only absolutely clear statement that can be made is that the results of these exercises all tend to depend strongly on the asset and time period. Further complicating matters is the use of the CAPM in many of these studies. Although the CAPM was the only way to go for systematic risk measurement when many of these early studies were undertaken, we know now that it is badly deficient as an asset pricing model and could account for spurious results in some of the studies mentioned here.

## Didn't We Argue That Only Systematic Risk Affects Asset Prices?

An add-on risk premium reflecting idiosyncratic risk makes little sense in the traditional world of asset pricing in which all agents are presumed to hold optimally well-diversified portfolios. But remember from Chapter 7 that incomplete markets wreak some havoc with this assumption that everyone is always perfectly diversified. In the specific case of derivatives and risk transfer, the reasons to suspect that incomplete markets might prevent full investor diversification and thus might explain a separate risk premium for idiosyncratic risk are twofold. First, if some firms cannot issue claims on their profits or if those claims are nonmarketable, investors cannot fully diversify away all the risks associated with their investments in those firms (Mayers, 1972). Second, nonparticipation in certain markets—usually arising from fixed start-up costs—can prevent investors in those firms from achieving optimal diversification of all idiosyncratic risks. If a firm believes it is at an informational disadvantage to derivatives market participants, for example, it may choose not to use derivatives, thereby leading to nonparticipation problems that affect asset prices (Merton, 1987).

Although nonmarketable claims and nonparticipation are probably the two most common motivators for market incompleteness that can justify the pricing of idiosyncratic risk in derivatives, these are not the only two reasons. Essentially any source of true market incompleteness that prevents all states of nature from being spanned by all securities and derivatives (see Chapters 1, 3, and 7) can potentially create enough market frictions that idiosyncratic risks will have an impact on equilibrium forward purchase prices (Bessembinder, 1992). The speculative risk premium thus is like an insurance premium paid by hedgers for the right to transfer some of the risks to which they are subject.

## An Integrated Approach to the Risk Premium

In an effort to identify the speculative risk premium, many of the empirical tests reviewed earlier (as well as many others *not* reviewed) looked at the question of pricing bias. In multiple studies, there is no bias to be found systematically, leading us to believe that forward and futures prices are in fact generally unbiased predictors of future spot prices. But if this is true, then we can also infer something useful about *systematic risk* in forwards and futures. Namely, the absence of an observed price bias in most forwards and futures not only debunks the mythology of a speculative risk premium, but also tells us *empirically* that most forwards and futures have payoffs that are uncorrelated with the stochastic discount factor.

There is, of course, another possibility. If we look at pricing bias alone, it is conceivable that the speculative risk premium exists but has the same magnitude *and opposite sign* as the systematic risk premium.

Several efforts have been made to distinguish between the systematic and speculative risk premiums in derivatives. In the model developed by Hirshleifer (1988, 1989, 1990), for example, the risk premium and pricing bias depend on the usual systematic risk premium plus a speculative risk premium based on idiosyncratic risk whose sign depends on the net hedging pressure in the market (i.e., the net position of hedgers).

Bessembinder (1992) empirically searches for a systematic risk premium and speculative risk premium across a huge range of derivatives based on both physical and financial underlyings. He finds that for most derivatives on physical assets, pricing bias is almost always nonexistent. Taken in isolation, both the systematic and the speculative risk premiums are small and statistically indistinguishable from zero.

Bessembinder (1992) also finds, however, that trading returns on nonfinancial derivatives are statistically different from zero when conditioned on the net position of hedgers in the market. This strongly suggests that the speculative risk premium and systematic risk premium may well exist and simply wash out with one another in the end. This provides some evidence, moreover, for the hedging pressure hypothesis and against the market balance model.

Numerous other studies of the risk premium have been undertaken over time, and most show that the bias present in most forward and futures markets is not meaningfully different from zero; futures and forward prices do tend to be good predictors of the expected future spot price. At the same time, a common theme emerges from almost all of these studies—namely, tests for pricing bias in derivatives tend to be highly sample dependent (both cross-sectionally and over time) and have fairly low power. Accordingly, the debate over the speculative risk premium continues.

## NOTES

1. See also Radner (1979) and Grossman (1981).
2. The term *bias* refers here to the statistical notion of bias, where we say that $x$ is an unbiased estimate of random variable $y$ if $x = E(y)$. If $x < E(y)$, we say that $x$ is a downward biased estimate of $y$. Conversely, $x > E(y)$ implies that $x$ is an upward biased estimate of $y$.
3. Recognize that these are *expected* as of time $t$; the actual time $t + 1$ spot price might be above or below the expected spot price, and the futures price would then be pulled to the *actual* spot price.
4. See, for example, Rockwell (1967).
5. Remember from earlier that we also technically need to assume some kind of market incompleteness here. Otherwise, the process of trading itself will force all expectations to reflect expectations relative to a martingale measure. If we have multiple stochastic discount factors, multiple probability measures against which expectations are evaluated can persist.
6. The leap from no speculative risk premium to unbiased forward and futures prices also assumes no systematic risk premium. Indeed, most proponents of the market balance approach do believe this, based mainly on empirical evidence. See, for example, Dusak (1973).

# CHAPTER 13

# Hedging Objectives

**D**etermining when and why a firm should hedge is no easy task. A value-maximizing corporation cannot be risk-averse in the same sense as an individual, so we must look for other explanations of why firms hedge. Specifically, we know that corporate hedging makes sense only if it increases the value of the firm by more than the costs of risk management at the margin. And we know that in order to increase the value of the firm, hedging must either reduce the firm's cost of capital or increase its expected cash flows. But how does a company make the leap from *why* it hedges to *how* it hedges?

We will begin this chapter with a very brief review of how and when corporations can benefit from hedging—an issue explored in much more detail in Culp (2001, 2002a). We then review the major types of commercial hedging that, despite their diversity, are all consistent with value maximization. The last two sections then review the process by which any given firm should attempt to draw an explicit connection between its underlying strategic rationale for hedging and its objectives in designing a hedge for a given exposure. Note that we do not propose to actually draw those specific connections here between why a firm hedges and how; that connection likely will be different for every company facing this decision. Instead, we focus on defining the process that a firm must undertake to translate its broad motives for hedging into a well-articulated set of objectives for any given hedge.

## RISK MANAGEMENT STRATEGY AND SOURCES OF GAINS FROM HEDGING

A firm's risk management strategy is its integrated approach to identifying, measuring, controlling, monitoring, reporting, and overseeing risk in a manner designed to ensure that the risks to which the firm *is* subject are the risks to which it *thinks it is* and *needs to be* subject as a part of its core business. The inner workings of the risk management process in place to implement a chosen risk management strategy at any given firm are discussed in Culp

(2001) and are well beyond the subject matter of this book. Nevertheless, as Culp and Miller (1999c) have forcefully argued, a firm cannot really know *how* to hedge if it has not first considered as a part of its risk management strategy *why* it should hedge.

When capital markets are perfect (i.e., no transaction costs, infinitely divisible securities, no taxes, no financial distress costs, etc.), all market participants have the same information, the investment decisions of a firm are made independently of its financial decisions, and all market participants can issue any securities on identical terms, the combined wealth of all security holders of the firm should not be affected by whether or not a firm hedges or retains any given risk. If the risk in question is systematic, the risk premium a firm's security holders will demand to retain the risk is equal in equilibrium to the risk premium the firm must pay to get rid of that risk. (See Chapters 7 and 12.) And if the risk is idiosyncratic, investors can diversify away the risk as easily as the firm can hedge it. So, under the aforementioned assumptions, firms' security holders should be indifferent to a firm's hedging decisions.

When one or more of the aforementioned assumptions are violated, however, hedging can raise the value of the firm either by lowering its cost of capital or by increasing its expected net cash flows (including decreasing its expected costs).

## Increasing Expected Net Cash Flows

Risk management as a process, and the use of risk transformation products, in particular, can be a means of increasing the firm's expected net cash flows either because it reduces the firm's expected or actual costs or because it actually increases the firm's revenues. This can occur for a number of possible reasons briefly summarized next.

### Reducing Expected Corporate Taxes

When a firm faces a *convex* corporate tax schedule, hedging can reduce expected tax liabilities and increase the firm's expected net cash flows. A convex tax schedule is one in which a firm's average tax rate rises as pretax income rises. This can occur because of progressivity in the corporate tax rate, the impact of the Alternative Minimum Tax, tax carryforwards and tax credits, and other tax shields that defer taxation.

The basic intuition here is straightforward. Suppose a firm has two possible pretax earnings levels, $X_1$ and $X_2$, that may occur with any probability $\rho$ and $(1 - \rho)$, respectively. Suppose further that the firm can lock in its earnings at level $X^*$ for a cost $C$, where $X^* = E(X) = \rho X_1 + (1 - \rho)X_2$. Hedged earnings thus are locked in at $X^* - C$.

Associated with each level of earnings is a tax liability $T(X_j)$ where $T$ is an increasing and convex function of $X$; that is, $T(X) \geq 0$ for all $X$, $\partial T/\partial X > 0$, and $\partial^2 T/\partial X^2 > 0$. If the firm locks in its earnings, its known tax liability is $T(X^*)$. Otherwise, the firm's expected tax liability is $E[T(X)] = \rho T(X_1) + (1 - \rho)T(X_2)$. By Jensen's inequality, we know that $T(\rho X_1 + (1 - \rho)X_2) < \rho T(X_1) + (1 - \rho)T(X_2)$ since $T(\cdot)$ is convex—that is, $T(X^*) < E[T(X)]$. Provided that $T(X^*) - E[T(X)] < C$, the tax savings from locking in earnings and avoiding the high tax rate on high earnings levels is less than the cost of hedging, and hedging thus can increase the firm's value.

## Reducing Expected Financial Distress Costs

Perhaps the most intuitive reason for firms to manage risk is to avoid the costs of financial distress or bankruptcy. Distress costs may begin to occur before a firm actually becomes legally insolvent, moreover, thus prompting firms to take actions designed to minimize these expected costs.

More formally, suppose the market value of a firm with a total outstanding debt of $FV$ has a value $V(A)$, where $A$ represents the market value of the firm's assets net of nondebt liabilities. The firm is economically insolvent when $A < FV$ but begins to encounter financial distress costs when $A \leq FV + k$ where $k > 0$. Distress costs are represented by the function $\phi(A)$, where $\phi(A) = 0$ for $A > FV + k$. When assets fall below $FV + k$, distress costs are presumed to become positive and begin rising at a rate that increases the further assets decline in value—that is, $\phi(A) > 0$ for all $A \leq FV + k$, $\partial \phi/\partial A < 0$, and $\partial^2 \phi/\partial A^2 > 0$. The value of the firm is then

$$V(A) = \begin{cases} A & \forall A > FV + k \\ A - \phi(A) & \forall A \leq FV + k \end{cases} = A - \phi(A)$$

Because $\phi$ is a convex function of $A$ and $V$ is a function of $-\phi$, $V$ must be a concave function of $A$ (Rockafellar, 1970). From there, the logic that hedging can increase the value of the firm is essentially similar to what we just reviewed in the tax case.[1]

Let a firm have two possible asset values, $A_1$ and $A_2$, that may occur with any probability $\rho$ and $(1 - \rho)$. Let $A_1 < FV + k$, and $A_2 > FV + k$. Suppose further that the firm can lock in its asset value at level $A^*$ for a cost $C$, where $A^* = E(A) = \rho A_1 + (1 - \rho)A_2$. To keep things simple, let us suppose the hedging cost $C$ is not so large that it drives the firm into distress if the firm hedges—that is, $A^* - C > FV + k$. If the firm hedges, its value is $V(A^* - C) = A^* - C$. If the company does not hedge, the value of the firm is then $E[V(A)]$. By Jensen's inequality, $E[V(A)] < V[E(A)]$ since $V$ is concave. As long as $V(A^*) - E[V(A)] > C$, hedging increases the value of the firm.

### Mitigating Underinvestment

If a positive net present value (NPV) project is rejected by the firm in the absence of a risk management program but accepted otherwise, then the benefit of risk management is fairly clear. One reason firms may decline positive NPV projects owes to "debt overhang" (Myers, 1977). If firm has too much debt, shareholders may opt to reject positive NPV projects because the benefits of a successful project will go mainly to pay off debt holders, whereas the risks of an unsuccessful project affect primarily equity holders. This is called "underinvestment" and can be mitigated if hedging is used to increase the firm's debt capacity and decrease its effective leverage.

Underinvestment may also occur if a firm's cash flows are depleted and the costs of issuing new securities to finance the new project are prohibitive (Froot, Scharfstein, and Stein, 1993, 1994). In this case, a firm may hedge its cash flows to try to ensure that enough internal funds are always available to exploit all positive NPV investment opportunities.

### Reducing Asset Substitution Monitoring Costs

If managers of the firm respond to shareholders more than creditors and if costly monitoring mechanisms like bond covenants are not used, managers may choose excessively risky projects to the benefit of equity and at the expense of debt. If the firm can selectively hedge the volatility of net cash flows on projects with positive NPVs but with high risks, managers may be discouraged from taking on excessively risky projects when they result in the expropriation of bondholders to the benefit of stockholders.

### Mitigating Excessive Managerial Risk Aversion

In general, when too much of a manager's wealth is tied up in his compensation package, his expected utility starts to depend on the value of the firm where he works. If the manager faces capital market imperfections or does not have equal access to the market, he may not be able to diversify away enough of these risks and thus may begin to behave more conservatively than security holders prefer. In an effort to keep the firm solvent and preserve his primary source of income, a manager might reject high-risk but high-NPV investment projects—again, underinvestment.

Selective hedging of catastrophic risks can help assuage managers' concerns in this regard and thus mitigate underinvestment.

### Exploiting Perceived Short-Run Profit Opportunities

The gains from hedging we have discussed thus far all trace to higher expected cash flows that arise from lower expected costs. A firm may also sometimes increase its expected cash flows through hedging programs designed to exploit perceived short-run deviations in firm-specific revenues or costs from their equilibrium values.

As discussed in Chapters 8 and 9, the convenience yield and liquidity premium on an asset—especially physical commodities—is often specific to individual firms. The own rate of interest for that firm may differ from the own rate in equilibrium that is reflected in the marginal forward contract. A firm may trade to exploit short-run deviations between the own interest rate it faces and the own rate reflected in derivatives.

Underlying this type of hedging is the important notion of an adjustment process in the market. This adjustment process admits the possibility of short-run financial decision making that is not really consistent with the standard neoclassical/Marshallian paradigm. We have already seen examples of the role played by this "market process" argument underlying Knight and at the root of much of the Austrian and neo-Austrian schools of economic thought.

In the traditional Marshallian and post-Marshall neoclassical paradigm, markets are viewed as being in a stationary state in which the relevant knowledge about demand and supply are known and market prices are static, or given, data to be taken and used by individuals and firms. In this world without change, we need not ask how this state of affairs came about. This knowledge simply falls into the category of irrelevant bygones.

Neoclassical economics does, of course, also deal with change. It does so by employing comparative statics. For example, we can conceive of a quasi-stationary state in which changes in the relevant knowledge in a market are few and far between, and the analysis of the full repercussions are dealt with by evaluating and comparing the stationary states before and after the changes in relevant knowledge occur. In the neoclassical world, prices act as signposts, guiding consumers to substitute goods for one another and producers to learn which lines of production to abandon or which to turn toward. In this neoclassical conception, the price system acts as a network of communication in which relevant knowledge is transmitted at once throughout markets that jump from one stationary state to the next.

In the neo-Austrian or disequilibrium-oriented context, by contrast, the market is viewed as a process that is in a constant state of flux. In consequence, there are no stationary or quasi-stationary states. Indeed, expectations about the current and future state of affairs are always changing because the state of relevant knowledge is always changing. And with those changing expectations, market prices are also changing. In consequence, the price system is functioning as a network for communicating relevant knowledge. It is also a discovery process that is in continuous motion, working toward creating a unity and coherence in the economic system. The speed of adjustment and the dissemination of knowledge in the price system depends on the scope and scale of the markets, however.

As it relates to our discussion here, the full force of market integration is realized when both spot and forward markets exist. Indeed, the function of forward or derivatives markets is to spread relevant knowledge about what market participants think will be. Forward markets connect and integrate those expectations about the future with the present in a consistent manner. Hicks (1939) argues that a principal economic function of forward and futures markets is to ensure the consistency of both prices and plans (*i.e.*, consumption and production) across heterogeneous and heterogeneously informed market participants. Lachmann (1978, pp. 67–68) elaborates:

> *It is precisely the economic function of forward markets to spread knowledge not about what is or has been, but about what people think will be. In this way, while the future will always remain uncertain, it is possible for the individual to acquire knowledge about other people's expectations and to adjust his own accordingly, expressing his own views about future prices by buying or selling forward, thus adding his own mite to the formation of market opinion as expressed in forward prices. In other words, forward markets tend to bring expectations into consistency with each other. . . . Price expectations involve intertemporal price relations, and intertemporal price relations cannot be made explicit, hence cannot be adequately expressed, without an intertemporal market.*

In a neo-Austrian world, the state of relevant knowledge and expectations are in a constant state of flux. And not surprisingly, spot and forward prices, as well as their difference (the basis), are constantly changing, too. Individuals' ever-changing expectations, therefore, keep the market process in motion. In consequence, disequilibrium is a hallmark of the neo-Austrian orientation. While the neo-Austrian market process is in a constant state of flux, it is working toward integrating and making consistent prices, both spot and forward prices.

This is all perfectly consistent with Knight's view of the world, which might be classified as somewhere between neoclassical and neo-Austrian. Knight seemed to believe in the idea of equilibrium, but what he called equilibrium looks a lot more like the neo-Austrian *disequilibrium* than the Marshallian *equilibrium*. Importantly, in Knight's view, spot and forward markets provide an integrated forum by which uncertainty is converted into risk, and this in turn makes the ideas behind a Marshallian equilibrium more palatable. If all uncertainty is turned into measurable risk through forward contracting, the zero-profit condition consistent with Marshall's long run becomes a plausible reality. Yet when a firm opts not to engage in forward transacting to manage intertemporal uncertainties, we have already seen in Part One that some kind of equilibrium exists in which firms can make positive economic profits. This may not be a long-run equilibrium in the sense that Marshall had in mind, but it does seem to conform to some of the other definitions of equilibrium described in Appendix 1.

We will return later in this chapter to examples of the type of hedging that this potential gain for the firm may motivate.

### Exploiting Perceived Informational Asymmetries in Spread Trades

For many of the same neo-Austrian reasons just discussed, firms may also engage in derivatives hedging in order to exploit perceived informational advantages. This is "speculation" by another name, so why discuss it as a potential gain *from hedging*? The answer lies in the other parts of this section—namely, that a firm wishing to engage in proprietary trading may still face problems like positive financial distress costs and potential underinvestment arising from debt overhang.

As a result, the firm may attempt to exploit is comparative informational advantage *through a hedge*, such as a spread trade. To take a simple example, suppose a large Swiss watchmaker is a major purchaser of platinum for its products. Thanks to its size and close relations with the dominant platinum producers, suppose the watchmaker expects a major negative supply shock to occur in six months. Following a period of falling inventories, this shock is expected to put a major strain on inventories and precipitate a major backwardation in the market. Because this information is nonpublic, the current six-month convenience yield will not yet reflect the anticipated inventory shortage, and the six-month cost-of-carry forward price thus will be too high relative to what it will be when the supply shock occurs.

The watchmaker could, of course, just go sell platinum six months forward. But this is a very risky transaction. If the information about the supply shock is wrong, mistimed, or offset by some other unanticipated shock, a price increase could cause serious losses for the watchmaker if it establishes a naked short forward position. The watchmaker producer thus might instead put on a calendar spread in which it is long a nearby delivery date and short the six-month forward. The spread risk is much lower than the price level exposure. In short, the firm established a speculative short and then hedged to avoid catastrophe by going long a contract that protects the total position but does not ruin the trading strategy.

Essential to this theory of gains from hedging is the notion that divergences in expectations can exist for long enough to be exploited. As we have discussed several times, trading itself is informative, so trading based on information asymmetries will invariably erase those asymmetries. This is the adjustment process to which Lachmann was referring in the quote referenced in the preceding section. But even if expectations are reconciled in the long run, the short-run adjustment period can be an important source of profits in a world where the same information is not shared by all.

Keynes (1936) viewed organized markets with some suspicion. He believed that divergent expectations would degenerate into chaos and result in prices that serve no role in resource allocation or risk transfer. Lachmann (1978) also seemed to feel that divergent expectations would lead to inconsistencies in plans unless rectified relatively quickly. But interpreted through Knight's lens, a stable system can comfortably coexist with heterogeneous expectations. This system may well involve inconsistencies *in short-run expectations*, but it is precisely this inconsistency that makes long-term profits sustainable for some firms in Knight's equilibrium world. These returns to entrepreneurship are, in a financial context, precisely the sorts of informationally motivated short-run trading decisions to which we are pointing in this section.

## Decreasing the Firm's Cost of Capital

Hedging can also increase firm value by decreasing the firm's cost of capital. In some cases, risk transfer is itself a source of contingent capital that may be obtained more cheaply than other more traditional sources of capital. In other cases, hedging can reduce the cost of capital by addressing some friction in the market.

### Reducing the Information Costs of Raising Capital

Hedging can lower a firm's cost of capital if the hedge reduces cash flow volatility by a sufficient amount to eliminate the need for the firm to issue new public securities to finance positive NPV investment projects. Similarly, hedging can reduce the amount of equity "risk capital" that a firm must hold to support a business activity and absorb potential losses on that business. In either case, the firm's cost of capital may fall to the extent the company can avoid the adverse selection costs of new public securities issues (Culp, 2002a,c).

Specifically, when managers are better informed than investors about the quality of the firm's investments, adverse selection costs can increase a firm's cost of capital, sometimes dramatically. Investors are likely to assume that firms will issue securities only when they are overpriced, and this expectation depresses the price investors are willing to pay for the securities. This more or less predictable chain of events in turn has the potential to create a self-fulfilling prophecy wherein firms indeed *do* prefer to issue new securities only when they are overpriced. The result is a pecking order in which companies prefer to use internal funds rather than issuing external securities—and, when outside capital is necessary, to issue less risky securities like debt rather than riskier equity instruments (Myers, 1984; Myers and Majluf, 1984).

The nature of the information asymmetry strongly influences the size of the discount attributable to adverse selection. Any source of external finance (except riskless debt) will change in value when more accurate information is revealed about the quality of the firm's investments. The more a security changes in value for a given information release (i.e., the riskier the security), the larger is the adverse selection discount. Similarly, firms with a significant proportion of intangible investments or "real options" will be harder for investors to evaluate and will hence suffer larger discounts arising from larger informational asymmetries. Such firms thus may benefit relatively more from hedging that protects capital or cash flows and abrogates the need for additional public securities offers.

### Synthetic Diversification

At a closed corporation whose owners cannot fully diversify their idiosyncratic risks, shareholders may be *incapable* of holding diversified portfolios because so much of their wealth is tied up in their own firm. In this case, hedging can reduce the cost of capital by lessening the impact of idiosyncratic risks on the firm's manager/owners.

## TYPES OF COMMERCIAL HEDGING

When we discussed in Chapter 12 the deficiencies underlying the assumption by Lord Keynes and Sir John Hicks that most hedgers are naturally long the asset and short futures or forwards, we emphasized that their view of hedging was far too simplistic. From our discussion in the previous section, we have further reasons to suspect that the types of hedging we observe are as diverse as the sources of gains to firms engaging in risk transfer that we just reviewed.

In this section, we follow Working (1953a,b, 1962) in an effort to classify the major types of hedging. This classification is based mainly on the motives of hedgers and thus helps us take a further step toward connecting the reasons a firm hedges with the mechanics of its hedging strategies.

### Pure Risk Avoidance Hedging

Pure risk avoidance hedging is undertaken by firms specifically seeking to eliminate the impact of a risk on some aspect of the firm's financials. This is the classic rationale for risk transfer and the use of derivatives—to shift the impact of one or more risks from the shareholders of the firm originally bearing the risk to the shareholders of some other firm.

Pure risk avoidance hedging is often thought to be hedging primarily motivated by a firm's efforts to reduce expected costs of financial distress. But in fact this type of hedging can be based on a much larger universe of potential gains in value for the firm. Shifting certain risks to other firms to avoid the financial impact of those risks also may help firms mitigate managerial risk aversion and asset substitution problems, as well as facilitating a reduction in effective leverage that leads to increased debt capacity and less underinvestment. Judiciously engaging in risk transfer can also reduce the equity capital and/or cash the firm needs to obtain from external securities markets to finance its operations or new investments, thus possibly leading to a lower cost of capital.

Pure risk avoidance hedging can be directed at essentially any risk—market and credit risk through the use of derivatives, operational and liquidity risk through the use of insurance and alternative risk transfer (ART) forms, and the like. Even in the narrow context of market risk management, pure risk avoidance hedging may be undertaken to manage the impact of risks on revenues, costs, asset or liability values, and so forth.

Pure risk avoidance hedging was surely the type on which Keynes and Hicks were focused when they assumed a speculative risk premium arose from longs in the market that all demanded short hedge positions. But even this is not strictly correct. A simple example will show how even pure risk avoidance hedging leads to behavior that is much richer than Keynes and Hicks believed.

Consider a typical corn farmer whose economic income in a single period is given by[2]

$$y_t = S_t q \theta_t$$

where $S_t$ is the random spot price of corn per bushel and the price at which we assume the farmer sells his crop. The constant $q$ denotes the average number of bushels brought to market and sold in any period, and $\theta_t$ represents a random weather-related shock to supply any period. Total quantity produced thus is $q\theta_t$. Assume $\theta_t$ is distributed symmetrically with an expected value of unity for all time periods $t$.

Now suppose the farmer hedges $z$ bushels of his income in the forward market at time $t - 1$. The farmer's realized income is then[3]

$$y_t = S_t q \theta_t + z(S_t - f_{t-1,t})$$

Let us suppose further that the risk management objective of the farmer is to reduce the variability of his income. (We will return to alternative hedging objectives later.)

First suppose that the correlation between $\theta_t$ and $S_t$ is positive. If output is high, then price is also high. Figure 13.1 illustrates the relation between income and the random shock to output in this case. If $\theta_t$ increases substantially, then income also increases substantially. Also shown on Figure 13.1 is the impact of hedging by going short $z$ bushels of corn. This has the effect of making income less sensitive to weather shocks by raising income in low $\theta_t$ states and raising income in high $\theta_t$ states.

Now suppose that the output shock is *negatively* correlated with price, but that price variability is lower than output variability. Income variability is thus lower than output variability. *A* given price decline, for example, is associated with a net *increase* in income because output rises by more than price falls. If the farmer sells forward as before, the effect thus will be to increase income variability, as shown in Figure 13.2. To reduce total income variability, the farmer would need to go *long* a forward or futures contract. When quantity falls, for example, price rises, but not by enough to offset the supply shock. So, income falls. But the long hedge pays off when price

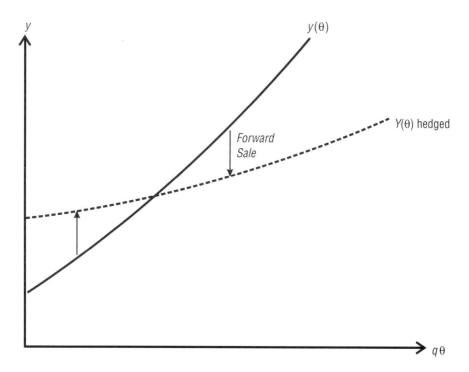

**FIGURE 13.1** Hedging with Positively Correlated Price and Supply Shocks

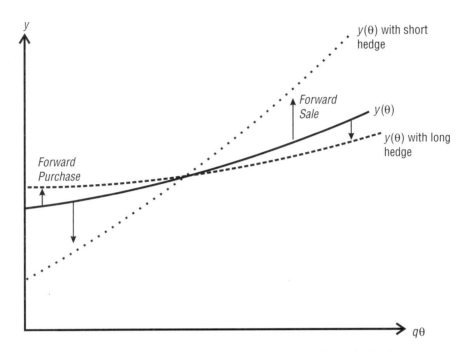

**FIGURE 13.2**   Hedging with Negatively Correlated Price and Supply Shocks

rises, thus mitigating the total income loss associated with the output contraction.

Now suppose that price and output are strongly negatively correlated—so much so that income now decreases when output increases. As Figure 13.3 illustrates, income variability can be reduced in this case through forward *sales*, as in Figure 13.1 when price and output were positively correlated. In other words, the short sale pays off when prices are low. When prices are low, output is high and income is lower. So, the forward generates additional income when income is declining as a result of rising output.

## Operational Hedging

Operational hedging is primarily undertaken by merchandisers or intermediaries in a physical supply chain and thus is associated mainly with physical commodities. The primary objective of operational hedging is *not* to change the firm's exposure to price risk, but rather to optimize the cost structure of a processing business. Indeed, operational hedges are often so short-lived that

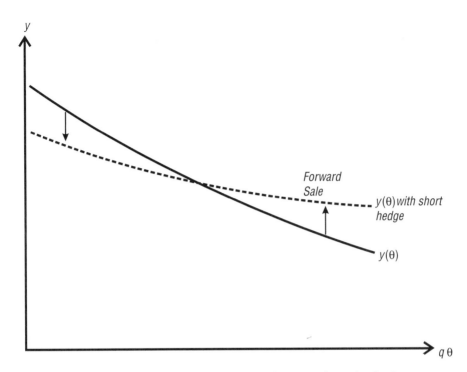

**FIGURE 13.3**  Hedging with Negatively Correlated Price and Supply Shocks

they have almost no price impact on the hedger whatsoever. In the context of the previous section, firms expecting a gain from operational hedging are most likely to realize it through short-run cost reductions, synthetic diversification, and perhaps reducing underinvestment or mitigating managerial risk aversion in a highly project-specific context.

The classic example of operational hedging is the flour-milling industry. Agricultural economist Holbrook Working studied flour milling in the mid twentieth century and found that it readily exemplifies hedging done for purely operational purposes. The key insight Working found after studying a number of mills was that millers found it easier to base their wheat purchase and flour sale decisions in terms of spreads over wheat prices rather than in absolute levels. For input purchasing, millers thus looked at the spread of particular lots of wheat prices relative to the prices of other lots of wheat (i.e., a quality spread). Similarly, output sales decisions were based on an analysis of the spread of the price of the flour sold by millers over current wheat prices (i.e., a calendar and quality spread) than to future actual wheat purchasing costs. Naturally, because millers were basing decisions on quality and calendar spreads in the futures markets, hedging those decisions over very short periods of time was also undertaken with futures.

Relying on futures markets for both short-term hedging and price signaling made sense to many flour millers because of the extremely low volatility of the quality and calendar bases they were using. On an intraday and day-to-day basis—the frequency with which flour millers were establishing and lifting these operational hedges—the correlation between the spot and futures prices was extremely high. For longer periods of time when the calendar basis risk became a real consideration, flour millers opted not to hedge. Similarly, Working (1962) noticed that millers west of the Rocky Mountains did not hedge with futures, presumably because the distance created a significant locational basis risk.

## Carrying-Charge Hedging

Carrying-charge hedging may be undertaken by firms whose operations involve both the use of derivatives and an underlying physical market position (Working, 1953a,b, 1962). Essentially a type of spread trading, carrying-charge hedging is intended to optimize the economic profits associated with a supply chain exposed to various basis risks. Carrying-charge hedging is principally undertaken by firms that wish to exploit a perceived short-run cost or profit advantage or an information asymmetry but desire to remained hedged against swings in absolute price levels while doing so. Examples of carrying-charge hedgers have included Metallgesellschaft and MG Refining and Marketing (see Culp and Miller, 1995b,c); Cargill; and, in its early days, Enron (see Culp and Hanke, 2003).

To take a simple example, suppose information is symmetric across market participants, but that not all firms face the same own rates of interest on all assets—especially physical commodities in which the cost of physical storage and the convenience yield can differ across firms. Firms may sometimes engage in spread hedging in order to reduce their total operating costs by better supply chain management.

Suppose we assume that the calendar basis for, say, natural gas is nonstochastic but differs across firms. Let us begin in a situation where $b^*$ is the calendar basis or cost of carry reflected in the market forward price of natural gas, and that $b^*$ is equal to the short-run marginal costs of all market participants at their production optima.

Now consider a new entrant into the natural gas market, and suppose that new entrant has a significant presence in the natural gas pipeline industry and strong economies of scale that leads to cost of distributing and transporting gas of $b^e < b^*$. In this case, the new entrant can *physically* move natural gas across time and space at a lower cost than gas can be moved synthetically using derivatives.

By going short or selling gas for future delivery using forwards or futures, the new entrant is selling gas at an implied net cost of carry of $b^*$. But its *own* net cost of carry—a cost that is quite relevant in the entrant's ability to move the gas across time and space in order to honor its own future sale obligation created by the forward contract—is less. Accordingly, in *disequilibrium*—or, more properly, on the way to a long-run equilibrium—the entrant can make a profit equal to the difference between its own net cost of storage and the cost reflected in the market.

The reason that this profit is a short-run profit inconsistent with a long-run equilibrium is that the entrant's sale of the forward contract drives the $b^*$ reflected in forward prices closer to be. If the new entrant is the lowest-cost producer and other firms can replicate its production techniques (i.e., the entrant owns no unique resources), ultimately $b^*$ will become $b^e$, which will also eventually approach the long-run minimum average cost of carry. The entrant's capacity to earn supranormal profits will vanish in this new equilibrium; in fact, zero economic profits earned by every producer is basically the very meaning of a long-run equilibrium, as we saw in Chapter 2.

For large commercial enterprises, however, the short run is an entirely relevant production period. Firms regularly engage in spread trading of the type just described as a hedge of their commercial operations. Perhaps a better way to describe this carrying-charge hedging is simply as marginal cost optimization. When synthetic storage is cheaper than physical storage in the short run, hedging with derivatives spreads can help producers exploit that cost reduction.

When we allow for the possibility that the supply chain participant may perceive itself as better informed than other market participants, carrying-charge hedging becomes even more comprehensive in what it covers. Working explains:

> *Whereas the traditional concept [of hedging] implies that hedging is merely a collateral operation that . . . would influence the stockholding only through making it a less risky business, the main effect of carrying-charge hedging is to transform the operation from one that seeks profit by anticipating changes in price level to one that seeks profit from anticipating changes in price relations. (Working, 1962, p. 438)*

Carrying-charge hedging, in other words, may be undertaken by value-maximizing corporations to exploit their superior information about price *relations* (i.e., the basis) while remaining market neutral with respect to spot prices.

Pure risk-avoidance hedging typically assumes that firms enter into forward contracting *and then* decide how to manage the risk of the position. Working's contribution was to recognize that the cash transaction and the hedge were two parts of a joint decision-making process. When information is asymmetric, he explains,

> *Hedging is not necessarily done for the sake of reducing risks. The role of risk-avoidance in most commercial hedging has been greatly overempha-sized in most economic discussions. Most hedging is done largely, and may be done wholly, because the information on which the merchant or processor acts leads logically to hedging. . . . To put it briefly, we may say that hedging in commodity futures involves the* purchase or sale of fu-tures in conjunction with another commitment, usually in the expectation of a favorable change in the relation between spot and futures prices. *(Working, 1953a, p. 326, emphasis in original)*

Absent superior information, value-maximizing firms may not only avoid the hedging, but may well shun the underlying activity itself. As Working notes:

> *Whereas the traditional hedging concept represents the hedger as think-ing in terms of possible loss from his stockholding being offset by a gain on the futures contracts held as a hedge, the carrying-charge hedger thinks rather in terms of a change in "basis"—that is, change in the spot-future price relation. And the decision he makes is not primarily whether to hedge or not, but whether to store or not. (Working, 1962, p. 438)*

That carrying-charge hedging may be undertaken by value-maximizing firms principally if not wholly to exploit a perceived informational advantage does *not* mean that carrying-charge hedging is speculation. Working also ar-gues that risks are, in fact, reduced by carrying-charge hedging, even though its primary motivation need not be risk reduction:

> *Hedging we found not to be primarily a sort of insurance, nor usually un-dertaken in the expectation that spot and futures prices would rise or fall equally. It is a form of arbitrage, undertaken most commonly in expecta-tion of a favorable change in the relation between spot and futures prices. The fact that risks are less with hedging than without is often a secondary consideration. (Working, 1953a, p. 342)*

In the previous section, we saw how firms might hedge to optimize their supply chain operations using spread trades even when information is sym-metric. Now suppose that the net cost of storage is a random variable about which some firms are better informed than others (e.g., the impact of supply or demand shocks on particular locational prices, the impact of pipeline congestion on the transportation basis, and the like). Now we are in a Knightian situation in which the zero-profit Marshallian long-run equilibrium no longer makes sense. Long-run equilibrium in Knight's world now may very well involve *positive* profits arising from the distinction between risk and uncertainty, and these positive profits are pursued through carrying-charge hedging.

In this case, firms like the entrant may engage in calendar-basis or spread trading in an effort to exploit their perceived comparative informational advantage. If a firm owns physical pipelines, for example, it may have a superior capability for forecasting congestion or regional supply and demand shocks. This creates a situation quite similar to a market that is out of or on the way to a Marshallian long-run equilibrium; that is, the net cost of carry that the *firm* observes may be *different from* the net cost of carry market participants expect, given the different information on which the two numbers are based. Just as in the disequilibrium case, firms may engage in basis trading to exploit these differences.

In a traditional rational expectations equilibrium, this type of behavior is akin to inframarginal firms attempting to exploit their storage cost advantage relative to the marginal price of storage reflected in forwards. In the traditional Marshallian model, this cannot go on for very long, because the trading actions of the lower-cost firm eventually lead them to *become* the marginal entrant, thus driving $b^*$ to $b^e$ for that firm. The same is true when trading *itself* is informative and transforms unobserved uncertainty into observed risk. Every time a well-informed trader attempts to exploit its superior information through a transaction, it reveals that superior information to the market. So, the paradox for the firm with better information is that the firm must either *not trade* based on that information in order to preserve its informational advantage or *give away* its informational advantage while simultaneously trying to exploit it in the short run through trading.

Culp and Miller (1995b,c) argue, however, that this sort of classic equilibrium assumes that the trading activities of the better-informed firm are, indeed, informative. But what if other market participants cannot *see* all the firm's trades? And what if the trades are occurring in highly opaque, bilateral markets rather than on an exchange? In this case, better-informed firms *can* profit from their superior information without necessarily imparting all of their valuable information into the new marginal price.

Trading to exploit disequilibrium, market imperfections, or Knightian uncertainty is hardly riskless. On the contrary, it can be *quite* risky (sic.). This helps explain why many firms engaged in trading designed to profit from uncertainty do so with *relative* or *spread* positions (see Chapter 11) rather than taking outright positions in one of the two explicit markets. Suppose, for example, that a firm perceives the true net cost of storage of gas to be $b^*$ (which is equal to the firm's own net cost of carry) but that the current net cost of carry reflected in listed gas futures prices is $b' > b^*$. It is a good bet that $b'$ will fall toward $b^*$. As such, an outright short position in forward contracts would make sense. But this is *extremely risky*. Even if the underlying source of randomness is uncertainty, as explained in Chapter 2, some firms may very well wish to manage this uncertainty as if it were a risk *if the costs are catastrophic to the firm*.

A position that exploits the same information asymmetry *without* the high degree of risk is to go short futures and *simultaneously* buy and hold gas. In this manner, the firm is protected from wild short-term price swings, and instead is expressing a view solely on the *relative* prices of storage as reflected in the futures market and storage by the firm itself.

## Selective Hedging

Working (1962, p. 440) describes selective hedging as a type of inventory risk management in which the amount of inventory hedged is determined by a firm "according to price expectations." In a world of symmetric information, selective hedging is equivalent to mixing pure risk avoidance hedging with a speculative component. But when information is asymmetric, selective hedging can be meaningfully distinct from speculation *for handlers of the asset*. Firms with a large position in an asset thus take a long or short position by *not* hedging; that is, they have a substantial natural exposure to the underlying source of randomness.

Selective hedging applies principally to *uncertainty* and to firms that have determined they would generally prefer to retain their natural exposure to uncertainty in order to benefit from it. In some cases, however, such firms may be induced to selectively hedge some or even all of their natural position purely to avoid anticipated losses—say, to increase debt capacity or avoid the costs of a financial catastrophe. Although the distinction is subtle, Working characterizes the purpose of selective hedging as "not *risk* avoidance, in the strict sense, but avoidance of *loss*." (Working, 1962, p. 440, emphasis added) To repeat an example from Chapter 2, a power company might perceive itself as in the business of bearing power price risk. At the same time, the company may not wish to incur the losses of being completely uncovered during a record-hot summer and thus may selectively hedge.

There is an inherent paradox to selective hedging, of course. As discussed in Chapters 2 through 4, firms transform uncertainty into risk when they hedge—whether they want to or not. A natural long that establishes a temporary short position using derivatives is revealing its own price expectations through the trading process and thus is giving away its information advantage in the process. The firm may, of course, try to keep its position anonymous by using futures, but the price impact of the hedge will still be widely known after the hedging transactions are put into place.

## Anticipatory Hedging

Another type of commercial hedging that presumes some degree of informational asymmetry and inconsistency in expectations is anticipatory hedging. Anticipatory hedging and selective hedging are close cousins. As we just saw, the latter might involve a firm with a natural long exposure going short futures and forwards if it anticipates a significant short-term price decline. Anticipatory hedging is also driven by price expectations, but it differs from selective hedging inasmuch as there is no specific asset or liability.

Anticipatory hedging is very common among firms with time lags in their production processes. Consider first a processor or manufacturer with raw material requirements. If the merchandiser expects a price increase, the merchandiser can go long a forward or futures contract to lock in the raw materials price today. By going long the derivative, the merchandiser is synthetically storing, or, in effect, buying the raw materials today for future delivery. Note that heterogeneous expectations are very important here: If everyone agreed that raw materials prices were going to rise, the forward price would reflect those expectations and not provide a potential source of savings to the merchandiser. Now consider the alternative situation of a producer that is selling is goods at future spot prices but on an indeterminate production schedule. That firm could hedge in order to lock in the value of its future sales.

Anticipatory hedging also often applies to financial hedging. A corporation with definite plans to issue fixed-rate debt three months hence, for example, may wish to protect itself against rising interest rates over the next three months by using derivatives to lock in today's interest rate.

## DEFINING A HEDGING OBJECTIVE

We began the chapter by discussing how companies could realize gains by hedging, and we then turned to review the very general types of hedging that are consistent with those gains. We now want to try to see how a firm operationalizes these lofty philosophical and economic concepts—how a company makes the real-world jump from a corporate risk management strategy into the tactics of day-to-day and exposure-by-exposure hedging decisions.

As we argued at the beginning, we cannot comment on the "right way" for a firm to connect its risk management strategy to individual hedges because this "right way" will depend on the nature of the firm's risk management process and the type of hedger the firm is. What we *can* do, however, is at least consider issues that a firm must resolve in order to make an explicit connection between *why* it is hedging and *how* it should do so.

The first such practical hedging issue with which a firm must struggle is to *define the financial focus of a hedge.* This is some metric that a firm can use to link transactional hedging decisions back to the broad financial condition of the firm. Not all hedging decisions will necessarily involve the same financial focus, but all hedging decisions must be predicated on *some* focus variable. Otherwise, there is no way for the firm to know how it should construct a particular hedge.

A second important issue involves the *definition of a specific hedging mandate* for a given hedging strategy. The financial focus of the hedge helps managers answer that question, but that is not enough. Managers must also decide what constitutes a successful risk transfer in the context of the relevant financial focus and the exact exposure to be hedged. As we saw in Chapter 4, risk transfer is not simply a question of one firm handing its risks to another. Rather, risk transfer is achieved when a firm constructs a hedge transaction so that its interaction with the risk exposure of concern results in a *net reduction* to that risk. A clearly articulated hedging mandate will help managers know just how to define when risk has been transferred and whether the amount transferred is enough.[4]

## The Financial Focus of a Hedge

Firms must associate a "financial focus" with every risk transfer transaction that serves to bridge the gap between why the firm decided to hedge and how the firm's managers should think about implementing that hedge. Although the firm as a whole may tend to prefer one financial focus variable over others, this is ultimately an issue to be decided for each hedging decision— whether involving a single risk exposure and hedge transaction or a portfolio of exposures.

In general, we can distinguish among the financial focus variables available to firms along four dimensions: value or capital, cash flows, economic profits, and accounting earnings.

### Value or Capital

"Value hedging" is a hedging strategy whose primary objective is the preservation of the net present value of a portfolio of assets and/or liabilities. To some firms, preserving the value of a stock of assets in isolation is the central hedging objective. Portfolio managers frequently adopt an asset protection perspective in their hedging activities, for example. Similarly, some firms may choose to concentrate their hedging activities on liability management (i.e., achieving the lowest-cost funding profile for a given set of liabilities). Still other firms consider the *net* asset/liability position (i.e., the present value of assets less the present value of liabilities) as the primary focus of their hedging activities.

Whether a firm is concentrating on managing the risks of its assets, liabilities, or the net of the two often depends on the distinction between risk and uncertainty explored in Chapter 2. Consider, for example, an insurance company whose primary business is the provision of insurance contracts. From an operational standpoint, the insurance company collects premiums for the policy lines it underwrites and then invests those premiums in assets to fund future claims arising from those policy lines. If the insurance company perceives itself as no better informed about the risks it is insuring than the purchasers of its insurance products, the firm is likely to adopt a net asset/liability management hedging perspective. But if the insurance company believes that incurring liabilities is akin to Knightian uncertainty, the company may choose to hedge only its assets—that is, only the part of its portfolio exposed to *risk* about which the firm has no comparative informational advantage.

To take another example, the Federal National Mortgage Association (Fannie Mae) issues debt to finance the acquisition of mortgage loan assets and mortgage-backed securities. The selection of assets to be held in the Fannie Mae portfolio is undertaken by portfolio and credit experts and is considered the core business function of Fannie Mae. As a result, all of Fannie Mae's hedging decisions are geared toward the liabilities incurred to finance its mortgage and mortgage-backed security acquisitions. Specifically, the risk management objective at Fannie Mae is to take whatever embedded optionality is in its asset portfolio as a given, and then to use derivatives to try to match the optionality of its liabilities as closely as possible to the optionality of its assets (Culp, 2003a).

A firm with a value orientation toward hedging may focus on value at a specific point in time (e.g., the date that a debt issue must be repaid) or may choose to consider changes in the market value of the firm over a given interval of time. In either case, the presumed objective of the risk management process is to take actions that impact the firm's market value.

Closely related to a value focus in a hedging program is some firms' focus on *capital preservation*, or the protection of equity capital and net worth. Whereas a value orientation can be applied narrowly to a specific portfolio of assets and/or liabilities, a capital preservation hedging objective tends to be an enterprise-wide hedging objective.

### Cash Flows

Cash flow–based hedging is distinct from value-based hedging mainly in the sense of timing. A value risk manager is concerned about the value of the firm or a portfolio, either at a specific point in time (e.g., when debt must be retired) or over regular intervals (e.g., monthly changes in value). A cash flow risk manager, by contrast, is concerned with cash flows *whenever* they might occur. Minimizing the volatility of changes in firm *value* does not necessarily imply the same hedging strategy as minimizing the volatility of *cash flows*.

Apart from different hedge ratios, the basic logic underlying the risk management strategy can differ between value and cash flow risk managers. Firms focused on preserving net asset values or their capital are generally hedging to avoid incurring costs of financial distress associated with very large losses. Hedging cash flows can be intended to help firms avoid financial distress, as well. But perhaps more common is for firms to manage their cash flow risks instead to reduce their reliance on what they may perceive as expensive external sources of funds to finance new investments. Especially when a firm's investments are intangible (e.g., research and development for a new drug), it can be less expensive for a firm to finance the R&D out of retained cash balances than by having to persuade new security holders about the viability of the project.

### Economic Profits

For many commercial hedgers, reducing input purchasing costs and/or putting a floor on output sale prices is a major motivation for hedging. We can think of this as hedging economic profits or the net profit margin.

Economic profits as a risk management focus variable lie somewhere between value and cash flow hedging. The value of a firm should equal its discounted net profits over time. Similarly, the net cash flows of a firm often closely track per-period profits. But not always. Consider a lumber company, for example, that owns timberlands and generates most of its profits from selling cut lumber in the market. Most of the firm's expenses will have been fixed costs incurred to maintain the forest and timberland and will have occurred well in advance of the first dollar of sales revenues obtained from lumber market sales. Hedging economic profits in this case probably means mainly hedging the lumber sales price against price declines. That may closely track cash *revenues*, but it ignores the sunk cash costs. And it also ignores the forest as a capital asset whose value must be preserved. Nevertheless, economic profits could well be the variable with which the firm is most concerned.

### Accounting Earnings

The accounting treatment afforded to different hedging strategies is relevant to a very large number of derivatives users. If a firm successfully uses derivatives to reduce its risks but cannot show that in its financial statements, the hedging program may be of limited use. In other words, many firms have hedging objectives that are defined in terms of how their hedging strategies impact certain accounting aggregates, such as earnings.

Note that some firms care more about this than others. To some companies, a hedge whose effectiveness is not clear to external investors may be worse than worthless. But to other companies like family-owned or closely held businesses, hedge accounting may be far less important than the economic impact of a hedge on value, capital, profits, or per-period cash flows.

## The Hedging Mandate

Defining the variable on which a derivatives hedging strategy will focus is an important link that connects a firm's broad risk management strategy with individual or portfolio hedging decisions. But this is not enough in isolation to tell managers how a given hedge should be constructed. In addition, a firm must define what it is about the focus variable that it is seeking to alter through its derivatives activity—that is, what specific risk it is trying to transfer away and how the hedge is intended to accomplish that.

### Hedging to Meet a Specific Threshold or Target

Depending on the financial focus variable that a firm chooses, the best way to accomplish a hedging objective may simply be to specify thresholds, targets, or specific hurdles for the hedging program. These may be numerical or relative.

Consider, for example, a refinery that purchases crude oil and sells refined oil products. As noted in Chapter 11, the crack spread will be the primary determinant of refining profits, and refining tends to become uneconomic when the crack spread falls below $3 per barrel (in crude-equivalent terms). A reasonable hedging objective for the refinery might be to implement a hedging strategy that locks in a minimum crack spread of $3 per barrel In this case, the financial focus variable is economic profits—the crack spread—and the guiding principle for the hedge in terms of risk measurement is simply that economic profits should not fall below $3 per barrel.

Alternatively, consider a mutual fund manager whose compensation and investor retention are based on the performance of an asset portfolio relative to a Russell 2000 benchmark calculated on a quarterly basis. In this case, the manager likely will have a value focus and will concentrate her hedging efforts on reducing the probability of underperforming the Russell 2000 in any given quarter. This would be an example of a relative threshold.

Or consider a defined-benefit pension plan sponsor whose pension liabilities are expected to grow at the nominal rate of 6 percent per year. A 6 percent minimum threshold nominal return on assets is a likely hedging objective function.

### Hedging to Match Sensitivities of Exposures

Rather than specify a formal hedging objective function of the form "maximize/minimize subject to constraints," some firms prefer instead to adopt operational guidelines to achieving their hedging ends. Of these the most popular and useful is probably the sensitivity analysis approach in which the sensitivity of a risk exposure to one or more variables of interest is matched as closely as possible with sensitivity of a corresponding hedge. Sensitivities may be defined in terms of any financial focus variable, which adds greatly to the appeal of this particular style of hedging.

Various forms of sensitivity-based hedging models are discussed in Chapter 14.

### Hedging to Reduce Volatility or Variance

Modern finance has for many years used variance as a statistical measure of risk. Defined broadly as the dispersion of some random variable around its expected value, variance is highly tractable and easily interpreted, and can usually be computed without a huge amount of effort. Accordingly, very popular hedging objectives include minimizing the variance of changes in the net value of an asset/liability position, minimizing the variance of net cash flows per period, minimizing the variance of income or economic profits, and the like.

Variance does have quite a few drawbacks associated with its use as a hedging objective function. Probably the most important is that the modern theory of corporate finance does not anywhere provide a clear link between the rationale for corporate risk management and the implementation of a variance-based hedging solution. (Culp and Miller, 1999c). In addition, variance itself has limitations as a risk measure; for example, it is a *symmetric* measure of dispersion around the mean and thus penalizes down deviations as much as up deviations.

Volatility is usually an inherently *historical* measure of risk, based on the estimated sample standard deviation of some time series of observed returns on assets and liabilities. The resulting estimate of the risk of an exposure will reflect any risks that impacted returns in the time series.

Consider, for example, a corporate bond for which you have the prior 50 trading days (i.e., 10 weeks) of data. Using all the data available, the volatility of the bond's daily returns calculated on day $t$ will be estimated as:

$$s_t = \sqrt{\frac{1}{50} \sum_{j=t-49}^{t} \left( r_{j-1,j} - \bar{r} \right)^2} \qquad (13.1)$$

where $\bar{r}$ is the sample mean daily return over the prior 50 trading days.

Now suppose that during the prior 50 trading days the bond experienced absolutely no fluctuations arising from changes in the perceived credit quality of the issuer. Returns varied solely based on nominal interest rate variations. The volatility estimate $s_t$ will thus reflect *only* credit-independent market risk in this case because credit-dependent market risk had no impact on returns over the period used for the calculation. A major drawback of using volatility as an estimate of the sensitivity of an asset or liability to changes in risk factors thus is its neutrality with respect to what risk factors cause the present value of the asset or liability to change. Volatility is a *total* risk measure, capturing both idiosyncratic and systematic risk and not differentiating between market, credit, liquidity, and other risks. *Anything* that causes the asset or liability to change in value over the period used for the sample volatility calculation is reflected in the number. A poor choice of sample period thus can lead to misleading inferences when volatility is used as the basis of risk measurement and reporting.

Numerous statistical methods are available to smooth volatility estimates over actual sample periods, as well as to produce predicted volatility numbers. To appreciate the differences in these methods, suppose a time series of daily bond returns is available going back 10 years. Taking the simple standard deviation of the whole series, as in equation (13.1), yields an "unconditional variance."

One of the simplest alternatives to taking the standard deviation of a whole time series is a moving average estimate of volatility, which keeps the number of observations constant for each day. In other words, an unconditional volatility estimate would add a new observation each day when new returns are realized without dropping any old observations, whereas a moving average drops the oldest observation each time a new return is realized. On date $t$, the moving average volatility over the past $N$ days is:[5]

$$s_t = \sqrt{\frac{1}{N} \sum_{j=t-N+1}^{t} r_{j-1,j}^2} \qquad (13.2)$$

where a zero mean daily return is assumed for simplicity. At time $t + 1$, $s_{t+1}$ is computed in the same manner, except the last observation—$r_{t-N+1,t-N}^2$—is dropped and replaced with the newest observation, $r_{t,t+1}$.

If we had a chosen a window of the prior 50 days, the moving average volatility estimate in equation (13.2) would be the same as the unconditional variance estimate in (13.1) as long as we assume in both cases that mean returns are equal to zero. Both unconditional volatility and moving average volatility thus *equally weight* all the observations in the calculation. In the unconditional case, because new observations are added without old ones being dropped, all available data is used, and, consequently, relatively less weight is given to more recent data. In the moving average case, recent observations are given more weight by keeping the moving average "window" (i.e., number of observations) constant each day.

Some firms prefer to give even more weight to recent history than the moving average. This can be done easily enough by using an exponentially weighted moving average (EWMA). For any day $t$, the EWMA *variance* is defined (assuming a zero daily mean return) as:

$$s_t^2 = \frac{\sum_{j=1}^{t} \lambda^{j-1} r_{t-j,t-j+1}^2}{\sum_{j=1}^{t} \lambda^{j-1}} \tag{13.3}$$

where $\lambda$ is a smoothing parameter. Using the properties of geometric sequences, this can be rewritten a bit more usefully as:

$$s_t^2 = s_{t-1}^2 + (1 - \lambda)(r_{t-1,t}^2 - s_{t-1}^2) \tag{13.4}$$

so that the current EWMA estimate of variance is equal to the prior day's EWMA estimate of variance plus the deviation of *today's* variance from that value weighted by one minus the smoothing parameter.

The summands in equation 13.3 both begin with $j = 1$ to reflect the fact that the EWMA uses *all* the available data. Nevertheless, much of the data vanishes from the calculation because of the smoothing term $\lambda$. In fact, the parameter $\lambda$ can be chosen so that a desired number of days $\tau$ impact the estimate using the following approximate relation between $\lambda$ and $\tau$:

$$\tau = \left(\frac{2}{1-\lambda}\right) - 1$$

A decay or smoothing factor of $\lambda = 0.9$, for example, means that only the prior 19 days of data are being reflected in the EWMA estimate of variance. A higher decay factor implies a higher weight on older observations, and a lower decay factor weights more recent observations relatively more.

A related approach for estimating variance involves the use of "conditional variance" time series methods. Perhaps the most common such conditional variance model is the generalized autoregressive conditional heteroskedasticity (GARCH) model.[6] A GARCH($m,n$) model expresses the variance of returns at any time $t$ as follows:

$$s_t^2 = \alpha + \sum_{p=1}^{m} \delta_p s_{t-p}^2 + \sum_{q=1}^{n} \gamma_q r_{t-q,t-q+1}^2 \tag{13.5}$$

In other words, the current conditional variance of returns is equal to a weighted average of prior conditional variances (the autoregressive component) and prior sample variances (the moving average component). A very popular special case of the GARCH(*m,n*) model is the GARCH(1,1) model, or

$$s_t^2 = \alpha + \delta s_{t-1}^2 + \gamma r_{t-1,t}^2 \qquad (13.6)$$

Note that the EWMA in equation (13.4) is a special case of the GARCH(1,1) model in (13.6) when $\alpha = 0$ and $\delta + \gamma = 1$, in which case $\gamma = 1 - \delta = 1 - \gamma$. This is called an integrated or IGARCH(1,1) model.

No matter what econometric methods are used to estimate volatility, however, all historical volatility measures are by definition limited by the historical data used to calculate them. One measure of volatility, however, does *not* rely on historical data.

## Hedging to Reduce Downside Semivariance

In certain situations, the use of volatility is problematic because it rests on an implicit notion that the risk being summarized is symmetric around the mean. When only losses are of interest *and* the distribution of the financial focus variable is not symmetric, an alternative measure of the sensitivity of an exposure to changes in market prices is "downside semivariance" (DSV). DSV may be defined for a time series of *N* daily returns as:

$$DSV_t = \frac{1}{N} \sum_{j=t-N+1}^{t} \left( \min[r_{j-1,j} - \bar{r}, 0] \right)^2 \qquad (13.7)$$

In other words, equation 13.7 takes the *negative* squared deviation of returns from the mean, disregards the positive squared deviations, and averages over the whole time series. The resulting risk measure is an indication of the tendency of returns on this asset to deviate from their expected value, but *only* on the downside.

## Hedging to Equate the Marginal Benefits and Costs of Risk Transfer

We do not spend much time in this chapter discussing the *cost* of hedging explicitly. Chapters 7, 8, and 12 should be sufficient for an understanding of the financial costs of hedging. Transaction costs like brokerage fees, bid/ask spreads, and commissions must also be factored into the cost. In the end, a hedge makes sense only if the marginal benefit of the hedge exceeds its marginal cost. Unfortunately, the marginal benefit of a hedge is usually defined at a level much more general than we can discuss here (e.g., the marginal benefit of reduced expected financial distress costs, the marginal benefit of reduced agency costs, the marginal benefit of avoiding underinvestment, etc.). See Culp (2001). Because we cannot digress into the benefits of hedging at that level, there is no need to go much further into costs than we already have.

Yet, worth noting is how a threshold-based approach to hedging can be especially useful for firms that have adopted an integrated risk management approach that, among other things, seeks to quantify systematically the benefits and costs of hedging. The usual way for a firm to accomplish this is using some type of risk-adjusted capital allocation scheme, such as those discussed in Merton and Perold (1993), Matten (2000), Shimpi (2001), Culp (2002a), and Stulz (2002). The basic metric in such a system is risk-adjusted return on capital (RAROC), which is defined for any activity as the expected economic profits from the activity divided by the capital at risk (CaR) required to support the activity.

Capital at risk is a member of the "at risk" family of risk measures that also includes *value* at risk (VaR), *cash flows* at risk (CFaR), and *earnings* at risk (EaR). The "at risk" measures involve several parameters that the hedger must select—chiefly, the probabilistic level of confidence the hedger wants to achieve (denote this percent) and the period over which changes in value, cash flows, or earnings will be examined. CaR (and the other measures) then is defined as the solution to the following equation:[7]

$$\int_{0}^{CaR} f(k)dk = (1 - \alpha)$$

where $k$ denotes capital and $f(k)$ is the probability distribution from which capital is drawn.

CaR and RAROC thresholds for hedging are becoming increasingly common for those firms seeking to implement hedges that have a greater contribution to the firm's marginal efficiency of capital than their marginal cost of capital. (It is also possible to define the benefits and costs of hedging in terms of VaR, EaR, and CFaR if the financial focus suggests that is important.) The marginal benefit of the hedge might be the marginal reduction in CaR times the firm's cost of capital, which then could be compared explicitly to the marginal cost of the hedge.

Stulz (2002) provides a useful framework for exploring the relations between CaR and individual hedging transactions. Unfortunately, all but the most sophisticated firms are likely to find these hedging criteria to be a bit advanced.[8]

## NOTES

1. Merton Miller used to argue that many early theories of why firms hedge were predicated on a need to "concavify" the firm's value function so that an otherwise linear function starts to *look like* a representative investor's

concave utility function. As a result, many of these early theories are plausible but rather oversimplified.

2. This example and the subsequent graphical analyses are based on the example, analysis, and graphs presented in Newbury and Stiglitz (1923).

3. We do not address the speculative risk premium here just yet. For now, go ahead and assume that the forward price is unbiased if it helps add concreteness.

4. It must be stressed that much of the literature on hedging does not make any explicit connection between the risk management strategy of a firm (i.e., why the firm's value can be increased by hedging) and the hedging mandate pursued in a given transaction or strategy. As a result, hedges are often judged failures simply because they successfully accomplished something other than the relevant hedging mandate. At the same time, outside commentators are quick to criticize hedges that do not conform to the usual models without regard to whether the *model* may simply be the wrong mandate for the firm in question. See Culp and Miller (1995a, 1999c).

5. Whether to divide by $N$ or $N - 1$ is debatable. $N$ is used here for consistency with other measures of volatility explored later.

6. A wide variety of similar models are also available, including the simple ARCH model of Engle (1982), GARCH-in-mean or GARCH-M, exponential or EGARCH, and so forth. For a survey of these models in general, see Engle (1995) and in financial applications see Gourieroux (1997).

7. Numerous different methods of actually measuring the "at risks" can be found. Interested readers are recommended to turn to Jorion (2002), Dowd (2002), Holton (2003), or Stulz (2002) for more detailed treatments of "at risk" calculations.

8. "Advanced" does not here refer to intellectual capability, but more to the *systems* and risk management infrastructure required to support a true enterprise-wide CaR- or RAROC-based hedging program.

# CHAPTER 14

# Hedge Ratios

**W**hen it comes to implementing a risk transfer arrangement using derivatives, a firm must define a hedge that properly implements the objectives articulated in the preceding chapter. This generally requires the hedger to make several important up-front choices about the design of the hedge:

- Will the hedge use OTC or exchange-traded derivatives, or both?
- Is the hedge forward- or option-based?
- How much of the underlying risk exposure should be hedged?
- Is the hedge static, or does it require dynamic rebalancing?

The first two questions must be answered by comparing the nature of the exposure to be hedged with the firm's broad risk management strategy and narrow hedging objectives. A hedge designed to reduce or eliminate cash flow volatility will likely involve OTC derivatives like swaps. A hedge intended to put a floor on the firm's input purchasing costs without eliminating cost savings associated with input price declines will likely involve an option-based solution, but whether the options are on- or off-exchange depends on factors such as liquidity and product availability, transaction costs, existing relationships to futures commission merchants (FCMs) and swap dealers, and the like. And so on. In short, we have pretty much said all that we are going to say on the first two issues of hedge design noted.

In this chapter, we address the last two issues in more detail—the size of the hedge and whether the hedge is static or must be rebalanced over its lifetime. These subjects fall into the rubric of what market participants call *hedge ratios*—the proportion of an underlying risk exposure that is hedged using derivatives at any given point in time.

## PRINCIPAL-MATCHED, QUANTITY-MATCHED, OR ONE-TO-ONE HEDGES

With a relatively complete menu of hedging objectives now behind us, we now turn to consider how these hedges can be implemented and how different objectives may imply different hedges. We begin in this section with one of the easiest (and not surprisingly common) hedging strategies: the principal- or quantity-matched hedge, also known as the one-to-one or one-for-one hedge.

The basic idea here is that a firm defines its risk exposure in terms of notional or actual principal (e.g., amount of debt, amount of foreign currency, etc.) or quantity (e.g., bales of cotton, ounces of gold, number of Treasury bonds, etc.), decides how much of that exposure to hedge, and then hedges it by matching the principal or quantity of the amount of the exposure to be hedged with the principal or quantity of the hedge instrument. The derivatives used might be forward- or option-based, depending on whether the firm wants to retain one side of its exposure and on how cost-sensitive the firm is.

Whether we are hedging with OTC or exchange-traded derivatives will affect how we construct our hedge. OTC derivatives generally can be customized, whereas exchange-traded derivatives often have no flexible terms apart from how much to go long or short. This is especially important when we are pursuing hedge objectives like value or cash flow targets in which the ability to match terms of the hedge contract with the terms of the exposure to be hedged can make a significant difference.

We define the underlying risk exposure of a firm to be hedged in terms of a quantity of physical goods or a principal amount to be hedged, either of which is denoted $Q$. The exposure $Q$ could be one million barrels of oil, a $1 million loan, a receivable of one million Hong Kong dollars, a single mortgage-backed security with a face value of $100,000, and so on. Some companies—especially what we called in Chapter 13 selective hedgers—may conclude that only some portion of their risk should be transferred to a counterparty using derivatives. Suppose a farmer plans to sell 1,000 bushels of corn in the future but wants price protection on only 500 bushels. In this case, we would define the exposure to be hedged as $Q = 500$ bushels. Because we are interested in hedge construction, we can ignore the part of its exposure that a firm opts *not* to hedge.

We then define the quantity or principal hedged as $Z$. We can express the hedge ratio at any time $t$ as the proportion of the risk exposure to be hedged ($Q$) that is actually hedged using derivatives ($Z$):

$$h_t = -\frac{Z}{Q} \qquad (14.1)$$

A principal- or quantity-matched hedge is a hedge in which $h = -1$; that is, for every long unit of principal or quantity exposure to be hedged, there is a unit of principal or quantity sold short (and for every short unit to be hedged there is a unit purchased long) using derivatives.

## Mechanics

Suppose a U.S.-based widget manufacturing company intends to sell its goods in Canada in six months. The price of the widgets is fixed in Canadian dollars at C\$100 per widget, and the firm has committed orders for the sale of one million widgets. Ignore credit risk and assume the quantity of widgets sold is firm and that all purchasers will honor their obligations. In six months, the firm will thus receive C\$100 million that must be converted back into dollars at the prevailing exchange rate.

Now suppose the firm wants to reduce the volatility of its profits as much as possible. In other words, the financial focus for this hedge is economic profits, and the hedging mandate is volatility reduction. In fact, we might suppose further that the firm would prefer, if at all possible, to reduce the volatility of its profits to zero, provided that can be accomplished without locking in a negative margin.

If the U.S. dollar price of Canadian dollars to be delivered in 180 days is \$0.6650, a principal-matched hedge involving a forward contract would require the firm to sell C\$100 million for delivery 180 days hence at a price of \$0.6650 per Canadian dollar. Recall from Chapter 6 that if the "settlement is initiated 180 days hence, the short is not likely to receive a final and irrevocable dollar payment until 182 days hence—and similarly for the long.

Table 14.1 shows the impact of this hedge for several different possible future exchange rates that might prevail 180 days after the trade date. The first column simply translates the 1,000,000 widgets sold at C\$100/widget into a US\$-equivalent revenue (or, since we have assumed no costs, profit) at several different possible future spot exchange rates—the possible rates at which Canadian dollars would have to be converted into U.S. dollars if the firm does not hedge. If the forward price of Canadian dollars is unbiased in the sense of Chapter 12, the second column shows expected profits and losses for the firm, which in this example are a function solely of exchange rate risk. The last two columns show the payoff on a quantity-matched forward sale of Canadian dollars and the net.

Do not forget that although the forward sale involves no cash outlay for the firm, the own interest rate may well be positive and the cost of carry negative. Even if the forward price is an unbiased estimate of the future spot price, the firm may still have to pay the negative cost of carry.

**TABLE 14.1** Principal-Matched Forward Hedge of Exchange Rate Risk

| Exchange Rate | US$ Revenues (Unhedged) | Expected Profit or Loss (US$) | US$ Payoff on Forward Hedge | Net Hedged US$ Profits |
|---|---|---|---|---|
| US$0.6600 | 66,000,000 | (500,000) | 500,000 | 0 |
| US$0.6625 | 66,250,000 | (250,000) | 250,000 | 0 |
| US$0.6650 | 66,500,000 | 0 | 0 | 0 |
| US$0.6675 | 66,750,000 | 250,000 | (250,000) | 0 |
| US$0.6700 | 67,000,000 | 500,000 | (500,000) | 0 |

Now suppose the same U.S.-based manufacturing company has received orders for one million widget sales in Canada at C$100/widget, but that orders are not considered firm until customers have been invoiced, which will occur in three months. For the next three months, customers thus can cancel their orders without penalty. If the firm waits three months to hedge, the forward price of Canadian dollars might rise in dollar terms, thus increasing the price at which the firm can hedge. But by going short Canadian dollars in the forward market now, the firm runs the risk of being overhedged in the event that customer orders are canceled.

Because the objective of the firm is to eliminate as much variability to profits as possible, the firm could buy three-month options on three-month forward contracts—provided, however, that the total premium paid on the options does not result in a negative profit margin for the widget seller. For any orders that become firm, the widget seller will exercise the options, thereby converting its options into three-month currency forwards at a forward price set today. For orders that cancel, the firm will allow the options to expire worthless.

## Slippage

Principal- or quantity-matched hedges tend to work fairly well when the principal or quantity being hedged is constant or has a very low volatility. If the amount being hedged is either unknown or variable, however, a principal-matched hedged can be subject to significant *slippage*. To see this, let us look at a simple sensitivity analysis of the American widget producer, now assuming that the quantity of widgets to be sold is *expected* to be one million but might well not be.

Table 14.2 shows a sensitivity analysis of the firm's U.S. dollar revenues and expected profits/losses, assuming it does not hedge. Whereas in Table 14.1 the only source of risk to the firm was exchange rate risk, you can now see that profits vary with the exchange rate *and* the quantity of widgets sold. Expected profits are calculated relative to an expected future spot exchange rate of US$0.6650 per Canadian dollar, and expected sales are one million widgets at the fixed price of C$100 per widget.

Table 14.3 now shows the impact of a principal-matched hedge, where the principal underlying the forward currency sale is matched to the *expected revenues* the firm hopes to repatriate (i.e., a forward sale of C$1,000,000 at US$0.6650). The payoffs on the hedge are the same as those shown in the third column of Table 14.1. As long as the quantity of widgets sold is really one million, we have eliminated our exchange rate risk and reduced the variance of profits to zero. But notice what happens if our actual sales differ from our expected sales. If we sell less than anticipated, we are *overhedged*. You can see this by comparing our first two columns with the first two columns in the profits/losses section of Table 14.2. For favorable exchange rate moves, we actually lose less than if we had not hedged. But for unfavorable exchange rate moves, losses on the hedge result in total losses *above* the total losses we would have incurred by not hedging. You can see a similar but opposite effect if we sell more than expected and are *underhedged*.

Notice also that the variability of profits rises the further our actual sales number is from its expected value. The range of potential losses is only

**TABLE 14.2**  Sensitivity Analysis of Profits to Exchange Rate and Sales Risk

| Spot Exchange Rate | Quantity of Widgets Sold at C$100/Widget | | | | |
|---|---|---|---|---|---|
|  | 500,000 | 750,000 | 1,000,000 | 1,250,000 | 1,500,000 |
| | Unhedged Revenues (U.S. Dollars) | | | | |
| US$0.6600 | 33,000,000 | 49,500,000 | 66,000,000 | 82,500,000 | 99,000,000 |
| US$0.6625 | 33,125,000 | 49,687,500 | 66,250,000 | 82,812,500 | 99,375,000 |
| US$0.6650 | 33,250,000 | 49,875,000 | 66,500,000 | 83,125,000 | 99,750,000 |
| US$0.6675 | 33,375,000 | 50,062,500 | 66,750,000 | 83,437,500 | 100,125,000 |
| US$0.6700 | 33,500,000 | 50,250,000 | 67,000,000 | 83,750,000 | 100,500,000 |
| | Unhedged Expected Profits/Losses | | | | |
| US$0.6600 | (33,500,000) | (17,000,000) | (500,000) | 16,000,000 | 32,500,000 |
| US$0.6625 | (33,375,000) | (16,812,500) | (250,000) | 16,312,500 | 32,875,000 |
| US$0.6650 | (33,250,000) | (16,625,000) | 0 | 16,625,000 | 33,250,000 |
| US$0.6675 | (33,125,000) | (16,437,500) | 250,000 | 16,937,500 | 33,625,000 |
| US$0.6700 | (33,000,000) | (16,250,000) | 500,000 | 17,250,000 | 34,000,000 |

**TABLE 14.3** Sensitivity Analysis of Profits Inclusive of Principal-Matched Forward Sale of C$100 Million

| Spot Exchange Rate | Quantity of Widgets Sold at C$100/Widget | | | | |
|---|---|---|---|---|---|
| | 500,000 | 750,000 | 1,000,000 | 1,250,000 | 1,500,000 |
| US$0.6600 | (33,000,000) | (16,500,000) | 0 | 16,500,000 | 33,000,000 |
| US$0.6625 | (33,125,000) | (16,562,500) | 0 | 16,562,500 | 33,125,000 |
| US$0.6650 | (33,250,000) | (16,625,000) | 0 | 16,625,000 | 33,250,000 |
| US$0.6675 | (33,375,000) | (16,687,500) | 0 | 16,687,500 | 33,375,000 |
| US$0.6700 | (33,500,000) | (16,750,000) | 0 | 16,750,000 | 33,500,000 |

$250,000 if sales are only 75 percent of what the firm expects, but the range of possible losses doubles if we sell only half the widgets we intended.

## Addressing Slippage

In general, a fixed-quantity hedge will perform relatively well when hedging fixed quantities, but slippage will cause the quality of the hedge to deteriorate the more variable the quantity being hedged. You may recall another version of this problem in Chapter 13 in the discussion of pure risk avoidance hedging under correlated quantity and price shocks.

Slippage can be addressed in several ways. The two most common ways are by turning a static hedge into a dynamic hedge or by adding optionality to the hedge.

### Dynamic Rebalancing

The fixed-principal or fixed-quantity hedge is generally a static hedge (i.e., the quantity hedged does not change over the life of the hedging transaction). To address slippage, one solution thus is to add a dynamic component in which the quantity hedged is changed periodically to match the changing exposure. Transaction costs can get high quickly in such cases, however, not to mention the operational troubles that such hedges can engender.

As you will recall, one distinct difference between OTC and exchange-traded derivatives is ease of offset. OTC derivatives must be unwound with permission of the original counterparty, whereas futures can be offset with the clearinghouse. As a result, any hedging strategy with a financial focus of profits or value that requires frequent rebalancing will generally involve some use of futures. (A later section shows why this is not true for cash flow hedges.) The whole hedge could be accomplished using futures, or, as an alternative, the firm might establish a principal-matched forward hedge at the beginning of the transaction and then use futures to rebalance the base position as required over time.

### Adding Optionality

Options and embedded options can also be combined with forwards, swaps, or futures to synthesize a dynamic component to the hedge. Such options may be either embedded into the original hedging instrument or purchased/written on a stand-alone basis.

In mortgage markets, for example, a principal-matched hedge of a mortgage portfolio will involve a principal that amortizes at a rate equal to the expected prepayment speed of the portfolio. That way the principal in the hedge declines at the same rate as the principal in the loan portfolio being hedged. But if mortgage prepayment speeds increase unexpectedly, the lender or mortgage portfolio owner will quickly be overhedged if using a principal-matched hedging strategy. As a solution, hedgers may opt to specify that principal on the hedge amortizes at a rate determined by some market price or reference rate presumed to be correlated with mortgage prepayments (e.g., LIBOR). This effectively embeds an option into the forward or swap and reduces slippage.

Alternatively, forwards and swaps can be customized with call provisions to allow for their partial or complete early termination. Suppose a firm issues 10-year fixed-rate bonds callable after year three. If the firm swaps fixed-rate for floating-rate debt by entering into a pay-floating rate swap whose settlement dates and principal match the coupon dates and principal of the bonds, the firm runs the risk that a call of the bonds after year three will leave the firm overhedged. This can be addressed if the firm includes a provision that allows the swap to be terminated early any time after year three. Equivalently, the firm could enter into a pay-fixed $3 \times 7$ swaption—an option that enables the firm to enter into a swap as a fixed-rate payer for seven years beginning three years hence. If the firm calls its debt, it can then simply exercise the swaption to neutralize the swap that is no longer needed to hedge the debt that has been called.

### Tailing and Present Value Adjustments for Futures

The example of a one-for-one hedge in the previous section involved the use of forwards. What if we had used futures? Would a one-for-one hedge still make sense?

### Mismatched Cash Flows

Because futures and futures options are resettled at least daily (usually twice daily), the cash flows on these products generally occurs much more frequently than the cash flows on the exposure the firm is hedging. Even if our hedging objective is defined in terms of value, profits, or earnings and not cash flows, the mismatch in the timing of the cash flows on the exposure being hedged and the hedging instrument can give rise to another form of slippage that will ultimately interfere with our hedging mandate of reducing the volatility of our profits.

Let us return to our example of the American widget manufacturer selling widgets in Canada (assume 1 million for sure) at a fixed price of C$100 per widget. Payment will be received on the widgets 180 days from now in Canadian dollars. Suppose the widget seller is interested in a quantity-matched hedge of its economic profits so that profits are as insulated as possible for exchange rate shifts. Suppose the current price of a *futures contract* on Canadian dollars with six months to maturity is $0.6650.[1] The contract, listed for trading on the CME, calls for delivery by the short of C$100,000 at maturity and has a minimum price fluctuation of $0.0001, which translates into $10 per contract.

Let's assume the widget maker pursues a hedging mandate of $h = 1$. Imagine that one day after the position has been initiated (i.e., 179 days prior to receiving payment on the widget sales), the spot exchange rate expected to prevail six months hence falls to $0.6545. If absolutely no further exchange rate movements are expected to occur, the firm expects to incur a $50,000 loss on its conversion of Canadian to U.S. dollars.

If as before the firm hedged using a forward contract to sell Canadian dollars for U.S. dollars, that contract is expected to pay off $50,000 ([$0.6550 − $0.6545] × C$100,000,000) in six months. If the six-month money interest rate is 4 percent per annum (with a day-count basis of 360 days) and we have 181 days until the *settlement* date on the forward contract (which is presumably two days after the contract matures, or 179 + 2 days from now), the present value of the $50,000 future payoff is:

$$\frac{\$50,000}{1+\dfrac{181}{360}.04} = \$49,014$$

This is exactly the same as the present value of the loss the firm expects to take on its conversion of Canadian dollar revenues back into U.S. dollars.

Now suppose instead that the firm opted to go short 1,000 six-month Canadian dollar futures on the CME at $0.6550 in lieu of a forward contract. When the exchange rate move occurs one day into the trade, thanks to the institutional design of futures, the widget maker receives a credit to its trading account *immediately* of $50,000 ([$0.6550 − $0.6545] × C$100,000/contract × 1,000 contracts). If the widget maker invests those proceeds at the current money interest rate for 181 days, the amount will be worth $51,006. The widget maker thus ends up with *more than enough* to cover the future value of the $50,000 decline in profits. The widget seller actually makes a $1,006 profit on the hedge if everything else goes as planned!

The exchange rate could, however, have moved against the firm. In that case, the firm would incur an immediate $50,000 *loss* that would have to be financed for 181 days. Assuming for simplicity that the firm can invest and borrow funds at the same 4 percent rate, the firm thus now *owes* $1,006 in interest costs 181 days hence, thus leaving the firm with only $48,994 in net gains on the hedge to apply to the $50,000 revenue loss.

Because the cash flows on exchange-traded derivatives occur at least daily, a quantity- or principal-matched one-for-one hedge ratio will result in a hedger being *overhedged*. When the underlying moves in favor of the hedge, the hedger *makes money*. But a move in the other direction *costs money*. Either way, the position is too big; some adjustment to the hedge ratio must be made to reflect this difference in the timing of cash flows.

### Present Value–Adjusted One-for-One Hedge Ratios

The adjustment the widget seller needs to make to its futures hedge should already be intuitively clear. Specifically, the present value (PV)–adjusted one-for-one hedge ratio the widget maker should hold on date $t$ to hedge a foreign currency payment that will settle on date $T$ is

$$h_t = PV_t[h] = -\frac{Z/Q}{1 + \dfrac{d_{t,T}}{DCB} r_{t,T}} \tag{14.2}$$

where $r_{t,T}$ is the money interest rate prevailing from $t$ to $T$. You may recall from Chapter 6 that $d_{t,T}$ is the number of days between dates $t$ and $T$ and that $DCB$ is the day-count basis for the money rate quotation—360 days in the United States, for example. The rate to use is the investment or financing rate actually available to the firm, or a simple average of the rate at which gains can be invested in a money market fund and the rate at which margin losses must be financed (e.g., interbank).

It is sometimes easier to express the present value adjustment using discount factor notation. Let $B_{t,T}$ denote the time $t$ price of a pure discount bond paying $1 on date $T$. Then we can rewrite the present value–adjusted hedge ratio in (14.1) as:

$$h_t = -\frac{ZB_{t,T}}{Q} \tag{14.3}$$

Note in both (14.2) and (14.3) that $Z$ is the quantity or principal hedged in total. For a forward contract, this was just the size of the contract negotiated. But because futures are standardized, it is sometimes useful to expand $Z$ into more practically useful terms. Specifically, let $N$ denote the number of futures contracts—this is what we really need to know—and let $Y$ denote the size of a single contract, so that $Z = NY$. In the one-for-one hedge, $Z = 1,000$ contracts $\times$ C\$100,000/contract = C\$100,000,000.

If you want to solve for the number of futures contracts directly, it is usually easiest to compute the present value adjustment *after* solving for the $N$ that yields your desired *nominal* hedge ratio—$h = -1$ in this case. In other words,

$$N = \frac{hQ}{Y} \tag{14.4}$$

In our example, $N = (-1)(C\$100,000,000)/C\$100,000 = -1,000$ contracts. With a 4 percent interest rate and 181 days to settlement, the present value–adjusted one-for-one futures hedge thus is:

$$PV_t[N] = \frac{-1,000}{1 + \left(\frac{181}{360}\right).04} = -980$$

You thus hold 20 fewer futures contracts to reflect the fact that cash flows on the futures position occur immediately, whereas the revenues being hedged will arrive six months in the future.

### Tailing the Hedge

For many years in the futures industry, the practice of making present value adjustments to hedge ratios involving futures contracts that were being used to hedge exposures with deferred payoffs was known colloquially as *tailing the hedge*. As an approximation of the present value adjustment in equation (14.2), hedgers could first solve the true one-for-one hedge ratio for the number of futures contracts to go long or short and then adjust for the mistiming in cash flows by adding the *tail* from the one-for-one hedge.

In our example, the one-for-one hedge ratio involves 1,000 futures contracts. In other words, if $h = -1$, $Q =$ C\$100 million, and $Y =$ C\$100,000/contract, then

$$N = \frac{hQ}{Y} = \frac{(-1)(\text{C\$}100,000,000)}{\text{C\$}100,000} = -1,000 \qquad (14.5)$$

The *tail* then is defined as

$$T = -N\left(\frac{d_{t,T}}{DCB}\right)r_{t,T} \qquad (14.6)$$

Note from (14.6) that the tail is always the opposite sign of $N$, the number of futures contracts in the one-for-one hedge. This is because the daily resettlement of futures results in a hedge that is *too large* in absolute value when paired with a risk exposure involving a deferred-maturity payoff. Indeed, the amount by which a futures position is overhedged is, all else equal, higher the further in the future the payoff being hedged.[2] The tail thus should always reduce the number of contracts in the hedge. A short one-for-one hedge thus has a long tail, and a long one-for-one hedge has a short tail.

In our example, the tail can be computed as:

$$T = -(-1,000)\left(\frac{181}{360}\right).04 = 20 \qquad (14.7)$$

The tailed hedge thus would be 980 short, which is exactly the same as the number of contracts we found using the present value calculation directly.

So, in general, the number of futures contracts that should be held on date $t$ in a *tailed* one-for-one hedge of a payoff occurring on date $T$ should be approximately equal to the number of futures contracts in a PV-adjusted one-for-one futures hedge of the same obligation:

$$N + T = \frac{hQ}{Y} - N\left(\frac{d_{t,T}}{DCB}\right)r_{t,T} \approx \frac{hQ/y}{1 + \left(\frac{d_{t,T}}{DCB}\right)r_{t,T}} \qquad (14.8)$$

### Is It Ever Sensible *Not* to Adjust for Present Values?

Basic finance theory would seem to tell thus that it is just plain wrong not to adjust the hedge ratios of exchange-traded derivatives for mismatched cash flows relative to a deferred payoff in the underlying exposure being hedged. But in the real world, this is not always the case.

In order for a present value–adjusted hedge ratio to be truly effective, it must be rebalanced essentially every time interest rates change or major cash flows on the futures leg of the position occur. With rounding, positions might not require adjustments each day, but adjustments will be frequent enough on any sizable hedge that transaction costs and operational headaches can mount quickly. Especially if the gains from tailing are small (e.g., the exposure being hedged is only a few months in the future), present value adjustments and the rebalancing of the hedge ratio they require may be more costly than the savings the practice generates.

In the real world, present value adjustments and tails also can greatly complicate *monitoring*. Suppose, for example, that a trade credit borrower pledges a soybean crop as collateral on a loan used to finance the transport of the beans from the fields to the crushing facility. The lender likely will insist that the borrower hedge the crop against price fluctuations that could erode the value of the collateral, and the lender will want to monitor that hedge. If the borrower adopts a one-for-one hedge, it will be obvious to the lender whether or not the borrower is properly hedged. But if the borrower adopts a dynamic present value–adjusted one-for-one hedge ratio, the hedge ratio will always be less than one and will be constantly changing. It may be hard for the lender to verify the calculations used to distinguish tailing from "speculative behavior" on the part of the borrower. Depending on the size of the gains from tailing, it may be easier on all fronts just to stick with the one-for-one hedge.

## CASH FLOW-MATCHED HEDGES

A principal- or quantity-matched hedge can be implemented using either OTC or exchange-traded derivatives by firms wishing to hedge value or capital, profits, or accounting earnings. A principal-matched hedge involving OTC derivatives can also function as a *cash flow* hedge. The principle is simple: Merely match the settlement dates on the derivatives contract with the settlement dates on the bundle of cash flows to be hedged and try to ensure that cash flows on the two positions are as highly correlated in absolute value as possible.

A cash flow–matched hedge is generally not generally possible with exchange-traded derivatives unless the exposure being hedged includes either other exchange-traded derivatives or an exposure with similarly frequent periodic cash resettlements. Even if matching is not the goal and the firm merely wishes to reduce substantially or minimize cash flow volatility, futures are not always a good choice.

We saw in the previous section that the size of a futures hedge can be adjusted to account for the differences in the present values of mismatched cash flows on the hedge and the exposure being hedged. But this adjustment equated *present values*. There is no way to change the *actual* pattern of cash flows on a futures contract. Although reducing the size of the position will reduce cash flow volatility somewhat, it is extremely unlikely that it will ever be enough to satisfy a cash flow hedger.

For the most part, firms with a very specific desire to reduce cash flows variability or to preserve cash balances are better off using OTC derivatives in which cash settlement dates can be exactly matched to the cash settlements on the exposure being hedged. There are exceptions, but very few.

## HEDGING THE SENSITIVITY OF AN EXPOSURE TO SMALL PRICE CHANGES

When we discussed hedging mandates, we saw that a very practical and commonly used technique is to try to match the sensitivities of a hedge and the underlying exposure to be hedged. But sensitivities to what?

This section specifically considers various hedges that try to equate the sensitivity of the value of an exposure to a small change in the underlying asset price with the sensitivity of the value of the hedge to a small change in the same asset price. Although this hedging technique is best illustrated with and probably most often used in value hedging, the principles discussed here can easily be extended to hedging earnings or economic profits, as well. Nevertheless, we will stick to value hedging for simplicity.

Denote the value of an exposure to be hedged as $U$ at some point in time. In this section, we suppose that only one source of risk—a single underlying price—affects $U$ in a manner that we wish to control through risk transfer. If $U$ is the total value of an exposure, we might be talking about the value of an inventory of copper where the quantity is fixed and the price is the sole source of risk to the copper stock. We often work with $U$ in per unit terms, moreover, in which case quite often $U$ is equal to the price of the underlying.

In general, the sensitivity of an exposure to a small change in the underlying price (or interest rate) is called the *delta* of the exposure and can be expressed analytically as:

$$\Delta_u = \frac{\partial U}{\partial P} \tag{14.9}$$

An alternative expression of delta is the elasticity of the value of an exposure with respect to a change in price. The elasticity of an exposure is just its delta scaled by the current price and the current value of the position:

$$\eta_{U \cdot P} = \Delta\left(\frac{P}{U}\right) = \left(\frac{\partial U}{\partial P}\right)\frac{P}{U} \qquad (14.10)$$

where the notation $\eta_{U \cdot P}$ is read "the value elasticity with respect to price."

## Computing Delta

Calculating the sensitivity of an exposure to a small change in the underlying price as given in equation (14.9) can be accomplished in several ways. The two most common computational methods are known as *analytical* and *numerical*.

### Analytical Deltas

An analytical delta is a sensitivity implied by the payoff of the asset or exposure in question or by some theoretical model for that payoff. When the underlying price affects the exposure linearly, the delta as of the date the payoff occurs is always unity. Consider, for example, a refinery that plans to sell an inventory of 42,000 gallons of heating oil in three months at the future spot price (gallons/cent). If we define $U$ as the value of the total inventory three months hence—$U = 42,000S_{t+3}$—then:

$$\Delta_u = \frac{\partial U}{\partial S_{t+3}} = 42,000$$

Alternatively, $\Delta_u = 1$ *per gallon*. The delta on a forward contract on any date over the life of the contract is always unity, and the delta on a futures contract on any date is always equal to the price on that date of a pure discount bond paying unity when the futures contract expires.

For exposures or assets whose payoffs do not depend on price linearly, the analytical delta is the delta based on some theoretical model of the price or exposure. In the celebrated Black-Scholes option pricing model, for example, the time $t$ price of a call option expiring at time $T$ on a non-dividend-paying asset whose current price is $P$ and whose volatility is $\sigma$ is:

$$C = PN\left(\frac{\ln\left(\frac{P}{K}\right) + \left(r + \frac{1}{2}\sigma^2\right)(T-t)}{\sigma\sqrt{T-t}}\right) - Ke^{-r(T-t)}N\left(\frac{\ln\left(\frac{P}{K}\right) + \left(r - \frac{1}{2}\sigma^2\right)(T-t)}{\sigma\sqrt{T-t}}\right)$$

$$(14.11)$$

where $K$ is the strike price and $N(\cdot)$ is the cumulative normal distribution. The analytical delta can be found easily by partial differentiation of equation (14.11) with respect to price:

$$\frac{\partial C}{\partial P} = N\left(\frac{\ln\left(\dfrac{P}{K}\right) + \left(r + \dfrac{1}{2}\sigma^2\right)(T-t)}{\sigma\sqrt{T-t}}\right) \qquad (14.12)$$

An analytical delta based on a theoretical model (rather than the true payoff) is only as useful as the model itself. *Model risk* can arise when an oversimplified or inaccurate model is used as the basis for a delta calculation. In the previous example, (14.12) is an absolutely correct expression for the delta of a European call as long as the Black-Scholes model is the *true model* for option prices. But if it is not, the model *and the analytical delta obtained from the model* are wrong.

### Numerical Deltas

Calculating a numerical delta is essentially measuring equation (14.9) "by brute force" using scenario analysis. If we denote a very small change in the underlying price as $\varepsilon$, the numerical delta can be found by literally repricing the exposure under the assumption of a price move of $\varepsilon$:

$$\Delta_u = \frac{U(P+\varepsilon) - U(P)}{\varepsilon} \qquad (14.13)$$

For very small price changes of $\varepsilon$, the delta *should* be symmetric whether we consider a price decline or increase. But sometimes discrete data and rounding prevent the use of truly small numbers, in which case we might want to calculate the numerical delta as:

$$\Delta_u = \frac{\dfrac{U(P+\varepsilon) - U(P)}{\varepsilon} + \dfrac{U(P-\varepsilon) - U(P)}{-\varepsilon}}{2} \qquad (14.13)'$$

Numerical deltas can be obtained by using payoff formulas or theoretical models. In the heating oil forward discussed in the previous section, we can again use the payoff formula directly. Suppose the fixed purchase price of heating oil is \$.8045 per gallon. The delta of the forward can be computed using equation (14.13) as:

$$\Delta_u = \frac{42,000(.8051 - .8045) - 42,000(.8050 - .8045)}{.0001} = 42,000$$

which is, of course, identical to the analytical delta for the position.

We can also compute a numerical delta by revaluing the position using theoretical models. For a call option, we can use the Black-Scholes model in equation (14.10) to find the numerical delta from (14.13):

$$\Delta_u = \frac{C(P + \varepsilon) - C(P)}{\varepsilon} \tag{14.14}$$

Equations (14.11) and (14.14) both rely on the Black-Scholes formula, even though the former is analytical and the latter numerical. As such, model risk is something to worry about using either approach. The primary difference comes from the difference between a discrete and a continuous change. The analytical delta in (14.11) holds for *infinitesimally small* changes in price, whereas the $\varepsilon$ price change used in (14.14) will be dictated by actual data considerations, such as the maximum decimalization of a price. The two approaches thus can yield slightly different numbers.

## Computing the Hedge Ratio

How do we go from our deltas to a hedge ratio? The answer is simple enough. Let us suppose we have computed the delta of our unhedged exposure as $\Delta_u$ and that using similar methods we compute the delta of a derivatives hedge as $\Delta_h$. Suppose further these are *per unit* deltas, not per exposure.

The value of the hedged position is:

$$V = QU + ZH \tag{14.15}$$

where $U$ and $H$ are the per unit values of the unhedged exposure and the hedge, respectively. $Q$ and $Z$ are the number of units to be hedged and in the hedge, as before. The delta of the combined position is:

$$\Delta_V = Q\Delta_u + Z\Delta_h \tag{14.16}$$

A delta hedge is a hedge that protects the combined position from changes in value if the underlying price moves by a small amount. We thus want a hedge $Z$ that solves:

$$\Delta_V = Q\Delta_u + Z\Delta_h \approx 0 \tag{14.17}$$

Or, using our definition of a hedge ratio from earlier, we want $h$ that solves:

$$\Delta_u + h\Delta_h = 0$$

$$\Rightarrow h = -\frac{\Delta_u}{\Delta_h}$$

(14.18)

Now let's consider some special cases of this.

### Duration Hedging

One of the oldest ways to measure market risk comes from the banking and insurance world and is called the "duration gap" model. Macaulay duration measures the delta sensitivity of the present value of an asset or a liability to a small change in interest rates:

$$D = -\left(\frac{\partial V}{\partial y}\right)\frac{1+y}{V}$$

(14.19)

where $V$ is the current value of a position and $y$ is the interest rate. Duration is thus the value elasticity of an asset or liability with respect to an interest rate. It is often convenient to define modified duration as:

$$MD = -\frac{D}{1+y}$$

(14.20)

in which case the risk of a position for a given change in rates is just:

$$\Delta V = V x M D x \Delta y$$

(14.21)

Duration and modified duration thus are deltalike measures commonly used in fixed income applications. "Duration immunization," for example, is the practice of matching (as closely as possible) the duration of assets and the duration of liabilities. Derivatives are often used to facilitate immunization.

In some cases, firms prefer not to manage the duration of assets *or* liabilities, but rather the net of the two. The "duration gap" for a business unit or portfolio of exposures is defined as:

$$D^{gap} = D^A - wD^L$$

(14.22)

where $D^A$ is the duration of all assets in the portfolio, $D^L$ is the duration of all its liabilities, and $w$ is the proportion of assets funded by liabilities. A commercial bank, for example, might have a loan portfolio with a seven-year duration that is 80 percent funded by a portfolio of demand deposit accounts and term deposits with an effective duration of six months.[3] The duration gap for the bank thus is 6.6 years.

If the bank wants to immunize itself against interest rate risk, it could employ a variety of hedging techniques using interest rate derivatives with the goal of constructing a derivatives hedge with a duration as close to 6.6 years as possible. Because the bank's duration gap is *positive* 6.6 years, an increase in rates leads to a decline in net asset value. The derivatives hedge thus would be long on rates (e.g., short Treasury derivatives or a pay fixed/received floating swap).

### Futures DV01 and PV01 Hedge Ratios

With exchange-traded futures, the delta is frequently called the DV01, or the dollar value of a basis point or one-tick change in the underlying. The DV01 of a futures contract is generally defined on a per contract basis and can be looked up or calculated using the contract specifications published by various exchanges.

For the most part, the DV01 is easy to calculate:

$$DV01 = \text{Contract size} \times \text{Minimum price fluctuation}$$

Consider, for example, the world sugar futures contract listed on the New York Board of Trade (NYBT). The contract calls for delivery of 112,000 pounds (50 long tons) of No. 11 sugar. The price is quoted in cents per pound and has a minimum fluctuation or tick size of .01 cents per pound. The DV01 for this contract thus is $0.0001/lb.

$$DV01 = 112,000 \text{ lbs.} \times \$0.0001/\text{lb.} = \$11.20/\text{contract}$$

Similarly, the Sydney Futures Exchange (SFE) futures contract on greasy wool has a contract size of 2,500 kilograms and a minimum price fluctuation of 1 cent per kilogram. The DV01 thus is A$0.01/kg.

$$DV01 = 2,500 \text{ kg.} \times \text{A\$0.01/kg.} = \text{A\$25/contract}$$

For financial futures, the DV01 is more often than not calculated in the same way as just shown for commodities. But things can get tricky. The futures contract on the German DAX stock index, for example, has a contract size defined as €25 per DAX index point. At an index level of 3,331.50, the contract thus is worth €83,287.50. In this case, however, the total contract size at any given time is irrelevant. The minimum price fluctuation is 0.5 index points. Because the contract is always worth €25 times the index level, a one-tick move is always worth €14.50. The DV01 thus is €14.5/contract. Similarly, the CBOT's futures contract on the Dow Jones Industrial Average has a value at any time of $10 times the level of the index. With a minimum price fluctuation of one index point, the DV01 thus is $10/contract.

Things can gets even trickier for interest rate futures. The "01" in DV01 generally means the per contract value of a tick. But in some cases, the "01" refers to a basis point. In interest rate derivatives, a basis point is .01 percent, or the interest rate expressed as a fraction multiplied by 10,000. An interest rate of 3.25 percent thus can be expressed as 325 basis points (.0325 × 10,000).

The real problem comes in when the minimum tick size of a contract is actually *smaller* than one basis point. Chicago Mercantile Exchange (CME) Eurodollar futures, for example, have a contract size of $1,000,000 that represents a hypothetical certificate of deposit (see Chapter 10). The price is some fraction of 100, which represents par value for the underlying CD. Subtracting the price from 100 gives the interest rate in percentage terms that market participants expect to prevail on a CD issued when the futures contract matures. A price of 98.5 indicates an expected future three-month rate of 1.5 percent, for example.

The minimum price fluctuation on a Eurodollar futures contract is generally 0.005, or half of a basis point. The contract specifications further indicate that one basis point (i.e., 0.01) is worth $25. How does this reconcile with a total contract size of $1,000,000? To see the answer, suppose the Eurodollar futures price is 98.5, implying an annualized rate of 1.5 percent. On a $1,000,000 CD, this represents interest income *over three months* of $3,750 ($1,000,000 × 1.5 percent per annum × $1/4$ year). Now suppose the price of the contract increases to 98.505. At the new rate of 1.495 percent, this represents interest income for three months of $3,737.50. The change in implied interest income is thus exactly $14.50, or the value of a single tick.

Now that we have made sense of the contract size, value of a basis point, and value of a tick, we need to decide which one to use! Earlier examples and common sense might lead us to pick the minimum tick size as the basis for the DV01. But in most cases, these futures will be used to hedge interest rates with a minimum quotation size of whole basis points. In other words, we do indeed want the dollar value of a basis point and not of a tick. So,

DV01 = $1,000,000 × 0.0001 bps per annum × 0.25 years = $25/contract

Now that we know how to compute the DV01 of a futures contract, how can we hedge with it? As long as we are hedging other futures contracts or positions with daily cash flows, we just use the DV01s of the hedge and the underlying position as approximations of our delta and compute the hedge ratio:

$$h = -\frac{\mathrm{DV01}_u}{\mathrm{DV01}_h} \tag{14.23}$$

As we have seen already, however, comparing the DV01 of a futures contract to the delta or DV01 of an exposure being hedged makes little sense if the payoff on the exposure being hedged occurs in the future and is not subject to periodic cash resettlement. In that case, we need to equalize the DV01s in present value terms using what we call a PV01 hedge ratio.

A PV01 is quite literally the present value as of date $t$ of a DV01 corresponding to a cash flow that will occur on date $T$. Not surprisingly, the adjustment looks just like the one we made earlier to go from a one-to-one hedge to a PV-adjusted one-to-one hedge, except the numerator is now the DV01 and not unity:

$$\mathrm{PV01} = \mathrm{PV}_t[\mathrm{DV01}] = \frac{\mathrm{DV01}}{1 + \left(\dfrac{d_{t,T}}{DCB}\right) r_{t,T}} \tag{14.24}$$

Because the futures pay off immediately, $\mathrm{DV01}_h = \mathrm{PV01}_h$ for the futures position. So, a PV01 hedge ratio is

$$h = -\frac{\mathrm{PV01}_u}{\mathrm{PV01}_h} = -\frac{\dfrac{\mathrm{DV01}_u}{\left(1 + \dfrac{d_{t,T}}{DCB} r_{t,T}\right)}}{\mathrm{DV01}_h} \tag{14.25}$$

To get to a number of futures contracts, we just substitute equation (14.4) to get

$$N = -\frac{\dfrac{\mathrm{DV01}_u}{\left(1 + \dfrac{d_{t,T}}{DCB} r_{t,T}\right)}}{\mathrm{DV01}_h} \frac{Q}{Y} \tag{14.26}$$

Let us work through an example. Suppose we are hedging a three-month forward sale of 100 million Canadian dollars using the CME Canadian dollar futures contract. The DV01 or delta of the forward contract is unity. To keep our units consistent, we express this as the smallest quoted fraction of the price, or $0.0001. And to avoid extremely small decimals, we can express this in something akin to basis points called "pips" in currency markets ($0.0001 = 1 pip). Suppose the payment will occur in 181 days and the money interest rate is 4 percent per annum as before; then the PV01 is 0.9803 pips. The minimum price fluctuation on the futures contract is one pip, and the size of the futures contract is C$100,000. So,

$$N = -\left(\frac{0.9803}{1}\right)\left(\frac{-C\$100,000,000}{C\$100,000}\right) = 980$$

We go long 980 futures contracts. Notice that $Q = -C\$100,000,000$ because the underlying position is *short*. With the negative in the hedge ratio definition, this ensures our futures position will be properly *long*.

The hedge in this example is the same size as the PV-adjusted or tailed one-for-one hedge ratio seen earlier using the same example. This should not surprise you at all. Both the exposure being hedged and the hedge instrument are linear in the underlying price, and delta thus is constant. The relation between a quantity hedge and delta hedge thus does not change over time.

### Slippage

For exposures that are linear in the underlying price, delta hedging is not that different from principal- or quantity-matched hedging. As such, both will be subject to slippage unless periodically rebalanced.

For exposures with a delta that depends on the level of the underlying price, the delta hedging approach has slightly less slippage. (Remember that we call this sort of risk *gamma* or *convexity* risk.) Delta hedging protects the underlying exposure from only *small* changes in the underlying price. If large changes occur, we get slippage in the hedge that increases with the size of the price change. The reason the delta hedge is a bit better than the principal-matched hedge is that at least we *start* in the right place. When the delta hedge is initiated, the position is in fact insulated from the risk of small price changes, whereas the principal-matched hedge may slip from the outset because it is not adjusted to current price levels.

## HEDGING THE SENSITIVITY OF AN EXPOSURE TO CHANGES IN MULTIPLE RISK FACTORS

A limitation of delta hedging is that it protects the value of a position from small changes in a single underlying price, but *only* to changes in that price.

What do we do if the position is sensitive to shifts in multiple underlying variables, such as the whole term structure of futures prices, price and price volatility, and the like?

Let the value of the position to be hedged $U$ now depend not merely on a single price but on a vector of $M$ state variables denoted **s**. We can express the change in the value of the position as a function of a small change in the state variables $\Delta$**s** using a Taylor series expansion:

$$\Delta U = U(\mathbf{s} + \Delta \mathbf{s}) - U(\mathbf{s}) \approx \sum_{j=1}^{M} \sum_{k=1}^{\infty} \frac{1}{k!} \frac{\partial^k U}{\partial s_j^k} (\Delta s_j)^k \qquad (14.27)$$

Suppose, for example, that some underlying exposure to be hedged is affected by changes in an underlying price $P$, the rate of change in the sensitivity of the position to small price changes (gamma), the volatility of price changes $\sigma$, the interest rate $r$, and the real own rate of interest on the asset $x$. We can express the sensitivity of the position to a small change in each of the underlying variables using a Taylor series expansion (from which we now drop any higher-order terms that do not correspond to an explicit source of risk):

$$\partial U \approx \frac{\partial U}{\partial P} \partial P + \frac{1}{2} \frac{\partial^2 U}{\partial P^2} (\partial P)^2 + \frac{\partial U}{\partial \sigma} \partial \sigma + \frac{\partial U}{\partial r} \partial r + \frac{\partial U}{\partial x} \partial x \qquad (14.28)$$

This is, of course, the familiar expression you have seen in prior courses for expressing the sensitivity of an option contract or portfolio to small changes in the underlying risk factors affecting the value of the position; thus it can be written in terms of the option Greeks:[4]

$$\partial U \approx \Delta_u \partial P + \frac{1}{2} \Gamma_u (\partial P)^2 + \kappa_u \partial \sigma + \rho_u \partial r + \frac{\partial U}{\partial x} \partial x \qquad (14.29)$$

Equating $\partial U$ to $\partial H$ is essentially the same as delta hedging in principle. In practice, the important difference is that we now need multiple derivatives. To hedge an exposure against changes in $M$ state variables, we generally need $M - 1$ different risk transfer contracts. We can solve for the hedge ratios on each of these contracts as a set of solutions to a system of simultaneous equations, each of which equates to zero the change in the value of the portfolio owing to a single source of risk. See Zimmermann (2002).

Suppose we are interested in hedging an underlying exposure against the risk of changes in the underlying price *and* changes in its delta. We thus want to hedge the portfolio in terms of both delta and gamma. Specifically, consider an electric utility that owns a generator that is never needed to satisfy its own local baseload or peaking demand. The generator can be turned on at no fixed cost, and power can be generated at the marginal cost of $K$ per megawatt hour (MWh). The generator is thus equivalent to a long option on power struck at $K$.

Even though we are not currently using the generator, the value of the generator is susceptible to changes in the price of electricity. If the utility adopts a hedging mandate of reducing the sensitivity of the value of the generator to power price fluctuations, the firm will need to hedge the generator viewed as a long call in both delta and gamma terms. The objective is for the combined generator and hedge portfolio to be both delta and gamma neutral—that is, $\partial V/\partial P = 0$ and $\partial^2 V/\partial P^2 = 0$ if $V$ is the value of the generator plus the hedge transactions.

With two risks, we know we need two hedging contracts. And because one of those risks we want to hedge is gamma, we know at least one of our hedge instruments needs to have a nonzero gamma. Because forwards have a constant delta, they have a zero gamma. Although we can use an electricity forward to hedge the delta component of our risk, we also need an option on electricity (or power forwards) to hedge the generator/call. Specifically, let $Z_1$ denote the amount of power we want to buy or sell using short-dated forwards, and let $Z_2$ denote the amount of power we want underlying the power option. Then let $Q$ denote the underlying position we want to hedge—the capacity of the generator (viewed as an option). To keep things clear, let's work with everything on a per-MWh basis and normalize $Q = 1$.

We have two equations—delta neutrality and gamma neutrality—and two unknowns—$Z_1$ and $Z_2$:

$$
\begin{aligned}
Z_1\Delta_1 + Z_2\Delta_2 + Q\Delta_u &= 0 \\
Z_1\Gamma_1 + Z_2\Gamma_2 + Q\Gamma_u &= 0
\end{aligned}
\tag{14.30}
$$

For example, suppose we estimate (using either numerical or analytical methods) the delta of the generator as 0.55 and the delta of the option we are using to hedge as 0.75. Suppose further that the gamma of the generator is 0.02 and the gamma of the option we are using to hedge is .015. We know that the delta of the forward is one in absolute value and its gamma zero. Substituting these numbers into equation (14.30), we have

$$
\begin{aligned}
Z_1 + Z_2(0.75) + 0.55 &= 0 \\
Z_2(0.015) + 0.02 &= 0
\end{aligned}
$$

Solving, we get $Z_1 = -1.55$ and $Z_2 = -1.33$. So, we can insulate the value of the power generation asset from both small and large swings in electricity prices by going short 1.55 electricity forward contracts and writing 1.33 electricity options for every MWh of capacity in the generator being hedged.

## VARIANCE-MINIMIZING HEDGE RATIOS

The sensitivity-matching approach to hedging has the virtue of being relatively robust and practical, but it has the drawback of working for only very small changes in the risk factors being hedged. One of the most popular alternatives to sensitivity matching is variance minimization. Like sensitivity matching, the process of identifying a hedge that minimizes the variance of the change in the value of an exposure over a certain period of time can also be applied to hedging changes in earnings or profits, as well.

### A Simple Value Hedge

We start as before by expressing the current value of a portfolio consisting of the exposure to be hedged $U$ and the hedge $H$, each represented by quantities $Q$ and $Z$, respectively, just as before. The value of the hedged position is:

$$V = QU + ZH \tag{14.31}$$

We can now express the *change* in value of the portfolio given in equation (14.31) over a discrete time period from $t$ to $t + 1$ as:

$$\Delta V = Q\Delta U + Z\Delta H \equiv Q(U_{t+1} - U_t) + Z(H_{t+1} - H_t) \tag{14.32}$$

Now let us examine the *variance* of per-period changes in the value of the hedged portfolio as given in (14.32):

$$\sigma_{\Delta V}^2 = Q^2 \sigma_{\Delta U}^2 + Z^2 \sigma_{\Delta H}^2 + 2QZ\sigma_{\Delta U \Delta H} \tag{14.33}$$

where $\sigma_{\Delta U \Delta H}$ is the covariance between changes in the values of the underlying exposure and the hedge.

To get the hedge that minimizes the variance of changes in the value of the combined position, we just partially differentiate the variance of the combined position with respect to the size of the hedge $Z$ and set the first-order condition to zero:

$$\frac{\partial \sigma_{\Delta V}^2}{\partial Z} = 2Z\sigma_{\Delta H}^2 + 2Q\sigma_{\Delta U\Delta H} = 0 \qquad (14.33)$$

$$\Rightarrow h = \frac{\sigma_{\Delta U\Delta H}}{\sigma_{\Delta H}^2}$$

where $h = -Z/Q$ as before.

The variance-minimizing hedge ratio shown in equation (14.33) also has a very nice feature. By definition,

$$h = \frac{\sigma_{\Delta U\Delta H}}{\sigma_{\Delta H}^2} = \beta_{\Delta U\Delta H}$$

where                                                                                             (14.34)

$$\Delta U = \alpha + \beta_{\Delta U\Delta H}\Delta H + \varepsilon$$

In other words, a least squares regression of changes in the value of the underlying exposure on changes in the value of the hedge product yields a beta coefficient estimate that is the same (at least in principle) as the variance-matching hedge ratio.

We still need to adjust the hedge ratio for the size of the underlying exposure. If we can customize the hedge, this is straightforward. Suppose, for example, we regress changes in the U.S. dollar value of a Hong Kong dollar–denominated business line of a U.S. firm on changes in U.S. dollar forward price of Hong Kong dollars and get a regression coefficient of 0.98. That means that every one-dollar increase in the forward price of the Hong Kong dollar is associated with a 98-cent increase in the value of the profits on the business line. If the firm expects to repatriate HKD100 million and wants to hedge the risk of USD/HKD changes in order to minimize the variance of U.S. dollar profits arising from exchange rate risk, the firm would sell a HKD98 million forward.

When hedging with futures, we need to convert this amount into a contract equivalent. We also may need to tail the hedge ratio to adjust for the present value mismatch between immediate cash flows on the futures and the payoff on the underlying at some time $T$. In general, we compute $N$ as follows:

$$N = \left(\frac{Q}{Y}\right)\left(\frac{h}{1 + \left(\frac{d_{t,T}}{DCB}\right)r_{t,T}}\right) \qquad (14.35)$$

If the size of a Hong Kong dollar futures contract is HKD1 million, for example, we would need:

$$\left( \frac{\text{HKD100,000,000}}{\text{HKD1,000,000}} \right) 0.98 = 98$$

or 98 futures without any present value adjustment.[5] If the same hedge is being used to hedge a receivable a year away and the money rate is 4 percent, then:

$$\left( \frac{\text{HKD100,000,000}}{\text{HKD1,000,000}} \right)\left( \frac{0.98}{1 + (365/360)0.04} \right) = 94$$

Note that we keep things in absolute values in this example. In fact, the hedge ratio is –.98 and the resulting hedge is short. It just so happens that we run the regression of dollar revenues on the exchange rate, which is tantamount to regressing a long HKD position on another long HKD position. Generally we would do the reverse, but in this case it is just as easy to simply recognize that we should be short.

## Hedging Profits under Price and Quantity Risk

We asserted that the preceding analysis is perfectly general and can also be applied to profits or earnings. Let's quickly convince ourselves of that. And while we're at it, let's see how this hedge ratio calculation method can *also* be used to capture correlated price and quantity risks.

Suppose we consider a chocolate bar producer that buys $Q_t$ metric tons of cocoa that is used to make and sell $\lambda Q_t$ chocolate bars in the same quarter at price $p_t$ per bar. The producer buys cocoa on the spot market each quarter at price $S_t$ per metric ton. Without hedging, the economic profits per quarter for the producer are:

$$\Pi_t = Q_t(\lambda p_t - S_t) \tag{14.36}$$

Now suppose the producer considers a forward hedge of its next-period profits consisting of $Z_t$ metric tons of cocoa purchased at the current one-period forward price. The hedged profits of the producer then are:

$$\Pi_{t+1} + Z_t(S_{t+1} - f_{t,t+1}) \tag{14.37}$$

Specifically, the producer wants to find the amount $Z_t$ that must be purchased forward in order to minimize the variance of next period's profits.

Profits may be affected by shocks to the price of chocolate bars, to the quantity of cocoa purchased, or to the price of cocoa. All these variables can increase the volatility of profits, and the covariances between these variables can either exacerbate or mitigate that volatility. But because we are hedging with a forward contract whose quantity is fixed, we can take into account *only* the cocoa price and how it covaries with the chocolate bar price, quantity sold, and cocoa purchasing costs. We need not look at the individual components, however, as the analysis in the foregoing section suggests.

Specifically, let us write the variance of quarterly profits as:

$$\sigma_\Pi^2 + Z^2 \sigma_s^2 + 2Z\sigma_{\Pi s} \qquad (14.38)$$

The variance-minimizing forward hedge thus will involve the forward purchase/sale of:

$$Z = -\frac{\sigma_{\Pi s}}{\sigma_s^2} \qquad (14.39)$$

We can calculate the size of the hedge using either the actual variances and covariances from time series data, or we can regress historical profits (as defined earlier) on the price of cocoa.

Recall from our discussion in Chapter 12 that when quantity and price are both variable, the right hedge may be either short *or* long. It depends entirely on the correlation between quantity and price. Fortunately, the variance-minimizing hedge ratio incorporates this correlation and thus provides us with the "right" answer.

Like virtually all of the hedge ratios we have discussed, however, variance-minimizing hedge ratios are notoriously unstable over time and thus must regularly be reestimated, perhaps leading to position rebalancing. The more frequently rebalancings are anticipated, the better off we may be implementing this type of hedge *using futures contracts* because of the ease with which we can get in and out of futures vis-à-vis comparable forwards. Even then, that may not be enough. As we shall now see, other changes to the basic model are quite often required to make this hedging technique useful.

## Conditional Variance Models

If variance minimization is the right hedging objective, variance-minimizing hedging seems to be the right solution to the hedging problem. Unfortunately, the proper implementation of variance-minimizing hedges can be a real challenge for two main reasons. First, the quality of the hedge ratio depends on the quality of the estimation method used to calculate the terms of the hedge ratio. Whether the required variances and covariances are computed explicitly or in a regression framework, measurement error can be severe.

Perhaps more problematic is the tendency for variances and covariances to change over time. Sometimes these changes are predictable or related to other observed market factors (e.g., very steep futures price term structures are associated with higher price volatility), but sometimes the changes can be completely driven by unforeseen structural phenomena (e.g., a shift in OPEC policy that hits the oil market hard). Yet, in an almost self-contradictory fashion, the traditional variance-minimizing hedge ratio discussed in the prior section used *unconditional* variance/volatility and covariance estimates obtained from OLS regression. The appeal of these hedge ratios, after all, is their capacity to capture hedge-changing market dynamics, so what sense does it make to use an estimation method that ignores precisely those dynamics in which we may be interested?

This is more a problem of statistics than economics, and it is a solvable one. If we want to incorporate time-varying volatility and covariances into our variance-minimizing hedge ratio estimates, we can look to employ one of the family of autoregressive conditional heteroskedasticity (ARCH) models developed by Engle (1982) and others. We already saw an elementary GARCH model earlier in the chapter when we looked at various definitions of volatility. And indeed, all we are really doing here is using statistics together with the properties of our time series data to improve our hedge ratios with better volatility numbers.

We begin by running what is known as an "error correction" model in which we regress the change in the value of the underlying exposure and the change in the value of the hedge contract on $M$ lagged values of both changes in the values of the underlying and the hedge:[6]

$$\Delta \ln U_t = \alpha_s + \sum_{j=1}^{M} \beta_{j,u} \Delta \ln U_{t-j} + \sum_{j=1}^{M} \gamma_{j,u} \Delta \ln H_{t-j} + \varepsilon_{t,u}$$

$$(14.40a)$$

$$\Delta \ln H_t = \alpha_s + \sum_{j=1}^{M} \beta_{j,h} \Delta \ln U_{t-j} + \sum_{j=1}^{M} \gamma_{j,h} \Delta \ln H_{t-j} + \varepsilon_{t,h}$$

We then define the conditional variances of the underlying and hedge instruments at any time $t$, as well as the conditional time $t$ covariance between the two. In this case, we will use a GARCH($m,n$) representation of the type we saw in equation (13.5), and, to keep the math simple, we will assume $m = n = 1$ so that we have a bivariate GARCH(1,1) model of the conditional variances of $U$ and $H$ and the conditional covariance between the two:

$$s_{u,t}^2 = \alpha_u + \delta_u s_{u,t-1}^2 + \lambda_u \varepsilon_{u,t-1}^2$$

$$s_{h,t}^2 = \alpha_h + \delta_h s_{h,t-1}^2 + \lambda_h \varepsilon_{h,t-1}^2 \qquad (14.40b)$$

$$s_{uh,t} = \alpha_{uh} + \delta_{uh} s_{uh,t-1} + \lambda_{uh} \varepsilon_{u,t-1} \varepsilon_{h,t-1}$$

If we assume the hedge and underlying have payoffs that occur at the same time, maximum likelihood estimation of (14.40) gives us what we need to solve for the conditional variance-minimizing hedge ratio:

$$h = \frac{s_{uh,t}}{s_{h,t}^2} \qquad (14.41)$$

from which we can compute the size of the OTC hedge. If we use this for a futures hedge, we need to remember to add the PV adjustment or tail.

## Incorporating Shifts in the Term Structure

Ng and Pirrong (1994) and Pirrong (1997) propose yet another improvement in the estimation methodology used to determine variance-minimizing hedge ratios. This method is especially useful for commodities with highly volatile own rates of interest. Unlike the previous section which mainly improves estimation by better taking into account the statistical properties of many financial time series, the adjustment discussed here also incorporates useful *economic* information into the hedge ratio. This backwardation-adjusted GARCH (BAG) hedge ratio not only incorporates time-varying volatility via the GARCH technique discussed in the prior section, but also reflects some of the empirical realities of forward and futures markets arising from the cost of carry model and the term structure of forward prices (see Chapters 8 through 10).

The cost of carry model has some important predictions for the behavior of market prices that can potentially provide significant additional information to would-be hedgers. We discuss most of these in Chapters 8 and 9, but it may be useful to summarize five of these empirical implications of the cost-of-carry model here:[7]

1. Spot and forward prices are more volatile for higher levels of the convenience yield.

2. The volatility of changes in spot prices rises relative to the volatility of changes in forward purchase prices as the convenience yield increases.
3. As the convenience yield rises, changes in spot and forward prices become less correlated at an increasing rate.
4. The variance of the calendar basis increases as the convenience yield rises.
5. When inventories are low and the convenience yield is high, spot prices move more than forward purchase prices in response to a given shock to demand or supply.

In order to implement the BAG hedge ratio estimation method, we need some measure of the equilibrium convenience yield reflected in a forward price at any given time. We can back this out using observed data, but the result is sensitive to our specification of the cost of carry model. Empirically, it has been common to use the continuously compounded version of the model for this purpose, so that we can define the instantaneous convenience yield prevailing for the period from $t$ to $T$ as:

$$q_t = c + r - l - \frac{\ln(f_{t,T}) - \ln(S_t)}{T - t} \tag{14.42}$$

We can then modify the system of equations shown in the last section to add the convenience yield to each equation as follows:

$$\Delta \ln U_t = \alpha_s + \sum_{j=1}^{M} \beta_{j,u} \Delta \ln U_{t-j} + \sum_{j=1}^{M} \gamma_{j,u} \Delta \ln H_{t-j} + \mu_u q_{t-1} + \varepsilon_{t,u}$$

$$\Delta \ln H_t = \alpha_s + \sum_{j=1}^{M} \beta_{j,h} \Delta \ln U_{t-j} + \sum_{j=1}^{M} \gamma_{j,h} \Delta \ln H_{t-j} + \mu_h q_{t-1} + \varepsilon_{t,h}$$

$$s_{u,t}^2 = \alpha_u + \delta_u s_{u,t-1}^2 + \lambda_u \varepsilon_{u,t-1}^2 + \phi_u q_{t-1}^2 \tag{14.43}$$

$$s_{h,t}^2 = \alpha_h + \delta_h s_{h,t-1}^2 + \lambda_h \varepsilon_{h,t-1}^2 + \phi_h q_{t-1}^2$$

$$s_{uh,t} = \rho \sqrt{s_{u,t} s_{h,t}} + \vartheta q_{t-1}^2$$

The parameters in the system of equations in (14.43) can be estimated using maximum likelihood. The BAG hedge ratio then takes the usual form:

$$h = -\frac{s_{uh,t}}{s_{h,t}^2} \tag{14.44}$$

Although BAG can be a very useful estimation methodology to add precision in computing variance-minimizing hedge ratios and is well-founded in the theory we have developed thus far in this book, it is important to remember that it is *only* an estimation methodology. No matter how much time we spend refining our calculations, we still face the operational difficulties and transaction costs of rebalancing, the need to pair the right hedge ratio with the right hedging mandate, and the need to monitor the effectiveness of the hedge on an ongoing basis.

## A WARNING ABOUT "OPTIMAL" HEDGE RATIOS AND MODEL RISK

There is an old saying that a perfect hedge can be found only in a well-tended garden. We discuss in Chapters 15 and 16 some of the issues associated with *imperfect* hedging—namely, basis risk, which is ignored altogether in this chapter. But before leaving this chapter and turning to that discussion, it is worth a moment of our time to consider what role expectations and information have in hedging.

Remember that we have been discussing *risk* in this section, not uncertainty. As a result, we have simply assumed that information is basically symmetric across hedgers and their risk transfer counterparties—or, if it is not, that the asymmetry is not substantial enough to give rise to a perceived comparative advantage on one side of the trade. Certainly we do not *need* informational asymmetries to motivate many types of hedging. As we discussed in Chapter 3 and again in Chapter 12, the Keynesian view of risk transfer is that one firm seeks to shift a risk to a specialist in risk bearing or financial intermediation.

Equally true is that informational asymmetries and differences in expectations are not required to explain why some firms opt for forward-based derivative solutions and others opt for option-based solutions. The former involve no up-front cost but can generate losses for the hedger; the latter require payment of an up-front premium but are limited liability. Yet, as we have seen in this chapter, the choice of instrument may have more to do with the nature of the exposure being hedged than with either cost or whether a firm is "strongly" or "mildly" bullish or bearish.

Nevertheless, our exploration of hedging would not be complete—nor consistent with numerous surveys of derivatives users—if we did not admit that different expectations can play an important role in the hedging decision. It is impossible not to recognize that a firm whose entire management has a strong view that interest rates cannot move much lower but could easily increase is more likely to seek protection on the upside than the downside of rates. Similarly, what about the coffee producer that is so convinced of a collapse in coffee prices that it does *not* hedge its coffee purchases?

As explained in Chapters 1 and 2, the focus in this book is very much on the *firm*. Nevertheless, a large amount of the hedging literature—and practice—still adopts the perspective of an *individual trader*. And in that world, a trade is either "speculative" or "hedge" with very little gray area in between. But for firms, the wide range of reasons that hedging can make sense also gives rise to a wide range of hedging strategies, not all of which can be viewed in the clean and neat world of "hedge" versus "speculation."

Especially in the family of variance-minimization models, there is a tendency even to decompose a single trade into a "hedge component" and a "speculative component." This traces to the early hedging models of Johnson (1960), Stein (1961), and Ederington (1979). And since then, the number of different models of "optimal hedging" intended to tweak the hedging problem in some way is too large to count—and certainly too large to survey here. But most of these models share a common framework: They consider how a risk-averse individual with a concave utility function approaches the hedging decision. And they conclude that being overhedged or underhedged relative to the optimal hedge ratio is speculation!

To take a concrete example, suppose we regress changes in the spot price of cotton on the cotton futures price and estimate a hedge ratio of 0.78. Every cotton bale that a producer sells thus should be hedged with 0.78 futures contracts—and tailed or PV-adjusted, as well. If we happen upon a cotton ginner with an inventory of 1,000 bales to sell that is hedging with 500 long futures contracts, most models will tell us that the ginner is a net speculator to the tune of 280 futures contracts. By hedging 280 lots less than the optimal hedge ratio, the ginner must be taking a bet!

Yet, there is a long distance between choosing a different hedge ratio than implied by a highly stylized model and outright speculation. And as Culp and Miller (1995a) strongly caution, to presume that the *model* is right and the *hedger* is either openly speculating or just plain wrong is quite a leap of faith in favor of financial modeling. Perhaps a more reasonable question would be to ask what variables the *model* omitted and make our leap of faith toward the actual observed behavior of the hedgers.

## NOTES

1. The futures price almost certainly will not equal the forward price, but we use the same number to keep the example clean. For explanations of the difference between futures and forward prices, see Cox, Ingersoll, and Ross (1981) and French (1983).
2. See Culp and Miller (1995a,b) for a practical exception to this.

3. Demand deposit accounts can be drawn at any time, so the bank must estimate the *effective* duration—usually the average repricing speed on its core deposits.
4. We have ignored time decay just to keep the example tractable.
5. There is no HK$ futures contract.
6. Five to 10 lags are plenty.
7. This is a slightly revised and reinterpreted redaction of the implications of this theory as presented in Ng and Pirrong (1994).

# CHAPTER 15

# Quality Basis Risk

**B**asis risk is the risk that the contracting structure chosen to facilitate the transfer of risk has a payoff that is not identical (but offsetting) to the risk the firm seeks to transfer. Remember from Chapter 4 that the essence of risk transfer is the combination of positions whose payoffs are negatively correlated. The lower that correlation in absolute value, the worse the hedge—the greater the basis risk.

Recall from Chapter 11 that we define the basis as the implicit price of transforming the spot price into something else—the price of the same asset for future delivery, the price of the same asset at a different location, the price of a related asset, and the like. As the phrase implies, basis risk refers to the imperfections in hedging that can arise when the transformation function applied to the spot price yields a *different exposure* than the exposure we are hedging. We explore how basis risk can impact hedging strategies in this chapter.

Our specific focus here is on *quality basis risk*, which arises when the asset underlying a derivatives transaction and from which the derivatives transaction "derives" its value is not the same as the exposure being hedged. This can result in the payoff on the derivatives transaction being an imperfect hedge of the original target payoff to be hedged. We consider here in particular the leading causes of quality basis risk, as well as the consequences of quality basis risk for hedgers. We also consider some solutions to quality basis risk problems. In many cases, quality basis risk can be addressed through hedge design—for example, better hedge ratios or alternative derivatives products. In other cases, it is simply part of the cost of risk transfer and should be factored in as such before a firm determines that hedging makes sense.

## IMPERFECT SUBSTITUTES

The first type of quality basis risk we consider here is the risk arising from using one asset (or a derivatives contract based on that asset) to hedge a different asset when the two assets are imperfect substitutes for one another. This risk is perhaps best illustrated by example.

## Hedge Involving Imperfectly Substitutable Assets

Suppose in particular we consider a hypothetical firm Copacabana, a Brazilian coffee exporter. Copacabana agrees on June 2, 2003, to sell 10,000 bags (60 net kilograms each) of type six "good cup" pure Arabica green coffee beans to Kestlé in a traditional forward contract. Kestlé will take delivery from Copacabana in Santos (the large port city near São Paulo) the day after the March 2004 futures contract expires. The contract expires March 23, 2004, so delivery will occur on March 24, 2004. Kestlé and Copacabana agree to a forward purchase price on June 2, 2003, of $f_{t,t+296}$ per bag. The subscripts denote calendar days relative to trade date $t$ (June 2, 2003) so $t+296$ is the delivery date (March 24, 2003, which is 296 days after the trade date).

Further suppose that Copacabana is worried about the weather this year. The firm can honor the physical delivery with its own harvest, but managers are concerned that bad weather could precipitate a major price increase over the life of the forward sale agreement to Kestlé. Its shareholders would question why Copacabana sold to Kestlé at such a low price in such a bull market, so Copacabana decides to hedge its profits with a one-for-one hedge using a cash-settled forward contract.

Unfortunately for Copacabana, a forward contract cannot be negotiated on type six or better good cup Arabica coffee. (We explore some reasons for this shortly.) Instead, Copacabana must enter into a forward on a coffee with a slightly lower quality grade than type six. We denote the spot price of this new grade of coffee underlying the forward hedge as $S_t^b$ for any time $t$, and the forward purchase price is $f_{t,t+296}^b$. Copacabana's hedged net profit on March 24, 2004, thus will be

$$600,000(f_{t,t+296} - S_{t+296}) + 600,000(S_{t+296}^b - f_{t,t+296}^b) \qquad (15.1)$$

or

$$600,000[(f_{t,t+296} - f_{t,t+296}^b) + (S_{t+296}^b - S_{t+296})] \qquad (15.1)'$$

Looking at equation (15.1)', the first term represents the hedged margin. This will represent the difference in the actual price at which Copacabana is selling coffee to Kestlé and the forward purchase price for the asset underlying the hedge. Whatever the first term, it is locked in as of June 2 when the hedge is put on.

Quality basis risk in this example arises from the fact that the underlyings of the two contracts are not exactly the same and thus have different prices. Specifically, the variance of profits on March 24, 2004, will be

$$600,000^2 (\sigma_h^2 + \sigma_u^2 - 2\sigma_{uh}) = 600,000^2 (\sigma_h^2 + \sigma_u^2 - 2\rho_{uh}\sigma_u\sigma_h) \quad (15.2)$$

where $\sigma_h^2$ and $\sigma_u^2$ represent the variances of the spot prices of coffee underlying the hedge and to be sold to Kestlé, respectively. The variables $\rho_{uh}$ and $\sigma_{uh}$ represent the correlation and covariances in the prices of the two coffee grades, respectively. As long as the spot price of the two different types of coffee are highly correlated, the variance will be small. (You can see that the variance of profits is zero if the two coffee prices are perfectly correlated.)

A variance-minimizing hedge ratio might help address this problem a bit. Rewriting equation (15.1) with an unknown quantity to be purchase forward Z, we can express profits as:

$$600,000(f_{t,t+296} - S_{t+296}) + Z(S_{t+296}^h - f_{t,t+296}^h) \quad (15.3)$$

The variance of profits shown in (15.3) then becomes:

$$600,000^2 \sigma_u^2 + Z^2 \sigma_h^2 - 1,200,000Z\sigma_{uh} \quad (15.4)$$

so that the variance-minimizing hedge is:

$$Z^* = 600,000 \left( \frac{\sigma_{uh}}{\sigma_h^2} \right) \quad (15.5)$$

In this particular example, however, variance reduction may not be the best hedging mandate—at least not on its own. Indeed, the term *basis risk* is a little misleading here because the "risk" to Copacabana comes from imperfect correlation in the spot price levels, not changes in the basis. Because the firm sold coffee forward and hedged with a forward, the true basis was locked in on June 2, 2003. The lack of variation over the life of the hedge in the basis does not mean, however, that the basis was the same in the two forward contracts. If the two coffee grades are significantly different, it is quite possible that not only are the spot prices different but that the own rates of interest are also different. Copacabana must absorb that difference as a cost if the own rate of interest is higher on the coffee it plans to deliver than the own rate on the coffee underlying the hedge.

Put in the same language we used in earlier chapters, Copacabana is selling type six good cup Arabica coffee to Kestlé in the future, but, as always, Kestlé is reimbursing Copacabana for the net cost of carry through the forward price as the long always does. Conversely, Copacabana is bearing the cost of carry of the lower-grade coffee it has purchased forward in its hedge. Even though the hedge is cash-settled, the forward price still reflects the true equilibrium own rate for that lower coffee grade. If the cost of carrying the lower-quality beans exceeds the cost of carrying the type six Arabica, Copacabana's profit margin will shrink.

This is also a good reminder that the hedge mandate is important. If Copacabana's managers are instructed to evaluate the quality of their hedging program purely in terms of the variance of profits, the hedge might be decent if the two grades of coffee have highly correlated spot prices. But if, say, the liquidity premium on type six Arabica beans is high relative to the lesser-quality beans, the own rate on Arabica beans will be higher than the lower grade and Copacabana's profit *level* will be eroded.

A "good hedge" in the sense of variance reduction may thus fail to meet a minimum profitability threshold test. Does this mean we should not use a variance-minimizing hedge ratio? Not necessarily. What it means is that we need to choose our hedging mandates carefully. In this case, we would almost certainly want a minimum profit margin constraint added. If the variance-minimizing hedge ratio can pass that test, fine. But if not, then Copacabana may be better off not hedging. What good is variance reduction on its own, after all, if it merely reduces the volatility of an operating *loss* for the firm?

## Why Ever Hedge with Imperfect Substitutes?

Deliberately hedging an exposure with a contract that is based on an imperfect substitute for the exposure being hedged may seem like a strange and potentially risky way to accomplish risk transfer. Nevertheless, the practical realities of the market often leave market participants with no choice for the simple reason that it is prohibitively expensive to define a derivatives transaction for every conceivable variation imaginable. In addition, some market participants hedge with imperfect substitutes deliberately.

### Costly Contracting and Limited Hedging Alternatives

Because exchange-traded derivatives are standardized and are costly for exchanges to list, it does not take much explanation or thinking to recognize why exchange-traded derivatives do not exist for every asset. That is discussed a bit in Chapter 5 when considering what assets are good candidates for futures.

OTC derivatives, however, can be fully customized to cover virtually any underlying asset, liability, payoff, or risk exposure on which the hedger and counterparty can agree. In theory, there is no reason for a firm ever to encounter quality basis risk in OTC derivatives hedging. In practice, however, a number of different factors can lead to a situation in which a hedger is unable at any reasonable cost to enter into a contract based on exactly the exposure being hedged.

Cost is the key consideration. With no transaction costs, a swap dealer would probably engage in any transaction a hedger proposes. But transaction costs are *not* zero. In that connection, consider some of the reasons that a hedger might not be able to negotiate a derivatives contract whose underlying asset is exactly the asset to be hedged or whose payoff is perfectly correlated with the exposure to be hedged:

- The cost to the swap dealer of identifying an offsetting counterparty or of hedging the transaction is prohibitive.
- The dealer and hedger cannot agree on a measure of price of the asset or exposure that will govern the cash flows on the derivatives agreement.
- The dealer does not have the capability to make or take physical deliveries at the location the hedger desires.
- The asset or exposure is influenced by noncompetitive supply considerations beyond the dealer's control.

A hedger searching for a derivatives contract with no basis risk can, of course, hope to identify a speculator to take the other side of the transaction. The aforementioned issues would not encumber a speculator, after all. But returning to our discussion in Chapter 12, the speculator would either demand a significant risk premium for agreeing to a risk transfer by the hedger or would need to have a market view countervailing the hedger's. Perhaps some hedgers can occasionally get lucky in finding the latter just when they need to, but it is not often the case.

In the end, swap dealing is a business, and although one virtue of OTC derivatives is their flexibility, dealers still prefer to focus on products that can be offered to more than one participant. The more exotic and customized the exposure to be hedged, the less likely it is that a counterparty can be found willing to negotiate at a fair price.

None of the above really applies to our example, though. High-grade Arabica coffee is the standard deliverable grade for many commercial coffee transactions and for coffee derivatives. High-quality Arabica beans are plentiful in supply, readily available, and regularly traded both in cash and derivatives markets, and even have a listed futures contract. It is very conceivable that a firm would have trouble finding a willing counterparty to a forward on a *low-grade* coffee, but not on Arabica.

Perhaps the reason Copacabana cannot hedge using the right product is simply that Copacabana has reached its maximum permissible credit limits with the major coffee swap dealers. As a result, no one active in the high-quality Arabica market is *able* to trade with Copacabana, even with substantial collateral posted. So, Copacabana is forced to look for smaller local counterparties, which, as it happens, may be willing to deal only in forwards based on lower-grade coffee beans.

### Cross Hedging

The practice of "cross hedging" involves the deliberate use of an imperfect substitute to hedge an underlying position. More often than not, a better alternative is available and is not chosen. The two common explanations for cross hedging are either to hide speculation or to try to reduce hedging costs.

Let's begin with the cynical interpretation. The term *cross hedge* is often a misnomer and an excuse for speculation. Consider, for example, a U.S. dollar–based portfolio manager of Canadian equities with a mandate to hedge the Canadian dollar/U.S. dollar exchange rate risk. Suppose a defined-benefit pension plan sponsor invested with this manager notices on a performance report that the manager is strongly short the South African rand against the U.S. dollar. When the pension plan inquires, the portfolio manager may claim she was "cross hedging" USD/CAD exchange rate risk with a rand/dollar derivatives contract. Her justification is that the historical correlation between changes in the USD/CAD rate and USD/SAR rate are strong. Another popular way to describe this is "hedging into" the SAR.

This is a case where common sense should take precedence over a regression. What economic tie is there between South Africa and Canada to justify such a cross hedge? How stable is the historical correlation given the almost arbitrary nature of the hedge? The pension plan manager must listen closely for good answers to these and other related questions. This cross hedge is extremely risky, and may not protect the pension plan against USD/CAD fluctuations in CAD-denominated equities. At the same time, it *exposes* the plan to USD/SAR risk as a *new* risk.

Sometimes, however, cross hedging can be well-intended and predicated on the desire for cost savings. It is an especially common practice in so-called "fixed exchange rate regimes" for currencies. The Hong Kong dollar has been linked to the U.S. dollar at the official rate of HKD7.8 = USD1 since 1983. For most of this period, the mechanism used to enforce the fixed rate has been a credible one (Culp and Hanke, 1995; Culp, Hanke, and Miller, 1999). As a result, many firms have hedged HKD positions using USD derivatives. And for the most part, the hedges have worked pretty well.

In contrast, the Exchange Rate Mechanism (ERM) of the European Monetary System was not a particularly credible regime (Culp, 1989, 1990a,b; Culp and James, 1989; Walters, 1990; Connolly, 1995). On "Black Wednesday"—September 16, 1992—the British pound and Italian lira devalued by over 30 percent against the Deutsche mark, to which both had been tied—in the case of Britain only briefly. In short, an unsustainable exchange rate regime linked Europe's currencies together in a delicate and kludgy system where nations were required to "defend their currencies" against devaluation and revaluations outside of prescribed bands. This was very different from the Hong Kong system and ultimately unsustainable.

Unfortunately, many people bought into the illusion of stability created by the ERM—so much so, in fact, that they deemed the exchange rate link/target between the pound and D-mark and the lira and D-mark to be immutable and indestructible. And as it happened at the time, some firms could achieve a cost savings by hedging sterling or lira positions with D-marks because of the relative shapes of the term structures of forward prices. This cross hedging was, of course, a disaster on Black Wednesday. When the sterling and lira literally fell out of bed, the D-mark hedges of sterling and lira positions became worse than worthless. Firms lost untold millions, and cross hedgers—in some cases a few of the top U.S. investment banks—learned an important lesson about cross hedging.

In summary, if a perfect substitute is available for hedging, a firm has an uphill battle in arguing why it should not be used—unless the objective is actually to trade or take on quality basis risk. One could argue, in fact, that successful cross hedging stories such as the HKD/USD are successes because the two currencies *really are perfect substitutes!* Occasionally, cross hedging does make sense and is indeed the right hedging solution, but a firm should use care to evaluate whether it is destined to be one of the few exceptions or one of the unfortunately numerous examples of the fallacy of cross hedging.

## TRANSPORTATION AND DISTRIBUTION BASIS RISK

Another type of quality basis risk arises in physical asset markets as a result of geographical disparities and unexpected changes in transportation costs. Let us consider a related example to the foregoing to illustrate the nature of geographical basis risk.

Suppose now that Copacabana and Kestlé rely on a merchant trading firm to intermediate the coffee purchase from Copacabana and resale to Kestlé at its port in Marseilles. Let's call this hypothetical firm Andermatt Fils & Cie. Andermatt owns a small fleet of ocean-going vessels that specialize in transporting soft commodities like coffee and orange juice from Latin America to Europe. Buying coffee in Brazil for resale in Switzerland is common.

In this example, suppose on March 19, 2004, Kestlé notifies that Andermatt that it would like Andermatt to purchase 10,000 bags of 60 net kilogram type six good cup Arabica green coffee beans in Santos for delivery to the Kestlé agent in Marseilles on April 30, 2004, for which Kestlé will pay Andermatt the fixed price of $f_{t,t+37}$ per kilo plus a negotiated mark-up of $T$ per kilo. The exact forward price will be computed on March 24, 2004. (Note that in contrast to the example in the prior section, we now treat March 24, 2004, as trade date $t$.) Andermatt notifies Copacabana that it would like to buy 10,000 bags of the specified coffee type at the spot price on March 24, 2004.

As is typical in trade finance, Andermatt arranges to post the coffee as collateral on a trade finance loan from the São Paulo branch of ABC Hambro Bank in the Netherlands. Funds will be available in Andermatt's account on March 24, 2004, in the exact amount of $600,000S_t$, based on whatever the posted coffee price is that day. Interest and principal are repayable to the bank's Marseilles branch on April 30, 2004, at the interest rate $r_{t,t+37}$.

In addition, Andermatt incurs lump-sum physical storage costs of $C_{t,t+37}$, which does *not* include the cost of transportation. Andermatt also earns the convenience yield and liquidity premium on the asset, expressed in April 30, 2004 dollars as $Q_{t,t+37} + L_{t,t+37}$ during the time it is shipping the coffee. Finally, denote the cost of transportation borne by Andermatt as $T_{t,t+37}$ per kilogram.

The allocation of transportation and distribution costs between buyer and seller in an international cross-border transaction is generally a part of the trading contract. *Incoterms* are standard definitions promulgated by the International Chamber of Commerce. The most popular incoterms are EXW (ex works), FOB (free on board), FCA (free on carrier), CIF (cost, insurance, and freight), DDU (delivered duty unpaid), and CPT (carriage paid to). Suppose Andermatt buys coffee from Copacabana FOB Santos and sells to Kestlé FCA Marseilles. That means that Copacabana pays all the transportation, freight, insurance, and other distribution costs to get the coffee from its warehouse into the container of Andermatt's cargo ship in Santos, whereupon Andermatt assumes the responsibility for all of those costs up to the point that Andermatt has delivered the coffee into the carrier (rail or truck) of Kestlé's choosing in Marseilles.

On April 30, 2004, Andermatt's profit is:

$$600,000[f_{t,t+37} + T - S_t(1 + r_{t,t+37}) - C_{t,t+37} + Q_{t,t+37} + L_{t,t+37} - T_{t,t+37}]$$

$$(15.8)$$

Assuming the Andermatt/Kestlé forward was at-market on date $t$, the cost of carry model can be used to rewrite equation (15.8) as:

$$600{,}000[T - T_{t,t+37} + S_t (r^b_{t,t+37} - r_{t,t+37}) + (C^b_{t,t+37} - C_{t,t+37})$$
$$- (Q^b_{t,t+37} - Q_{t,t+37}) - (L^b_{t,t+37} - L_{t,t+37})] \tag{15.8}'$$

where the $b$ superscript indicates the various terms as reflected in the at-market forward basis.

Andermatt is what we call a "logistics firm." It is not in the business of bearing outright price risk, and equation (15.8) confirms that it does not. Instead, it is in the business of transporting commodities. But if the forward price is competitive rather than set to reflect Andermatt's actual cost of carrying the coffee, then the basis risk on this transaction can be significant. If the ship sinks, breaks down, loses a refrigeration unit, encounters bad weather and must put to port, or anything else similar, the *actual price paid* by Andermatt to transport coffee may well exceed the equilibrium cost of carry reflected in the forward selling price negotiated with Kestlé.

Transportation basis risk is especially common in derivatives. Even OTC derivatives tend to have only a few authorized delivery points. The contract may allow the parties to agree mutually that delivery will occur at a point not specified, but the at-market price will reflect *authorized* delivery points. It thus will be up to the parties to negotiate a suitable markup—$T$ in equation (15.8)—to cover these additional costs. But the actual transport costs paid might be quite different from the estimated costs.

Logistics and transportation firms like Andermatt are essentially spread traders—in this case, the transportation spread. It is their business to try to operate such that their markup is more than enough to cover the outlays that are not explicitly included in the forward price, but the firms could stand to lose *a lot* if they are wrong in estimating those outlays.

## DELIVERY AND LOCATION BASIS RISK

Transportation differentials can also give rise to another type of quality basis risk that is sometimes called delivery or location basis risk. This is a form of *price risk* arising from locational pricing.

To illustrate this in the context of our previous example, suppose that Andermatt decides to buy another 5,000 bags of coffee from Copacabana and plans to sell them on the spot market in Marseilles to any interested commercial parties. Andermatt thus contacts ABC Hambro Bank and requests that the loan to be made March 24, 2004, be increased to $900{,}000S_t$. Andermatt explains what the additional amount is for.

Recall that the coffee inventory was pledged to ABC Hambro as collateral on the trade loan. If Andermatt goes bankrupt on April 15, 2004, the bank can seize the inventory and, more likely than not, can still sell the coffee to Kestlé at the prenegotiated forward price. Similarly, ABC Hambro will demand the additional 300,000 kilograms of coffee as collateral, but this time the bank will insist that Andermatt hedge the excess 300,000 kilos on its own. Because Andermatt has not identified a buyer or locked in a sale price for this extra coffee cargo, the bank is at risk to declining prices in the event Andermatt defaults.

Andermatt decides to hedge as cheaply and cleanly as possible using MAY04 Arabica coffee futures listed on the Bolsa de Mercadorias & Futuros (Brazilian Mercantile & Futures Exchange, or BM&F). Table 15.1 summarizes the important features of the contract. Note in particular that all the authorized delivery points are in Brazil.

From the Bank's standpoint, its risk is that Andermatt fails financially and the bank inherits 300,000 kilograms of coffee *in Marseilles*. At the bank's behest, Andermatt thus opts to hedge the variance of monthly changes in the cargo. Because the cargo will be sold at the Marseilles spot price for Arabica coffee, Andermatt runs the following OLS regression to get its variance-minimizing hedge ratio:

$$\Delta S = \alpha + \beta \Delta F$$

where $\Delta$ represents monthly price changes obtained from a historical time series. If the estimated beta is 0.78 and the money interest rate is 2.5 percent per annum, we can use the formula we saw in equation (14.35) and the information in Table 15.1 to compute the size of the futures hedge:

$$N = \left(\frac{300,000}{10,000}\right)\left[\frac{-0.78}{1+\left(\frac{37}{360}\right).025}\right] = -23$$

This hedge, however, could be quite risky. And in fact, a lot of banks active in the trade finance area have lost substantial sums of money in the past decade on losses associated with collateral mishedging. By hedging a *Marseilles* sale with a contract tied to a *São Paulo* price, the bank (and Andermatt) is at risk of transportation cost changes, other basis fluctuations, and a substantial difference in the spot prices as in the previous section because of the imperfect substitutability of coffee sold on the spot in Marseilles and coffee sold on the spot in Brazil. A supply glut in Marseilles, for example, could depress the price there without changing the price much in Brazil.

**TABLE 15.1** BM&F Arabica Coffee Futures

| Underlying Asset: | Green Brazilian coffee beans of the *coffea Arabica* variety, type six or better, good cup or better |
|---|---|
| *Price Quotation:* | US$ per 60 net-kg bag |
| *Tick Size:* | US$0.05 per 60 net-kg bag |
| *Contract Size:* | 100 bags, 60 net kg each |
| *Delivery Months:* | MAR, MAY, JUL, SEP, DEC |
| *Expiration:* | Sixth business day preceding the last day of the delivery month |
| *Authorized Delivery Points:* | *In the State of São Paulo:* São Paulo, Santos, Batatais, Espírito Santo do Pinhal, Franca, Garça, São José do Rio Pardo, Leme<br>*In the State of Paraná:* Londrina, Rolândia<br>*In the State of Minas Gerais:* Andradas, Elói Mendes, Araguari, Patrocínio, Machado, Varginha, Guaxupé, Poços de Caldas, Piumhi, Ouro Fina, São Sebastião do Paraíso, Três Corações, Campos Altos, São Gotardo, Manhuaçu, Carmo do Paranaíba, Monte Carmelo<br>*In the State of Bahia:* Vitória da Conquista e Luiz Eduardo Magalhães |
| *Delivery Terms:* | FOB in the city of São Paulo—freight costs are deducted for any other delivery point. |
| *Delivery Procedures:* | *Notice:* Sellers may notify the BM&F of their intent to make delivery any time from the second day of the delivery month to 18:00 on the seventh business day preceding the last day of the delivery month.<br>*Allocation:* Buyers shall be offered to match with seller delivery notifications on a first-in basis with priority going to the longs that have been in the market the longest time—if not enough buyers voluntarily match to sellers, BM&F will assign delivery obligations to the remaining longs on a first-in basis.<br>*Settlement:* Physical or cash settlement (if agreed upon). |

## TIMING OF DELIVERY

Quality basis risk can also arise from what standardized contracts say about delivery dates and times. The light, sweet crude oil futures contract on the NYMEX, for example, specifies ratable delivery from Cushing, Okalahoma, over the entire delivery month. A short that does not offset a position prior to the expiration day (i.e., the third business day prior to the 25th business day in the month preceding deliveries), for example, is required to pump oil to Cushing *daily* over the whole delivery month.

A firm hedging a single wellhead purchase thus could encounter major basis risk by hedging with a ratable delivery contract. Note, however, that *spot* oil market purchases are *also* usually for ratable delivery. Going long 28 FEB04 light, sweet crude contracts on January 14, 2004, for example, requires the long (if he does not offset his position prior to expiry) to buy 1,000 barrels of crude every day in February at the futures settlement price. If a firm bought 28,000 barrels in the spot market on the same oil on the same day, the purchase obligation would be economically indistinguishable. Crude spot and futures transactions both create a portfolio of daily forward contracts on a fixed quantity of oil maturing on each successive day in the delivery month.

## SWITCHING UNDERLYINGS AND CONTRACT PRICING FOR PHYSICALLY SETTLED FUTURES

All of the sections thus far represent quality basis risks that could in principle arise whether OTC or exchange-traded contracts are being used. In this section, we turn our attention briefly to physically settled futures, in particular.

With OTC contracts, "the underlying" is clear. It may not always be exactly what every firm wants nor will it always track every exposure perfectly, even with the ability to customize. But it is *usually* clear what the underlying *is*. With exchange-traded futures, by contrast, the contract specifications on physically settled futures almost always allow for the delivery of more than one asset or instrument. Especially for commodity futures, numerous different grades and levels of quality exist in a single commodity, and futures based on a single commodity thus must accommodate this somehow.

Determining the deliverable assets for a futures contract is more art than science for the listing futures exchange. If too narrow a range of qualities are eligible for delivery into the contract, deliverable supply will be too tight and hedging demands for the product will be low. Liquidity will suffer, and the product will die from lack of use. But if the exchange allows too much quality variability, basis risk will drive away hedgers. Again liquidity will suffer, and the product will die from lack of use. The trick is to be somewhere in between.

The NYMEX futures contract on light, sweet crude oil is the most actively traded commodity futures contract in the world. It provides us with an instructive example of quality basis risk. The contract allows oil to be delivered as long as the oil contains no more than 0.42 percent sulfur by weight and has an API gravity of between 37° and 42°. The following domestic crude streams are deliverable into the NYMEX contract at par (i.e., at exactly the settlement price): West Texas Intermediate, Low Sweet Mix, New Mexican Sweet, North Texas Sweet, Oklahoma Sweet, and South Texas Sweet. (Sweet means low sulfur.)

In addition to the crude streams that are deliverable at par, the NYMEX light, sweet crude contract also permits delivery of certain other streams *off* par. U.K. Brent and Forties crude and Norwegian Oseberg Blend may be delivered at a $0.30 per barrel discount to par (i.e., the seller receives $0.30/bbl. below the final settlement price for crude delivered from these streams). Nigerian Bonny Light crude and Columbian Cusiana, by contrast, may be delivered at a $0.15 per barrel premium to par. Nigerian Qua Iboe may also be delivered, but at a $0.05 premium.

Considering the various categories of light, sweet crude oil that constitute the deliverable supply for this contract, it is no surprise that the price of the contract will not perfectly track the prices of all deliverable crude streams all the time.

Most futures contracts are offset prior to delivery. So, why is it a problem to have multiple assets deliverable into the same contract? The answer is that there is only one *contract price*. As long as the prices of the multiple deliverables (at par) are similar, the price of the futures contract with multiple underlyings is generally just the weighted average of the permissible underlying where the weights are market-assessed probabilities that any given asset type will be delivered. If the prices of the deliverable assets are fairly variable relative to one another, then the price of the futures contract is the price of the *cheapest to deliver* asset.

Let's consider some examples. First, consider the light, sweet crude contract again. The price of this contract is generally considered to track most closely the price of West Texas Intermediate Crude delivered in Cushing, Oklahoma, or into TEPPCO pipelines from a Midwestern inventory block known as "PADD 2." Fortunately, the price of crude is based more on sulfur content and specific gravity than on the name of the crude stream. The major distinction then is location and transportation, and this can be addressed by adding or subtracting a differential to the Cushing delivery point. One reason the NYMEX contract is so successful is that it does indeed appeal to most hedgers without causing a significant amount of basis risk, and the basis risk that it does exhibit is often relatively easy to deal with using markups or discounts to the futures price for cash deliveries.

Quality basis risk can be particularly problematic on futures available all year that are based on seasonal commodities. Wheat futures are traded year-round, for example, but the deliverable grade switches during the year depending on the harvest. The precise timing of that switch, however, is unknown and variable, and this can give rise to quality basis risk. A farmer that *thinks* the price of a wheat futures contract is tracking spring wheat and is hedging accordingly could be in serious trouble if the contract unexpectedly switched to a pricing basis off the winter wheat crop. Even if the types of wheat contain comparable amounts of protein, the price behavior may shift when the pricing of the contract shifts from spring wheat to winter wheat.

Now consider the futures contract on the long-term U.S. government bond listed on the Chicago Board of Trade. Although a futures contract on a *financial* asset, the contract requires physical delivery by shorts that do not offset prior to maturity. Specifically, the short may deliver any noncallable bond issued by the U.S. Treasury with at least 15 years remaining to maturity (or, if the bond is callable, with at least 15 years remaining to its first call date). The last trading day for a given contract is the eighth to the last business day of the contract month, and delivery can occur at any time during the contract month.

When a bond is delivered by the short in the CBOT long bond futures contract, the invoice price paid by the long is equal to the futures price times a "conversion factor" plus accrued interest. Because such a wide range of bonds can be delivered into the CBOT contract, the Chicago Board of Trade tries to equalize invoice prices across bonds by adjusting the quoted futures price with a conversion factor calculated as the approximate decimalized price at which the delivered bond would yield 6 percent to maturity or first call.

Because the short can choose among a variety of deliverable bonds, the short will virtually always select the cheapest-to-deliver, which is determined largely by the bond's duration, convexity, and changes in rates. The difference between the cash price of the bond adjusted by the conversion factor and the futures price is a version of the "futures quality basis" for the bond in question and indicates the return to holding the bond for delivery against the futures contract. For high yields, high-duration bonds are often cheapest to deliver and thus have a relatively small chance of becoming more expensive relative to other lower-duration delivery-eligible bonds, especially if the futures contract is close to expiration. As yields fall, the cheapest-to-deliver bond changes and the price of the futures contract changes to reflect the new cheapest to deliver.

How the single quoted futures price responds to changes in the cheapest-to-deliver underlying can be challenging as a modeling exercise. As a hedging exercise, this problem of switching underlyings can be a real problem. It can reduce the correlation of the *quoted contract price* to almost any given actual bond; that is, while making the contract itself more accommodating through its multiple deliverables, the delivery features of the contract also can sizably increase the basis risk of hedgers trying to manage the price risk or interest rate risk of a single, specific obligation or investment.

Worth noting, however, is that the imprecision associated with modeling options like cheapest to deliver often generates *speculative interest* in a contract, thus increasing liquidity and the range of potential counterparties available to trade at any given time. In this sense, eliminating all the quality basis risks and imperfections associated with standardized delivery contracts *may not be desirable* even if it is possible.

## MANAGING QUALITY BASIS RISK

The preceding section contains comments throughout on different ways that firms might address quality basis risk. Some degree of quality basis risk may be inevitable, but judicious hedge design can go a long way toward reducing that risk. In this section, we focus on two types of market responses to quality basis risk separate and apart from some of the hedge design solutions already mentioned.

### EFPs

Because of their standardization, exchange-traded futures have long been thought to engender more quality basis risks than comparable OTC products. As a result, many exchanges have taken steps over time specifically intended to address market participants' concerns about certain sources of quality basis risk. If quality basis risks affect futures *prices* though design features like the cheapest-to-deliver option, not much can be done without restructuring the contract. Instead, exchanges have tried to develop avenues such that customization of the *delivery process* can help eliminate certain quality basis risks.

Many exchanges increasingly allow market participants to address delivery concerns leading to basis risk either by negotiating a separate arrangement, usually called alternative delivery procedure (ADP), or through EFPs—exchange for product or exchange for physicals. Provided they are based on the same asset, futures and cash markets are already completely integrated; the threat and sometimes the actual practice of arbitrage ensures virtually negligible price deviations that can persist across futures and spot markets for the same asset. EFPs make that arbitrage process easier *and* assuage some participants' delivery basis risk concerns by allowing futures to be literally exchanged into equivalent cash market positions, or vice versa.

EFPs were designed mainly for energy futures as a way of helping commercial hedgers use standardized futures without sacrificing their demands for customization *at delivery*. EFPs thus enable firms essentially to specify delivery on their own terms—with a counterparty of their choosing, at a location of their choosing, at a time of their choosing, and in a quality grade of their choosing.

Suppose two companies, JR Ewing and Blake Carrington, are both NYMEX members—Ewing is long and Carrington is short. These firms can arrange a delivery on any terms they wish by doing an EFP. Mechanically, they need only register the EFP with the exchange. Ewing takes delivery from Carrington *off exchange* on terms the two counterparties may specify, and the two futures positions are booked out against one another (NYMEX, 1999).

## Insurance, ART, and Information

Why not design derivatives contracts that simply directly reimburse hedgers for the financial losses they actually incur? Would this not eliminate the discussion of quality basis risk once and for all? The answer is yes, it would—and this kind of solution is called *insurance*.

### Basis Risk versus Moral Hazard and Adverse Selection

Because insurance contracts reimburse purchasers for actual economic damage sustained, they must in fact sustain damage to request reimbursement. This obviously implies that the insurance purchaser must be capable of sustaining damage from the risks underwritten in insurance contracts—the purchaser of insurance must have a so-called "insurable interest."

In some cases a firm may be forced to incur basis risk instead of entering into a contract with a payoff that is perfectly correlated to the exposure being hedged as a result of information costs. In particular, *pure* quality basis-risk-free risk transfer can be hindered or rendered impossible in two situations.

The first situation that can be troubling for a risk-bearing specialist is when the hedger seeks to manage the risk of an exposure about which it is significantly better informed than any potential counterparty. If the exposure in question is either genuine uncertainty or a risk about which there is such asymmetric information, adverse selection problems can become significant. Suppose, for example, that all firms agree that the firm with the original exposure is also the best-informed about that exposure. This immediately leads to an expectation that the original firm will hedge only when it is advantageous to do so—when it is *dis*advantageous for risk-bearing specialists to agree to be counterparty to the trade. Knowing this, prospective trading partners thus may set a huge bid/offer spread or may simply refuse to trade.

Adverse selection problems are often called problems of *hidden information*. The close cousin of adverse selection is moral hazard, which is also an information cost but of a different nature. In the case of moral hazard, the hedger and would-be swap dealers may be equally well informed about the nature of the risk, but the transaction may fail to occur because of *hidden action*. If the hedger is capable of influencing the probability or severity of a loss arising from a given risk, counterparties may be reluctant to agree to full risk transfer.

Adverse selection and moral hazard are classic problems in insurance markets, and this is an important distinction between insurance and derivatives. Insurers have evolved numerous methods for dealing with moral hazard and adverse selection, some of which are discussed in Chapters 2 and 3. These mitigants of either moral hazard or adverse selection include better monitoring and classification of risks in the population of insurance purchasers, mechanisms that force the insured party to participate in some part of the loss (e.g., deductibles, policy limits, co-pays, co-insurance), and strict due diligence of the underwriting risk.

Derivatives dealers have chosen to address this problem instead by making the payoffs of derivatives dependent on variables about which no single user has either undue informational advantage or undue influence. This, however, immediately introduces quality basis risk. The less able a firm is to influence the variable determining the payoff on the derivatives contract, the less that variable is likely to be correlated with the hedger's actual losses. At the same time, derivatives do not restrict participation to firms with an insurable interest; for example, firms going long the Swiss franc against the dollar need not actually have a franc/dollar exposure. Derivatives thus still allow speculation, whereas insurance really does not.

So, there's the rub. Introducing some quality basis risk by tying a contract payoff to a variable outside the direct control of the hedger limits moral hazard and adverse selection—and we call those derivatives. Reimbursing a firm for an actual financial loss eliminates quality basis risk at the expense of creating moral hazard and adverse selection—and we call that insurance.

## ART Forms

The proliferation of alternative risk transfer products in recent years is closing the gap between insurance and derivatives, and the latter are becoming increasingly more firm-specific in their payoffs. Credit derivatives, for example, are highly firm-specific but do not restrict participation to firms with an insurable interest.

Similarly, "multitrigger" structures are becoming increasingly common as ways of reducing the quality basis risk faced by firms without creating excessive moral hazard and adverse selection problems. A typical multitrigger contract requires at least two conditions to be met before the contract pays off. One trigger is likely to be that the purchaser has sustained actual economic damage, whereas the other trigger is likely to be based on a variable outside the hedger's direct control. Because the second trigger limits moral hazard, the *payoff* on such transactions is often expressed as a reimbursement to the hedger for actual losses sustained. Quality basis risk thus affects the hedger *through the second trigger* and not through the payoff. In other words, the hedger experiences quality basis risk concerning *when* the hedge pays off, but not on *what* the hedge pays.

As an example, Switzerland's Compagnie Financière Michelin (the financial and holding company for French tire maker Michelin) wanted to purchase a put option on its own subordinated debt to guarantee itself access to future debt capacity *at a prenegotiated price.* Swiss Re entered into an agreement with Michelin in late 2000 called Committed Long-Term Capital Solutions (CLOCS) in which Swiss Re gave Michelin the option for up to five years (through end-2005) to issue subordinated debt maturing in 2012 that Swiss Re would purchase at a fixed price. The CLOCS option also has a second trigger: Michelin can exercise the put only when the combined average growth rate of gross domestic product (GDP) in the European and U.S. markets in which Michelin is active falls below 1.5 percent (from 2001 to 2003) or below 2 percent (from 2004 to 2005).

Tying CLOCS to a second trigger that was an external macro variable beyond Michelin's control helped limit potential moral hazard problems. At the same time, Michelin's earnings are highly correlated with GDP growth in the specified markets, thus limiting the quality basis risk inherent in the second trigger. Notice that the first trigger is that Michelin's cost of debt finance in the market is above the price specified in the CLOCS structure—a completely firm-specific trigger because it involves settlement in actual Michelin debt.

Another area in which the trade-off between quality basis risk and moral hazard has long been finessed is the use by reinsurance companies of "cat bonds" to obtain additional catastrophic reinsurance capacity for property claims arising as a result of a natural disaster or catastrophe (e.g., hurricane, tornado, earthquake). In a typical cat bond structure, a special purpose entity (SPE) is established that is a separately capitalized stand-alone licensed reinsurance firm in which some sponsoring reinsurance company owns the small residual interest. The SPE sells catastrophe reinsurance to the sponsoring reinsurance company, which in turn pays premiums to the SPE. The SPE invests those premiums in low-risk securities, along with the proceeds from its issuance of cat bonds. In the event no losses occur, the cat bond holders receive a very high coupon rate, financed from the premium payments made by the reinsurer to the SPE. But if losses do occur and the premium collected by the SPE is insufficient to cover them, interest and/or principal may be withheld from bondholders by the SPE to pay the reinsurance claims.

The source of potential quality basis risk for the sponsoring reinsurance company is the residual interest it has in the SPE. If the bonds issued by the SPE specify that interest and/or principal will be withheld based on the actual reinsurance losses and claims made by the reinsurer on the SPE, then the sponsoring reinsurer has no basis risk. Claims made on the reinsurer are fully passed on to cat bond investors as losses.

Some investors in such structures, however, were concerned about the moral hazard that might create—the temptation for the resinsurer to exaggerate its claims so it could be reimbursed by the SPE at the expense of cat bond investors. Two solutions have been proposed that mitigate moral hazard but in turn create quality basis risk. First, some cat bonds withhold interest and principal from investors based on losses reported *in a broad index*, such as the Property Claims Services index of catastrophic property losses. If the actual claims made by the reinsurer are well above the index of losses, the SPE will be unable to withhold enough principal and interest to fully reimburse the reinsurer. This basis risk, however, is precisely what reassures investors that the structure cannot be manipulated by the sponsor.

A second alternative, called "parametric cat bonds," specifies a principal and interest withholding schedule based on some parameter unrelated to insurance claims, such as the size of an earthquake on the Richter scale. This parameter is likely to be highly correlated with the reinsurer's losses, but remains beyond the control of the resinsurer. The cost of controlling moral hazard is, of course, the quality basis risk that the parametric measure to which cat bond payoffs are indexed is a poor approximation for the actual losses sustained by the sponsoring reinsurer.

# CHAPTER 16

# Calendar Basis Risk

Calendar basis risk is the risk that unexpected changes in the slope of the term structure of futures/forward prices (i.e., unexpected changes in own rates of interest and the net cost of carry) will result in unexpected losses. Calendar basis risk can arise from calendar spreads in isolation—either those deliberately established using derivatives or those that are naturally occurring—or can arise from hedging strategies in which the maturity of the exposure does not match the maturity of the hedging instruments used. The latter is often called *rollover risk*.

## CALENDAR BASIS RISK AND SPREADS

Establishing a calendar basis spread trade invariably exposes the firm to calendar basis risk. Just consider some examples:

- Simultaneously short the front-month (i.e., nearest to expiration) silver futures contract and buy the back-month contract (i.e., the most deferred maturity)—you get killed if the term structure of futures prices flattens out of contango or moves into backwardation.
- Go long the front-month futures contract on a Treasury bill and short the front-month futures contract on the long-term treasury bond—you benefit from a steepening of the Treasury yield curve and get hurt from the reverse.
- Write short-dated puts and buy longer-dated calls on a currency—a devaluation of the currency in the very near future could wipe you out.
- And so on.

In short, it is not difficult to identify calendar basis risk that is created through spread trading.

More subtle are the numerous *natural* calendar basis risks to which some firms are subject. Careful attention to these risks must be paid in hedge design, or else the hedge could actually exacerbate—and certainly fail to address—the firm's risk control concerns.

Throughout this discussion, it is also important to keep in mind that bearing calendar spread risk naturally may be synonymous with the primary business of the firm—it may represent what the firm views as a source of uncertainty rather than risk. So, just because a firm has a natural calendar basis risk does not mean a priori that the risk should be hedged.

## Input-Output Calendar Spreads

Input-output spreads, discussed in Chapter 11, are a combination of quality and calendar spreads in which inputs are purchased by a firm, transformed somehow into outputs, and then sold in output form. The crack spread involves purchasing crude, refining it, and selling the refined products; the crush spread is the crushing of soybeans into meal and oil; the spark spread is the purchase of gas to power gas-fired electric turbines; and so on.

Input-output spreads usually rely on some transformation or production process that takes time. It takes time to refine crude into gasoline and fuel oil; it takes time to crush beans into meal and oil; it takes time to move natural gas through a pipeline to a combined-cycle gas turbine; it takes time to mill wheat into flour; and so on.

If the timing of the input-output cycle is predictable, the firm can hedge the risk without a great deal of difficulty. If it takes a miller one month on average to turn wheat into flour and both are bought/sold spot, a wide range of derivatives solutions are available, depending on the miller's hedge objective. Ignoring quality basis risk, the miller's margin could be locked in by going long wheat forwards or futures in the month of the planned wheat purchase and then shorting wheat futures one month later. (As noted when we discussed operational hedging in Chapter 13, milled flour prices are often set proportional to wheat prices.) Alternatively, if the miller is willing to pay to protect its margin from narrowing but does not want to be deprived of gains from a wider margin, a solution would be purchasing calls on spot wheat for the planned purchase date and purchasing puts with a maturity of one month later.

Unfortunately, the timing is not always predictable in input-output systems, which can complicate the hedging problem. In that situation, American-style options on forwards or futures would make sense. Once the timing of the cycle becomes clear, the miller can just exercise the options into the relevant forwards—or not if they are out-of-the-money.

## Transportation-Related Calendar Spreads

Lags in the movement of assets can create calendar basis risk exposures. In physical asset markets, such lags are usually a result of transportation and distribution issues.

The trade finance example involving Andermatt Fils & Cie in Chapter

15 already provides us with an example of how a firm can hedge its calendar basis risk. In that example, it was the trade financier, ABC Hambro, that insisted Andermatt hedge. But if Andermatt did not default, the hedge would actually have been unnecessary—and, in fact, would have been the equivalent of a speculative position. A better alternative might have been to use options that could be exercised into in-the-money forwards in the event of a default by the firm.

Alternatively, consider an oil company that owns oil in the ground and refineries. The refineries are subject to input-output calendar spread risk, but the firm as a whole is also subject to the risk of price fluctuations from the time the oil is pumped to the time it is delivered to the refineries. Hedging with a calendar spread could make sense.

Specifically, suppose the crack refining process takes three months on average for the hypothetical company Gatsby Oil. And suppose it takes another month on average to pipe oil from a wellhead or a tank far to the refinery. The refining division of Gatsby Oil would be looking to do a long crude hedge with a maturity of one month after the planned production dispatch date and a short hedge in heating oil and gasoline with a maturity three months after the crude contract matures. But this is not enough. Gatsby as a firm also bears the risk of oil price changes in the first month. For this Gatsby might hedge its sales to refineries using a one-/two-month calendar spread—going long the front month as protection against the opportunity cost of spot price increases that cannot be realized because the oil has been committed to a refinery, and then going short the second month to hedge the fixed transfer or explicit price paid by the refinery. Augmenting the natural crack spread position with such a hedge essentially synthetically bring the refining process forward to the time when oil is first pumped from the ground.

## Settlement Lags

In financial asset markets, calendar basis risk can be created because of the lag between the initiation of a final settlement and the achievement of irrevocability in finality in the settlement cycle. Analogous to the transportation basis risk on physical assets, the settlement cycle is essentially a "midmarket" or "midstream" component of the financial asset's supply chain. And some firms may wish to hedge this.

Currency transactions, for example, take two days to reach final settlement after instructions are issued to initiate the required funds transfers. Some firms may wish to prolong that settlement window and can do so using transactions called "spot-next" and "tom-next" rolls. These products were virtually built to help currency dealers conduct short-dated calendar basis trading.

## Other Exposures and "Real Options"

Calendar-basis risk is so common that it would exhaust the remainder of this book—as well as the patience of many readers *and* this author—to cover the different sources of it. A key thing for firms to bear in mind, however, is the frequency with which calendar basis risk is naturally embedded into commercial and financial contracts through "real" or implicit options.

Options embedded in callable bonds, for example, create "extension" and "compression" risk for their investors and issuers. In other words, the exercise of the option—or even its moneyness—can impact the effective maturity of the instrument, thus giving rise to problems, for example, in immunization and duration-matched hedging programs. Unexpected changes in prepayment speeds on mortgages can have the same impact.

In summary, calendar basis risk that arises naturally from a firm's business profile is usually a manageable risk. The hard part is simply *spotting* that risk in the first place.

## ROLLOVER RISK

A trading strategy is subject to *rollover risk* if unexpected shifts in the term structure of futures prices expose the trader to the risk of losses. Rollover risk is present only in multiperiod trading strategies for which the time horizon of the strategy exceeds the maturity of the instruments used to execute the strategy. Nevertheless, the lack of derivatives with maturities extending out to the most deferred maturity of an exposure being hedged is fairly common. Rollover risk is an important risk that demands a firm's serious attention.

Rollover risk is best illustrated by a simple two-period example. We will assume that futures are conditionally unbiased predictors of expected future spot prices, so that:

$$F_{0,1} = E_0[S_1]$$
$$F_{1,2} = E_1[S_2] \quad (16.1)$$
$$F_{0,2} = E_0[S_2]$$

Futures prices $F_{0,2}$ and $F_{0,1}$ are known and observable at time 0, whereas $F_{1,2}$ is not. We will find it useful to write the time 0 expectation of $F_{1,2}$—using the law of iterated expectations:

$$E_0[F_{1,2}] = E_0 E_1[S_2] = E_0[S_2] = F_{0,2} \quad (16.2)$$

Now consider a producer with a commitment to sell one unit of the asset at time 2 for the prenegotiated price of $K$ (presumably the two-period forward price plus some profit margin or markup). The financial focus of the producer's hedge is time 0 profits. We will return to the hedging mandate later. For now, let's just characterize the hedges to see the nature of what rollover risk really is.

## Maturity-Matched Hedge versus a Rollover Hedge

Define a *hedging strategy* as a vector of hedge ratios $\mathbf{Z} = (Z_{0,1} Z_{0,2} Z_{1,2})$ where $Z_{j,k}$ denotes the number of futures maturing at time $k$ held as of time $j$. (Normalize the physical position to one unit so that the hedge ratio and the true quantity of futures held are the same.) For now, we consider two possible hedging strategies: $\mathbf{Z}^1$ is what we call a "maturity-matched PV-adjusted one-for-one hedge," and $\mathbf{Z}^2$ is what we call a "PV-adjusted one-for-one rollover hedge."

### Maturity-Matched PV-Adjusted One-for-One Hedge
We first consider a strategy involving a two-period futures contract entered at time 0 and held through time 2. Assume the hedger or trader decides to PV-adjust or tail the hedge but otherwise opts for a one-to-one hedge ratio. So,

$$\mathbf{Z}^1 = \left( 0 \ \ \frac{1}{1+r} \ \ 1 \right) \tag{16.3}$$

where we assume $r$ is a constant one-period money interest rate for simplicity. The realized cash flows on trading strategy $\mathbf{Z}^1$ each period are:

$$\pi_1 = Z_{0,2}(F_{1,2} - F_{0,2}) = \frac{(F_{1,2} - F_{0,2})}{1+r}$$

$$\pi_2 = Z_{1,2}(S_2 - F_{1,2}) = (S_2 - F_{1,2}) \tag{16.4}$$

The *terminal value* of the cumulative cash flows on the hedge as of time 2 plus the physical position represent the net profit from the strategy expressed in time 2 dollars:

$$\begin{aligned} \Pi_2 &= (K - S_2) + \pi_1(1 + r) + \pi_2 \\ &= (K - S_2) + (F_{1,2} - F_{0,2}) + (S_2 - F_{1,2}) \\ &= K - F_{0,2} \end{aligned} \tag{16.5}$$

No matter what the realized mark-to-market value of $F_{1,2}$ happens to be at time 1, the net profits of the position will be unaffected and have no risk. The net profit is equal to the fixed asset sale price $K$ less the two-period futures price at time 0.

We can rewrite (16.5) using (16.1) so that time 2 profits can be expressed as:

$$\Pi_2 = K - E_0(S_2) \qquad (16.6)$$

We will also find it useful to express (16.5) in terms of the calendar basis:

$$\Pi_2 = K - S_0(1 + b_{0,2}) \qquad (16.7)$$

so that the net time 2 profit for the producer is the sales price of the product less the synthetic cost of storage.

Notice in equations (16.5), (16.6), and (16.7) that all these variables are known as of time 0. The actual profit and expected profit thus are the same and the variance of profits at time 2 is zero.

What is the interpretation of the two-period basis $b_{0,2}$ in (16.5) and (16.7)? Of course it is just the two-period money interest rate minus the two-period own rate of interest. But we can actually say a bit more than that, which will prove very useful to us when comparing the two strategies. Specifically, we know that at-market futures like other derivatives are priced to yield a zero expected profit. But because futures are marked to market and re-settled at least daily, we can make the stronger statement that in an efficient market, the *daily cash flow expected on a futures transaction should be zero.* This allows us to write $F_{0,2}$ differently as:

$$E_0(F_{1,2} - F_{0,2}) = 0 \quad \Rightarrow \quad F_{0,2} = E_0(F_{1,2}) \qquad (16.8)$$

So, the two-period futures price observed at time 0 is equal not only to the time 0 conditional expectation of the time 2 spot price, but also to the time 0 conditional expectation of the one-period futures price prevailing one-period hence. This is not particularly surprising. Were it not the case, either everyone would want to hold the two-period contract or no one would. This is the only way to guarantee indifference in the two contracts as of time 0.

At time 1, the one-period futures price is a known function of the time 1 spot price and the one-period basis prevailing at time 1. So, let's rewrite (16.8) using the cost of carry formulation:

$$F_{0,2} = E_0(F_{1,2}) = E_0[S_1(1 + b_{1,2})] \qquad (16.9)$$

which simplifies again to:

$$F_{0,2} = E_0[S_1(1 + b_{1,2})] = E_0(S_1) + E_0(S_1 b_{1,2}) \tag{16.10}$$

Equation (16.10) yields an important insight. It says that we can write the two-period futures price at time 0 as the one-period futures price at time 0 plus the time 0 expectation of the one-period basis that will prevail at time 1. Or, more interestingly,

$$S_0(1 + b_{1,2}) = S_0(1 + b_{0,1}) + E_0(S_1 b_{1,2}) \tag{16.11}$$

so that we can again rewrite the guaranteed net profit from the maturity-matched hedge in equation (16.5) as:

$$\Pi_2 = K - S_0(1 + b_{0,1}) - E_0(S_1 b_{1,2}) \tag{16.12}$$

We already knew from equations (16.5) through (16.7) that using the two-period maturity-matched futures contract locked in the two-period basis for us as of time 0. We can now interpret that further and say that the two-period cost of carry we have locked in is the one-period cost of carry plus the *one-period basis expected to prevail one period from now.*

### PV-Adjusted One-for-One Rollover Hedge
Now consider a trading strategy:

$$\mathbf{Z}^2 = \begin{pmatrix} \dfrac{1}{1+r} & 0 & 1 \end{pmatrix} \tag{16.13}$$

The realized cash flows on trading strategy $\mathbf{Z}^2$ each period are:

$$\pi_1 = Z_{0,1}(S_1 - F_{0,1}) = \frac{(S_1 - F_{0,1})}{1+r} \tag{16.14}$$

$$\pi_1 = Z_{1,2}(S_2 - F_{1,2}) = S_2 - F_{1,2}$$

The *terminal value* of the cumulative cash flows on the hedge as of time 2 plus the physical position represent the net profit from the strategy expressed in time 2 dollars:

$$\begin{aligned} \Pi_2 &= (K - S_2) + \pi_1(1 + r) + \pi_2 \\ &= (K - S_2) + (S_1 - F_{0,1}) + (S_2 - F_{1,2}) \\ &= K + (S_1 - F_{0,1} - F_{1,2}) \end{aligned} \tag{16.15}$$

Unlike equation (16.5), all of the terms in (16.15) are *not* known as of time 0. We can take a conditional expectation to get expected profit:

$$
\begin{aligned}
E_0(\Pi_2) &= K + [E_0(S_1) - F_{0,1} - E_0(F_{1,2})] \\
&= K + [E_0(S_1) - E_0(S_1) - E_0(S_2)] \\
&= K - E_0(S_2)
\end{aligned}
\tag{16.16}
$$

which is the same as equation (16.6). So, the conditional expected profit on the rollover hedge is exactly the same as the actual profit expressed in terms of conditional expectations on the maturity-matched hedge.

Before taking a conditional variance, it will be useful to rewrite the time 2 realized profit in (16.15) again, this time using the cost of carry formula:

$$
\begin{aligned}
\Pi_2 &= K + [S_1 - S_0(1 + r_{0,1} - x_{0,1}) - S_1(1 + r_{1,2} - x_{1,2})] \\
&= K - S_0(1 + r_{0,1} - x_{0,1}) - S_1(r_{1,2} - x_{1,2}) \\
&= K - S_0(1 + b_{0,1}) - S_1 b_{1,2}
\end{aligned}
\tag{16.17}
$$

We can again verify using (16.17) that the conditional expected profits on the two hedging strategies are the same. From here, we can compute the conditional variance of the strategy as:

$$
\text{var}_0(\Pi_2) = \text{var}_0(S_1 b_{1,2})
\tag{16.18}
$$

The term $S_1 b_{1,2}$ in the preceding expressions is our calendar basis risk of the position. Remember that we expressed the components of the basis as proportional to the spot price, so the whole term taken together is essentially just the basis that will prevail from time 1 to time 2. We don't know this at time 0. In the maturity-matched hedge, we could observe and lock in the two-period basis. In the rollover hedge, we do not commit ourselves to the two-period cost of carry. Improvements in the basis help us, but deteriorations hurt us.

## Rollover Gains/Losses and the Slope of the Term Structure

We can see the difference in the two hedges most clearly if we compare not the expected profits or conditional variances, but rather the *realized profits*. Think of this as going short the two-period futures contract and hedging it with two long one-period futures so that your net profit from the two combined strategies can be obtained by subtracting equation (16.12) from (16.17) to get

$$E_0(S_1 b_{1,2}) - S_1 b_{1,2} \qquad\qquad (16.19)$$

With the two-period contract, you lock in the two-period basis which we saw is the one-period basis plus the time 0 expectation of the one-period basis one period hence. With the rollover, your profit depends on the *realized* one-period basis at time 1.

A very common misperception of rollover strategies holds that you "make money on the rollover" when the market is in backwardation and "lose money on the rollover" if the market is in contango. We can see from (16.19), however, that this is plainly wrong. First, if the actual basis is equal to its time 0 conditional expectation, it does not matter what the slope of the term structure is—the two strategies generate the same profits. Second, suppose the market is expected to be in contango at time 1. Then at time 1, the basis is weaker than anticipated *but still positive*. You make a rollover gain *even though the market stayed in contango*. Conversely, if the market is expected to be in backwardation at time 1 and the basis strengthens, the strategy loses money *even if the market remains in backwardation*.

What matters to a rollover hedger thus is not the *actual* slope of the term structure, but rather the slope of the term structure *relative to expectations*. If the basis weakens relative to expectations, the strategy generates rollover gains. If the basis strengthens relative to expectations, rollover losses result.

## Graphical Illustrations

Figures 16.1 to 16.4 will help illustrate the nature of this calendar basis or rollover risk. Figures 16.1 and 16.2 depict markets in which everything turns out just as was expected the period before. The black lines indicate variables being observed or expectations taken *as of time 0*. The solid line represents the *expected future spot price* at times 1 and 2, and the actual spot price is assumed to be realized at exactly these expected values. The two dashed lines in turn correspond to our three quoted futures prices.

Figure 16.1 depicts a market that is in strong contango at time 0 and in which nothing changes at time 1. At time 1, the actual spot price $S_1$ is exactly equal to its time 0 expectation, and the basis $b_{1,2}$ is exactly equal to what it was expected to be at time 0. Figure 16.2 shows a similar situation for a market initially in backwardation. In both cases, the graphs illustrate that when the one-period basis *realized* at time 1 is the same as it was expected to be at time 0, the two hedging strategies are no different *ex post*. Of course the two-period strategy has no risk *ex ante*, and the rollover strategy does. But, as we will now see, no risk also means no reward.

In Figures 16.3 and 16.4, we now add some more lines. These new lines are shaded gray to represent variables observed or expectations evaluated *at time 1*. In Figure 16.3, the market is in steep contango at time 0, but unlike

*Futures/Spot Prices*

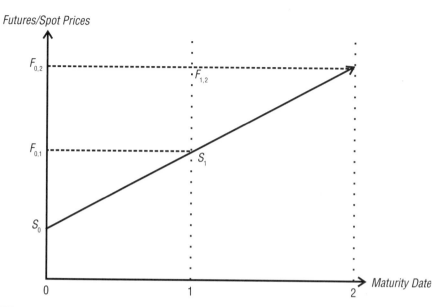

**FIGURE 16.1** Expectations Met, Contango

*Futures/Spot Prices*

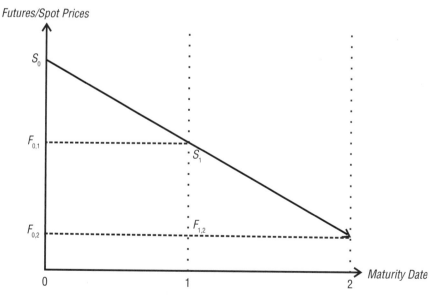

**FIGURE 16.2** Expectations Met, Backwardation

*Futures/Spot Prices*

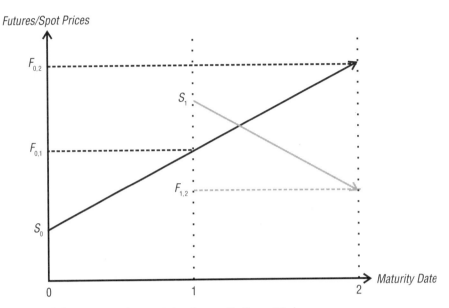

**FIGURE 16.3**   Backwardation Gains from a Rollover Hedge

*Futures/Spot Prices*

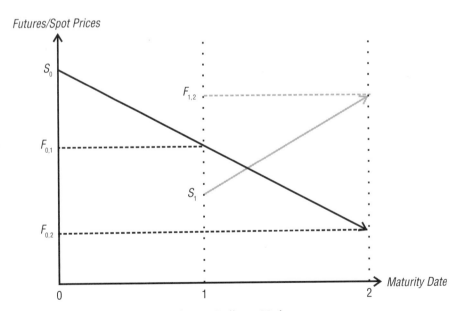

**FIGURE 16.4**   Contango Losses from a Rollover Hedge

Figure 16.1 now some kind of shock occurs that causes the market to shift into steep backwardation at time 1. The newly listed one-period futures price $F_{1,2}$ reflects this and is well below the realized time 1 spot price. Note that the *realized* spot price at time 1, moreover, is well above what it was expected to be at time 0.

In the maturity-matched strategy, absolutely nothing that happens at time 1 is relevant in a present value sense—not the true realization of the time 1 spot price $S_1$, not the new conditional expected time 2 spot price $E_1(S_2)$, and not the newly listed one-period futures price $F_{1,2}$. By opting for a two-period futures contract, the hedger *locks in* the two-period calendar basis, which is positive and very high as of time 0. The hedger is going to pay close to full carry, but the strategy involves no risk and time 2 realized net profits have a zero variance.

Now consider the rollover hedge. At time 0, the hedger locks in the *one-period* basis $b_{0,1}$. This is a positive number representing a positive net cost of carrying the asset one period into the future. But at time 1, the sharp increase in the spot price together with a shift of the market into backwardation results in a *very* substantial cost savings (if not outright profit) to the hedger. Recall that the rollover hedge results in a net hedged profit of $K - S_0(1 + b_{0,1}) - S_1 b_{1,2}$. The hedger is stuck with $b_{0,1}$ in *either* strategy—that is simply the cost of carry when the hedge is initiated. But now the rollover hedger benefits strongly from the massive deterioration in the basis; $S_1$ has gone up substantially and $b_{1,2}$ has become quite negative. The term $-S_1 b_{1,2}$ thus *becomes positive* and represents a *rollover gain* for the hedger.

Figure 16.4 shows the opposite scenario—a market that starts in backwardation and slips into contango at time 1. This strategy imposes *losses* on the rollover hedger. The two-period basis locked in with the maturity-matched hedge is the one-period basis plus the expected one-period basis one period from now, and both of those terms reflect backwardation.

## HEDGING LONG-TERM EXPOSURES WITH SHORT-DATED DERIVATIVES

Some companies with a clear risk transfer mandate have no choice but to incur calendar basis risk in their hedging strategies. Derivatives for maturities that precisely match the maturities of the exposure being hedged are just not available all the time. The reasons are the same as we discussed in Chapter 15 for why derivatives on all assets are not always available: costly contracting.

There are a range of hedge construction issues to which calendar basis risk gives rise. Some of the more important ones are discussed in the next several sections.

## Hedge Ratios

If a firm is forced to use rollover hedging to hedge a long-dated exposure using a sequence of short-dated derivatives, various adjustments to the hedge ratio can be made to try to reduce the calendar basis risk to which the hedger will inevitably be subject. As discussed in Chapter 14, the choice of a hedge ratio depends strongly on the hedging objectives of the firm (see Chapter 13).

To take the obvious and oft-used example, suppose the hedger wants to minimize the variance of a rollover hedge used to hedge a long-dated forward commitment. As discussed in Chapter 14, probably the simplest solution is to collect a time series of price changes in the derivatives contract that the hedger can and plans to use and then regress a time series of changes in the comparable forward exposure on those short-dated futures price changes. The PV-adjusted regression beta is then an approximate variance-minimizing hedge ratio.

As an example, Edwards and Canter (1995) estimated variance-minimizing hedge ratios from 1990 to 1992 for heating oil and gasoline assuming one-month futures are used to hedge a nine-month forward contract. Their hedge ratios were around 0.50, suggesting that only about half of the underlying nine-month exposure should be hedged with one-month futures. Of course as the underlying exposure gets closer in time, the position would have to be rebalanced, as well as if the regression estimates exhibit time variation.

More sophisticated techniques would take into account either the presumed stochastic properties of the market—see, for example, Brennan and Crew (1999), Hilliard (1999), and Ross (1999)—or the empirical properties of the market. As an example of the latter, Pirrong (1997) uses the BAG hedge ratio estimation method discussed in Chapter 14 to compute hedge ratios in crude oil when one-month futures are used to hedge 13-, 14-, and 15-month deferred commitments. His hedge ratios average about 0.50 over a two-year period.

## Multiple Settlement Dates

Numerous exposures that firms may wish to hedge involve more than one settlement date. Firms with a cash flow hedging mandate invariably do (and almost certainly should) turn to swaps in this situation. Firms with a value or profit risk management orientation, moreover, also may turn to swaps in an effort to match as many maturities as possible in the hedge and underlying position. But this is not always possible, and sometimes can even conflict with the objectives of the hedging program.

Market participants that resort to futures in this situation practice several techniques when dealing with a multisettlement exposure whose last settlement date is beyond the last listed futures date. These techniques are often combined with one another, but we discuss them separately for simplicity.

### Stripping

A "futures strip" is a combination of futures contracts with multiple maturities held simultaneously to hedge multiple settlements. Suppose $t$ denotes a given calendar time increment and a firm has settlement obligations whose value it wishes to hedge on dates $t$, $t + 1, \ldots, t + N$. To accomplish this hedge, the firm can simply enter into futures contracts with maturities matched to the settlement dates—if possible.[1]

Now suppose the most deferred futures maturity at any point in time is $M$ periods in the future where $M < N$. A "pure strip" hedge simply ignores the periods from $M + 1$ to $N$ until the corresponding contracts become available. For example, if a firm is hedging quarterly interest payments for 10 years using Eurodollar futures, the CME actually lists contracts quarterly out to 10 years. A full strip can be constructed to hedge each interest payment completely. But if the exposure to be hedged has four additional settlements beyond year 10, futures are not available. In the pure strip solution, those four quarterly payments would simply not be hedged from the beginning.

One quarter into the life of the hedging program, however, the first quarterly settlement on the underlying exposure has occurred and the corresponding futures hedge has been lifted. In addition, a *new* 10-year maturity contract is now on the board. So, one quarter into the program, the strip covers all but three future settlement dates. And so on, until one year into the program the first four quarterly settlements have elapsed, their corresponding hedges offset or settled, and four new quarterly maturities have been added. A strip thus can fully hedge 11 years of settlements *one year into the life of the hedge*.

In terms of hedge ratios, firms can choose the quantities to hedge for each maturity that best fulfill its hedge mandate. In interest rate hedging, PV01 hedge ratios are often used to construct strips (see Chapter 14). For commodities, it is often variance-minimizing hedge ratios. As always, the right hedge ratio depends on the financial focus and hedge mandate adopted by the firm.

### Stripping and Stacking

Many hedgers are uncomfortable with a pure strip when not all the maturities to be hedged are covered with existing derivatives products. Leaving the deferred maturities totally unhedged even for a year can be quite risky.

A very popular solution (especially in interest rate markets) is the combination of stripping with a so-called *stack-and-roll* hedge. In such a hedge, a strip is constructed up to the most deferred available futures contract using the preferred hedge ratio calculation. The hedger then essentially "pretends" that additional futures are available beyond that maturity by using the price of the most deferred contract as a substitute for the missing contract prices. Corresponding hedge ratios are computed for those missing contracts, and the *sum* of the hedge size for all the missing contracts is added to the hedge size for the last-listed contract. The hedges corresponding to the missing maturities are thus *stacked* in the last contract month.

As time moves on and near-term maturity contracts expire, new contracts are listed. The stack that covers the missing contracts is then rolled forward into the newly listed contract *minus* that part of the stack that actually hedges the old back-month settlement date. And so on until the stack is redistributed into a full strip.

To take an example, suppose a firm calculates PV01 hedge ratios to hold Eurodollar futures for every quarter out to 10 years but in fact needs to hedge four more quarters out to 11 years. Suppose the PV01 for the 10-year contract is 100. The hedger then computes hypothetical PV01s for the missing contracts at years 10.25, 10.50, 10.75, and 11. The price of the 10-year is used for the four missing contract prices, but the present value adjustment is actually carried out to the correct time of the future settlements. Suppose the result is PV01 hedges of 100, 100, 99, and 98 contracts for the four missing contract maturities.

When the hedging program begins, the 10-year futures contract will have a total of 497 contracts—100 for the settlement in year 10, 100 for the settlement at year 10.25, 100 for the settlement at year 10.50, 99 for the 10.75-year settlement, and 98 for the 11-year position.

One quarter into the program, the firm recalculates the PV01s for all contracts in the strip, including the hypothetical PV01s for now three missing contracts at 10.25, 10.50, and 10.75 years. Suppose the PV01s for years 10 through 10.75 are now 100, 99, 99, and 98, respectively. When the new 10-year contract is listed, the firm will roll forward 396 contracts into the new 10-year. The old 10-year contract—now the 9.75-year contract—has only as many contracts as indicated by its new PV01 hedge ratio. And so on until the strip is completed.

Stripping and stacking in this manner makes good sense especially if the long end of the term structure of futures prices is stable. In interest rates, this is often the case. Using the most deferred contract price as a proxy for the missing prices works pretty well. But in a market like equity and in some commodities, the approach is not very realistic.

### Stack-and-Roll

A stack-and-roll hedge need not be implemented in the last-listed futures contract. Suppose, for example, a firm plans to make monthly purchases of gold for one year and wants to hedge using gold futures. To keep things easy, suppose the firm opts for a tailed one-to-one hedge ratio that suggests each month should have one contract in the hedge. The firm could do a full strip from the get-go, entering one short position for each listed contract month out to a year.

Alternatively, the firm could stack and roll the hedge in a maturity of its choosing. The hedger could put all 12 contracts in the 12-month contract. Each month when a new one-year contract is listed, the position would be rolled forward *minus* one contract to reflect current-period deliveries. Or the hedger could stack all 12 in the front-month and do the same thing at the other end of the term structure.

Stacking in this manner depends very much on the hedge objectives of the firm. If the objective is to minimize calendar basis risk, stacking everything in, say, the front month may be a very bad idea indeed. For a carrying-charge hedger seeking to trade the calendar basis against a physical position, however, stacking in the front month may make perfect sense (Johnson, 1960; Culp and Miller, 1995a).

## METALLGESELLSCHAFT

Practitioners, journalists, policy makers, and academics alike originally perceived the Metallgesellschaft AG (MG) fiasco as just another derivatives-related loss.[2] Yet, unlike the other derivatives disasters (e.g., Barings with its rogue trader and Procter & Gamble with its leveraged interest rate bet), a feature of the MG episode that immediately distinguished it from the rest of the pack was that this firm had apparently lost over a billion dollars *while hedging*.

The analysis and debate among various academics, practitioners, and policy makers over what happened at MG in 1993 is both instructive and confusing—instructive because the MG case does indeed contain many lessons for would-be hedgers and risk managers, and confusing because several different debates were actually occurring, all at the same time, all involving the same events at the same company, and all bearing on the current theory and practice of corporate hedging. This section makes no attempt to summarize all of those debates, but focuses instead on the three most interesting issues raised by MG for risk managers.

### The MGRM Program

At the end of 1992, MG was a century-year-old industrial conglomerate with 251 subsidiaries involved in trade, engineering, and financial services activities. Owned largely by institutional investors, including Deutsche Bank, Dresdner Bank, Daimler-Benz, and the Kuwait Investment Authority, MG's subsidiary responsible for petroleum marketing in the United States was MG Refining and Marketing (MGRM).

In December 1991, MGRM recruited from Louis Dreyfus Energy Corporation Arthur Benson and his management team, whose key marketing strategy was to offer firm price guarantees to mostly retail customers for 5 to 10 years on gasoline, heating oil, and diesel fuel purchased from MGRM. By September 1993, MGRM had sold forward the equivalent of over 160 million barrels of petroleum products in these contracts. The firm hedged its resulting exposure to spot oil price increases with futures contracts and futures-equivalent commodity swaps. The bulk of MGRM's futures positions were on the New York Mercantile Exchange in the most liquid contracts of between one and three months to maturity.

MGRM's hedging strategy was called a one-for-one stack-and-roll hedge. At any given time, an amount equivalent to the total remaining delivery obligation on the customer contracts was stacked in the short-dated futures. When the futures contracts matured each month, the total position (less current deliveries) was rolled forward into the next contract maturities.

When futures prices fall unexpectedly, cash drains must be incurred to meet variation margin payments. After OPEC failed to reach production quota agreements in late 1993, oil prices did indeed plunge. Faced with rising margin calls, the supervisory board of MG AG in December ordered the liquidation of substantial portions of MGRM's futures hedge and subsequently canceled up to 40 million barrels of its customer contracts. The early termination of the hedge and cancellation of the customer contracts resulted in an estimated net loss of about $1.08 billion, earning MGRM its place as one of the largest derivatives-related disasters.

The unfortunate end of MGRM's program has given rise to numerous questions about issues ranging from corporate governance to the valuation of long-dated commodity derivatives. The questions most relevant to risk management discussed in the remainder of this section can be separated into three general categories:

1. Given the obvious funding risks, did the program make economic sense when it was first started?
2. Did MGRM get its hedge ratios wrong?
3. Was the program terminated at the right time and in an appropriate manner?

### *Ex Ante* Value of the Program

Many doubtless still believe that MGRM's program was so fatally flawed that it was doomed to failure before it ever started, but the evidence in favor of that conclusion is far from compelling. Bollen and Whaley (1998) show, for example, that despite the funding risks of MGRM's program, it would have resulted in substantial economic profits for the firm in almost any reasonable scenario. In addition, the position that the program was flawed *from its inception* is hard to sustain if it can be shown that the program had a positive initial discounted expected net present value, and Culp and Miller (1995a,d) attempted to demonstrate exactly that.

True, the funding risks of MGRM's program were huge. Indeed, the inherent liquidity risk of using futures that are resettled once or twice daily to hedge a long-dated forward exposure is itself a major lesson to be learned from the MGRM debacle. But despite this risk—a risk of which MGRM's managers were apparently keenly aware—MGRM undertook the program anyway. Why?

It now seems that MGRM's management at the time believed that the firm had access to a "contingent capital" facility designed to provide up to $1.3 billion in cash in the specific event of a liquidity crisis.[3] The "guarantee" from banks that were acting both as creditors to *and* major shareholders of MG AG was designed to provide an infusion of capital in exchange for revolving senior debt, the proceeds from which were to be used by MGRM to buy puts on oil futures. This would have converted MGRM's futures hedge into synthetic calls and completely terminated the huge margin outflows required to keep the hedge in place as oil prices fell.

The total cost of the puts that would have been required to halt the cash drain totally would have been about $126 million—a far cry from the $1.3 billion in the facility, and clearly worth it to preserve the $800 million of value that Culp and Miller (1995a) estimate was locked up in the customer contracts when they were canceled. Unfortunately, it seems that the only person authorized to draw on the facility was the chairman of the MG AG management board, Heinz Schimmelbusch, who was removed by the MG AG supervisory board before he had the chance to invoke the facility.

## Basis Risk, Present Values, and Hedge Ratios

Probably the most common criticism of MGRM's program was that although the firm may have correctly calculated the *expected value* of its strategy, it failed to construct a hedging strategy appropriate to reduce the *risk* of its strategy. For most of MGRM's critics—for example, Brennan and Crew (1997), Edwards and Canter (1995), Hilliard (1999), Mello and Parsons (1995), Neuberger (1999), Pirrong (1999), and Ross (1997)—the firm's central failing was getting its hedge ratios wrong, either because it did not adopt a maturity-matched hedge like a commodity swap, did not tail its hedge to account for differences in the present values of the cash flows on the underlying contracts relative to the futures,[4] or did not choose a hedge ratio to minimize the variance of the changes in the value of the program.[5]

Despite the prominent role of variance in any mechanical discussions of how firms hedge, surprisingly little work has been done to substantiate the role of variance at the theoretical level. Classic articles about why risk-averse *traders* hedge—for example, Johnson (1960), Stein (1961), Ederington (1979)—imply a variance minimization objective, but articles on *corporate* hedging simply argue for the reduction in risk, usually with no specific attention to variance as a source of reduction in the value of the firm. Total variance is treated as a "bad" rather than a "good," as in the classic Markowitz investment paradigm, virtually by assumption.

The simplest example of the actual costs supposedly contributed by variance arise when increases in cash flow volatility force firms to turn to external financing sources, as in the models of Myers (1977) and Froot, Scharfstein, and Stein (1993) (hereinafter FSS). Myers (1977) argues that agency costs of external finance are most significant for firms with private information about intangible assets and investment opportunities. Those companies find it more difficult to convey the positive NPVs of their investments to external creditors and consequently face a higher cost of debt. FSS suggest that firms plagued with this problem would be well-advised to rely as little as possible on external finance and to eliminate their cash flow volatility by hedging.

Most of the variance in the cash flows of MGRM's program, of course, was a result of the calendar basis risk associated with using short-dated futures to hedge a long-dated commitment. For a firm whose risk management objective was to reduce the costs of external finance or financial distress as in the models of Myers or FSS, the MGRM program would have made little sense. Mello and Parsons (1995) and others thus argued that MGRM should have used maturity-matched swaps. A properly calculated hedge ratio as presented by Pirrong (1997) and others is also broadly consistently with this risk management objective.

But the objective of reducing the costs of external finance through cash flow variance reduction is only a *presumptive* risk management goal. Evidence from MGRM's annual reports and elsewhere suggests that the firm's business mandate was essentially "basis trading." In this case, a risk management program designed to minimize basis risk would have subverted the very reason that the firm was in business and thus would have made virtually no sense.[6]

The Myers and FSS analysis adopted by many of MGRM's critics, moreover, cannot have applied to MGRM for a variety of reasons. MGRM's hedged marketing program was not an *intangible* asset at all. On the contrary, it had a significant positive NPV—easily verifiable by outside calculations—that would have served as ample collateral to prospective lenders. True, some *generic* firm following an MGRM-like strategy might have found it difficult to secure external financing *quickly* after a period of sharply declining oil prices. A company forced into the capital market for liquidity when prices fall can be forced to pay what some might consider "distress costs" for that liquidity, even if the long-run expected NPV of the program is positive.

External financing costs are all almost totally irrelevant, however, as applied to MGRM. As noted earlier, this company's major shareholders *and* creditors were the two largest banks in Germany *and* members of the parent company's supervisory board. MGRM's financing thus was virtually all *internal* from "delegated monitors" who should have had no trouble seeing the positive NPV of MGRM's program. Even in the models of Myers and FSS, internal financing does not impose any deadweight costs, and thus does not provide an a priori rationale for hedging designed to minimize cash flow volatility (see Culp, 2001, 2002a).

## Was the MGRM Program Ended at the Right Time and in the Right Manner?

If the positive NPV of MGRM's hedged marketing program was so obvious, why, then, was it closed down at such great cost? The answer lies in one of the hardest problems in all of corporate finance—to wit, when is it rational to throw good money after bad? A simple example may help illustrate the poignancy of this dilemma. Suppose a multinational corporation has a subsidiary in France that is currently incurring net cash flow deficits at the rate of $1 million per year. The multinational could shut the operation down, but severance pay and other termination expenses required under French law would run about $12 million cash, net after tax recoveries. Efforts to find a buyer for the subsidiary have not been successful. Suppose that consultants report one of the problems to be inadequate production capacity for some of the plant's products. Additional equipment can be purchased for a current expenditure of about $4 million and will cut the net cash deficit to about $500,000 per annum. Suppose the cost of capital is 10 percent, and the planning horizon is 25 years.

The multinational faces three alternatives: (1) continue operating at a loss of $1 million per year; (2) shut down the plant for a current expenditure of $12 million; or (3) invest $4 million now to reduce losses to $500,000 per annum. The NPV of each alternative can be calculated as follows:

$$\text{NPV} = \sum_{j=1}^{25} \frac{X_{t+j}}{(1+r)^j} - I_t$$

where $r$ is the firm's cost of capital (i.e., 10 percent by assumption), $X_{t+j}$ is the net cash flow at time $t + j$, and $I_t$ is the current investment cost (i.e., expansion or shutdown). The NPV of the immediate shutdown alternative clearly is −$12,000,000. To maintain the status quo yields a current NPV of −$9,077,040. And to invest the additional $4 million today and cut losses to

$500,000 per year thereafter yields a current NPV of –$8,538,520. Counter-intuitive as it may seem, the best alternative clearly is to invest the additional $4 million today in plant improvements, even though the French subsidiary is a losing operation.[7]

When the problem is given in the classroom, less experienced students faithfully compute the present values in the French subsidiary example and get the right answers. Experienced executives, however, often refuse to do the calculations at all. They say the solution is obvious: shut the plant down, and blame the previous management for the loss!

MGRM's situation may well have been no different from the example. MG AG officials argued that the course of action they took—winding down the program by liquidating part of the futures/swaps hedge and canceling some of the customer contracts *with no compensation required from customers*—was the only alternative, given the "untenable" situation into which MGRM's former management had put the firm. But as noted earlier, the firm might instead have purchased puts to abrogate the cash drains on its futures hedge, thereby allowing the program to have been continued.

Even assuming that MG AG management was unwilling to continue the program, the firm still had alternatives for *how* it ended the program. The supervisory board might, for example, have directed that MGRM's hedged customer contracts be sold to another firm. Culp and Miller (1995a) estimated that if MGRM had been able to sell the combined program for its year-end 1993 capital asset value, it would have received nearly $800 million from the sale. MGRM's *net* 1993 loss would still have been about $200 million—roughly the same as if the program had been continued. But the sale would at least have halted the cash drains with which the supervisory board had become so obsessed.

Alternatively, the MG AG supervisory board could have instructed MGRM to buy back its customer contracts by unwinding them. As swap dealers know, when the market smells trouble, unwinding bilateral contracts rarely nets the unwinding firm a cash flow equal to the actual capital value of the contract. That MGRM might not have collected from its customers the same $800 million it could have made by selling the program to another firm is thus plausible. But between the time MGRM negotiated the fixed prices on its customer contracts and year-end 1993, the oil spot price had fallen by nearly $5.75 per barrel. Unless MGRM negotiated its contracts at a *massive initial loss*, customers should have been willing to pay *something* to get out of their contracts.[8]

So, contrary to its assertions, MG AG's supervisory board thus had several viable alternatives in December 1993. Instead, the supervisory board chose to liquidate much of the hedging program and then let its customers off the hook, and then blamed former management for forcing it to pursue this financially catastrophic solution—the French subsidiary example redux.

## SUMMARY

Did the MGRM disaster occur because the MG AG supervisory board truly believed it was throwing good money after bad and had reached some kind of "optimal stopping rule"? Or did the disaster occur because the old MG AG management board *thought* the supervisory board was supporting the basis trading activities of MGRM when it actually was not? Or did the supervisory board support the program initially and then subsequently abandon MGRM, perhaps in an effort to justify the ouster of the old management board that the supervisory board seemed to have been attempting for some time?

Unfortunately, even with the many separate lawsuits in which MG ultimately became involved, the settlements invariably had "shut-up" clauses that specified the closure of files to outside inspection. Thus, alas, the answers to these questions and the full story of MGRM—who did what to whom, when, and why—will probably never come out.

## NOTES

1. In the event that the settlement dates of the exposure to be hedged do not correspond to futures maturities, the resulting "stub" risk can sometimes be hedged using a combination of other instruments. In this situation, however, it is easier and more common to simply use swaps in lieu of futures.
2. The discussion in this section draws heavily from Culp and Miller (1995a, 1999c) and Culp (2003c).
3. For a discussion of contingent capital, see Culp (2002a,b,c).
4. Critics like Ross (1997) who concentrated on MGRM's failure to tail its hedge can generally be separated from critics like Edwards and Canter (1995) who were more concerned with reducing the basis risk of the combined program. The issue of why MGRM may not have tailed its hedge—for example, the shortened *effective* maturity of the program created by the presence of early termination options, as well as the need to be able to monitor and report a "fully hedged" position to customers—are explored in Culp and Miller (1995b,c).
5. Virtually all of the major academic articles analyzing MGRM's hedging strategy—both for and against—are reprinted in Culp and Miller (1999a).
6. For more discussion of the relation between the strategy and tactics of risk management and the use of "selective hedging" methods, see Stulz (1996) and Culp (2001).
7. The unadjusted NPV criterion, of course, is not actually the best way even to answer this question. Following on the early work by Myers (1977) and Brennan and Schwartz (1985), the numerous recent developments in real

options can help managers develop better and more systematic criteria than the NPV criterion alone.

8. A former MGRM employee explained in a critique of the special audit of MG that on December 22, 1993, one of MGRM's biggest customers paid MGRM $2 million to unwind its fixed-price contracts. Two months later when many of MGRM's similar contracts had been canceled with no compensation required from customers, MG refunded the $2 million it had been paid earlier. Although there is no easy way to assess whether the $2 million paid was a fair estimate of that customer's actual contract value, it is likely that if one of them was willing to pay, so were others.

# PART Four

# Appendixes

# Economic Theory and Equilibrium

*Practical men, who believe themselves to be quite exempt from any intellectual influences, are usually the slaves of some defunct economist.*

—J. M. Keynes (1936)

One of the most important concepts in both economics and finance is the notion of *equilibrium*. Strange as it may seem, however, it is a concept about which there has been much disagreement historically and about which there remains significant confusion. Nevertheless, invoking the concept of equilibrium is the deus ex machina by which we accomplish many of our tasks in finance and economics. Consider some examples:

- The prices of risky assets and bundles of cash flows typically depend on some kind of equilibrium concept.
- Entry and exit of new competitors or participants in markets occurs when we are "out of equilibrium" but stops when we are "in equilibrium."
- The ability of firms to sustain positive economics profits over time depends on our conception of an equilibrium and whether we are "in one" or "out of one."

Clearly, we need to add some teeth to this concept.

In some ways, developing a more precise concept of what is meant by "equilibrium" is the issue at the very heart of economic theory itself. For many, an exploration into theoretical economics—and its history—is out of place in a book like this, even in an appendix. But even at a deeply theoretical level, economics has a surprising amount of relevance for many of the problems this addresses. This Appendix thus begins with a brief introduction to why readers might want to consider what economic theory has to say about some of the concepts discussed here. We then turn to discuss more broadly what alternative theories of economics have said—and say—about equilibrium.

# RELEVANCE OF ECONOMIC THEORY

Lionel Robbins described economics as "the science which studies human behavior as a relationship between ends and scarce means which have alternative uses" (Robbins, 1932, p. 16). Especially when we recognize that scarce resources go well beyond hard assets like oil and include less tangible but equally important assets like knowledge, information, and human capital, it is hard to argue that economic theory is irrelevant. But at the day-to-day level of corporate decision making, economic theory has been so marginalized that it *is* viewed as being largely irrelevant.

The now almost universal aversion to economics in practical discussions is not confined to business practitioners. *Everyone* outside the economic profession has probably at one time or another regarded economists as overly theoretical and abstract creatures disconnected from the operations of "the real world." Several reasons account for this general unpopularity of economics and its perceived general lack of real applicability.

The first is a self-inflicted wound for which economists have only themselves to blame. Namely, scholarly economics journals and studies have over the years become increasingly reliant on highly mathematical and technical modeling approaches. The *methodology* of economics has in effect erected a barrier to entry around the academic side of the profession. Within the academic profession of economics, those without either the mathematical skills required to be a theorist or modeler or the statistical skills required to be an empiricist or econometrician are regarded as "not very good." They do not get tenure at the coveted universities, and their papers appear in second- and third-rate journals. Paradoxically, the better the economist by most current metrics of the profession, the less likely it is that an average person with a B.A. from a liberal arts school will be able to digest what they say and write. Although not, to be sure, universally true, the correlation between work that the economics profession tends to reward and work that outsiders cannot understand is disturbingly high.

Despite the preponderance of technical modeling that goes on in economics today, this was not always the case. In fact, the only stumbling block to reading Smith or Ricardo or Mill or any of the other great classical economists—basically anyone writing before 1870 about the behavior of humans in the face of resource scarcity—is their use of older styles of written English. The "barriers to entry" for the classical works, though, are small.

Also important to recognize is that the classical economists were *not* marginalized. On the contrary, they were quite frequently very important members of society, and their works received mainstream attention and significant debate from virtually all classes of society. Historically, economics was neither a science nor a subject aimed primarily at the intellectual. The major works of two of the greats—Smith and Ricardo—actually were direct responses to *political legislation* of their day concerning restraints on international trade.

A second reason for the marginalization of economic theory today must surely be the widespread perception its general failure as a science. Although I shall have more to say on the methodology of economics as teleology a bit later, suffice it to say now that this criticism is largely correct, albeit frequently misunderstood. An example will suffice to illustrate the point. In physics, the law of gravity says that when an apple becomes detached from the tree, it will fall to the ground. No matter how much data you collect, this will be true 100 percent of the time. In economics, the criteria for determining the "success" of models are much laxer. The law of demand, for example, states that the price someone is willing to pay for a good is inversely proportional to the quantity demanded—that is, "demand curves" slope down. Although every fiber of our being may agree that this is intuitively true, economists would regard a regression R-square of 30 percent to be a wild success. Tell a physicist that you can explain only 30 percent of apple falls and she will laugh at you.

Finally, the history of economics is fraught with tremendous disagreement *within the profession* about certain nontrivial issues. For many years, a central subject of debate among economists concerned the importance of the supply of land in determining economic profits. Today, most economists do not even consider land as a separate and distinct factor of production. And if reputable members of the profession cannot agree, how can those outside it agree?

Essentially the same problem is encountered in theology. Even within Christianity, the often vitriolic and always impassioned disagreement among members of the pastorate and clergy in different Protestant denominations and in the Catholic Church lead many laymen to be fairly confused. People tend more often than not, at least initially, to be biased to what they are used to hearing, rather than to what might be considered "correct." Add to that that both economics and religion often deal with inherently "untestable" propositions—you cannot *prove* that a demand curve slopes downward any more than you can *prove* God exists—and you have a generally befuddled population.

An important difference between economics and religion—and the two are indeed often compared—is that at least in religion the layman has access to "primary source documents" and to the same data as the clergy. People can pick up the Bible or the Koran and read them for themselves, drawing their own conclusions as they see fit. And they can supplement those conclusions by listening to debates by the experts of their field.

Economics, by contrast, is a highly data-intensive field in which many professionals do not even have the raw materials required to engage in statistical inference. And, as noted earlier, outsiders are doomed to be forever locked out of reading the debates economists have with themselves without a strong background in calculus and regression analysis.

To keep the analogy going, however, let me quote the pastor of my own church, Erwin W. Lutzer, who likes to remind people that "Everyone is entitled to their own opinion, but everyone is *not* entitled to their own truth." If for the purpose of this example assuming that there *is* an absolute truth, the question then is how best to find it out. In this regard, disagreements among theologians do not alter the fundamental principles of what is true about God. Likewise, the inability of economic theories to be reconciled with the data and communicated effectively to the public does not alter the truisms that may well underlie the behavior of humans and firms facing resource scarcity. In other words, economics may be *inaccessible* to many, and it may be *abstract* in theoretical form and empirical practice. But it is absolutely not *irrelevant*.

To draw one final parallel between economics and religion in the context of the prior statement, it is often true that much can be gained by the struggle to find the truth, even when the quest for 100 percent "proof" is doomed to fail from the start. In theology, self-examination together with careful study of the extant doctrinal beliefs, primary documents, exegetical controversies, and the like can lead one to become quite comfortable with an absolute belief system. And this may well be true despite the absence of physics-like laws that can be postulated and either proven or disproved.

German historian Karl Popper criticized much of economics as resting on a set of "nonfalsifiable" propositions—they could not be *disproved*. Nevertheless, he was the first to recognize that the analysis of the problem was the source of the greatest intellectual gain, not the resolution of the underlying question.

In the spirit of Popper, certain parts of this book take a fairly close look at competing economic theories. You are encouraged not to be put off by this, however, but rather to be stimulated into drawing *your own* conclusions. Some of the theories we discuss in this book *are* testable, and, indeed, have been tested. They are falsifiable by their nature and thus true or false. That does not mean we have clear answers to the questions underlying these theories. As noted, the methodology of economics may never give us a clean answer to whether a falsifiable theory is correct. And in still other cases, we will deal with theories that are nonfalsifiable—for example, Frank Knight's belief that profits can arise only from sources of randomness that cannot be measured. If they cannot be measured, they cannot be tested.

The use of derivatives in risk transfer is an extremely practical and narrow field of interest. That does not make this subject free of significant debate, both methodological and empirical. And like it or not, the economic theories we put forth *do matter* and they *do affect* how people view these products and markets and participate in derivatives activity. Take an example. J. M. Keynes believed that establishing an uncovered, naked short position in a derivatives contract based on a physical commodity would generate positive average profits over time. This is strong stuff—it says that being short makes money on average. If this is true, it should affect the way firms hedge, the way individuals construct their portfolios, and the way practical market mechanisms address "long" versus "short" positions. We thus have an obligation to take a hard, serious look at this theory.

## SCHOOLS OF ECONOMIC THOUGHT AND CHARACTERIZATIONS OF EQUILIBRIUM

The so-called "professionalization of economics" did not begin until the end of the nineteenth century, mainly in England and the United States. Prior to that, the analysis of economic problems was undertaken by theologians, lawyers, philosophers, businessmen, and statesmen—those who had "day jobs" other than "economist" who either analyzed economic problems as part of those other jobs or on their own time. Consider the number of great early economists throughout history for whom economics was not their actual profession: Adam Smith was a moral philosopher; Richard Cantillon was a merchant banker and real estate speculator; Thomas Malthus was a clergyman in the Church of England; John Stuart Mill and David Ricardo were Members of Parliament; Antoine Augustin Cournot was a professor of mathematics; and Karl Marx was a journalist (only later in his life a revolutionary).[1]

The beginning of economics as a true profession was marked by the emergence of the *Quarterly Journal of Economics* as the first scholarly journal of the field in 1886, followed quickly by the *Economic Journal* in 1890 and the *Journal of Political Economy* in 1892. Commensurate with the creation of "true economists" was the beginning of the field's progression toward increasingly more mathematical formalism and to a shift from what economic historians like to call the classical and neoclassical periods.[2] Both the classical and neoclassical periods are also considered "schools of thought" in economics today. There are several other schools of thought, moreover, that do not conform to specific periods of time. Most of these are not discussed here, with one exception.

### Classical Period

The classical period began with Adam Smith's *Wealth of Nations* published in 1776 and ran roughly up to the period from 1870 to 1890. This period of economics arguably contains the greatest advances in thought of any period—

relative to where things started, of course—but lacked the development of a consistent and coherent theme. Indeed, throughout most of the period the major players were arguing with one another. These players included Adam Smith, David Hume, Thomas Malthus, John Stuart Mill, David Ricardo, and Karl Marx.

A central preoccupation of the classical economists was what we now call *capital theory*. Most classical economists considered there to be two or three factors of production, depending on how you define the terms: labor, land, and capital. Capital theory seeks to clarify what exactly is meant by the slippery term, as well as what gives capital its "value." As an example of the lack of agreement, Malthus (1820) believed that the value of capital was what determined the value of what capital produced, whereas Ricardo (1817) considered the value of capital to be the value of labor sacrificed to capital-intensive production. Marx (1859) later extended the Ricardian "labor theory of value" into the theory that the value of capital came from the ability of its owners to *exploit* labor during capital-intensive production.

A major theme of the classical period that is evident to at least some degree in all the major works is the belief that production capabilities were determined totally exogenously by a mixture of the available land and resources, the state of knowledge, and the supply of capital. This assumption came to characterize *Ricardian economics* after its initial developer. Disagreement occurred, however, about distribution. Ricardo also felt that the distribution of resources occurred to ensure that all participants earned an essential constant profit, and resources moved around to ensure that fact. Mill and others argued instead that the distribution of wealth was driven by human behavior and was endogenous.

Another major precept of the classical period was the belief that most things in an economy tend toward some *natural rate*, and it was in this belief that the core concept of equilibrium was defined for the classical economists. According to the classicists, the value of resources in the market tended toward the natural rate, and shifts in supply were required to bring about that tendency. The tendency of supply shifts to cause a convergence between market and natural rates is essentially the Classical or Ricardian definition of an equilibrium.[3]

## The Marginalist Revolution and the Neoclassical Period

The birth of the neoclassical period is generally credited to William Stanley Jevons (a meteorologist and chemist turned economist) and Léon Walras (an economist in Lausanne, Switzerland) (Backhouse, 2002). Jevons and Walras—together with Carl Menger—led the so-called "marginalist revolution" that turned much of classical economic theory—including its characterization of equilibrium—on its head.

Specifically, Jevons and Walras believed that market values of assets and factors of production were determined by interactions between supply and demand "at the margin." As Hicks (1989) notes, however, Jevons and Walras did a better job of identifying the problem with the classical theory (i.e., ignoring the importance of incremental benefits and costs) than in proposing a solution.

Jevons (1871) introduced us to the Law of One Price—identical goods of uniform quality must sell for the same price. Jevons's "law of indifference" then stated that the market price of a good was the price at which the marginal or incremental unit of that good would sell. The problem with that idea is that he never really explained how the market reached that point. In addition, if equilibrium is taken to mean the equality of supply and demand, then Jevons's proposition implied that markets are always and constantly in equilibrium.

Walras (1874) was working without knowledge of Jevons but reached essentially the same theoretical impasse (Hicks, 1989). Walras argued that the market price of a good was the price at which supply and demand curves intersected. Walras is often credited with being one of the first two economists to recognize, moreover, that demand schedules trace to a concept known as *marginal utility*—the idea that the incremental quantity demanded of something depends on the incremental value or utility that the economic agent gets from the good (Schumpeter, 1954; Robbins, 1998). (Menger was the other economist to recognize this, as we shall see.)

What Walras did *not* do, however, was contemplate any realistic adjustment mechanism by which the market forces of supply and demand were reconciled. Instead, Walras merely supposed the existence of an auctioneer who literally called out prices. In his famous adjustment process of *tatônnement*, the auctioneer continued calling out prices until the marginal utility of some agent (i.e., the demand) was equal to supply. But especially on the supply side, Walras was fairly silent on where this auctioneer got her information.

Edgeworth (1881) refined the notion of a Walrasian equilibrium by introducing the possibility of *recontracting*. If the Law of One Price or Jevons's law of indifference was violated, economic agents would simply amend their prior price agreements. A buyer who purchased at an excessive price would recontract by repudiating his first purchase agreement and then identifying a new seller from whom the good could be purchased at a lower price. Or a buyer who had unfilled demand at a given price could entice suppliers to provide more of the good by offering a higher price. Either way, the uniform price would tend to equate supply and demand at the margin.

The "equilibrium" postulated by Edgeworth, however, did not necessarily result in the same allocation of resources as the "equilibrium" postulated by Walras. In Edgeworth's case, gains and losses on trades conducted "out of equilibrium" would generate income effects that dictate where the final equilibrium would occur, which might happen to be exactly the same as a Walrasian equilibrium but probably would not be.

Marshall (1890) is often regarded as having applied formalistic and mathematical principles to the early classical economists. In some sense this is accurate as concerns his notions of equilibrium. One of the most important concepts developed by Marshall was the notion of a *short run* and a *long run*. The short run was essentially Edgeworth's recontracting period in which profits and losses were possible because of deviations in supply and demand with their "true" long-term values. In the long run, all profits were driven to their natural rate of zero. *Only imperfect competition can explain positive long-run profits in a Marshallian equilibrium.* On the production side, entry by new firms occurs until the marginal entrant has a minimum average cost. The long-run demand supply curve is then the long-run minimum average cost curve, and a long-run equilibrium is one in which price (demand or marginal revenue) is equal to minimum average cost, which in turn is equal to marginal cost (supply).

## The Neoclassical School

For the most part, Marshall's *Principles* is regarded as the defining price theory text of the neoclassical school of the price system. The basic tenets of the neoclassical school include the following: the Law of One Price; the distinctions between short-run and long-run behavior of market participants and markets; the inability of firms to earn positive economic profits in the long run in a perfectly competitive market; returns to sale in production; nonsatiation and diminishing marginal utility in consumption; and market efficiency.

## Menger and the Austrian Critique

Around the same time that the neoclassical period and school began to emerge with Jevons, Menger, an Austrian, led (perhaps unintentionally) a move in a slightly different direction—later to become known as the Austrian school, so named because most of the contributors to this theory were resident at the University of Vienna.

The Austrians had several major points of departure with neoclassical economists; chief among them was the disdain of most Austrians after Menger to embrace mathematics as a tool of economic analysis. Unfortunately, as the neoclassical paradigm became steadily more rooted into the intellectual fabric of the times, the Austrian school was quickly marginalized. Defenders of the neoclassical approach argued that Austrians simply lacked the technical acumen to use mathematics, and in some cases that was probably an accurate criticism (Schumpeter, 1954).

The criticisms of the Austrians, however, were unfortunate inasmuch as some significant developments in economic theory were made by Austrians—for example, the work on capital theory by Böhm-Bawerk (1891) and Lachmann (1978). But many of these concepts did not work their way into conventional economic thinking until they were ultimately championed by someone deemed closer to the neoclassical school, such as Nobel laureates F. A. Hayek and Sir John Hicks, who were sympathetic to the Austrian school but regarded as and accepted by the neoclassical establishment.

Although it is easy and tempting to point at the use of mathematics as the major distinction between the neoclassical and Austrian schools, this is a severe oversimplification of what actually were fairly serious methodological disagreements.[4] An important gulf between the neoclassical and Austrian schools concerned the definition of value or marginal utility. Menger (1871) deserves probably as much credit as Walras (1874) for recognizing the role of marginal utility in governing consumption optimality. But unlike Walras and other neoclassicals, Menger (1871) advanced the theory of *subjective value*, which held that each individual's values and utilities were subjective, relative, dependent on the psychology and wants of that particular individual, and—importantly—not directly comparable across different economic agents. So, the *concept* of marginal utility was identified in Menger, but, along with it, the impossibility of operationalizing the concept also was born.

The differences between the Austrian and neoclassical schools in areas apart from utility often had a parallel with the disagreement on value. Namely, neoclassical economics tends to stress objective and knowable quantities, whereas the Austrian school tends to stress subjective and unknowable quantities. Apart from the objective versus subjective value debate, this chasm is perhaps nowhere more obvious than in the notion of equilibrium.

The neoclassical theory of equilibrium essentially postulates an equilibrium as a balance of forces—supply and demand—that lead to either a state of rest or a steady state of uniform motion in a system. Adjustments occur discretely as the economic system jumps from one state into another until it reaches a point of stability and balance.

In the Austrian theory, equilibrium can be better defined as a situation in which knowledge and expectations lead to consistent plans. Hayek (1937) defines an equilibrium as a situation in which "the different plans which the individuals composing [an economic system] have made for action in time are mutually compatible." To Austrians, equilibrium thus is more of a *tendency* than a stationary or steady state. Importantly, perhaps the richest insights from the Austrian school thus are not its analyses of equilibrium, but rather its analysis of *disequilibrium*.

In the neoclassical paradigm, disequilibrium is simply not very interesting. It is just a condition in which markets do not clear and must adjust toward a market-clearing set of prices. In the Austrian paradigm, disequilibrium is basically the constant state of affairs. Markets still *tend* toward equilibrium, but the constant changes in information, knowledge, and expectations of individuals make the market much more of a *process* than a state of nature.

The consequences of the divergence between the Austrian and neoclassical schools are significant. The neoclassical picture is a fairly choppy one in which individuals and firms jump discretely toward a Marshallian long run in which everyone believes the same thing and no firm can make positive profits. But what if the Austrian school were right and there is essentially no such long run? That would imply some form of stable situation in which profits *are* possible and information is *not* equal across market participants.

### The Neo-Austrian Middle Ground

Importantly, it is not really necessary to pick a philosophical allegiance to explore these issues. Perhaps no one understood this more than Sir John Hicks, who liked to call himself a "neo-Austrian." Himself a Nobel laureate in economics, Hicks was deeply rooted in the neoclassical tradition. And yet, Hicks recognized the importance of some of the Austrian concepts. Like many, he did not believe that the Austrian school had put forth an alternative theory of economics to the neoclassical or even the classical school. But he did believe there was much about neoclassical economics that could benefit from Austrian insights. For example, Hicks adopted a Hayekian notion of equilibrium as consistency in plans in most of his work, recognized the importance of heterogenous expectations and information in the process by which markets adjust, and fundamentally disagreed with the Marshallian notion of a clean dichotomy between a short run and a long run. Yet, he embraced these Austrian beliefs without ever giving up the standard tools of formal economic analysis pioneered by Jevons and Walras.

The vast majority of this book takes a methodological approach quite similar to that of Hicks. Throughout most of the book we essentially retain the core features of the neoclassical paradigm (the Law of One Price, marginalism, rising supply price, etc.), but we remain openly sympathetic to the Austrian critique and to the Austrian views of the market as a process and equilibrium as a consistency in plans rather than a balance of forces. Indeed, as we see throughout this book, it becomes quite hard to explain a lot of financial and derivatives market activity without being *a little bit* Austrian.

## NOTES

1. For those seeking a good introduction to the history of economics and the great economists, Backhouse (2002) is a good place to start. More seasoned veterans may prefer a deeper look, such as Schumpeter (1954) or Robbins (1998)—both are classics but neither is "light beach reading."

2. Certainly there were intellectual contributions to and developments in the theory of "economics" before the classical period. Robbins (1998) refers to these early works as comprising two groups. "Anticipations" of what was to come more systematically later includes all the early works, such as Plato and Aristotle. Between those who anticipated economics and the classical period was the "Emergence of Systems" in which several key intellectuals advanced theories that recognized some of the fundamental organizing principles of classical (and in some cases neoclassical) economic theory. Major contributors to this period include Cantillon, the Physiocrats (Mirabeau, Quesney, Law, and Turgot), Locke, and Hume.

3. Ricardian economics is here equated with classical economics because Ricardo first took natural rates to the extreme and truly *systemized* them. To Ricardo, *everything* had a natural rate—a natural rate of profits, a natural rate of interest, a natural rental rate for land and labor, and so on—and shifts in supply of all these variables were required to bring market and natural rates into equality. See Hicks (1989).

4. See White (1977).

# Derivation of the Fundamental Value Equation

To describe what an investor likes and dislikes, and hence to think about how the investor values an asset, we employ the standard economist's model that investors want to find the highest value of a "utility function"[1]:

$$U(c_t, c_{t+1}) = u(c_t) + \xi E_t[u(c_{t+1})]$$

$u(c_t)$ describes how more consumption at time $t$ makes the investor happier. We typically assume that investors always prefer more to less [$u_c(c) > 0$], and each incremental unit of consumption brings slightly less happiness than the unit before it [$u_{cc}(c) < 0$].

Now think of a financial asset whose price at time $t$ is $p_t$ and whose payoff (total value) at time $t + 1$ is $x_{t+1}$. The investor can freely buy or sell as much of this asset as she likes at time $t$. How much will she buy or sell? To find the answer, denote $e(t)$ as her consumption level before she buys any of the asset, and denote by $\xi$ the amount of the asset she chooses to buy. Then, her problem is to choose the $\xi$ that solves:

$$\max_\xi u(c_t) + E_t[\xi u(c_{t+1})]$$
$$s.t. \quad c_t = e_t - \xi p_t$$
$$s.t. \quad c_{t+1} = e_{t+1} - \xi x_{t+1}$$

Substitute the two constraints into the objective, and take a derivative with respect to the $\xi$. Set the derivative equal to zero to characterize the maximum. The result is that the investor's optimal consumption-investment choice satisfies:

$$p_t u'(c_t) = E_t[\xi u'(c_{t+1}) x_{t+1}]$$

or, rearranging with price on the left and the rest on the right,

$$p_t = E_t \left[ \xi \frac{u_c(c_{t+1})}{u_c(c_t)} x_{t+1} \right]$$

## NOTES

1. This simple formulation treats all consumers as alike and presumes that utility is "additively separable" across time. Numerous alternatives to this simple setup have been proposed. See, for example, Constantinides (1990). Many alternatives are reviewed in Cochrane (1997, 1999a,b).

# Relation between the Cost of Carry Model and the Fundamental Value Equation

$\mathbf{R}$ecall that the fundamental value equation in (7.2) allows us to write the time $t$ price of any time $T$ payoff as:

$$p_t = E_t[m_T x_T] \tag{A3.1}$$

and the time $t$ price of any sequence of $N$ payoffs as:

$$p_t = \sum_{k=1}^{N} E_t\left[m_{t+t_k} x_{t+t_k}\right] \tag{A3.1}'$$

where the $k$th payoff occurs at time $t + t_k$.

Recall further that the payoff on a contract negotiated at time $t$ for the delivery of one unit of some asset at time $T$ at the price $f_{t,T}$ is:

$$x_T = S_T - f_{t,T} \tag{A3.2}$$

Substituting (A3.2) in (A3.1), the payoff on a traditional forward must have the following true price at time $t$:

$$p_t = E_t[m_T(S_T - f_{t,T})] \tag{A3.3}$$

If the forward is at-market when negotiated, we know by definition that the true price is zero at time $t$. Recognizing that $f_{t,T}$ is nonstochastic, we thus can rewrite (A3.3) as:

$$E_t[m_T S_T] = E_t[m_T] f_{t,T} \tag{A3.4}$$

Now consider the underlying asset. Suppose the Keynesian liquidity premium is zero and the asset pays an explicit distribution of $Q_{t+k}$ each period. In addition, suppose it costs $C_{t+k}$ each period to store the asset. The distributions (e.g., dividends or coupon payments) and storage costs are known at time $t$. We can then use (A3.1)′ to express the time $t$ price of the underlying asset as:

$$S_t = \sum_{k=1}^{T-t} E_t\left[m_{t+k}Q_{t+k}\right] - \sum_{k=1}^{T-t} E_t[m_{t+k}C_{t+k}] + E_t[m_T S_T] \qquad \text{(A3.5)}$$

which can be rewritten more usefully for our purposes here as:

$$E_t[m_T S_T] = S_t - \sum_{k=1}^{T-t} \frac{Q_{t+k}}{(1+r_{t,t+k})} + \sum_{k=1}^{T-t} \frac{C_{t+k}}{(1+r_{t,t+k})} \qquad \text{(A3.6)}$$

Remember from Chapter 7 that $E[m_{t+k}] = 1/(1 + r_{t,t+k})$.
    Now substitute (A3.6) into (A3.4):

$$\frac{f_{t,T}}{(1+r_{t,T})} = S_t - \sum_{k=1}^{T-t} \frac{Q_{t+k}}{(1+r_{t,t+k})} + \sum_{k=1}^{T-t} \frac{C_{t+k}}{(1+r_{t,t+k})} \qquad \text{(A3.7)}$$

Simplifying,

$$f_{t,T} = S_t(1+r_{t,T}) - \sum_{k=1}^{T-t} Q_{t+k}(1+r_{t+k,T}) + \sum_{k=1}^{T-t} C_{t+k}(1+r_{t+k,T}) \quad \text{(A3.8)}$$

Now define:

$$q_{t,T} = \frac{\sum_{k=1}^{T-t} Q_{t+k}(1+r_{t+k,T})}{S_t} \quad \text{and} \quad c_{t,T} = \frac{\sum_{k=1}^{T-t} C_{t+k}(1+r_{t+k,T})}{S_t} \qquad \text{(A3.9)}$$

Multiply and divide the second and third terms of (A3.8) by $S_t$:

$$f_{t,T} = S_t(1+r_{t,T}) - S_t \left( \frac{\sum_{k=1}^{T-t} Q_{t+k}(1+r_{t+k,T})}{S_t} \right) + S_t \left( \frac{\sum_{k=1}^{T-t} C_{t+k}(1+r_{t+k,T})}{S_t} \right) \quad \text{(A3.10)}$$

Finally, substitute (A3.9) into (A3.10) to get:

$$f_{t,T} = S_t(1 + r_{t,T} - q_{t,T} + c_{t,T}) = S_t(1 + r_{t,T} - x_{t,T}) \quad \text{(A3.10)}$$

which was to be shown. Q.E.D.

# References

Alchian, A., and H. Demsetz. 1972. "Production, Information Costs, and Economic Organization." *American Economic Review* 62.

Allen, F., and D. Gale. 1994. *Financial Innovation and Risk Sharing.* Cambridge: MIT Press.

Anderson, R. W., and J. P. Danthine. 1983. "Hedging Diversity in Futures Markets." *Economic Journal* 93.

Arrow, K. A. 1953. "Le rôle des valeurs boursières pour la repartition la meilleure des risques." *Colloques Internationaux du Centre National de la Recherche Scientifique* 11: 41–47. Translated into English in 1963–1964 as "The Role of Securities in the Optimal Allocation of Risk-Bearing," *Review of Economic Studies* 31.

Arrow, K. A. 1970. *Essays in the Theory of Risk Bearing.* Amsterdam: North-Holland.

Arrow, K. A. 1978. "Risk Allocation and Information: Some Recent Theoretical Developments." *Geneva Papers on Risk and Insurance* 8.

Backhouse, R. E. 2002. *The Ordinary Business of Life: A History of Economics from the Ancient World to the Twenty-First Century.* Princeton, N.J.: Princeton University Press.

Banz, R. W. 1981. "The Relationship between Return and Market Value of Common Stocks." *Journal of Financial Economics* 9.

Barenboim, D., and E. W. Said. 2002. *Parallels and Paradoxes: Explorations in Music and Society.* New York: Pantheon Books.

Baumol, W. J. 1957. "Speculation, Profitability, and Stability." *Review of Economics and Statistics* 39(3).

Berle, A. A., Jr., and G. C. Means. 1932. *The Modern Corporation and Private Property.* New York: Macmillan.

Bernardo, A. E., and O. Ledoit. 2000. "Gain, Loss, and Asset Pricing." *Journal of Political Economy* 108(1) (February).

Bessembinder, H. 1992. "Systematic Risk, Hedging Pressure, and Risk Premiums in Futures Markets." *Review of Financial Studies* 5(4).

Billingsley, P. 1995. *Probability and Measure.* New York: Wiley Interscience.

Black, F. 1972. "Capital Market Equilibrium with Restricted Borrowing." *Journal of Business* 45.

Black, F., and M. Scholes. 1973. "The Pricing of Options and Corporate Liabilities." *Journal of Political Economy* 81.

Black, F. 1985. "Noise." *Journal of Finance* 41(3) (July).

Blommenstein, H. J., and B. J. Summers. 1994. "Banking and the Payment System." In *The Payment System: Design, Management, and Supervision.* B. J. Summers, ed. Washington, DC: International Monetary Fund.

Bodie, Z., and V. Rosansky. 1980. "Risk and Return in Commodity Futures." *Financial Analysts Journal* 36.

Böhm-Bawerk, E. von. 1890. *Capital and Interest: A Critical History of Economic Theory.* London: Macmillan.

Böhm-Bawerk, E. von. 1891. *The Positive Theory of Capital.* London: Macmillan.

Bollen, N. P., and R. E. Whaley. 1998. "Simulating Supply." *Risk* 11(9).

Breeden, D. 1979. "An Intertemporal Asset Pricing Model with Stochastic Consumption and Investment Opportunities." *Journal of Financial Economics* 7.

Brennan, M. J. 1958. "The Supply of Storage." *American Economic Review* 48.

Brennan, M. J., and N. I. Crew. 1999. "Hedging Long-Maturity Commodity Commitments with Short-Dated Futures Contracts." In *Corporate Hedging in Theory and Practice: Lessons from Metallgesellschaft.* C. L. Culp and M. H. Miller, eds. London: Risk Publications.

Brennan, M. J., and N. I. Crew. 1997. "Hedging Long Maturity Commodity Commitments with Short-Dated Futures Contracts." In *Mathematics of Derivative Securities.* M. A. H. Dempster and S. R. Pliska, eds. New York: Cambridge University Press.

Brennan, M. J., and E. S. Schwartz. 1985. "Evaluating Natural Resource Investment." *Journal of Business* 58(2).

Brennan, M. J., and E. S. Schwartz. 1979. "A Continuous-Time Approach to the Pricing of Bonds." *Journal of Banking and Finance* 3.

Bromberg, B. 1942. "The Origin of Banking: Religious Finance in Babylonia." *Journal of Economic History* 2(1) (May).

Burghardt, G. D. 2003. *The Eurodollar Futures and Options Handbook.* New York, and Chicago: McGraw-Hill and Chicago Mercantile Exchange.

Burghardt, G. D., T. M. Belton, M. Lane, and J. Papa. 1994. *The Treasury Bond Basis.* Revised ed. New York: McGraw-Hill.

Burghardt, G., T. Belton, M. Lane, G. Luce, and R. McVey. 1991. *Eurodollar Futures and Options.* Chicago: Probus.

Campbell, J., A. Lo, and C. MacKinlay. 1996. *The Econometrics of Financial Markets.* Princeton, N.J.: Princeton University Press.

Carlton, D. W. 1984. "Futures Markets: Their Purpose, Their History, Their Growth, Their Successes and Failures." *Journal of Futures Markets* 4(3).

Cassell, G. 1903. *The Nature and Necessity of Interest.* London: Macmillan.

Chang, E. 1985. "Returns to Speculators and the Theory of Normal Backwardation." *Journal of Finance* 45.

Chen, N.-F., R. Roll, and S. A. Ross. 1986. "Economic Forces and the Stock Market." *Journal of Business* 59.

Chicago Board of Trade (CBOT). 1989. *Commodity Trading Manual.* Chicago, Ill.: Chicago Board of Trade.

Chicago Board of Trade (CBOT). 2003. "An Explanation of the Soybean 'Crush.' " CBOT Knowledge Center. www.cbot.com/cbot/www/cont_detail/0,1493,14+477+6173,00.html.

Coase, R. H. 1937. "The Nature of the Firm." *Economica* 4 (November).

Coase, R. H. 1988. *The Firm, the Market, and the Law.* Chicago, Ill.: University of Chicago Press.

Coase, R. H. 1995. *Essays on Economics and Economists.* Chicago, Ill.: University of Chicago Press.

Cochrane, J. H. 1991a. "Production-Based Asset Pricing and the Link Between Stock Returns and Economic Fluctuations." *Journal of Finance* 46.

Cochrane, J. H. 1991b. "Volatility Tests and Efficient Markets: A Review Essay." *Journal of Monetary Economics* 27.

Cochrane, J. H. 1996. "A Cross-Sectional Test of an Investment-Based Asset Pricing Model." *Journal of Political Economy* 104.

Cochrane, J. H. 1997. "Where Is the Market Going? Uncertain Facts and Novel Theories." *Federal Reserve Bank of Chicago Economic Perspectives* 21.

Cochrane, J. H. 1999a. "New Facts in Finance." *Federal Reserve Bank of Chicago Economic Perspectives* 23.

Cochrane, J. H. 1999b. "Portfolio Advice for a Multi-factor World." *Federal Reserve Bank of Chicago Economic Perspectives* 23.

Cochrane, J. H. 2001. *Asset Pricing.* Princeton, N.J.: Princeton University Press.

Cochrane, J. H. and J. Saá-Requejo. 2000. "Beyond Arbitrage: Good Deal Asset Price Bounds in Incomplete Markets." *Journal of Political Economy* 108.

Cochrane, J. H., and C. L. Culp. 2003. "Equilibrium Asset Pricing and Discount Factors: Overview and Implications for Derivatives Valuation and Risk Management." In *Modern Risk Management: A History.* London: Risk Books.

Connolly, B. 1995. *The Rotten Heart of Europe: The Dirty War for Europe's Money.* London: Faber & Faber.

Constantinides, G. M. 1990. "Habit Formation: A Resolution of the Equity Premium Puzzle." *Journal of Political Economy* 98.

Constantinides, G. M., and D. Duffie. 1996. "Asset Pricing with Heterogeneous Consumers." *Journal of Political Economy* 104.

Constantinides, G. M., and T. Zariphopoulou. 1999. "Bounds on Prices of Contingent Claims in an Intertemporal Economy with Proportional Transaction Costs and General Preferences." *Finance and Stochastics* 3.

Cootner, P. H. 1960a. "Returns to Speculators: Telser versus Keynes." *Journal of Political Economy* 48 (August).

Cootner, P. H. 1960b. "Returns to Speculators: Rejoinder." *Journal of Political Economy* 48 (August).

Cox, J. C., J. E. Ingersoll, and S. A. Ross. 1981. "The Relation between Forward Prices and Futures Prices." *Journal of Financial Economics* 9(4).

Cox, J. C., J. E. Ingersoll, and S. A. Ross. 1985. "A Theory of the Term Structure of Interest Rates." *Econometrica* 53.

Cox, J. C., S. A. Ross, and M. Rubinstein. 1979. "Option Pricing: A Simplified Approach." *Journal of Financial Economics* 7.

Crouhy, M. D. Galai, and R. Mark. 2000. *Risk Management*. New York, N.Y.: McGraw-Hill.

Culp, C. L. 1989. "In the EMS, a Quiet Struggle to Pay the German Piper." *London Times* (October 13).

Culp, C. L. 1990a. "Britain and the European Monetary System: An American Perspective." *Economic Affairs* 10(6) (August/September).

Culp, C. L. 1990b. "The Perils of ERM." *Wall Street Journal* (August 24).

Culp, C. L. 1995a. *A Primer on Derivatives*. Washington, D.C., and Chicago, Ill.: Competitive Enterprise Institute and Chicago Board of Trade.

Culp, C. L. 1995b. "Regulatory Uncertainty and the Economics of Derivatives Regulation." *The Financier* 2(5).

Culp, C. L. 1996. "Some Characteristics of a Successful Futures Contract." *Futures and Derivatives Law Report* 16(5).

Culp, C. L. 1997. "The Role of Eurodeposit Futures in Swap Rate Determination: An Empirical Analysis." Unpublished Working Paper, Graduate School of Business, University of Chicago (December).

Culp, C. L. 2001. *The Risk Management Process: Business Strategy and Tactics*. New York: John Wiley & Sons.

Culp, C. L. 2002a. *The ART of Risk Management: Alternative Risk Transfer, Capital Structure, and the Convergence of Insurance and Capital Markets*. New York: John Wiley & Sons.

Culp, C. L. 2002b. "Clearing: A Risk Assessment." *Futures Industry* (July/August).

Culp, C. L. 2002c. "The Revolution in Corporate Risk Management: A Decade of Innovations in Process and Products." *Journal of Applied Corporate Finance* 14(4).

Culp, C. L. 2003a. "Demystifying Derivatives in Mortgage Markets and at Fannie Mae." *Fannie Mae Papers* 2(4).

Culp, C. L. 2003b. "Derivatives Can Help Manage Risks." *Financial Times* (August 12).

Culp, C. L. 2003c. "Metallgesellschaft." In *The Growth of Risk Management: A History*. London: Risk Books.

Culp, C. L. 2003d. "Modigliani-Miller Propositions." In *The Growth of Risk Management: A History*. London: Risk Books.

Culp, C. L. 2003e. "Playing the Odds." In *Risk, Control, and Performance*. New York: McKinsey & Co. for the World Economics Forum, September 2003.

Culp, C. L., and S. H. Hanke. 1995. *An Anatomy of Hong Kong's Currency Board*. Unpublished Working Paper, Department of Geography and Environmental Engineering, Johns Hopkins University.

Culp, C. L., and S. H. Hanke. 2003. "Empire of the Sun: A Neo-Austrian Interpretation of Enron's Energy Business." In *Corporate Aftershock: The Public Policy Lessons from Enron and Other Recent Disasters*. C. L. Culp and W. A. Niskanen, eds. New York: John Wiley & Sons.

Culp, C. L., and H. James. 1989. *Joining the European Monetary System: For and Against*. London: Centre for Policy Studies.

Culp, C. L., and B. T. Kavanagh. 2003. "Structured Commodity Finance after Enron: Uses and Abuses of Pre-Paid Forwards and Swaps." In *Corporate Aftershock: The Public Policy Lessons from Enron and Other Recent Disasters*. C. L. Culp and W. A. Niskanen, eds. New York: John Wiley & Sons.

Culp, C. L., and R. J. Mackay. 1996. "Structured Notes: Mechanics, Benefits, and Risks." In *Derivatives Risk and Responsibility*. R. A. Klein and J. Lederman, eds. Chicago: Irwin Professional Publishing.

Culp, C. L., and R. J. Mackay. 1997. "An Introduction to Structured Notes." *Derivatives: Tax, Regulation and Finance* 2(4).

Culp, C. L., and M. H. Miller. 1995a. "Auditing the Auditors." *Risk* 8(4).

Culp, C. L., and M. H. Miller. 1995b. "Hedging in the Theory of Corporate Finance." *Journal of Applied Corporate Finance* 8(1).

Culp, C. L., and M. H. Miller. 1995c. "Metallgesellschaft and the Economics of Synthetic Storage." *Journal of Applied Corporate Finance* 7(4).

Culp, C. L., and M. H. Miller, eds. 1999a. *Corporate Hedging in Theory and Practice: Lessons from Metallgesellschaft*. London: Risk Publications.

Culp, C. L., and M. H. Miller. 1999b. "Postscript: How the Story Turned Out." In *Corporate Hedging in Theory and Practice: Lessons from Metallgesellschaft*. C. L. Culp and M. H. Miller, eds. London: Risk Publications.

Culp, C. L., and M. H. Miller. 1999c. "Introduction: *Why* a Firm Hedges Affects *How* a Firm Hedges." In *Corporate Hedging in Theory and Practice: Lessons from Metallgesellschaft*. C. L. Culp and M. H. Miller, eds. London: Risk Publications.

Culp, C. L., and A. M. P. Neves. 1999. *A Primer on Securities and Multi-Currency Settlement Systems: Systemic Risk and Risk Management*. Washington, D.C.: Competitive Enterprise Institute.

Culp, C. L., and W. A. Niskanen, eds. 2003. *Corporate Aftershock: The Public Policy Lessons from Enron and Other Recent Disasters*. New York: John Wiley & Sons.

Culp, C. L., and F. L. Smith Jr. 1989. "Speculators: Adam Smith Revisited." *The Freeman* (October).

Culp, C. L., S. H. Hanke, and M. H. Miller. 1999. "The Case for an Indonesian Currency Board." *Journal of Applied Corporate Finance* 11(4).

Culp, C. L., S. H. Hanke, and A. M. P. Neves. 1999. "Derivatives Diagnosis." *The International Economy* 13(3)(May/June).

Culp, C. L., M. H. Miller, and A. M. P. Neves. 1998. "Value at Risk: Uses and Abuses." *Journal of Applied Corporate Finance* 10(4)(Winter).

Danthine, J.-P. 1978. "Information, Futures Prices, and Stabilizing Speculation." *Journal of Economic Theory* 17(1).

Davidson, P. 2002. *Financial Markets, Money and the Real World*. Northampton, Mass.: Edward Elgar.

De Roover, R. 1948. *Money, Banking and Credit in Mediaeval Bruges*. Cambridge, Mass.: Mediaeval Academy of America.

De Roover, R. 1963 [1999]. *The Rise and Decline of the Medici Bank*. Washington, D.C.: Beard Books.

Debreu, G. 1959. *Theory of Value*. New York: John Wiley & Sons.

DeRosa, D. F. 1998. *Currency Derivatives*. New York.: John Wiley & Sons.

DeRosa, D. F. 2000. *Options on Foreign Exchange*. New York.: John Wiley & Sons.

Diamond, D. W., and R. E. Verrecchia. 1981. "Information Aggregation in a Noisy Rational Expectations Economy." *Journal of Financial Economics* 9.

Doherty, N. A. 2000. *Integrated Risk Management*. New York: McGraw-Hill.

Douglas, M., and A. B. Wildavsky. 1982. *Risk and Culture: An Essay of the Selection of Technical and Environmental Dangers*. Reprint ed. Berkeley, Calif.: University of California Press.

Dowd, K. 2002. *Measuring Market Risk*. New York: John Wiley & Sons.

Duffie, D., and R. Rahi. 1995. "Financial Market Innovation and Security Design: An Introduction." *Journal of Economic Theory* 65.

Duffie, D., and G. M. Constantinides. 1996. "Asset Pricing with Heterogeneous Consumers." *Journal of Political Economy* 104(2) (April).

Dusak, K. 1973. "Futures Trading and Investor Returns: An Investigation of Commodity Market Risk Premiums." *Journal of Political Economy* 81.

Ederington, L. H. 1979. "The Hedging Performance of the New Futures Markets." *Journal of Finance* 34(1).

Edgeworth, F. Y. 1881. *Mathematical Psychics: An Essay on the Application of Mathematics to the Moral Sciences*. 1932 ed. London: London School of Economics.

Edwards, F. R., and M. S. Canter. 1995. "The Collapse of Metallgesellschaft: Unhedgeable Risks, Poor Hedging Strategy, or Just Bad Luck?" *Journal of Applied Corporate Finance* 8(1) (Spring).

Emmett, R. B. 1999. "Introduction." In *Selected Essays by Frank H. Knight: Volume I, "What Is Truth" in Economics?* Chicago: University of Chicago Press.

Engle, R. 1982. "Autoregressive Conditional Heteroskedasticity with Estimates of the Variance of United Kingdom Inflation." *Econometrica* 50.

Fama, E. F. 1976. "The Effects of a Firm's Investment and Financing Decisions on the Welfare of Its Security Holders." *American Economic Review* 68(3).

Fama, E. F. 1980. "Agency Problems and the Theory of the Firm." *Journal of Political Economy* 88(2).

Fama, E. F. 1991. "Efficient Markets II." *Journal of Finance* 46.

Fama, E. F., and K. R. French. 1993. "Common Risk Factors in the Returns on Stocks and Bonds." *Journal of Financial Economics* 33.

Fama, E. F., and K. R. French. 1996. "Multi-factor Explanations of Asset-Pricing Anomalies." *Journal of Finance* 47.

Fama, E. F., and M. H. Miller. 1972. *The Theory of Finance.* New York: Holt, Rinehart, and Winston.

Farrell, M. 1966. "Profitable Speculation." *Economica* 33.

Ferson, W., and C. R. Harvey. 1999. "Conditioning Variables and the Cross-Section of Stock Returns." *Journal of Finance* 54.

Fisher, I. 1907. *The Rate of Interest: Its Nature, Determination and Relation to Economic Phenomena.* New York: Macmillan.

Fisher, I. 1925. *The Purchasing Power of Money.* New York: Macmillan.

Fisher, I. 1930. *The Theory of Interest as Determined by Impatience to Spend Income and Opportunity to Invest It.* New York: Macmillan.

Francis, J. C., W. W. Toy, and J. G. Whittaker. 1999. *The Handbook of Equity Derivatives.* Revised ed. New York: John Wiley & Sons.

French, K. R. 1983. "A Comparison of Futures and Forward Prices." *Journal of Financial Economics* 12(3).

French, K. R. 1986. "Detecting Spot Price Forecasts in Future Prices." *Journal of Business* 59(2–2) (April).

Friedman, M. 1953. *Essays in Positive Economics.* Chicago: University of Chicago Press.

Froot, K. A., D. S. Scharfstein, and J. C. Stein. 1993. "Risk Management: Coordinating Investment and Financing Policies." *Journal of Finance* 48(5).

Froot, K. A., D. S. Scharfstein, and J. C. Stein. 1994. "A Framework for Risk Management." *Harvard Business Review* (November–December).

Gibson, R., and E. S. Schwartz. 1990. "Stochastic Convenience Yield and the Pricing of Oil Contingent Claims." *Journal of Finance* 45.

Global Derivatives Study Group. 1993. *Derivatives: Practices and Principles.* Washington, D.C.: The Group of Thirty.

Gollier, C. 2001. *The Economics of Risk and Time.* Cambridge, Mass.: MIT Press.

Gourieroux, C. 1997. *ARCH Models in Financial Applications.* Amsterdam: Springer Verlag.

Grabbe, J. O. 1996. *International Financial Markets.* 3rd ed. Englewood Cliffs, N.J.: Prentice Hall.

Gray, R. W. 1961. "The Search for a Risk Premium." *Journal of Political Economy* 69.

Gray, R. W. 1962. "The Seasonal Pattern of Wheat Futures Prices under the Loan Program." *Food Research Institute Studies* 3(1).

Gray, R. W. 1967. "Price Effects of a Lack of Speculation." *Food Research Institute Studies* (7 Supp.).

Grossman, S. J. 1977. "The Existence of Futures Markets, Noisy Rational Expectations and Information Externalities." *Review of Economic Studies* 44.

Grossman, S. J. 1981. "An Introduction to the Theory of Rational Expectations under Asymmetric Information." *Review of Economic Studies* 48.

Grossman, S. J. 1988. "Program Trading and Stock and Futures Price Volatility." *Journal of Futures Markets* 8(4).

Hakansson, N., J. G. Kunkel, and J. Ohlson. 1982. "Sufficient and Necessary Conditions for Information to Have Social Value in Pure Exchange." *Journal of Finance* 37.

Hanley, W. J., K. McCann, and J. T. Moser. 1995. "Public Benefits and Public Concerns: An Economic Analysis of Regulatory Standards for Clearing Facilities." Working Paper, Federal Reserve Bank of Chicago WP-95-12 (September).

Hansen, L. P., and R. Jagannathan. 1991. "Implications of Security Market Data for Models of Dynamic Economies." *Journal of Political Economy* 99.

Hansen, L. P., and S. F. Richard. 1987. "The Role of Conditioning Information in Deducing Testable Restrictions Implied by Dynamic Asset Pricing Models." *Econometrica* 55.

Hansen, L. P., and K. J. Singleton. 1982. "Generalized Instrumental Variables Estimation of Nonlinear Rational Expectations Models." *Econometrica* 50.

Hardy, C. O. 1923. *Risk and Risk-Bearing.* 1999 ed. London: Risk Books.

Harris, M., and A. Raviv. 1989. "The Design of Securities." *Journal of Financial Economics* 24.

Harrison, J. M., and D. M. Kreps. 1979. "Martingales and Arbitrage in Multiperiod Securities Markets." *Journal of Economic Theory* 20.

Hart, O. D., and D. M. Kreps. 1986. "Price Destabilizing Speculation." *Journal of Political Economy* 94(5).

Hartzmark, M. L. 1991. "Luck Versus Forecast Ability: Determinants of Trader Performance in Futures Markets." *Journal of Business* 64.

Hayek, F. A. 1931. *Prices and Production*. London: Routledge.

Hayek, F. A. 1932. "Reply to Sraffa." *Economic Journal* 42.

Hayek, F. A. 1937. "Economics and Knowledge." *Economica* 4.

Hayek, F. A. 1945. "The Use of Knowledge in Society." *American Economic Review* 35(4).

Hicks, J. R. 1939. *Value and Capital: An Inquiry into Some Fundamental Principles of Economic Theory*. 1957 ed. London: Oxford University Press.

Hicks, J. R. 1965. *Capital and Growth*. Oxford: Oxford University Press.

Hicks, J. R. 1973. *Capital and Time: A Neo-Austrian Analysis*. London: Oxford University Press.

Hicks, J. R. 1989. *A Market Theory of Money*. London: Oxford University Press.

Hilliard, J. E. 1999. "Analytics Underlying the Metallgesellschaft Hedge: Short-Term Futures in a Multiperiod Environment." In *Corporate Hedging in Theory and Practice: Lessons from Metallgesellschaft*. C. L. Culp and M. H. Miller, eds. London: Risk Publications.

Hirshleifer, D. 1988. "Residual Risk, Trading Costs, and Commodity Futures Risk Premia." *Review of Financial Studies* 1(2).

Hirshleifer, D. 1989. "Determinants of Hedging and Risk Premia in Commodity Futures Markets." *Journal of Financial and Quantitative Analysis* 24(3).

Hirshleifer, D. 1990. "Hedging Pressure and Futures Price Movements in a General Equilibrium Model." *Econometrica* 58.

Ho, T. S. Y., and S.-B. Lee. 1983. "Term Structure Movements and Pricing Interest Rate Contingent Claims." *Journal of Finance* 41.

Holton, G. 2003. Value-at-Risk: Theory and Practice. New York: Academic Press.

Hooker, R. H. 1901. "The Suspension of the Berlin Produce Exchange and Its Effect on Corn Prices." *Journal of the Royal Statistical Society* 64(4).

Houthakker, H. S. 1957. "Can Speculators Forecast Prices?" *Review of Economic Statistics* 39.

Houthakker, H. S. 1959. "The Scope and Limits of Futures Trading." In *The Allocation of Economic Resources*. M. Abramovitz et al., eds. Stanford, Calif.: Stanford University Press.

Houthakker, H. S. 1961. "Normal Backwardation." In *Value, Capital, and Growth: Essays in Honour of Sir John R. Hicks*. J. N. Wolfe, ed. Chicago: Aldine.

Hull, J. C. 2003. *Options, Futures, and Other Derivatives*. Upper Saddle River, N.J.: Prentice Hall.

Jaffe, J. F., and R. L. Winkler. 1976. "Optimal Speculation against an Efficient Market." *Journal of Finance* 31.

Jagannathan, R., and Z. Wang. 1996. "The Conditional CAPM and the Cross-Section of Expected Returns." *Journal of Finance* 51.

Jarrow, R. A., and S. M. Turnbull. 1999. *Derivatives Securities*. 2nd ed. Cincinatti: South-Western College Publishing.

Jastrow, M. 1911. *Aspects of Religious Belief and Practice in Babylonia and Assyria*. New York: American Academy of Religion.

Jensen, M. 2001a. *A Theory of the Firm: Governance, Residual Claims, and Organizational Forms*. Cambridge: Harvard University Press.

Jensen, M. 2001b. *Foundations of Organizational Strategy*. Cambridge: Harvard University Press.

Jensen, M. C., and W. H. Meckling. 1976. "Theory of the Firm: Managerial Behavior, Agency Costs and Ownership Structure." *Journal of Financial Economics* 3(4).

Jevons, W. S. 1871. *The Theory of Political Economy*. London: Macmillan.

Johnson, L. L. 1960. "The Theory of Hedging and Speculation in Commodity Futures." *Review of Economic Studies* 26.

Jorion, P. 2002. *Value at Risk: The New Benchmark for Managing Financial Risk*. New York: McGraw-Hill.

Kaldor, N. 1939. "Speculation and Economic Stability." *Review of Economic Studies* 7.

Kane, E. J. 1988. "Interaction of Financial and Regulatory Innovation." *American Economic Review* 78.

Kat, H. M. 2001. *Structured Equity Derivatives*. New York: John Wiley & Sons.

Keynes, J. M. 1921. *The Collected Writings of John Maynard Keynes: A Treatise on Probability*. Vol. VIII, 1973 ed. London: Macmillan.

Keynes, J. M. 1923. *The Collected Writings of John Maynard Keynes: A Tract on Monetary Reform*. Vol. V, 1973 ed. London: Macmillan.

Keynes, J. M. 1930a. *A Treatise on Money: Volume I, The Pure Theory of Money*. 1950 ed. London: Macmillan.

Keynes, J. M. 1930b. *A Treatise on Money: Volume II, The Applied Theory of Money*. 1950 ed. London: Macmillan.

Keynes, J. M. 1936. *The General Theory of Employment, Interest, and Money*. Cambridge: Cambridge University Press.

Knight, F. H. 1921. *Risk, Uncertainty, and Profit*. 1931 ed. New York: Macmillan.

Knight, F. H. 1932. "Capital, Time, and the Interest Rate." *Economica* (August).

Knight, F. H. 1933. *The Economic Organization*. 1951 ed. New York: Augustus M. Kelley, Inc.

Kolb, R. W. 1992. "Is Normal Backwardation Normal?" *Journal of Futures Markets* 12(1).

Kolb, R. W., and J. A. Overdahl. 2003. *Financial Derivatives*. New York: John Wiley & Sons.

Kramer, A. S. 2003. *Financial Products: Taxation, Regulation, and Design*. 3rd ed. Aspen Publishers.

Kreps, D. M. 1977. "A Note on 'Fulfilled Expectations' Equilibria." *Journal of Economic Theory* 14.

Kreps, D. M. 1990. *A Course in Microeconomic Theory*. Princeton, N.J.: Princeton University Press.

Kyle, A. S. 1985. "Continuous Auctions and Insider Trading." *Econometrica* 53.

Lachmann, L. M. 1978. *Capital and Its Structure*. Kansas City, Mo.: Sheeds Andrews & McMeel, Inc.

Laffont, J.-J. 1989. *The Economics of Uncertainty and Information*. Cambridge: The MIT Press.

Lettau, M., and S. C. Ludvigson. 2001. "Consumption, Aggregate Wealth, and Expected Stock Returns." *Journal of Finance* 56.

Lewin, P. 1999. *Capital in Disequilibrium: The Role of Capital in a Changing World*. New York: Routledge.

Lintner, J. 1965. "The Valuation of Risky Assets and the Selection of Risky Investments in Stock Portfolios and Capital Budgets." *Review of Economics and Statistics* 47.

Lucas, R. E. 1972. "Expectations and the Neutrality of Money." *Journal of Economic Theory* 4.

Lucas, R. E. 1978. "Asset Prices in an Exchange Economy." *Econometrica* 46.

MacDonald, R. L. 2003. *Derivatives Markets*. New York: Addison Wesley.

Machina, M. J., and M. Rothschild. 1987. "Risk." In *The New Palgrave: A Dictionary of Economics*. J. Eatwell, M. Milgate, and P. Newman, eds. London: Macmillan.

Magill, M., and W. Shafer. 1991. "Incomplete Markets." In the *Handbook of Mathematical Economics: Volume IV*. W. Hildenbrand and H. Sonnenschein, eds. Amsterdam: Elsevier.

Malthus, T. 1820. *Principles of Political Economy*. 1989 ed. Cambridge: Cambridge University Press.

Marcus, A. J. 1982. "Risk Sharing and the Theory of the Firm." *Bell Journal of Economics* 13(2).

Markowitz, H. 1952. "Portfolio Selection." *Journal of Finance* 7(1).

Markowitz, H. 1959. *Portfolio Selection: Efficient Diversification of Investments*. 1990 ed. London: Blackwell.

Marshall, A. 1890. *Principles of Economics*. 1964 ed. London: Macmillan.

Marx, K. 1859. *Das Kapital (Capital)*. 1885 ed. London: Lawrence and Wishart.

Matten, C. 2000. *Managing Bank Capital*. 2d edition. New York: John Wiley & Sons.

Mayers, D. 1972. "Non-Marketable Assets and Capital Market Equilibrium Under Uncertainty." In *Studies in the Theory of Capital Markets*. M. Jensen, ed. New York: Praeger.

McKinnon, R. 1967. "Futures Markets, Buffer Stocks, and Income Stability for Primary Producers." *Journal of Political Economy* 75.

Mello, A. S., and J. E. Parsons. 1995. "Maturity Structure of a Hedge Matters: Lessons from the Metallgesellschaft Debacle." *Journal of Applied Corporate Finance* 8(1) (Spring).

Menger, C. 1871. *Principles of Economics*. 1994 ed. New York: Libertarian Press.

Merton, R. C. 1973. "An Intertemporal Capital Asset Pricing Model." *Econometrica* 41.

Merton, R. C. 1987. "A Simple Model of Capital Market Equilibrium with Incomplete Information." *Journal of Finance* 42.

Merton, R. C. 1989. "On the Application of the Continuous-Time Theory of Finance to Financial Intermediation and Insurance." *Geneva Papers on Risk and Insurance* 14.

Merton, R. C. 1992. "Financial Innovation and Economic Performance." *Journal of Applied Corporate Finance* (Winter).

Merton, R. C. 1995a. "Financial Innovation and the Management and Regulation of Financial Institutions." *Journal of Banking and Finance* 19.

Merton, R. C. 1995b. "A Functional Perspective of Financial Intermediation." *Financial Management* 24.

Merton, R. C., and A. F. Perold. 1993. "Management of Risk Capital in Financial Firms." In *Financial Services: Perspectives and Challenges*. Boston: Harvard Business School Press.

Milgrom, P., and N. Stokey. 1982. "Information, Trade, and Common Knowledge." *Journal of Economic Theory* 26.

Miller, M. H. 1986. "Financial Innovation: The Last Twenty Years and the Next." *Journal of Financial and Quantitative Analysis* 21.

Miller, M. H. 1992. "Financial Innovation: Achievements and Prospects." *Journal of Applied Corporate Finance* 4(4).

Miller, M. H. 1997. "Risk and Return on Futures Contracts: A Chicago View." In his *Merton Miller on Derivatives*. New York: John Wiley & Sons, 1997.

Mises, L. von. 1949. *Human Action*. 1996 ed. London: Routledge.

Modigliani, F., and Miller, M. H. 1958. "The Cost of Capital, Corporation Finance, and the Theory of Investment." *American Economic Review* 48(A2.2).

Morris, S. 1994. "Trading with Heterogeneous Prior Beliefs and Asymmetric Information." *Econometrica* 62(6).

Myers, S. C. 1977. "The Determinants of Corporate Borrowing." *Journal of Financial Economics* 5.

Myers, S. C. 1984. "The Capital Structure Puzzle." *Journal of Finance* 39(3).

Myers, S. C., and N. S. Majluf. 1984. "Corporate Financing and Investment Decisions When Firms Have Information That Investors Do Not Have." *Journal of Financial Economics* 13.

Neuberger, Anthony. 1999. "Hedging Long Term Exposures with Multiple Short Term Futures Contracts." *Review of Financial Studies* 12(3) (Autumn).

Neumann, J. von, and O. Morgenstern. 1944. *Theory of Games and Economic Behavior.* Princeton, N.J.: Princeton University Press.

Newbury, D. M. G., and Stiglitz, J. E. 1983. *The Theory of Commodity Price Stabilization: A Study in the Economics of Risk.* Oxford: Clarendon Press.

New York Mercantile Exchange (NYMEX). 1999. *A Guide to Energy Hedging.* New York: NYMEX.

Ng, V. K., and S. C. Pirrong. 1994. "Fundamentals and Volatility: Storage, Spreads, and the Dynamics of Metals Prices." *Journal of Business* 67(2) (April).

O'Driscoll, G. P., and M. J. Rizzo. 1996. *The Economics of Time and Ignorance.* 2d ed. London: Routledge.

Ogus, S. L. 2003. *Economic Freedom in Post-1949 China.* Doctoral Dissertation in Economics, University of London (January).

Outreville, J. F. 1998. *Theory and Practice of Insurance.* London: Kluwer Academic Publishers.

Pastor, L., and R. F. Stambaugh. 2001. "Liquidity Risk and Expected Stock Returns." NBER Working Paper No. w8462 (September). Forthcoming *Journal of Political Economy.*

Petzel, T. E. 1989. *Financial Futures and Options.* New York: Quorum/Greenwood Press.

Pigou, A. C. 1923. *Essays in Applied Economics.* London: P. S. King.

Pirrong, S. C. 1997. "Metallgesellschaft: A Prudent Hedger Ruined, or a Wildcatter on Nymex?" *Journal of Futures Markets* 17(5).

Powers, M. J. 1970. "Does Futures Trading Reduce Price Fluctuations in Cash Markets?" *American Economic Review* 60.

Radner, R. 1968. "Competitive Equilibrium Under Uncertainty." *Econometrica* 36.

Radner, R. 1972. "Existence of Equilibrium in Plans, Prices and Price Expectations in a Sequence of Markets." *Econometrica* 47.

Radner, R. 1979. "Rational Expectations Equilibrium: Generic Existence and the Information Revealed by Prices." *Econometrica* 47.

Rendleman, R. J., Jr. 1992. "How Risks Are Shared in Interest Rate Swaps." *Journal of Financial Services Research.*

Ricardo, D. 1817. *On the Principles of Political Economy and Taxation.* 1951 ed. Cambridge University Press.

Ritchken, P. H. 1985. "On Option Pricing Bounds." *Journal of Finance* 40.

Robbins, L. C. 1932. *An Essay on the Nature and Significance of Economic Science*. 1935 ed. London: Macmillan.

Robbins, L. C. 1998. *A History of Economic Thought: The LSE Lectures*. S. G. Medema and W. J. Samuels, eds. Princeton, N.J.: Princeton University Press.

Robinson, J. 1951. "The Rate of Interest." *Econometrica* 19(2).

Rockafellar, R. T. 1970. *Convex Analysis*. Princeton, N.J.: Princeton University Press.

Rockwell, C. S. 1967. "Normal Backwardation, Forecasting, and the Returns to Commodity Futures Traders." *Food Research Institute Studies* 8 (suppl.). Reprinted in *Classic Futures: Lessons from the Past for the Electronic Age*. L. G. Telser, ed. London: Risk Books, 2000.

Rolfo, J. 1980. "Optimal Hedging under Price and Quantity Uncertainty: The Case of a Cocoa Producer." *Journal of Political Economy* 88.

Roll, R. 1977. "A Critique of the Asset Pricing Theory's Tests, Part I: On Past and Potential Testability of the Theory." *Journal of Financial Economics* 4.

Roncaglia, A. 2000. *Pierro Sraffa: His Life, Thought, and Cultural Heritage*. London: Routledge.

Ross, R. L. 1975. "Financial Consequences of Trading Commodity Futures Contracts." *Illinois Agricultural Economics* 15(2).

Ross, S. A. 1976a. "The Arbitrage Theory of Capital Asset Pricing." *Journal of Economic Theory* 13.

Ross, S. A. 1976b. "Risk, Return and Arbitrage." In *Risk and Return in Finance: Volume I*. I. Friend and J. Bicksler, eds. Cambridge, Mass.: Ballinger.

Ross, S. A. 1989. "Institutional Markets, Financial Marketing, and Financial Innovation." *Journal of Finance* 44(3).

Ross, S. A. 1999. "Hedging Long-Run Commitments: Exercises in Incomplete Market Pricing." In *Corporate Hedging in Theory and Practice: Lessons from Metallgesellschaft*. C. L. Culp and M. H. Miller, eds. London: Risk Books.

Rothschild, M., and J. Stiglitz. 1976. "Equilibrium in Competitive Insurance Markets: An Essay on the Economics of Imperfect Information." *Quarterly Journal of Economics* 90(4).

Rubinstein, M. 1975. "Security Market Efficiency in an Arrow-Debreu Economy." *American Economic Review* 65.

Rubinstein, M. 1976. "The Valuation of Uncertain Income Streams and the Price of Options." *Bell Journal of Economics* 7.

Savage, L. 1954. *The Foundations of Statistics*. New York: John Wiley & Sons.

Schumpeter, J. A. 1954. *A History of Economic Analysis*. 1996 ed. London: Oxford University Press.

Sharpe, W. 1964. "Capital Asset Prices: A Theory of Market Equilibrium under Conditions of Risk." *Journal of Finance* 19.

Shimpi, P. 2001. *Integrating Corporate Risk Management*. New York: Texere.

Simon, H. A. 1959. "Theories of Decision Making in Economics and Behavioral Science." *American Economic Review* 49.

Smith, A. 1776. *An Enquiry into the Nature and Causes of the Wealth of Nations*. 1981 ed. Indianapolis: Liberty Classics.

Smith, C. W., Jr., C. W. Smithson, and L. M. Wakeman. 1986. "The Evolving Market for Swaps." *Midland Corporate Finance Journal* 3.

Smith, C. W., Jr., C. W. Smithson, and L. M. Wakeman. 1988. "The Market for Interest Rate Swaps." *Financial Management* 17.

Smith, F. L. 1992. "Environmental Policy at the Crossroads." In *Environmental Politics: Public Costs, Private Rewards*. M. Greve and F. Smith, eds. New York: Praeger.

Smith, F. L. 2003. "Cowboys vs. Cattle Thieves: The Role of Innovative Institutions in Managing Risks along the Frontier." In *Corporate Aftershock: The Public Policy Lessons from Enron and Other Recent Disasters*. C. L. Culp and W. A. Niskanen, eds. New York: John Wiley & Sons.

Solow, R. 1956. "A Contribution to the Theory of Economic Growth." *Quarterly Journal of Economics* 70.

Sraffa, P. 1926. "The Laws of Returns under Competitive Conditions." *Economic Journal* 36.

Sraffa, P. 1932a. "Dr. Hayek on Money and Capital." *Economic Journal* 42.

Sraffa, P. 1932b. "Rejoinder to Hayek." *Economic Journal* 42.

Sraffa, P. 1960. *Production of Commodities by Means of Commodities: Prelude to a Critique of Economic Theory*. 1973 ed. Cambridge: Cambridge University Press.

Steele, G. R. 2002. *Keynes and Hayek*. London: Routledge.

Stein, J. L. 1961. "The Simultaneous Determination of Spot and Futures Prices." *American Economic Review* 51.

Stigler, G. J. 1987. *The Theory of Price*. 4th ed. London: Macmillan.

Stulz, R. 2002. *Risk Management and Derivatives*. New York: South Western College Publishing.

Stulz, René M. 1996. "Rethinking Risk Management." *Journal of Applied Corporate Finance* 9(3) (Fall).

Telser, L. G. 1958. "Futures Trading and the Storage of Cotton and Wheat." *Journal of Political Economy* 66.

Telser, L. G. 1959. "A Theory of Speculation Relating Profitability and Stability." *Review of Economics and Statistics* 41(3).

Telser, L. G. 1960. "Returns to Speculators: Reply." *Journal of Political Economy* 48.

Telser, L. G. 1967. "The Supply of Speculative Services in Wheat, Corn, and Soybeans." *Food Research Institute Studies* 7 (suppl.).

Telser, L. G. 1986. "Futures and Actual Markets: How They Are Related." *Journal of Business* 59(2-2).

Tirole, J. 1982. "On the Possibility of Speculation under Rational Expectations." *Econometrica* 50.

Tufano, P. 2003. "Financial Innovation." In *Handbook of the Economics of Finance*. G. M. Constantinides, M. Harris, and R. M. Stulz, eds. Amsterdam: Elsevier.

Turnbull, S. M. 1987. "Swaps: A Zero Sum Game?" *Financial Management* 16.

Vasicek, O. 1977. "An Equilibrium Characterization of the Term Structure." *Journal of Financial Economics* 5.

Verrecchia, R. 1980. "Consensus Beliefs, Information Acquisition, and Market Information Efficiency." *American Economic Review* 70.

Walras, L. 1874. *Elements of Pure Economics or the Theory of Social Wealth*. 1954 ed. London: George Allen & Unwin.

Walters, A. A. 1990. *Sterling in Danger*. London: HarperCollins.

Weller, P. and M. Yano. 1992. "An Introduction to the Theory of Hedging and Speculation in Futures Markets." In *The Theory of Futures Markets*. P. Weller, ed. London: Blackwell.

White, L. W. 1977. *The Methodology of the Austrian School Economists*. New York: Center for Libertarian Studies.

Wicksell, K. 1898. *Interest and Prices*. 1936 ed. London: Macmillan.

Wicksell, K. 1906. *Lectures on Political Economy*. 1935 ed. London: Routledge.

Wildavsky, A. B. 1988. *Searching for Safety*. New Brunswick, N.J.: Transaction.

Wildavsky, A. B. 1991. *The Rise of Radical Egalitarianism*. New York: National Book Network.

Williams, J. 1986. *The Economic Function of Futures Markets*. Cambridge: Cambridge University Press.

Williamson, O. E. 1975. *Markets and Hierarchies: Analysis and Antitrust Implications*. New York: Free Press.

Williamson, O. E. 1998. *The Economic Institutions of Capitalism: Firms, Markets, Relational Contracting*. New York: Free Press.

Williamson, O. E., and S. G. Winter. 1993. *The Nature of the Firm: Origins, Evolution, and Development*. New York: Free Press.

Wilson, R. 1969. "The Structure of Incentives for Decentralization." In *La Decision*. Paris: Centre Nationale de la Recherche Scientifique.

Wörhmann, P. 1998. "Swiss Developments in Alternative Risk Financing Models." *European America Business Journal* (Spring).

Wörhmann, P. 1999. "Finite Risk Solutions in Switzerland." *European American Business Journal* (Spring).

Wörhmann, P. 2001. "Alternative Risk Financing—Developing the Market Potential of Small and Medium-Sized Companies." *European America Business Journal* (Spring).

Wörhmann, P., and C. Bürer. 2001. "Instrument der Alternativen Risikofinanzierung." *Schweizer Versicherung* 7.

Working, H. 1948. "Theory of the Inverse Carrying Charge in Futures Markets." *Journal of Farm Economics* 30.

Working, H. 1949a. "The Investigation of Economic Expectations." *American Economic Review.*

Working, H. 1949b. "The Theory of Price of Storage." *American Economic Review* (December).

Working, H. 1953a. "Futures Trading and Hedging." *American Economic Review* 52(3).

Working, H. 1953b. "Hedging Reconsidered." *Journal of Farm Economics* 35.

Working, H. 1958. "A Theory of Anticipatory Prices." *American Economics Review* 48.

Working, H. 1960a. "Price Effects of Futures Trading." *Food Research Institute Studies* 1.

Working, H. 1960b. "Speculation on Hedging Markets." *Food Research Institute Studies* 1(2).

Working, H. 1962. "New Concepts Concerning Futures Markets and Prices." *American Economic Review* (June).

Working, H. 1963. "Futures Markets under Reserved Attack. *Food Research Institute Studies* 4.

Zimmermann, H. 1999. "Financial Innovation, the Transfer of Knowledge, and Postgraduate Education." In *The Transfer of Economic Knowledge.* E. Mohr, ed. London: Edward Elgar.

Zimmermann, H. 2002. "The Value of Convexity Implicit in Option Prices." Working Paper, WWZ Universität Basel (November).

# Index